A WORLD WAITING TO BE BORN

Educated at Harvard and Case Western Reserve, Dr M. Scott Peck has served in administrative posts in the government during his career as a psychotherapist. He is currently Medical Director of the New Milford Hospital Mental Health Clinic and a psychiatrist in private practice in New Milford, Connecticut.

A WORLD WAITING TO BE BORN

TO BE BORN

The Search for Civility

M. Scott Peck, M.D.

ARROW

Published by Arrow in 1994

3 5 7 9 10 8 6 4 2

First published in the UK in 1993 by Rider, an
imprint of Random House UK Ltd.

Arrow Books
20 Vauxhall Bridge Road, London,
SW1V 2SA

Random House Australia (Pty) Limited
20 Alfred Street, Milsons Point, Sydney, New South
Wales 2061, Australia

Random House New Zealand Limited
18 Poland Road, Glenfield, Auckland 10, New
Zealand

Random House South Africa (Pty) Limited
PO Box 337, Bergvlei, South Africa

Random House UK Limited Reg. No. 954009
ISBN 0 09 932821 6

Typeset in 10/11 Ehrhardt by Deltatype Ltd,
Ellesmere Port, Cheshire
Printed and bound in the United Kingdom by
Cox & Wyman Ltd, Reading, Berks

To the mission of
The Foundation for Community
Encouragement (FCE) and the calling of
all the past and present staff, directors,
leaders, donors, and other volunteers who
have given it life.

Grateful acknowledgment is made for permission to
reprint the following:

Excerpts from *The Prophet* by Kahlil Gibran.
Copyright 1923 by Kahlil Gibran and renewed 1951
by Administrators C.T.A. of Kahlil Gibran Estate
and Mary G. Gibran. Reprinted by permission of
Alfred A. Knopf, Inc.

'For Julia, in the Deep Water' by John N. Morris.
Reprinted by permission; copyright © 1976 The
New Yorker Magazine, Inc.

From 'Story of a Soul,' translated by John Clarke,
O.C.D. Copyright © 1975, 1976 by Washington
Province of Discalced Carmelite Friars, Inc. ICS
Publications, 2131 Lincoln Road, N.E., Washington,
D.C. 20002.

Excerpt from 'Little Gidding' in *Four Quartets*,
copyright 1943 by T. S. Eliot and renewed 1971 by
Esme Valerie Eliot, reprinted by permission of
Harcourt Brace Jovanovich, Inc.

BOOK DESIGN AND DIAGRAMS BY BETH
TONDREAN DESIGN

We shall not cease from exploration
And the end of all our exploring
Will be to arrive where we started
And know the place for the first time.

T. S. ELIOT
Four Quartets

Contents

Contents

Contents

Acknowledgments

It is particularly appropriate in this book about organizations to note that there is no such thing as a significant solitary endeavor. Although I am identified as its sole author, innumerable souls have played a role in the creation of this work. I cannot personally thank them all for their contributions. Special credit, however, is publicly acknowledged to those who have most directly participated: Ann Harris, my editor, for her wise discernment; Phil Mirvis for his loving and painstaking suggestions; Jonathan Dolger, my agent, for his championing; Kathy Fitzpatrick, my personal manager, for her enthusiasm and research assistance; Gail Puterbaugh, my program director, who helps me on my travels where I get to do most of my yellow-pad work; Susan Poitras, our office manager, who teaches machines what to do with it; yet once again, Lily Peck, general manager, who keeps it all going; and finally the hundreds of FCE pioneers who created the book's 'Epiphany.'

A
World
Waiting
To Be Born

Part One

THE
CORNERSTONES OF
CIVILITY

1

Something is Seriously Wrong

Toward a Redefinition of Civility

There is an illness abroad in the land.

On Monday, January 29, 1990, the *USA Today* newspaper carried a full-page advertisement. Tiny print in the left lower corner identified the advertiser as Dun & Bradstreet (D&B), a large financial analysis firm specializing in 'The Fine Art of Managing Risk.' Otherwise, the entire page was devoted to four brief sentences in bold type:

I'M 30,000 FEET OVER NEBRASKA AND THE GUY NEXT TO ME SOUNDS LIKE A PROSPECT.

I FIGURE I'LL BUY HIM A DRINK, BUT FIRST I EXCUSE MYSELF AND GO TO THE PHONE.

I CALL D&B FOR HIS COMPANY'S CREDIT RATING. THREE MINUTES LATER I'M BACK IN MY SEAT BUYING A BEER FOR MY NEW BEST FRIEND.

Something is seriously wrong.

A year earlier, I received a hint as to what is wrong—the nature of the illness involved—when I had the opportunity to meet for four days with the Commissioners of Education of the United States. These 'Chief State School Officers' had gathered together to consider a profound and controversial issue: the teaching of values in public schools. During the first day, we listened to scholars present papers on the history of public education in the United States. I was surprised to learn that in the early days of the nation there had been great and heated debate over whether there even

3

should be public education supported by taxation. The debate was resolved on the grounds that in order to sustain a democratic society, public education was required for the widespread teaching of 'civics.'

By civics, our leaders two hundred years ago meant something far broader than a simple intellectual knowledge of the Constitution and legislative processes. Primarily they meant a deep-seated set of values that would be a foundation for responsible citizenship—values encouraging interest and involvement in large social issues as opposed to mere self-centeredness, values necessary to maintain the health of democracy.

Closely allied to civics is another word: *civility*. It has an old-fashioned, almost quaint ring to it, doesn't it? Why is this so?

In *The Different Drum* I attempted to take a word, *community*, that had lapsed into obsolete meaningless and both resurrect and redefine it.[1] This book is a similar attempt. I wish to resurrect and redefine the meaning of civility. This is necessary for the healing of our society.

To most people, civility means only politeness or good manners. Indeed, this is essentially the dictionary definition. But there are enormous problems with such a definition. In the advertisement the businessman flying over Nebraska was perfectly polite. He excused himself when he got up to go to the phone, and he had the good manners to pay for his seatmate's drink. Yet his behavior was utterly self-serving and manipulative. It was not at all what I would call civil.

Then what is civility? Politeness and good manners are designed to avoid hurting people's feelings. But I began to arrive at a better definition of civility when I ran across an amusing yet profound quote from Oliver Herford, who once said, 'A gentleman is one who never hurts anyone's feelings unintentionally.'[2] In other words, civility might have much

[1] M. Scott Peck, M.D., *The Different Drum: Community-Making and Peace* (New York: Simon & Schuster, 1987).
[2] Oliver Herford (1865–1935), *Franklin Pierce Adam's Book of Quotations* (New York:

more to do with conscious intention—awareness—than with not hurting feelings. In fact, on occasion, it might actually be civil to hurt someone's feelings as long as you know what you're doing.

Although a far more complex matter than superficial politeness, civility certainly does have to do with how we humans relate with each other. Whenever there is a relationship between two or more people, an organization of some sort is involved. Genuine civility is then, in part, consciously motivated organizational behavior. And this is a book about organizational behavior.

Organizational behavior is the term given to the study of how human beings behave in organizations. This study includes not only how individuals behave, but also how groups—and even organizations themselves—behave.

In its very broadest sense, organizational behavior encompasses virtually the entire field of human psychology, since almost all human behavior occurs in the context of one or more organizations. Consider the businessman in the ad. He is employed by an organization, as is his seatmate. He strikes up a relationship with his seatmate in the hope of establishing a relationship between their organizations. In the process of doing so, he is using the services of four other organizations: a financial analysis firm, a telephone company, an airline, and a beer-manufacturing business. Moreover, he is doing all this within the context of an organization called society—which, in this case, seems to encourage rather than discourage manipulative organizational behavior.

We are organizational creatures. We are born not only into a society and culture but usually into a specific, complex organization: a family. Our marriages are organizations. We study in schools that are organizations; we earn a living in businesses that are organizations; at some time or another

Funk-Wagnall's, 1952).

5

we will likely worship in an organization; and when we die there will be organizations to usher us out of this world.

This is not a textbook. Although broad in approach, it makes no attempt at a thorough coverage of the field of organizational behavior. Furthermore, the usual purpose of a textbook is to objectively present organizational behavior as it is; in focusing on the issue of civility, my ultimate purpose is to suggest what I believe it can and ought to be.

The following chapters of this section will delineate the interlocking cornerstones—the underlying prerequisites—for civil behavior. Through this delineation, we shall gradually arrive at the more accurate and complete re-definition of civility that we so desperately need.

The second section will be devoted to an exploration of these cornerstones in the most common of organizations: marriage and the family. The third will examine civility in the context of business or the larger organizations for which we work. The differences between businesses and families will be noted, but so will many of the organizational dynamics they have in common. Finally, there will be a fourth, concluding, section on community in the workplace. It is entitled 'Epiphany' because the mode of organizational behavior that I call genuine community is the vehicle par excellence for both the teaching and the practice of civility. Here lies our most exciting and unrecognized of frontiers.

Earlier I said that there is an illness abroad in the land. A full-page advertisement in *USA Today* costs a great deal of money. The scenario of a businessman checking the credit rating of his seatmate's company before buying him a drink is not, in itself, so remarkable. What is remarkable is that such an expensive ad, literally extolling the virtues of uncivil, manipulative organizational behavior, must have met the overall approval of executives in the advertising agency that created it, the company that purchased it, and perhaps the newspaper that published it. This is why there is something seriously wrong not so much with the advertisement as with the culture that produced it. It seems we may live in a society that has almost forgotten the glory of what it means to be human. We are in need of healing.

2
Salvation and Suffering

The Ambiguity of Pain and Disease

I write as a physician, one who attempts to heal disease.

Virtually all who have sought my ministrations have done so because they were in pain. Indeed, they have generally regarded pain and disease as synonymous. This is natural. Does not the very word *dis-ease* equate with *dis-comfort*, with pain and suffering?

Yet a major part of my patients' predicament has frequently been a misunderstanding of the nature of disease. The fact is that pain and disease are seldom identical. In other words, the ignorance of this fact — ignorance of the reality of disease—is itself a frequent cause of disease. Healing, therefore (particularly in the case of emotional and social disorders), usually requires education concerning the distinction between disease and suffering. So it is for the serious cultural 'illness' of which that 1990 Dun & Bradstreet advertisement was a symptom.

When I was seven years old, a Boy Scout handbook happened to fall into my hands. Instantly the deepest desire of my life was to become a Scout, only I was five years too young. But in the back of the handbook was an advertisement for the official Boy Scout hatchet. The notion came to me that if I could just lay my hands on that hatchet, then I could begin my career as a Scout on my own. There was but one thing I asked of my parents for my eighth birthday.

They gave it to me. It was beautiful, its sharp blade protected by a sweet-smelling, fresh leather snap-on sheath. In anticipation of that birthday morning I had my target picked out for weeks: a small birch tree with a four-inch-thick trunk on the edge of our rural property. At the first possible opportunity I escaped from the house, unsheathed my lovely present, and went to work.

It is surprisingly difficult to chop down even a small tree with a hatchet. Halfway through the job I stopped to rest. At that moment I was horrified to notice blood streaming down my right leg. Somehow—either because the blade was so sharp or my concentration so intense—I had managed, without any awareness, to hatchet a two-inch-long gash in my right knee. Grabbing tool and sheath, I ran home crying.

The doctor was called. They made house calls in those days. To the best of my recollection novocaine was not yet routinely available. So the three stitches he took to close the wound hurt like hell—although not much more than injections of local anesthetic would have.

My parents took away my hatchet. I was not old enough for it, they said. Maybe in a couple of years they would give it back to me. I was heartbroken.

Over the next few days the skin surrounding my stitched gash became reddened, slightly swollen, and tender to the touch. It was several weeks—well after the stitches were removed—before this mild inflammation went away, before the skin returned to its normal color and I could press on the area without pain.

In terms of pain, the injury—the disease, if you will—caused me no hurt whatsoever. I would not even have known about it had it not been for the frightening sight of blood. What did hurt, however, was the medical intervention taken to repair the disease. And what hurt far more, on an emotional level, was the preventive medicine of my parents taking the hatchet away from me so that such an injury was much less likely to happen again in the future.

Then there was the mild inflammation. While it was the least of my pains, it is the most instructive of all. At the time—and for years thereafter—I considered inflammation a disease. But one of the very first things we learned about in medical school was 'the inflammatory response,' which, we were taught, is the essential part of the healing process.

The body in its wisdom (through mechanisms we still do not completely understand) responds to an injury or infection with a dilatation of the little blood vessels, or capillaries, in the vicinity of the disease. This dilatation, or engorgement, of the tiny blood vessels in the skin around the wound is what causes the skin to look so red; the fiery redness (from which we get the term *inflammation*) is a result of an increased blood flow to the area of the disease.

Not only do these little blood vessels dilate but their walls become more porous to allow the escape of blood plasma (or *transudate*) into the surrounding tissues. This is what causes the swelling. The blood vessel porosity also allows the selective escape of white blood cells (but not the more passive red cells). Moving through the transudate, the white blood cells (often called *phagocytes* or, literally, 'eating cells') go to the diseased spot and gobble up dead cells, bacteria, dirt, and other debris. They actually digest this debris and then return through the transudate into the blood vessels. It is a remarkably efficient, microscopic garbage collection and removal service.

The transudate, by surrounding the minute nerve endings in the skin and putting increased pressure upon them, has the effect of making these nerves more sensitive. Hence the increased tenderness of inflamed tissue. But the result of this tenderness is to encourage the individual to protect the area from unusual pressure or activity so as to prevent any interference with the healing process.

Finally, because it so dramatically increases the blood supply to the diseased area, inflammation provides an increased amount of oxygen and other nutrients essential to the rapid growth of new cells—new skin cells if it is a simple scrape or, in the case of a deeper cut like mine, new connective tissue cells that form the scar. Once the debris has been carted away and the damage repaired, the dilatation of the vessels ceases and the blood supply returns to normal. The inflammation is over because the disease has been healed.

There are, of course, a few morals to the story.

The first is that health is a process. If a physician had examined me at any time during the three weeks between when the gash in my knee was sutured and when the last vestiges of inflammation had vanished, she would have pronounced me a perfectly healthy eight-year-old. Not in spite of the inflammation, but because of it. A reason I was perfectly healthy was precisely because the inflammatory response was proceeding well.

We creatures are always being subjected to little nicks and bruises, pimples and bug bites, and besieged by hordes of alien bacteria and viruses. Some part of us is always in the process of healing. Consequently, the condition of health is not a static state of perfect wellness; it is, among other things, a condition of ongoing healing.

For example, a possible explanation for the cause of cancer is referred to as the 'scanner theory.' This theory holds that various cells in the healthy body routinely become cancerous; but the body remains healthy because within it there is some not-quite-yet identified mechanism that scans the body for such malignant cells, spies them out, and proceeds to kill them before they multiply into a growing tumor. What causes cancer then, according to the theory, is not a cancerous cell but rather the failure of the 'scanner' to detect it. While there are some suggestions, we do not yet know why such a defensive healing mechanism ceases to operate effectively. The theory is offered not because it is proven, but because it demonstrates the way in which physicians are increasingly coming to think about disease: that most disease may best be defined as a failure of the healing process.

Please do not think of this theory as some harebrained speculation cooked up by a wild-eyed scientist in his isolated laboratory. There is much to support it. If we physicians know anything at all, it is the reality of what we call the 'immune system.' The immune system is an extremely complex, multifaceted orchestration of various blood cells and antibody-producing mechanisms that elegantly serves as the body's defense system against disease. The inflammatory response itself is but one example of the immune system in action.[1]

The point that health is not so much the *absence* of disease as it is the *presence* of an optimal healing process is crucial for understanding our lives. It is crucial because the principle applies not only to our physical health but also to our mental health and to the health of our organizations and institutions. A healthy organization—whether a marriage, a family, or a business corporation—is not one with an absence of problems, but one that is actively and effectively addressing or healing its problems.

Perhaps the most dreaded disease of all history has been leprosy.[2] What made it so dreaded were the ghastly deformities it caused: twisted joints, amputated toes and fingers, chronic ulcers. But few today realize the reason for most of these dreadful effects. The primary way in which the causative agent, Hansen's bacillus, wreaks its havoc is its affinity for settling along those nerve fibers that carry the sensation of pain and then destroying them. It thereby creates a condition of painlessness. A leper who broke his ankle would continue to walk on it, unaware that anything had happened to him. Or severely burn her fingers while not

[1] To my mind, the most dramatic cutting edge in medical research today is the field of 'psychoneuroimmunology.' The name may sound esoteric, but the purpose of the field is quite simple. Scientists working in it are attempting to discern how psychological functioning may affect the brain in such a way as to cause breakdowns in the immune system or in bodily defenses, like the proposed 'scanning mechanism' in the case of cancer.

[2] No longer so dreaded because there now are drugs that stop its progress and render it no longer infectious.

realizing she had placed them too close to the flame. Pain is a signal of disease, not the disease itself. Indeed, it is primarily a disease-preventing mechanism. Without it we would all quickly become crippled. So a second moral is that we need to experience pain for our healing and health.

Since physical pain is so often either a disease-preventing mechanism or a normal part of the healing process, we obviously cannot define disease as the presence of pain, nor health as its absence. Then how do we define these conditions?

Simply, health is an ongoing process, often painful, of an organism becoming the most—the best—it can be. And disease is anything, sometimes painful, often painless, that interferes with the process of health.

I use the word *organism* to signify that these definitions apply not only to individual creatures but also to organizations. The similarity between the words *organism* and *organization* is no accident. Any organized system, whether an individual or a group, is an organism. Schools, churches, businesses, government agencies, and entire nations are organisms as well, and each may also be healthy or diseased.

These definitions further apply not only to physical health and disease but also to psychological and spiritual health and disease. As in my previous books, I make no distinction between the psychological and the spiritual, so will henceforth use the word *psychospiritual*. The words *health* and *healing* come from the same Anglo-Saxon root as *whole* and *holy*. The leper does not have a whole nervous system. The man who will not face certain obvious issues is not using his whole mind. A corporation that is blind to its own problems cannot be healthy. Mental health—the ongoing process of becoming the most that we can be psychospiritually—is the ongoing process of becoming whole and holy.

Becoming the most that we can be is also the definition of *salvation*. The term literally means 'healing.' As we apply 'salve' to our skin to heal it, so we can learn to apply the principles of mental health in our lives to heal, to make us whole, to save our souls, individually and collectively.

It is a familiar tale. Deeply in love, Bill and Mary are married. But three years after their wedding, the bloom of romance has faded, leaving each with an empty ache. Bill is afraid to tell Mary of his ache because it will hurt her. So he pretends that nothing has changed. Meanwhile, to ease his pain, he begins a series of one-night stands. Mary also pretends that everything is the same for fear of hurting Bill and, in order to fill her emptiness, starts binge shopping. Both cover up their behavior. A year goes by. Simultaneously, Mary discovers Bill's infidelity and Bill discovers they are deeply in debt. Bill blames his affairs on Mary's excessive spending, and Mary blames her spending on Bill's unfaithfulness. They decide that the divorce court is the only route out of their impasse.

Here's another familiar tale. In its short history the Jones Company has expanded rapidly to where it has over a hundred employees. Suddenly there is a drop in new orders. Similar companies are also experiencing declining revenues. The government states the country is not in a recession. Management, not wanting to hurt its employees or otherwise bear the pain of downsizing, decides that prosperity is just around the corner. It sinks all its capital into an expensive marketing campaign. Orders continue to drop, and by the time the government admits to a recession a year later, the Jones Company must file for bankruptcy. These tales are not apocryphal. They are so familiar precisely because they are so agonizingly common.

As a physician, I do not like *unnecessary* pain. I hate it. But we shall continue to suffer it egregiously until we learn to distinguish far more clearly between that pain which is indeed needless and that which is essential for our healing. This is because much disease is actually the result of the attempt to avoid the necessary pain of living and the frequent need for repair. Such disease we call *neurosis*. Carl Jung explained, 'Neurosis is always a substitute for legitimate suffering.'[3] He was referring to individual psychospiritual disorders, but the dynamics are the same for those of organizations. As we talk of the incivility involved in dysfunctional families and businesses, we shall often be speaking of collective neuroses.

I cannot guarantee you that Bill and Mary's prototypical marriage could have been saved had they been willing early on to face the psychospiritual pain of the loss of the romance in their relationship. Such pain is intense. It would have raised profound psychospiritual questions about the nature of marriage and their humanity—questions to which there are neither clear nor easy answers. But there is no doubt that their choice to facilely escape the pain of their legitimate issues doomed the relationship.

Similarly, I cannot guarantee that an incisive downsizing would have assured the long-term survival of the prototypical Jones Company. Its management's reluctance to lay off employees was understandable. There is no more painful decision a humane manager can make than to render competent subordinates unemployed through no fault of their own. Nonetheless, it is probable that its immediately comfortable choice to not cut back ultimately put over a hundred good people out on the street instead of fifty.

Note that in both these instances the suffering involved in hurting others may be at least as excruciating as—and sometimes inseparable from—the experience of being hurt oneself. Individuals do not exist in isolation, and we are addressing organizational behavior. Note also the considerable amount of ambiguity involved. This too is prototypical. Clear-cut decisions are relatively easy. The more ambiguous our choices, the more painful they are likely to be.

---

[3] *Collected Works of C. G. Jung*, Bollingen Series, no. 20, 2nd ed., *Psychology and Religion: West and East*, trans. R. F. C. Hull (Princeton, N.J.: Princeton University Press, 1973), vol. II, p. 75.

Inherently, there are no rules for dealing with such ambiguities. A few soft guidelines may emerge as we consider cases in greater depth in the sections to come.

For the moment, however, we can quite clearly state two of the interrelated cornerstones of civil behavior: (1) the capacity, on both an individual and corporate level, to distinguish between necessary, legitimate (healthy) suffering (including that inherent in ambiguity) and that which is unnecessary or excessively convoluted; and (2) the willingness to bear—to meet head-on and work through—that suffering which is a proper portion in both our individual and collective lives.

A corollary of these principles is that civility is ultimately healing behavior. The effect of a civil individual upon herself and others will be even-greater health. And a civil organization will have the same effect.

My purpose, therefore, is not to make people or organizations more pain-free, but to assist us organizational creatures to be healthier, happier, and more alive. To that end, it is necessary that we become more conscious not only of the varieties of our suffering but also of the nature of organizations. And realize that, unlike the superficial politeness we use to smooth ruffled feathers or gloss over problems, genuine civility is a form of healing behavior that demands often painful honesty and the scalpel of candor.

3

Selves and Systems

The reality and illusion of the self

The first three chapters of Genesis, along with their other insights, constitute a surprisingly accurate account of evolution. The sequence of creation recorded in Genesis 1 over three thousand years ago—first light and stars, then land and water, then plants and the other creatures, and finally human beings—corresponds exactly to our twentieth-century scientific understanding of the developmental order.

But, as a psychiatrist, what fascinates me still more is Genesis 3, for this is the essential account of human psychospiritual evolution. Specifically, while the account is filled with ambiguity, it is the story of how we humans evolved into consciousness. The first thing that happened after Adam and Eve ate the fruit of the Tree of Knowledge of Good and Evil is that they became conscious. And having become conscious, they became conscious of themselves as separate from the other creatures and the rest of nature; they became self-conscious. How was it that God knew they had eaten the fruit? She/he knew precisely because they had become shy and modest—that is, self-conscious. 'Who told you you were naked?' God demanded rhetorically, realizing full well that no one had, that they had figured it out for themselves because they were now conscious of themselves.

This consciousness, or awareness, of ourselves as entities separate from the rest of nature—this sense of separation —is symbolized by our having immediately been kicked out of Eden, out of that warm, fuzzy state of oneness with the

17

rest of the world. We come then to yet another great truth (among others) that this rich story teaches us: We cannot go back to Eden. For the way is forever barred by cherubims with flaming swords. We cannot (except at the peril of our souls) reverse evolution. We can only go forward through the desert into deeper and ever-deeper levels of consciousness for our salvation.

This is such an important truth because an enormous amount of psychospiritual disease—including the abuse of drugs—arises out of the attempt to get back to Eden. So it is that Mark Vonnegut, in writing about his own mental illness and drug abuse, entitled his book *The Eden Express*.[1] Why do we drink at cocktail parties except to diminish our shyness, our self-consciousness? And, indeed, if we take just the right amount of alcohol (or pot or coke or some combination thereof) we may, for a few minutes or hours, regain that lost state of oneness with nature and feel that we have returned home to the womb. But the feeling never lasts for long and the price isn't worth it. It is a form of what Dietrich Bonhoeffer referred to as 'cheap grace.'[2] For the reality, as the great story tells us, is that we cannot go back to Eden; we can only evolve, for our salvation, into ever-more conscious beings.

This drama of developing self-consciousness is repeated throughout the lifetime of each one of us—of every human being, past, present, or future. As far as psychologists can ascertain, the newborn infant has no sense of self. It cannot distinguish between itself and the rest of the world. But then, at almost exactly the age of nine months in healthy development, something rather extraordinary happens. The infant develops 'stranger anxiety.' Prior to that age the child will be unperturbed whenever a stranger enters the room. But now, suddenly, with the appearance of a stranger it will scream in obvious terror, or if it is in its mother's arms, it will

[1] Mark Vonnegut, *The Eden Express* (New York: Praeger Publishers, 1975).

[2] Dietrich Bonhoeffer, *The Cost of Discipleship* (New York: Macmillan, 1963). First published in German, 1937.

turn away and fearfully burrow into her bosom for protection. What has happened here? Clearly, the infant has learned to discern the stranger as someone different from its parents. But there is something more. Equally clearly it also perceives the stranger as a threat. A threat to what? To itself. For this to happen, however, it must have a sense of self. It is now aware of itself as a separate and very vulnerable entity.

Thereafter, the consciousness of self continues to develop throughout childhood, adolescence, and hopefully adulthood. Painfully. Consciousness and pain are inextricably interwoven. If someone has severe enough physical pain, what do we do? We give him an anesthetic to render him unconscious. Similarly, people will anesthetize themselves to deal with their emotional pain—either with drugs or, more commonly, through a variety of psychological tricks called 'defense mechanisms.' While sometimes necessary—even life-saving—these defense mechanisms are more often employed in an unhealthy fashion to limit consciousness so as to ward off existential, 'legitimate' suffering. When used this way they are the cause of psychospiritual disease. As self-imposed limitations of consciousness they prevent the person from moving forward through the desert and becoming all that she or he can be. Conversely, psychotherapy—the healing of the psyche—is a process of relinquishing these defenses so as to directly face the painful issues of life. As the Twelve Step programs put it, 'No pain, no gain.'

So the further you proceed through the desert, the more conscious you become, the more healthy and 'saved' and civil you are, the more it will hurt. You will become ever-more aware of the aging process inexorably working within you, more aware of your own sins and psychopathology. You will also become more aware of the pschopathology of others and the games they play—as well as the sorrows and burdens they bear. And finally you will become ever-more conscious of the sins and evils of society. That's the bad news.

19

The good news is that simultaneously—paradoxically—you will experience more joy. These principles hold true for groups as well as individuals. Organizations, too, are either more or less conscious. Families, churches, businesses, and governments become sick by refusing to face painful realities. If they allow themselves to become conscious of their painful issues, however, then they can work on organizational healing and grow into painful but joyful maturity. Another part of the good news of this book is that, yes, there can sometimes be joyful and civil organizations.

Upon occasion I used to tell my patients, 'Psychotherapy is not about happiness; it is about power. If you go the whole route, I cannot guarantee you will leave here one jot happier. What I can guarantee is that you will leave more competent. There is a kind of vacuum of competence in the world, however, so that as soon as a person becomes more competent, life or God will give her greater problems to work on. So you may leave here worrying about far larger issues than when you came in. But there is a kind of joy that comes from knowing that you're worrying about the big things and no longer getting bent out of shape over the little ones.'

We ourselves are not the only object of our awareness. My medical school education had some surprising benefits. One of the greatest was the opportunity to study micro-scopic anatomy. With that study, the evolution of my own consciousness took a giant leap forward.

When we are young, some of us by good fortune may be quite physically beautiful on the outside. But it is at best a very temporary beauty. It fades along with the bloom of youth into a mass of wrinkles and blemishes and pockmarks and sagging flesh. Look beneath this flesh, whether young or old, with the naked eye and there is nothing particularly beautiful to behold either. At this level of gross anatomy not even surgeons can become very rhapsodic. The fat clings together in clumps. The heart is a bunch of tough muscle. The intestines are as squishy as they look. The brain, for the most part, resembles thick gray mush. Our limbs and livers essentially appear no different than those of a cow lying on our butcher's counter. Textbooks of gross anatomy are worth their price, but not as works of fine art.

All external appearances to the contrary, our bodies are mostly water. Consequently, when you look at thin slices of our relatively unattractive organs under a microscope, you can't see much except pallid and indistinguishable filaments. But if you take these same slices, soak them for a few days in selected formulas and sequences of dyes, or 'stains,' and look again: Voilà! Suddenly you have entered a fairy world, a garden of delights compared to which Disney-land is downright insipid.

The first thing that struck me seeing the delicate blue tentacles of our intestinal villi, the complex red swirls of our kidney glomeruli, the orange mosaics of our liver, and the silver spiders that are our brain neurons was the unimaginable beauty of this microscopic realm. No matter what our age, station, species, or even state of health, at this level we are all very beautiful on the inside.

More gradually, however, as I peered at one beautiful cell after another, microscopic slide after slide, month after month, something even more important dawned on me. Each and every cell was a minuscule part of a complex system. The absorbing villi cells, the smooth muscle cells, and the connective tissue cells holding them together were all an integrated part of an organ—in this case, the small intestine. The small intestine was, in turn, a part of the digestive system: the teeth, tongue, salivary glands, mouth, esophagus, stomach, ileum, jejunum, colon, anus, liver, gall bladder, and pancreas, each with its own unique cells and configurations of cells. And the digestive system was integrated with other systems. The fine filaments of the autonomic nerve cells that stimulated the digestive muscles to relax or contract and the glands to rest or secrete were minute parts of the nervous system, connecting all the way up through the spinal cord to other cells in the brain. Throughout each organ were the tiny cells of arteries or veins, all connected ultimately to the heart as part of the circulatory system. And in each artery or vein I could spy varieties of blood cells, originally manufactured in the bone marrow as little individual parts of the hematopoietic system.

Actually, I had 'known' for years that the human body—and the body of every other living thing, animal or plant—was a system. But prior to medical school I had not been aware of the extraordinary complexity of these systems. This new awareness was also an aesthetic one; the complexity was so great as to be magnificent, so elegant as to be beautiful.

I was now able to make another leap of consciousness, once again to something I had long 'known' but only dimly. Since each individual cell was a component of an organ, and each individual organ a component of a body system, and each such system a component of the body, was it not possible that my body was also part of a larger system still? In other words, might I—my individual self—be but a single cell of an organ of some gigantic organism?

Of course. As a fledgling physician I was connected, directly or indirectly, to countless other individual human selves. To my parents who paid my tuition. To the older physicians who taught me. To the laboratory technicians who conducted the tests I ordered. To hospital administrators. To manufacturers who made the equipment I used. To the patients I used that equipment on. To growers in Mississippi and California who sold cotton to the North Carolina textile workers who made the clothes I wore. To ranchers in Kansas who grew the beef and farmers in New Jersey who grew the lettuce I ate. To the truck drivers who transported all these things to me. To my landlord. To the barber who cut my hair. And on and on.

So it was (although I had not even yet heard the term) that

I became a foursquare believer in systems theory. The basic tenet of systems theory (which actually is not a theory but a fact) is that everything is a system. As nuclear physicists have discovered, even the atom, once thought to be the irreducible element of matter, is a system whose complexities they have hardly begun to unravel. Moving up the scale of size, every one of those little cells I used to look at under my microscope was, in itself, a system not only of millions of molecules but also of multiple larger components with different functions. Each liver cell, for instance, serves as a chemical factory processing hundreds of different raw materials into multiple product lines. On a level more macroscopic than organs or individuals, all of us are component parts of the fabric of human society. We are just beginning to wake up to the fact that the whole of that society is connected to the waters, to the land, to the forests, and the atmosphere: the 'ecosystem.' Indeed, systems theorists often envision the entire planet as a single organism. And, of course, our Earth is a part of the solar system. It is probable that as we begin to reach even further into outer space, we will increasingly perceive a systemic nature to the galaxies and to the universe itself.

The most mature recorded thinkers have always been mystics and, by definition, systems theorists. One of the constant characteristics of mystics of all cultures and all religions in all ages has been their ever-present consciousness of an invisible interconnectedness beneath the surface of things. Consequently, each of their teachings, one way or another, has de-emphasized the separation between self and other.

This de-emphasis of self reached its acme in certain Hindu and Buddhist mystical writings in which the entire concept of self is declared a total illusion (maya), where all human suffering is ascribed to this illusion, and where spiritual progress is completely defined by one's capacity to transcend the consciousness of oneself as an entity. It is no accident that in some of this literature the infant, who has not yet learned how to distinguish itself, is glorified as having a pure mind—a mind liberated from maya, the illusion of self. It is also no accident that in this same literature the distinction between good and evil is considered illusion as well. Buddhists and Hindus do not use the Genesis story. It is as if they identified their heaven — nirvana, or the state of mind free from illusion—with the human condition in the Garden of Eden before we had partaken of the fruit of the Tree of Knowledge of Good and Evil, before we had become self-conscious.

From my own point of view, although I have learned much from it, this Eastern tradition of mystical theology has carried matters too far. It was the Eastern tradition that schooled me in the paradoxical nature of virtually all truth. Yet the Western tradition's attitude toward the self is the more paradoxical—and hence, I believe, the more accurate. Western mystics have also repeatedly spoken of Unity, identified the self with God, blurred the distinction between self and others and between self and nature. But they have never, to my knowledge, gone so far as to deny the reality of the self or to declare it to be without consequence, or to totally denigrate self-consciousness.

Jesus was an example of the Western mystic. He integrated himself with God: 'I am in the Father and the Father in me.'[3] He blurred the distinction between himself and others: 'Inasmuch as you have done it unto one of the least of these, my brethren, ye have done it unto me,' and, 'Inasmuch as ye did it not to one of the least of these, ye did it not to me.'[4] Over and again he taught that we should pay less heed to ourselves in many ways, for example, by concerning ourselves less with clothing, food, and security. But he also taught that we needed to pay *more* attention to ourselves in other ways, such as being concerned with motes in our own

[3] John 14:11.
[4] Matthew 25:40 and 45.

24

eyes and the quality of our prayer lives. Finally, he gave the ultimate expression of the proper paradoxical attitude toward the self when he proclaimed, 'Whosoever will save his life [self] will lose it, and whosoever will lose his life [self] for my sake [i.e., in the right way] will find it.'[5] In common with Jewish mystics before him and Jewish, Christian, and Muslim mystics thereafter, Jesus never said there was no self. Rather, he urged us to cease clinging to our lesser selves in order that we might find our greater true selves.

I do not believe it bad that we have been kicked out of the womb of Eden. That thrusting forth is *evolutionary*. And the point is not to stop as soon as we can, finding what looks like a safe place, and burrow into the sand, settling for limited consciousness and a lesser self-awareness. Instead, the point is to plunge ahead as pilgrims, through thorns and sharp stones of the desert into deeper and ever-deeper levels of consciousness, becoming ever more able to distinguish between those varieties of self-consciousness that are ultimately destructive and those that are life-enhancing, even godly.

Richard Bolles once labeled us humans as 'the comparing creatures.'[6] It is an apt designation. By virtue of our awareness of self, we are endlessly comparing ourselves with others. Are we bigger or smaller? More or less beautiful, handsome? Younger or older? Richer or poorer? Smarter or more stupid? Less or more powerful? Et cetera, et cetera *ad infinitum*. Our destiny as comparing creatures, ceaselessly measuring ourselves against our fellow beings, is simultaneously one of the greater blessings and curses of the human condition.

Take the matter of grades in school. They may give rise to

---

[5] Matthew 16:35 (brackets mine).
[6] The Reverend Richard N. Bolles, sermon preached at St. John's Episcopal Church, Passaic, New Jersey, Sunday, October 6, 1986.

an utterly false sense of either adequacy or personal inadequacy. An A student with a disagreeable, self-centered personality may judge himself to be wholly competent when the reality is that he has light-years of psychospiritual growth to go. Conversely, a C student who is a truly fine person may consider himself unnecessarily incompetent and inferior in comparison to the first youth. How frequently have I seen the C students ultimately far outstrip the A students in this journey of life!

On the other hand, high grades may allow a young woman to feel sufficiently comfortable about herself to be able to venture forth into challenging new areas of psychospiritual development. Or low grades may stimulate a girl to buckle down to her studies, perhaps even to appropriately seek psychotherapy and other forms of assistance to correct her poor performance. Comparisons are not always odious.

Comparisons may work for the good in other ways. Our fellow humans may serve us not only as positive role models but also as negative ones. My father, for instance, despite his many virtues, was an outspoken male chauvinist. His chauvinism was such a glaring, negative trait as to cause me to want to be different. It made it easier for me to cleanse myself or much of my own chauvinisim and thereby gradually become a less imperfect husband, father, and friend. Through comparison, as we grow up, we partly define ourselves against other people. Such a self-definition process may be very healing and healthy.

The great psychiatrist Carl Jung labeled the self-defining, self-differentiation process individuation. Indeed, this process was so central to his thinking that his followers have called their body of theory individual psychology. It regards completion of the individuation process as the ultimate goal of psychospiritual growth. Unfortunately, it is a goal most of us never fully reach. Most of us, one way or another, will die still partly tied emotionally to our parents' apron strings or still mindlessly allowing our ideas and opinions to be dictated by the media. Relatively few of us ever fully learn to think for ourselves, to become full individuals. Yes, we live within systems, but it is also our task not only to preserve but to fulfill our individuality. We are called to become our true, unique selves, and not mere organization men and women.

Another enormous virtue of self-consciousness becomes apparent when we study ego psychology. The ego is the governing part of our personality. A very simple way to look at ego development—the maturation of this governor—is in terms of three stages. The first stage, that of early childhood, is one of an absolute or almost absolute lack of self-consciousness. Here the ego is totally down at the level of the emotions and enmeshed with them. It is the lack of self-consciousness at this stage that makes young children so frequently charming. When they are joyful, they are one hundred percent joyful. They are marvelously spontaneous. But it is this same spontaneity that can so often make them difficult. For when they are sad, they are also one hundred percent sad, sometimes to the point of being inconsolable. And when they are angry, they are one hundred percent angry and sometimes violent or vicious.

As indicated, there are glimmerings of self-consciousness by the age of nine months. This capacity for self-awareness very gradually increases throughout childhood. In adolescence, however, it undergoes a dramatic growth spurt. For the first time young people have a quite obvious 'observing ego.' Now they can observe themselves being joyful or sad or angry *while* they are feeling so. This means that the ego is no longer wholly confined to the level of the emotions. Now a part of it—the observing ego—is detached from the emotions, above them looking on. There is a certain resulting loss of spontaneity.

The observing ego is still not fully developed in adolescence. Thus, adolescents are frequently spontaneous, sometimes dangerously so. At other times, however, they seem to be nothing but a mass of affectations as they self-consciously try on one new identity after another by donning outrageous hairstyles, outfits, and behaviors. Constantly comparing themselves with peers and parents, these seemingly flamboyant creatures are often painfully shy and suffer innumerable spasms of excruciating embarrassment.

Perhaps because the process can be so painful, the majority of people fail to further develop their observing egos once they enter adulthood. Their self-observing capacity becomes modulated (and less painful), but often this occurs only because it actually shrinks. There is a real loss when this happens. When, unwittingly, the majority settle for a limited—even diminished—awareness of their own feelings and imperfections, they have stopped short on the journey through the desert, thereby failing to fulfill their human potential or grow into true psychospiritual power and civility.

But a fortunate minority, for reasons both mysterious and graceful, continue the journey, ever strengthening their observing egos rather than allowing them to atrophy. One of the reasons that psychoanalytically oriented psychotherapy may be profoundly effective is because it is a vehicle for the exercise of the observing ego. What the patient is doing as he lies on the analyst's couch is not merely talking about himself but observing himself talking about himself and observing his feelings as he does so.

The exercise of the observing ego is crucial because if it becomes strong enough, the individual is then in a position where she can proceed to the next stage and develop what I call a 'transcendent ego.' It is analogous to being an orchestra conductor. The individual with the transcendent ego has become so aware of her emotions that she can actually orchestrate them. She may be feeling some sadness, but she is in command of herself, so she can essentially say, 'This is not the time for sadness or violins; it is a time for joy. So hush now, violins. And come on, horns, blow forth.' Note that she does not repress or quash her sadness any more than an orchestra conductor would stomp on the violins. She simply sets her sadness aside, or 'brackets' it.

Similarly, she would be able to address the joyful part of herself: 'I love you, horns, but this is not a situation for joyful expression. It is one that calls for anger. So beat the drums.'

I was attempting to explain the concept of transcendent ego to a patient one afternoon. This particular patient, who was seeing me because of a problem expressing his anger, had some years before been high in the administration of a university at a time of student riots. 'Aha!' my patient suddenly exclaimed. 'Now I understand what you're talking about.' He recounted how at the height of the riots the president resigned and a new university president was immediately brought in to replace him:

We went from meeting to meeting to meeting. More often than not, the discussions were very heated. The new man mostly just listened. Occasionally he would very calmly comment that university policy was probably such and such, but he wasn't sure because he was still learning the ropes. I admired how he kept his cool. But I also began to wonder if he wasn't being too passive, possibly even ineffective. Finally we were at a huge meeting in the amphitheater, open to the entire faculty. The issue was particularly critical. A very young faculty member went into a long diatribe about how the entire administration was nothing but a collection of insensitive and unresponsive fascist pigs. When he was finished the new man stood up and strode to the lectern. 'I have been with you for three weeks now,' he said with his usual calm, steady voice, 'and you have not yet had the occasion to see your new president get angry. This morning you are going to have that opportunity.' Then he proceeded to utterly blast the arrogant, young fool away. It was very impressive. Maybe that's an example of what you mean by a transcendent ego at work.

I don't know enough about either the university or its new president in those turbulent times to make an accurate historical assessment of the situation. Nonetheless, this secondhand tale is an ample illustration of how consciousness is another critical cornerstone of civility.

My patient labeled his president's behavior in this instance as 'impressive.' Occurring in an auditorium filled with important members of a large institution, it was specifically an impressive instance of organizational behavior.

What made it so impressive? My patient, who was terrified of giving vent to his own angry feelings, admired his president's self-control. Not the kind of overcontrol from which he himself suffered, but a far more developed self-control that allowed healthy flexibility. It was not that in the course of the first three weeks the new man had never felt irritated, annoyed, angry, or even outraged. Nor was it that he had any problem expressing such emotions. It was that he saved his anger for the most propitious moment. He had learned how to orchestrate his feelings with the situation. It was a matter of timing. Most music is a matter of timing. The power of that moment lay in the kind of artfulness of leadership.

Underlying that artfulness, that elegant self-control, was a high degree of consciousness. The president was clearly conscious of his own feelings. It was clearly his conscious choice to single out that particularly unreasonable young faculty member for public criticism. And he seemed to do so out of a clear awareness of the needs of the institution at that particular moment. Thus, he was simultaneously conscious of the self, conscious of the other, and conscious of the organization.

Remember Herford's famous line that 'a gentleman is one who never hurts anyone's feelings unintentionally.' Certainly, the president knew he would be hurting the feelings of that arrogant young faculty member, but he also appeared to be utterly intentional about it. The moment was so impressive precisely because he seemed to know exactly what he was doing in a complex situation.

I have already defined civility, in part, as consciously motivated organizational behavior. For behavior to be so motivated, there must be consciousness in the first place. And in this oxymoron lies a critical cornerstone of civility: To become more civil, humans must become ever more conscious of themselves, of others, and of the organizations that relate them together.

The converse of this cornerstone or simple principle is that incivility generally arises out of unconsciousness. It will be demonstrated again and again in Parts Two and Three, where cases of incivility in family and business life are considered in depth. They are cases of unconsciously motivated organizational behavior, or people who literally did not know what they were doing. Usually incivility is uncivil because it is unintentional.[7] We will be exploring many ramifications of the fact that consciousness is a cornerstone of civility. One is that just as individual humans vary in the degree of their consciousness, so do the organizations to which they belong. This will be a particular focus of the concluding section, where it will be observed that whole businesses may be either more or less conscious of themselves and how they are behaving. It also follows that the more unconscious organizations are, the more likely that they, like individuals, will be perpetrators of incivility, albeit on an even grander scale.

Another ramification is already obvious. Since children are born as primarily unconscious creatures, we humans are not born civil. We only become civil through development and learning. This is also true for organizations. Many factors can either retard or enhance such development and learning. The most mysterious of these factors is free will. Individually and collectively, we can *choose* to become more conscious and more civil, although it is seldom totally explainable why the choice is made or fails to be made.

It was mentioned that the very existence of a significant observing ego implies a certain loss of spontaneity. Since the development of a transcendent ego—such as that apparently possessed by the new university president—is based on the prior foundation of an observing ego, the obvious question then arises as to whether the price isn't a

---

[7] It was to the unconscious nature of uncivil behavior of his murderers that Jesus was referring when he asked, 'Forgive them, Father, for they know not what they do.'

renunciation of spontaneity. Paradoxically, the answer is yes and no. Yes, because the fully conscious civil person is often not free to do whatever she simply feels like doing. No, because she has the flexibility to consciously decide when she can be spontaneous as opposed to when the time calls for caution. There is a small loss of freedom associated with constant self-examination and consciousness. But those who have become accustomed to it have found, on balance, that consciousness and civility make for a way of life that is profoundly *liberating*.

4

The Hole in the Mind

The Lack of Group Consciousness

It will be recalled that public school education was established in the United States for the purpose of teaching civics. The chief state school officers who gathered together in the summer of 1988 to consider the teaching of values in schools did so because of their sense that American public education has failed its purpose.

The failure of schools to teach values in recent years is, I believe, but one part of a larger problem. By virtue of trucks and planes that distribute national daily newspapers to our doorstep every morning and television that brings the most polished news commentators into our living rooms each evening, no people on earth have ever been more exposed than Americans to public issues. Yet the fascist demagoguery of Joseph McCarthy is allowed to captivate the nation for over two years before being checked. Oliver North, revealed to be a dissembling player in secret and illegal government operations, comes to be hailed as a hero by the majority. It is discovered a year after the fact that Congress granted President Johnson authority to wage full-scale war in Vietnam on the basis of a total scam. The obviously ill-begotten war proceeds unabated for another eight years. Why? Is there a hole in our minds?

As consciously motivated organizational behavior, civility (like healthy civics) requires consciousness of one's self, consciousness of the other person, and consciousness of the organization, or larger system, relating the self and other. The consciousness of the self has already been briefly addressed and consciousness of the other will be shortly. The hole in our minds under discussion relates primarily to the poverty of our consciousness of organizations and systems.

This mental poverty is perhaps reflective of human nature at this point in its evolution. It is probably natural that we should be next most conscious of those others most like us and near to us: our neighbors or the person across the table. The larger system relating to us is less tangible or visible. The problem is not so much one of physical as one of mental distance. Actually, the organization is every bit as close as our neighbor, so close that it may be hard to see the threads binding us as we talk across our desks or backyard fences. Being invisible, however, the web of such threads —the organization—is abstract and tends to seem, therefore, far more distant than it really is.

Natural though it may be, the prevailing lack of organizational consciousness lies at the root of our failure of civics, our severe problem in diagnosing our systemic ills and implementing timely treatment. As I travel around the nation, I find the vast majority of its citizens to be very decent sorts. They generally like to take care of themselves. They are generally concerned about their neighbors and behave in a kindly fashion toward them. But, despite their bombardment by newspapers and TV, they are generally unconcerned about the broader social or systemic issues that affect them. They seem remarkably unaware of the exorbitant personal price they and their neighbors are paying to support the military-industrial complex or a health care system that is almost out of control. They may have opinions about such matters. But their opinions are usually thoughtless and uneducated. Their concern is shallow. They don't seem to feel any responsibility for the systems in which they are caught up, and they don't seem to *want* any responsibility. They want a mythical 'someone' to take care of it for them. The system seems beyond them, something in which they are somehow not involved, something that is out of sight and out of mind.

Never was this made more painfully clear to me than in the spring of 1987. Jim Bakker, a prominent evangelist, and Gary Hart, a prominent politician, had recently been exposed as adulterers. I was leading an all-day seminar for four hundred participants in Chicago. Usually I give three different lectures at such events, but this time the sponsoring organization wanted to focus the whole day on just one of my lectures: 'Self-Love vs. Self-Esteem,' a talk that wrestles with the issues of individual sin, guilt, remorse, and contrition. It struck me as unbalanced to begin with this hour-long lecture, and then spend the entire rest of the day on questions and answers. So I decided to do something different. I announced to my audience that I would start with my customary talk and we'd spend the rest of the morning on it, but after lunch I would begin with a new talk that would focus the remainder of the day on issues of corporate guilt, sin, remorse, and contrition. By corporate sin, I explained, I meant the evil we do not as individuals alone, but as *bodies* of individuals together. We would be examining our collective responsibility for the sins of our business corporations, our churches, our government, and the many other organizations to which we belong as members of society.

The morning went splendidly, but the afternoon was another matter. At first I thought the audience's lack of responsiveness was merely the effect of a new talk for which I had not yet worked out enough appropriate light moments and jokes. Yet as we got into the question-and-answer period—usually a lively time—the atmosphere in the room grew heavier still. Was it because they had all had a large lunch? I wondered. But I discarded that thought as the mood became still more oppressive. Something was going seriously wrong, I realized, thinking frantically about what sort of intervention I might make to uncover the problem.

But I did not need one. A woman had her hand raised with seeming eagerness. I called on her. She stood up. 'I just want to tell you, Dr Peck,' she said, 'how seriously disturbed

I am by the way you have been blessing the sexual behavior of Jim Bakker and Gary Hart!' Two hundred people immediately broke out in applause of agreement with her. The group's anger was out in the open.

Not that I knew how to deal with that anger. 'Thank you,' I responded. 'Your statement obviously reflects the feelings of a great many in this room and makes it equally obvious I have been failing to communicate well. I am sorry if I have been unclear. Because I have never, for a moment, intended to bless their behavior or otherwise approve of it. What I have been trying to do—apparently rather poorly—whenever questions about their behavior have been raised is to wonder with you why we spend so much concern on the sexual acts of these few public individuals, for which we have no responsibility, and so little concern on such issues as the insanity of the arms race or the sickness of our unbalanced budget, for which we do have some responsibility.' Perhaps as many as a hundred applauded this response. Yes, the conflict was out in the open—with me on the minority side—but it was hardly resolvable. I had lost over half my audience. The rest of the afternoon was stormy and the day ended on a distinctly sour note.

The people who paid a significant sum to come and hear me on that day, like most of my audiences, were not an average cross-section of the American public. My audiences are generally college-educated, white-collar, upper-middle-class women and men. More specifically, the vast majority have not only had psychotherapy but also see themselves as being on a spiritual journey. Envisioning themselves growing toward something, most feel they still have a way to go and they acknowledge their imperfections. As relatively advanced spiritual travelers, they usually have a well-developed sense of their own sin and are familiar with personal guilt, remorse, and contrition. Furthermore, a large percentage are themselves in the 'helping professions.' As physicians and nurses, pastors, psychotherapists, and social workers, they are not only accustomed to assisting others with their issues of sin, guilt, and forgiveness but have actually been trained to be sensitive to others and conscious of their needs. Yet when confronted with their involvement in diseased organizations, they were uninterested, petulant, and missed the point.

Yes, there is a hole in the mind.[1]

The problem goes deeper and is far more extensive than our difficulty dealing with great social issues. Quite possibly, it is unrealistic to expect the average citizen to deeply concern himself with the complexities of the nation's health care system or the unhealthy dependence of the national economy upon the military-industrial complex. The key decisions will be made in Washington, and it is not surprising that, on this level, 'the system' should seem beyond him.

If you look at this man's organizational behavior, you will likely find that he takes pride in his job because he knows it well. He is interested in the lives of his coworkers on the assembly line and is usually happy to cover for them when necessary. But you are also likely to find that he has no interest in what goes on in the front office. He probably has no idea of the company's budget. He may be utterly unknowledgeable about the company pension plan in which he participates. He has little understanding of the production department, of which he is a member, and quite possibly never thinks of it in terms of a system.

It is this close-to-home organizational unconsciousness that causes far greater unnecessary psychospiritual disease and suffering than that caused by broad social problems. In Parts Two and Three, case after case will be examined in

[1] Our lack of social consciousness—this hole in the mind—has been the subject of several major books. See Christopher Lasch, *The Culture of Narcissism: American Life in an Age of Diminishing Expectations* (New York: Norton, 1978). Also Robert Bellah, et al., *Habits of the Heart: Individualism and Commitment in American Life* (Berkeley: University of California Press, 1985).

depth where the hole in the mind wreaks havoc at the grass-roots level of the family and in day-to-day business dealings. At this point, it will suffice to give two brief examples of unnecessary psychospiritual suffering—one in marriage and one in business—to glimpse how much destructive pain could be averted were we to elevate our organizational consciousness and learn even the simplest organizational principles.

Virtually everyone who joins an organization—whether by joining IBM or by joining another individual in matrimony—does so with two needs: to give something and get something. Obviously we want to get something. Money and status, for instance, are among the 'motivators' for people seeking organizational employment. And nowadays certainly most of us expect to receive love and affection when we marry. What may be less obvious is how much—how almost desperately—we humans want to give as well as receive. Most of us have a profound need to be of genuine service to the agencies for which we work, to be truly useful, even essential, in our jobs. And how many of us are so hardhearted that we enter marriage without any desire to give, to bring delight and joy to our spouse, our beloved?

The problem comes when the organization doesn't have what we want to receive from it or doesn't want what we desire to give it. As I look back on our wedding day thirty-three years ago, I realize I pledged my troth to Lily with two inchoate but very deep fantasies in mind. One was that in and through the institution—the organization—of our marriage I would be able to 'make' Lily happy. The other was that as a result of this union I would no longer suffer from loneliness.

Our marriage has had unanticipated joys, but the disillusionment of the next two decades was intensely painful for both of us. There were a number of important 'things' that Lily wanted from me that I found myself eventually either unwilling or unable to give her. They ranged from mundane offerings of roses to theological agreement. And vice versa.

It gradually dawned on me that I could not fulfill my fantasy to *make* Lily happy. And as a consequence of our various mutual mis-matches, each of us has experienced times — frequently prolonged—of profound loneliness within our married relationship.

How much of our suffering might have been prevented, I wonder, if I had known from the outset the truth that it is generally not within one person's power to fully make another person happy in this life? A stable and reasonably healthy marriage can meet some terribly important human needs. Our committed relationship has provided both Lily and me with a very meaningful center to our lives. But it might have been much less painful had we not had to discover for ourselves that it is not within the nature of the institution of marriage to provide anything like a total surcease of loneliness.

The problem of unmet expectations in marriage is primarily a problem of stereotyping. Each and every human being on this planet is a unique person. Since marriage is inevitably a relationship between two unique people, no one marriage is going to be exactly like any other. Yet we tend to wed with explicit visions of what a 'good' marriage ought to be like. Then we suffer enormously from trying to force the relationship to fit the stereotype and from the neurotic guilt and anger we experience when we fail to pull it off.

The absence of any overall formula for marriage would be obvious if we were educated about organizations. Read any textbook on organization theory, for instance, and if you do not get lost in the details, you will realize that the whole book is basically an elaboration of what is called 'contingency theory.' Contingency theory states simply that there is no one best structure for an organization—that the best type of structure will be contingent upon the particular organization's size and product or function. The text will go on to examine a whole variety of organizational structures and how, for better or worse, different types of structures fit different types of businesses.

Given the hole in our minds, however, mere study is not enough. Many businesspeople with graduate degrees from schools of business administration have read such textbooks and personally applied contingency theory to their jobs, yet they have neglected to apply it to their marraiges. To fill the hole in our minds, it is necessary not only to become educated about organizational principles but also to *think* about them and become conscious of their relevance to any and all of the systems in which we participate.

Contingency theory (which is also not a theory but a fact) is a major subprecept of systems theory. Systems theory, it will be remembered, begins by stating that every 'thing' is a system of component parts. It goes on to state that the nature of a system (organization) is not only contingent upon its function but also depends upon the nature of its parts.

Like everything else, a marriage is a system. While it consists of merely two component parts—usually a husband and a wife—its varieties are innumerable. The nature of a marriage will vary not only according to the unique personalities of the two partners involved but also according to the functions it serves and the conditions under which it operates. In some ways the nature of my marriage changed as soon as Lily and I had children. It changed again when the children were out of diapers. It changed once more when the children entered adolescence. Once again it changed when they left home. Similarly, it had to change when we shifted from being relatively poor monetarily to becoming relatively wealthy. And when we moved from being the recipients of philanthropy to roughly twenty years of breaking even, and then once more when we became significant financial donors. It will certainly change again as we shortly move from middle age into old age.

Another principle of systems theory is a corollary to the fact that a system will vary according to the nature of its component parts: that if you change a part, the whole system has to change—which is to say that the other parts also have to change, at least in relationship to each other. Many people have had the experience of taking their car to the shop for a minor engine repair only to have that car conk out on them as they are driving back home from the shop. Usually when this happens they will swear at the mechanic for having done some evil deed. But as a rule, no evil deed has been done at all. It is just that the presence of a brand-new part will cause a subtle change in the entire engine, requiring an adjustment from the older parts—sometimes an adjustment those older parts are not able to make without themselves breaking down.

Whenever a married person came to see me for psycho-therapy—even when the problem had nothing to do with the marriage—I knew from the moment he or she walked through my office door that the chances were better than even that if the therapy was successful, it would eventuate either in a divorce or in the person's spouse also entering therapy. Psychotherapy is successful by definition only when the patient changes for the better. But if you put a better part back into an old marriage, it means that the marriage has to change or break down.[2] Sometimes the spouse would be quite able to make the needed changes in himself or herself on his or her own. As often as not, however, the spouse would need professional assistance in making the necessary adjustments. With unfortunate frequency he or she would refuse to change, to adjust, and divorce would be the necessary and inevitable outcome of the patient's growth.

Lily entered psychotherapy in 1965, distressed over a weight problem. Almost a year to the day later I entered psychotherapy because of a problem with anxiety. Note that neither of our problems related directly to our marriage. But any good systems theorist would suspect that that timing was more than accidental.

Lily and I have been fortunate. Our marriage has not merely survived; it has been and continues to be a gradually

---

[2] So it was that Jesus advised that new wine not be put in old wineskins.

evolving adventure. But often a painful one, particularly in its early days. Some of that pain was the result of our natural ignorance of each other as individuals, but more was the result of our ignorance of the institution of marriage. Why such astonishing ignorance? Yes, love tends to be blind, but we live in a culture that encourages such blindness, such a lack of group consciousness. When we married, both Lily and I had had five years of college. Yet neither of us ever received even a minute's worth of formal instruction on the subject of marriage. No one ever taught us that marriage as an organization cannot be expected to meet all of the partners' needs or conform to their stereotypes.

After completing my psychiatry residency training in mid-1967 I owed the army three years of 'payback' time. To fulfill this obligation I was assigned, at the age of thirty-one, to be the director of psychiatry at the U.S. Army Medical Center in Okinawa. In this position I was to manage a department of approximately forty. One senior sergeant was considerably older than I. The three other psychiatrists were approximately my age. Two junior officers were in their late twenties. The remaining thirty-five personnel were enlisted men and women in their late teens or early twenties.

Until that time I had never managed anybody. Through college, medical school, internship, and residency I had always been at the very bottom of the hierarchy. Nor, typical of such schooling, had I ever received anything faintly resembling management training. Yet from the moment I took over the department I was perfectly clear in my own mind about what my management style would be: I was going to be just as different from every authoritarian boss who had ever been in charge of me as I could possibly be.

I had no idea how to define consensus, but I was going to strive for it. Certainly my model was a highly consultative one. Not only did I never make an administrative decision without consulting everyone involved; I did my very best to see that, within the constraints of professional competence, the people under me made their own decisions wherever possible about the matters that affected their own lives. Because ours was a medical, 'professional' department, I felt we could ignore the matter of rank. I discouraged them from addressing me as 'Major Peck.' Soon everyone was calling me Scotty. I was 'Mr Nice Guy.' And it worked. The mood was euphoric. Everybody spoke glowingly of what a good leader I was and how relieved they were to be free of that stupid old lieutenant colonel, their previous commander. The work ran smoothly. The department morale was superb.

After just about six months, however, things began to go sour. It was almost imperceptible at first. The euphoria was gone. The men stopped talking about what a great place it was to work. 'All right,' I told myself, 'the honeymoon's over. What else could you expect? Now it's work as usual, but nothing's wrong.' But by the nine-month mark it began to get worse. While the work went on, petty bickering started. I wondered whether there might be a problem, but I could see nothing to account for it. Certainly it had nothing to do with me, for hadn't I shown myself to be a born leader? By the year mark, however, it was clear there was a problem. The bickering had escalated and the work was beginning to suffer. Little things were being left undone. At this point fate seemed to come to my rescue. A major new outpatient medical complex was in the final stages of construction, and the hospital commander told me that the clinic, the largest part of our department, would move there. Our current offices were cramped, cold, and gloomy. The new ones would be modern and airy, with views out over the Pacific and wall-to-wall carpeting. Surely the morale would improve at the prospect of such a pleasant move.

Only it didn't. It got worse. As moving day approached the entire staff grew ever more irritable. They began to squabble with each other over who would get which office in the new building. The packing of the files fell way behind schedule. It was now finally obvious it was my responsibility to do something. But what? I announced to the staff that we were going to meet over in the new conference room for the entirety of the next morning. And that we would continue to meet in that way every successive morning—even though it meant working in the evenings—until we got to the bottom of the problem.

The two four-hour meetings we had were two of the stormiest I have ever attended. Everyone took potshots at me and at each other. Everyone was angry. Everyone had something to complain about. Yet all the complaints were picky, superficial, and seemingly unreasonable. It was unrelieved chaos. But toward the end of the second morning one of the enlisted men said, 'I feel I don't know where I stand.' I asked him if he would elaborate. He couldn't. He became inarticulate and the group continued with its random conflict. But the young man's words reverberated through my mind. Earlier that morning someone else had said, 'Everything's vague around here.' And the day before another young man had voiced the complaint: 'It's like we're at sea.' I told the group that I needed time to think, that they should get back to work, and that we would not have any more of these meetings for the foreseeable future.

We returned to the old building, and I sat in my office staring at the ceiling, my lunch on the desk beside me, uneaten. Was it possible the department needed more structure than I had provided it? What kind of structure? A clearer sense of rank? What did they want me to do—boss them around like a bunch of children? That was totally against my nature. But then most of them were rather young, after all. Could it be that they wanted me to be some kind of father figure? Yet if I started ordering them around like an autocrat, wouldn't they hate me? I wanted to be Mr Nice Guy. But, come to think of it, it was not my job to be popular; it was my job to run the best possible department I could. Maybe they did need a stronger kind of leadership from me.

I called the noncommissioned officer in charge (NCOIC) of the department, asked him to find the plans for the new building, and bring them to me as soon as possible. When he arrived, we unrolled the floor plan for the psychiatry outpatient clinic onto my desk. I pointed to the larger corner office. 'That will be mine,' I announced. Then, intermittently pausing just long enough for him to write each assignment, I proceeded along the blueprint through the smaller offices: 'We'll put Captain Ames here, you here, Sergeant Ryan there, Lieutenant Hobson here, Private Coopermen there, Captain Marshall here, Sergeant Mosely here, Private Enowitch there,' and so on down the map. 'Now please go inform each of them of the office I've assigned him to.'

You could practically hear the howls of dismay across the island. But by evening the morale had begun to improve. The next day I watched it escalate. By the end of the week it was back to where it had been at its best. They still called me Scotty and my overall style of leadership continued to be relatively—although no longer rigidly—nonauthoritarian. Yet the morale stayed high for the remaining year of my tour of duty.

You could think of this as a success story. I did eventually acknowledge that there was a problem and that it was my responsibility. I finally took the correct steps to diagnose it. I was able to readjust my behavior to meet the needs of the organization. Indeed, the story is used in part precisely because it is such a dramatic example of how a system can be successfully changed by a single simple intervention.

I prefer, however, to regard it as a story of failure. For the fact of the matter is that the department—the organization and the individuals within it—*suffered* for over six months on account of my poor leadership. It was indelibly clear that we had a significant morale problem at least six months before I took corrective action. Why did I take so long?

One reason was my self-esteem. I simply did not want to believe that there was anything wrong with Scott Peck or that his leadership was anything other than perfect.

Fueling that conceit, however, were my needs: my need to offer the department a simplistically compassionate, non-authoritarian style of supervision, and my need to receive back the constant affection and gratitude of my subordinates. Until that final day I never even stopped to ask whether my needs were in consonance with those of the organization. It almost required a veritable relevation for me to realize that it was not necessarily my job—my role in the organization—to be popular.

It also never occurred to me that there was anything other than one best way to run any organization. I had never heard of contingency theory. My group consciousness was so limited I gave no thought to how remarkably young the members of the department were, and hence no thought to the possibility that the department might require a different style of leadership than an organization whose personnel were more mature. So it was that we suffered needlessly for months.

Would it have been different had I received some management training before being assigned to Okinawa? Would Lily and I have suffered substantially less, I wonder, had we had the benefit of some instruction on marriage before the fact? These questions are too hypothetical to answer with certainty, but at the very least, the response should be a guarded yes.

It must be a guarded response since, being different, individuals have different styles of learning. Some children learn better in open classrooms while others do best in more structured situations. Some young adults benefit far more from formal instruction than from experience, while others do far better with experiential learning. Moreover, certain types of instruction are more or less suitable depending on the type of material being presented. Contingency theory again! I cannot be sure how much I could have benefited from management training until I actually became a manager. Or how much a course in marriage would have meant before I had an actual marriage to deal with.

Certainly, as a psychiatrist, I would have been at a total loss working with my first patients had I not had at least some previous grounding in Freud and other personality theories. On the other hand, I must admit that I have learned considerably more, on the whole, from my patients than from textbooks. Would it not be safe to assume that it is not an either/or issue—a question of whether education is better before the fact or after the fact—but more properly a both/and issue?

Because consciousness of the organizations, groups, and systems to which we belong is such a critical cornerstone of civility, the matter of education to such consciousness will be the primary focus of the concluding section of this work. There it will be described how, over the past decade, major breakthroughs in the field of 'group learning' have occurred that offer us new and better means to fill the hole in the mind. Some of the teaching 'technologies' involved will then be examined in depth. For the moment, it need only be mentioned that we now know that group or organizational consciousness can be developed in almost every human being through training. We know not only that such training is far more effective when it is experiential but also that the effectiveness can be enhanced when it is immediately followed by some more or less didactic instruction to reinforce it. We know such training can be effective with people at least as young as fifteen. Finally, we know that its effectiveness is vastly increased through repetition.

So at issue is not whether such things as marital instruction, 'parent effectiveness training,' or management training should be given before the fact or after the fact. These are simply varieties of education that develop our group or organizational consciousness, and hence our civility. Such education should begin before we are spouses, parents, or employees or managers, and should clearly continue long after we have assumed these organizational roles. Its teachings can be used both as preventive medicine and for reconstructive surgery. Learning to elevate our consciousness of the larger systems to which we belong is a learning for all seasons.

5

Enter God, Stage Left

Ethics and Submission

I have a friend who was one of the first American pilots to be shot down and captured by the North Vietnamese. In the early days of his seven-year captivity, he and his fellow prisoners of war were systematically tortured. In an extraordinary book about his experiences, he made it quite clear how his captors were engaging in fully conscious organizational behavior.[1] They knew exactly what they were doing. They were conscious of their intent and the effect their beatings and even more brutal practices had on their victims. They knew that anyone will break under enough pain and that their torture would extract confessions—no matter how false—useful for propaganda purposes in serving their organizational mission. Yet, even those of us who were horrified by the incivility of America's prosecution of the Vietnam War would never consider that torture to have been a civil response or in any way justified.

So civility is something more than organizational behavior that is merely 'consciously motivated.' It must be *ethical* as well. And all but the morally insane would agree that torture is inherently and grossly unethical. Instances of gross incivility—torture, rape, murder, criminal child abuse, and so on—abound. In making its points, however, this book will generally employ illustrations of more subtle, everyday incivility for several reasons. Their subtlety will compel us to an even deeper analysis so that we can put our

[1] Gerald Coffee, *Beyond Survival* (New York: G. P. Putnam's Sons, 1990).

fingers on the very essence of civility. As horrifying as outrageous incivility is, our everyday incivility is responsible for a vaster amount of human misery. Finally, such misery eventually tends to become itself a cause of overt brutality.

Thus, the advertisement described at the beginning of this book portrayed an example of apparently 'acceptable' incivility. The businessman who called to get a credit rating on the company of his seat-mate before buying him a beer was certainly not doing anything criminal. Yet I proclaimed that the ad indicated that something was seriously wrong. What? What harm could there be in such organizational behavior? So what if the businessman was so shallow as to consider the seatmate his 'new best friend' simply on the basis that the man represented a good business prospect?

Approximately sixty years ago, the great Jewish theologian Martin Buber wrote a dense, scholarly, almost unreadable book whose title has been translated into English as *I and Thou*.[2] By virtue of its profundity, which inspired many others to build upon it,[3] the work is one of the most important books ever written on the subject of human relationships—organizational behavior—in general and on the subject of human narcissism in particular. It is the place to start our ethical analysis.

As its title indicates, Buber labeled the most healthy or mature relationship possible between two human beings as the 'I-Thou' relationship. In such an instance, I recognize you to be different from me, but even though you are different—a 'You' or other—you can still be beloved to me; namely, a 'Thou.' Such relationships are relatively rare. Indeed, one should not even aspire to too many of them since they require a lot of work. For instance, I do not have an I-Thou relationship with my tax lawyer. I do recognize him to be different from me: a You. Indeed, it is precisely

[2] Martin Buber, *I and Thou* trans. Walter Kaufmann (New York: Charles Scribner's Sons, 1970).
[3] See Maurice Friedman, *The Confirmation of Otherness* (New York: The Pilgrim Press, 1983).

because he is different from me—because he has gifts different from mine—that he is so valuable to me, but I have not yet taken the energy (nor am I likely to do so) to make him particularly beloved to me. Most of the time we go around having I-You relationships. There is nothing un-ethical about this as long as we recognize and respect the essential humanity of each other.

But the problem comes, as Buber indelibly pointed out, when we lose sight of the humanity of the other simply because he or she is other. Consequently, Buber contrasted the I-Thou relationship with what he called the I-It relationship. This occurs when I see you as a subhuman, even inanimate, object—an 'It'— simply to be used, as we might use a chair or shovel. What was so seriously wrong with that advertisement was its implication that I-It rela-tionships are perfectly acceptable, if not downright virtuous, forms of organizational behavior. The depicted business-man was pretending that his seatmate was a Thou or his 'new best friend' when, in fact, he was an object, an account to be checked out, and if the results warranted it, to be buttered up with a pretense of civility.

So what? Why is it necessarily wrong to treat our fellow people like objects? Granted, we don't have outright slavery anymore, but this is certainly a common practice in our military and business affairs, where workers become mere numbers to be moved around. There are, in fact, rare times when top executives may have little other choice, and the ambiguities involved will be addressed in some depth much later in a chapter on business and ethics. For the moment, however, let me simply state that it is *wrong* to regard any other human being, a priori, as an object, or an 'It.' This is so because each and every human being—you, every friend, every stranger, every foreigner—is *precious*.

The attitude that all human beings are precious is referred to as humanism. By itself, however, it is merely an attitude. It doesn't say anything about *why* humans are precious. This is the reason conservative Christians in recent years have been decrying 'secular humanism.' Many such conservative Christians behave with far les civility than the secular humanists they criticize. With this caveat, however, the criticism needs to be taken seriously. For secular humanism is like a house built on sand. When the going gets rough—when a business is bad or strife is abroad—such humanistic attitudes may easily be blown away.

For this reason, I do not believe that secular ethics — ethics without theology—can be adequate. They do not relate us to the larger system. They leave God out of the picture. Mind you, secular humanists may be quite conscious of systems theory and the most active of ecologists. But the larger system they have in mind is solely that of the 'visible,' material world.

The word *religion* comes from the Latin *religio*, a root that has received a remarkable number of different translations. The translation most meaningful to me is 'to connect.' William James defined religion as the attempt to be in harmony with an *unseen* order of things.[4] In other words, theology attempts to delineate our proper *connection* to a spiritual, as opposed to purely material, universe.

This matter of connection is the essence of Michael Novak's distinction between what he called the 'secular' and the 'sacred' mentality.[5] The person with a secular mentality feels himself to be the center of the universe. Yet he is likely to suffer from a sense of meaninglessness and insignificance because he knows he's but one human among five billion others—all feeling themselves to be the center of things — scratching out an existence on the surface of a medium-sized planet circling a small star among countless stars in a galaxy lost among countless galaxies. The person with a sacred mentality, on the other hand, does not feel herself to

[4] William James, *The Varieties of Religious Experience* (New York: Random House, 1978), p. 53. Originally published in 1902.
[5] Michael Novak, *Ascent of the Mountain, Flight of the Dove*, rev. ed. (New York: Harper & Row, 1978).

be the center of the universe. She considers the Center to be elsewhere and other. Yet she is unlikely to feel lost or insignificant precisely because she draws her significance and meaning from her relationship, her connection, with that center, that Other.

More specifically than in the Eastern religions, the Western religions designate the Other or God to be Creator. And here we have a theological foundation for the humanism civility requires. Human beings are special because God created them. By virtue of their relationship with the sacredness of their Creator, they themselves are sacred creatures.[6]

Indeed, Islam holds that God not only created human beings but actually created them higher than the angels.[7] In Judaism our creation in some ways is seen as an ongoing process. Yahweh is a 'God of Presence,' speaking to us, listening to us, and actively intervening in our lives. Note the intimacy of the Psalms. And in Christianity, God is still more present and intimately involved, even to the point of coming down 'to live and die as one of us' and, as the 'Holy Spirit,' whispering daily in the ears of each one of us.

The idea that God has a direct, perpetual, loving relationship with each human being has extraordinary significance in every aspect of our lives, including our organizational behavior. Glenn Tinder, a political scientist, has recently and compellingly argued that it provides the only ideological foundation for humane ethics.[8] From it is derived the concept of what he calls 'the exalted individual.'

---

[6] The belief that we are sacred creatures has enormous implications in regard to our treatment not only of others but also of ourselves. It is the essential reason—to give just one instance—for the religious prohibition against suicide. From one vantage point, suicide may be looked upon as the ultimate act of arrogance. Being sacred creatures, we are not our own creatures in large part. What right have we, then, to be our own destroyers? Many who commit suicide think, 'It's my life to do with as I want,' as if their life were an 'It'—a thing—of their own creation.

[7] The Koran, Sura II, verses 30–36. These verses suggest that Satan, an angel, rebelled against God precisely because of God's elevation of Adam above the angels.

[8] Glenn Tinder, 'Can We Be Good Without God?: On the Political Meaning of Christianity,' *The Atlantic Monthly*, December 1989, pp. 69–85.

He is careful to point out that our exalted nature is but one side of a paradox; the other side is our 'fallen,' sinful nature. The entirety of the paradox must be embraced for us to keep our spiritual feet on the ground. But since God, despite our sin, considers each of us worthy of his/her unconditional love, it is incumbent upon us to afford each other in our organizational lives at least some faintly corresponding measure of dignity.

As Tinder puts it, 'The concept of the exalted individual implies that governments—indeed, all persons who wield power—must treat individuals with care.' It is a cornerstone of civility.

Tinder's article was entitled in the form of a question: 'Can We Be Good Without God?' I would answer, 'Yes . . . when the living is easy.' So I now complete the definition of civility not as merely 'consciously motivated organizational behavior that is ethical,' but specifically 'ethical in submission to a Higher Power.' Without such submission, our ethics are likely to fly out the window in times of trouble. Secular humanism tends to become less humanistic when the climate is harsh. By civility, I mean something deeper —more radical and fundamental—than a fair-weather phenomenon.

The term 'Higher Power' was coined, or at least initially popularized, by the Twelve Steps of Alcoholics Anonymous. In the definition of civility, I have used it rather than the name of God for two reasons.

One is that the term is simultaneously both more broad and more specific. If I used God, it would imply one would have to be a believer in order to be a civil person. That is not the case. Some atheists and many agnostics or secular humanists are immensely civil human beings. Although none is adequate, there are synonyms for God: God is light; God is love; God is truth. Anyone deeply dedicated to love, light, and truth will be civil indeed, no matter what her formal belief system or lack of it is.

Conversely, there are legions of believers who are not so dedicated. The word *praxis* means the integration of belief with behavior or practice. The opposite of praxis is blasphemy. Blasphemy is not the use of bawdy language or swearing. Rather, as in using the name of God in vain, it refers to a public espousal of belief in God while failing to make any significant attempt to behave in accordance with such expressed faith. It is a failure of praxis, a failure to 'walk your talk.' Unfortunately, it is very common, if for no other reason than we have a great capacity to subvert the will of God to our own. There are many who believe in God while lacking any taste for submitting themselves to God—to love, light, and truth. Consequently, all manner of incivility through the ages has actually been committed in the name of God.

The other reason I use the term *Higher* Power, therefore, is that it not only implies that there is something 'higher' than us as individuals, but it also implies the appropriateness of our submitting ourselves to that something higher, be it love, light, truth, or God. 'Thy will, not mine, be done' was a glorious expression of desire for such submission. The key word is *will*. Submission, particularly as used in our now complete definition of civility, implies an effective submission of the human will to something higher than itself.

While always free, the human will seems to vary in its strength from person to person. In the course of my psychiatric practice I saw many women and men whose tenacity was truly extraordinary. They either held on to obviously maladaptive patterns with enormous vigor or with equal vigor made giant steps away from such patterns towards health. Other patients, however, struck me as strangely lacking in 'oomph,' as if they had been born apathetic. Because they quickly drifted out of therapy, I was never able to get a sense of whether their lackluster nature was genetic or the result of some unknown but devastating defeat in childhood that had extinguished their spark. The causes of strength and weakness of will are mysterious. Be that as it may, I believe a strong will is the greatest blessing that can be bestowed upon a person—not because it guarantees success, but because a weak will guarantees failure.

All blessings are potential curses. It is a strong will that creates a Hitler as well as an Albert Schweitzer. And even when beneficial, major blessings have potential side effects that must be dealt with. One of the side effects of a strong will, for instance, is the tendency to temper. It is strong-willed people who wrap golf-clubs around trees because that damn little ball won't go where they *want* it to.

Having a weak will is like having a little donkey in your backyard. It can't do much for you, but it can't hurt you very much either. About the worst it can do is chomp on your tulips. Having a strong will, on the other hand, is more like having a dozen Belgian horses in your backyard. Unless they are properly trained, disciplined, and harnessed, then with them you can literally move mountains.

The notion of harnessing the will raises a profound issue: What is it to be harnessed *to*? It cannot simply be harnessed to itself, because then it will remain unharnessed. No, if the will is to be voluntarily harnessed, one must choose to harness it to something *higher* than oneself, than one's own will. It can only be harnessed to a Higher Power.

The distinction between the harnessed and the unharnessed will was made with great clarity by Gerald May in his book, *Will and Spirit*, notably in the first chapter entitled 'Willfulness and Willingness.'[9] Willfulness refers to the unharnessed will, which by definition is merely willful. By willingness May did not mean being a pushover, but a trait of those of strong will who have placed their wills in God's service, who are *willing* to move whenever and wherever God calls.

This matter of harnessing the will to a Higher Power is of such importance that the playwright Peter Shaffer made it

[9] Gerald May, *Will and Spirit: A Contemplative Psychology* (San Francisco: Harper & Row, 1982).

the conclusion of his masterpiece, *Equus*.[10] As the title suggests, horses are the motif of this play, which is superficially about a disturbed adolescent who blinded six horses. On a deeper level the play is about his psychiatrist, Martin Dysart, who, in the process of working with the young man, resolves his own mid-life spiritual crisis. The final lines come when Dysart says in soliloquy, 'I cannot call it ordained of God. I can't get that far. I will, however, pay it so much homage. There is now, in my mouth, this sharp chain. And it never comes out.'

Dysart says cautiously that he cannot refer to himself as 'ordained of God,' and, indeed he does not have to. A decade ago I attended a week-long intensive course on ethics. Ethics is defined simply as that branch of philosophy that attempts to answer 'the ethical question.' This question is, 'What makes an act good?' Over the millennia philosophers have answered it in a variety of ways, which are the various ethical theories. Perhaps because the discipline of philosophy has come to be divorced from that of theology, none of these theories has ever proven itself to be wholly adequate. However, the theory to which the course devoted the greatest attention was called the 'ideal observer theory.'[11] It states, 'That act is good which appears good to an ideal observer.' Sometimes philosophers seem to talk in circles, but in this case the professor went on to define an ideal observer as 'a being who is more knowledgeable than you, more objective than you, yet who still cares.'

It won't take long to realize that when we are talking about a caring being who is more knowledgeable and objective than us, we are likely talking about God—except that if you talk about God in academic philosophy you might lose your tenure. Certainly, one of the things I am most commonly doing when I am in prayer is checking out my life with my Ideal Observer. Struggling to respond to the myriad of

[10] Peter Shaffer, *Equus* (New York: Avon Books, 1974), p. 125.
[11] See Charles Taliaferro, 'The Environmental Ethics of an Ideal Observer,' *Environmental Ethics* 10 (Fall 1988), pp. 233–50, for a recent discussion of the theory.

questions in my life, I am continually asking, 'Hey, God, how does this look through your eyes? From up there in your position as a Higher Power?'

When I had the opportunity to address the commissioners of education at that meeting to examine the issue of teaching values in public school education, I began by saying that God is 'the bottom line.' For the reasons stated, I explained to them that there can be no such thing as a totally adequate secular ethic. Without including God in the system there may be no way to ultimately justify a bottom line any nobler than this quarter's profitability without regard to consequences, which seemed to be the prevailing 'ethic' of the eighties. I recounted how in his early years Einstein had hoped to develop a 'unified field theory' that would explain everything and thereby explain away God. Having failed to do so, toward the end of his life Einstein pronounced, 'Subtle is the Lord.'[12] Since God is indeed subtle, I suggested to the commissioners that it would behoove us to teach godly values with subtlety. Ideal observer theory, it seemed to me, would be a perfect vehicle in this regard. God need not even be mentioned by name. Yet by practicing ideal observer theory, students would not only be exercising their own observing egos; they would also be attempting to be in harmony with an unseen order, with a Higher Power.

I have no idea whether any of the commissioners ever took my recommendation. It gives me pleasure, however, to fantasize about a society in which all citizens by the end of adolescence learned to routinely put ideal observer theory into practice. Just think of what it would be like if all husbands and wives, all parents, all employees and executives automatically considered their organizational behavior from the vantage point of a caring being more knowledgeable and objective than themselves! Might it not be a considerably more civil world?

[12] Abraham Pais, *Subtle Is the Lord: The Science and the Life of Albert Einstein* (New York: Oxford University Press, 1982), p. 113.

Having explained my rationale for using the term 'Higher Power' in place of the name of God in the formal redefinition of civility, I believe I must immediately back-pedal. Throughout the rest of the book, whenever theology is relevant, I will usually not be talking about a Higher Power but about God—and specifically the God of my Christian orientation. It is not my desire to exclude anybody of a different religious orientation, and I hope that non-Christians will be able to reference this material to the God of their own understanding and forgive me my parochialism. As a particular and inevitably limited human, I simply do not know how to adequately address many issues of the relationship between organizational behavior and a Higher Power without specific reference to my *particular* kind of God.[13]

One such issue (which will be repeatedly addressed) is that of vocation. In its purely secular usage, the word *vocation* refers merely to whatever job one performs (usually for an organization). It bespeaks nothing of the meaning of that job. For instance, when it finally dawned upon me in Okinawa that my job was not necessarily to be popular, I became a more civil human being. My organizational consciousness enlarged sufficiently to take therapeutic action as a manager, a simple action which dramatically improved the health of a small organization. But so what? Is that the goal: merely to become a better organization man? No matter what the organization—whether it be the U.S. Army Medical Corps or the Third Reich?[14]

The answer provided by the Adolph Eichmanns of the world is obviously NO. There is clearly a higher human destiny than selling your soul to an organization, and he who

[13] Probably the greatest virtue and problem of Christianity has been labeled 'the scandal of Particularity,' that is, the question its theology raises of why God should have incarnated himself (or herself) in that particular person (Jesus) in that particular culture at that particular time, and no other.

[14] It is reported that Albert Speer was interested in applying the most modern and humane motivating theories to the management philosophy and structure of the Nazi death camps.

makes the organization his Higher Power has dramatically lost his way.

Yet it is also not proper to regard the organization as an 'It,' something lower or utterly inferior to oneself. To do so is to fall into the opposite trap from that of the organization man. It is an equally common trap. There are many who regard their organizations—their businesses and sometimes even their families—solely as things to be used. They have no qualms about undermining the organization for their own advancement, subverting it for their own needs. They feel no loyalty to it for its nurturance. They are essentially predators.

The proper relationship between the individual and the organization, then, is a *lateral* one. Civil people regard their organizations as they would the other person: neither superior nor inferior to themselves. The proper relationship between the individual and God, on the other hand, is a *vertical* one, with God on top and in the driver's seat. Ideally, God should be submitted to at all times, whereas one should submit herself to husband, child, family, neighbor, and organization only some of the time. The great commandment might be rewritten: 'Love thy Lord, your God, with all of your heart and mind and soul, and your neighbor (or organization) *as* yourself.'

Occasionally, I find myself wishing I could write a book that totally left God out of the picture. It would be easier for me and simpler for the reader. But I cannot. Either God belongs in the system or does not. As both a believer in the 'unseen order of things' and a systems theorist attempting to be in harmony with that order, I must try to bear God, or my Higher Power, in mind at all times—even when it places a burden upon my audience.

And a burden it is. We see now that civility requires not merely consciousness but more specifically four types, or foci, of consciousness: the self, the other, the organization, and now God, or a Power Higher than the first three. Just to comprehend it, the reader must exercise his civility as this book requires him to continually bounce back and forth — literally vibrate—between these four levels of consciousness. And if that was not enough, yet another issue will repeatedly be left dangling: Is there such a thing as collective consciousness? In other words, can an organization itself become conscious above and beyond the consciousness of its individual members? Is the most civil organization something more than the sum of its parts? Only in the final section will this question be directly addressed, and even then the answer will be ambiguous.

So this is a lot of consciousness. It will be recalled that no matter how much joy may be its reward, pain is the inevitable and continual price of consciousness. There is only so much pain a body or mind can bear. We need to sleep. We need some of our defenses. We need to take time off now and then. Total consciousness is probably an impossibility in this life. 'Now we see through a glass darkly,' said the Apostle Paul, 'but then face to face.'[15] It behooves the reader to be civil to herself. Should you find yourself feeling overwhelmed by the darkness, by your own blindness and the limits of your consciousness, be gentle with yourself. Remember that unfailing civility is an ideal. We will inevitably fall short. We are not born perfect creatures. Still, it is an ideal toward which we should continually strive, and by so striving, with the help of God's grace, we will *become* more perfect.

This chapter has uncovered three additional interlocking cornerstones of civility. One is an attitude of humanism, which may be defined as the ethical consciousness of other people, individually and collectively, as precious beings. A second is a foundation for humanism in theology, in a belief that humans are so precious because they are created by a divine and Higher Power, reflecting in themselves some of

[15] I Corinthians 13:12.

the divinity of their Creator. The third is that the civil individual must be in a relationship of willing submission to that Higher Power.

Just as consciousness is ever expanding, leading us to the awareness of an even larger system, so civility is an ever-expanding process. It is but a small step from seeing other people as precious by virtue of their Creator to seeing all creation as precious. The practice of civility inevitably leads us into larger systems, ecological consciousness, and a loving concern for the integrity of the whole.

While the definition of civility as 'consciously motivated organizational behavior that is ethical in submission to a Higher Power' is now complete, more is needed to complete this introduction. God is inherently mysterious, but certain questions are crying out to be answered. I have spoken of a relationship with God or a Higher Power. But what is the nature of such a relationship? How does God relate to us? And how do we relate to God? I have said we should relate to God in submission, but what does that actually mean? What does such submission look like? What does it require of us? What can we do to nurture such a relationship? And, finally, can't we be a little more specific about the connection between this relationship and our organizational behavior? My Christian theology does have some answers to these questions, imperfect though they may be. It is to these answers in the next three chapters we now turn.

The Apostle Paul also said that it is terrifying to fall into the hands of the living God. That falling—the submission required—may be excruciating. Don't listen to any false prophet who tells you that the ethical life can somehow be a perfectly comfortable one. The definition of civility implies that the higher authority, or God's will—the ethical imperative—is frequently at odds with either the individual's will or the organization's goals or both. And so it is. We often must work out such conflicts in fear and trembling. But remember our starting point—the fact that health is often a painful process. Civility is never painless. In fact, it is usually more painful to be civil than it is to be uncivil. Incivility comes easily. Nonetheless, relatively and understandably rare though it may be, civility is the path of growth, the road to personal and collective salvation or healing. Civility is hardly the only way to live, but it is the only way that is worthwhile.

6

Yes, Virginia, There Is Unconditional Love

Covenant

'Unconditional love' has become a popular phrase these days. But I am not sure there is such a thing between human beings—unless it is the love of parents for their infant, and even then it is based on the fact that it is *theirs*. And as soon as the infant grows up enough to talk back to them, that love becomes conditional indeed. I'm not saying that unconditional love isn't, like civility, an ideal toward which we should strive. Indeed, the more we strive the closer we come to that ideal, and such striving has much to do with civility. All I'm saying is that, as 'comparing creatures,' we're invariably judgmental to a greater or lesser degree. Unconditional love does not come naturally to us humans. But God is another matter.

We left off the Old Testament account of human evolution when Adam and Eve were expelled as conscious beings from the Garden of Eden. Let us pick up the story again. Is it an accident that the very next significant occurrence is murder? Cain slays Abel in Genesis 4. And apparently this sort of incivility continued through the succeeding generations, with the result that by Genesis 6 God is fed up with his creation. He determines to get rid of all animal life by wiping the slate clean with a flood. At the last moment, however, he decides to spare the life of a just man, Noah, and that of his wife and his sons and their wives, along with an assorted selection of all the other creatures. So at God's instruction they ride out the flood together on the ark. And when the waters recede, he directs them to proceed forth, multiply on the face of the earth, and begin the whole business all over again.

But at this point, something truly extraordinary happens. In Genesis 8 and 9 God decides 'in His Heart' never again to destroy his creation, *no matter how wicked or uncivil we creatures might be*. It was not that the slate was wiped clean. The decision is made with no illusions. He makes it with full knowledge that 'the imagination of man's heart is evil from his youth.' And he proclaims this decision to Noah and his sons in the form of a promise to them *and their seed* and to all creatures, despite their evil, 'for perpetual generations.' This promise is called a covenant, and God makes its token the rainbow, saying, 'And it shall come to pass, when I bring a cloud over the earth, that the bow shall be seen in the cloud: and I will remember my covenant, which is between me and you and every living creature of all flesh; and the waters shall no more become a flood to destroy all flesh.'[1]

This is the earliest example in the Bible—and, as far as I know, in all literature—of unconditional love. A covenant is not a contract. It goes far deeper. A contract is always both bilateral and conditional. It is executed between two or more parties under specified conditions, saying, 'I will do this on the condition that you do that, and if you do not do what is specified, than you will be in violation of contract and I am released from any obligation to you.' But here God is saying unilaterally, on his own initiative, 'I will behave in such a way as to not destroy you or your seed, regardless of how you behave.' No ifs, ands, or buts. No conditions. A covenant implies unconditional caring.

Although unconditional love does not come as naturally to human beings as to God, nonetheless, from time to time, we humans have attempted to care unconditionally for each other. I am told that the early Hebrews would occasionally

[1] Genesis 9:14–15.

covenant with one another—and *on behalf of their seed* or offspring. As a token of such covenant, it was apparently customary for them to cut their forearms and place their wounds together so that their blood would mingle, in the same way that American Indians would reputedly make themselves 'blood brothers.'[2] The best-known example of a covenant between humans in the Old Testament was between David and King Saul's son, Jonathan.[3]

After Saul and Jonathan were slain by the Philistines, what little remained of the House of Saul went into hiding and David was made king over Israel. A few years pass before David learns that Jonathan had a son, Mephibosheth, a crippled youth, surviving in the squalor of an outcast camp. Because of his covenant with Jonathan, David has the young cripple brought to him, and not only restores his land but invites the lad to always dine with him amid the splendor of the king's table.[4] Mephibosheth apparently does so, but then shortly vanishes to return to the outcast camp. Many more years pass, and suddenly one day Mephibosheth, in rags, shows up once again at King David's palace. When David asks him why he left, Mephibosheth in essence replies, 'My people told me you were not to be trusted, and I believed them. I thought it was too good to be true. But after watching you from afar I have come to realize, even though I do not deserve it, that your charity, your love and covenant, is for real.' And so it was that the poor, lame man returned to the splendor of the royal table.[5]

Ever since I first heard this rather obscure little story, it has continued to grow on me. Like Mephibosheth, we are all crippled in one way or another. It *is* hard to trust unconditional love. But we have the power of choice. Just

---

[2] I am indebted for this information, and the exegesis that follows, to William Linden, a lawyer and lay minister.
[3] I Samuel 18:3; 20:42; 23:18.
[4] II Samuel 9.
[5] II Samuel 19:24–30.

because it is there doesn't mean we have to accept a covenant or believe in it. We can turn away from it. But since it is there, unconditionally, we always have the right to change our minds and return to it. These points are critical, for it is within the context of God's covenantal relationship with us that the call to civility exists. We can accept or we can reject our true vocations. We can choose to hear and attend to the still small voice of conscience or God. It is also within our power to refuse to hear and ignore it. And, finally, we can always change.

As expressed to Noah, God's covenant initially seemed to be with the entire human race, even the entirety of the animal kingdom. Yet within ten generations or so he seems to have become quite selective about it. Certainly he seemed to have no compunction about destroying whole cities—for example, Sodom and Gomorrah—because of the wickedness of their inhabitants. And he begins to have a covenant, a special relationship, with a particular tribe, the family of Abraham, and then more specifically with the progeny of Abraham's grandson, Jacob. Thereafter the Old Testament seems to suggest that God's covenant is not with all humanity but only with Israel.

Not that this is a covenant with a group—a tribe or nation. It is not an individual matter. God does speak to individuals, to Moses and the prophets, but his purpose in doing so seems to be not so much for the individual's benefit as for the benefit of Israel. The primary theme of the Old Testament is that God is using individuals to assist in his designs for the group.

From the very beginning of the New Testament, however, the nature of this covenant starts changing. Simeon, after witnessing the circumcision of the infant Jesus, sings: 'Lord, you now have set your servant free to go in peace as you have promised, for these eyes of mine have seen the Savior, whom you have prepared for *all the world* to see, a light to enlighten *the nations* and the glory of your people, Israel.'⁶ Jesus is Israel's glory, but that glory is prophesied to be for the benefit, once again as in Noah's time, of all humanity.

Then there is the relationship between Jesus and God, so different in flavor from that of the Old Testament prophets to God. It is not so much one of awe as one of intimacy and equality. Jesus, who calls God 'Abba,' or 'Daddy,' seems to be on a best-friend kind of footing with his Father.

Moreover, Jesus's relationship with the Jews, with Israel, is not predominantly special. He grieves over Jerusalem and has some of his own tribal prejudice to overcome. But he makes himself available not only to Jews but to anyone who seems to need him enough, to Canaanites and Samaritans and Romans—to *people*.

Finally, on the night before he dies, Jesus serves his disciples wine and tells them, 'This is my blood of the *New* Covenant, which is shed for you and for *many* for the forgiveness of sins.' In the months and years that followed, those disciples and other early Christians heatedly debated what Jesus meant by the word *many*. Many Jews or many people? Within a decade or so the debate was resolved: the blood, the communion, the covenant will be offered to anyone who accepts it, to the Jew and to the Gentile, to the circumcised and the uncircumcised, to all willing people.

So this is my belief as a Christian: that God covenants—has covenanted—with everyone. But I think there is something else that is 'new' about this covenant beyond its universality. I do not believe this covenant is simply with us humans as a species, like God's covenant spoken to Noah. Instead, I believe it is with each of us human beings as *individuals*, that God unconditionally loves you and me and every other single person in the world.

⁶ Luke 2:25–32 (emphasis added).

Indeed, Christian doctrine holds that not only *did* God once die for all of us and each of us, but also that she/he continues to suffer over each of us *today*, tomorrow, and for eternity. Before he died Jesus promised us this direct, ongoing, individual relationship with God through the aegis of something he called either the 'Comforter' or the 'Holy Ghost.'[7] Today this aegis is generally referred to as the 'Holy Spirit,' a term that I will occasionally employ. For the most part, however, I will simply talk in terms of God speaking to us to signify the directness of the 'hotline' that each of us has with her/him.

I have already spoken of the immense significance that this direct, perpetual, unconditionally loving relationship or covenant with each of us holds for our organizational behavior. I agree with Tinder that, by virtue of its 'exaltation of the individual,' God's covenantal, ongoing caring for us is the ground of ethical behavior and civility.

But God's covenant with us as individuals has another profound implication for our organizational behavior—one which, to my knowledge, has not received attention elsewhere. It is that God *only* covenants with individuals and does *not* covenant—at least any longer—with organizations. In other words, while individuals are exalted, their organizations—the family, the clan, the church, the business, the government, and so on—are not. Indeed, we get in serious difficulty whenever we attempt (as we so often do) to exalt our human institutions.

I do not mean to imply that God has no interest in organizations. To the contrary, God actively loves, blesses, and nurtures those organizations that suit her purposes. But unlike her love for individuals, God's love for organizations is fully conditional. It is not covenantal. If the organization is sufficiently sinful, God will dump it, desert it, even if it is a church supposedly operating in God's name. It is vitally

[7] John 14.

important for people to bear this in mind as they work out their vocations and seek to practice civility.

Bearing it in mind, we should continually be asking ourselves a series of questions. Is this organization in which I participate a godly one? Is it a civil organization that genuinely serves people well, thereby serving God? If not, what role can I play to make it more civil, more godly? And if there is nothing creative I can do in this regard, does God desire me to remain in such an uncreative role? Or might God be calling me elsewhere, to an organization more civil and a role more creative? These are some of the often painful questions of vocation in its deeper sense. They are ethical questions that are difficult to ask without reference to—without a relationship with—God or a Higher Power. They are also so critical to our organizational lives that the issue of vocation needs now to be examined in greater depth.

7

Tell Them I Came but No One Answered[1]

Vocation

To most people vocation simply means what one does for a living, one's occupation or career. For many religious, however, the definition is more literal, yet far more complex.

The word *vocation* literally means 'calling.' It is derived from the Latin verb *vocare*, 'to call'—the same verb that is the root of the adjective *vocal*. The religious meaning of vocation, therefore, is what one is called to do, which may or may not coincide with one's occupation, with what one is actually doing.

In this sense vocation implies a relationship. For if someone is called, something must be doing the calling. This something is God. As a Christian, I believe that God calls us human beings—whether skeptics or believers, whether Christian or not—to certain, often very specific activities. Furthermore, since God relates—covenants — with us as individuals, so this matter of calling is utterly individualized. What God is calling me to do is not at all necessarily what God is calling you to do.

And just as we, like Mephibosheth, are free to reject the covenant, so we are free to refuse to heed God's call. The fact that we have a vocation doesn't necessarily mean that we will follow it. Conversely, the fact that we want to do something doesn't necessarily mean it is what God wants us to do, calls us to do.

Monks and nuns tend to be the experts on the subject of

[1] A line from a poem by Walter De la Mare, 'The Listeners,' *Collected Poems 1901–18* (New York: Henry Holt and Co., 1920), vol. 1, p. 144.

vocation, for it is in monastic life that the issue has traditionally been regarded as most central. Is this aspiring nun or monk truly called to the monastery? Did God create, design him or her for the cloistered life or for this particular type of religious order? For celibacy? Does God actually desire this man to be a monk, yearn for this woman to be a nun? These are key questions, debated at extraordinary length within monastic halls. The periods of postulancy and novitiate preceding the taking of monastic vows have been established not only to train aspirants for the life but also to 'test' their vocations. And it is not uncommon for a novice who has spent two or more years in the mother house and seemingly adjusted well to be called in to the office of the Superior or novice mistress and told: 'I'm sorry, my dear, but we have decided you don't have a vocation.' Or the same for a man who eagerly desires to be a monk. And he or she must then leave the order. These seemingly brutal judgments about vocation may not always be made correctly, but they are always made with great seriousness.

As some may not be called at the deepest level of their being to something they superficially want to do, so also may some spend years—even a lifetime—fleeing their true vocation. A forty-year-old sergeant major in the army consulted me for a mild depression that he ascribed to an upcoming reassignment to Germany in two weeks' time. He and his family were sick and tired of moving, he claimed. It was unusual for top-ranking enlisted men (or officers) to seek psychiatric consultation, especially for such a minor condition. Several other things were also extraordinary about this man. People do not get to be sergeant major without considerable intelligence and competence, but my patient exuded wit and gentility as well. Somehow I was not surprised to hear that painting was his hobby. He struck me as being artistic. After learning he had been in the service for twenty-two years, I asked him, 'Since you're so fed up with moving, why don't you retire?'

'I wouldn't know what to do with myself.'

'You could paint as much as you wanted,' I suggested.

'No, that's just a hobby. It's not something I could make a living on.'

Having no idea of his talent, I was not in a position to rebut him on that score, but there were other ways to probe his resistance. 'You're an obviously intelligent man with a fine track record,' I countered. 'You could get lots of good jobs.'

'I haven't been to college,' he replied, 'and I'm not cut out for selling insurance.'

'Why don't you go to college then? You could make it on your retirement pay.'

'No, I'm too old. I wouldn't feel right around a bunch of kids.'

A minor intuition grabbed me. 'Over the course of your career did anyone ever suggest you go to Officer's Candidate School, that you become an officer?'

He blushed. 'Well, three times actually.'

'But you never took them up on it?'

'No,' he answered, still blushing slightly. 'If you keep looking at the horizon, sooner or later you're going to stumble over a root or rock.'

We had time for only one more appointment before his reassignment. I asked him to return and bring with him some of his more recent paintings.

He came back the following week with the minimum number: two, one an oil and the other a watercolor. Both were magnificent. They were modern, imaginative, even flamboyant, with an extraordinarily effective use of shape, shade, and pigment. 'How many more of these do you have at home?' I inquired.

'Maybe four or five. I don't paint very often. I do only three or four a year.'

'Have you ever had a show?'

'No.'

'Or attempt to sell any of them?'

'No, I just give them away to my friends.'

73

'Look,' I said, 'you've got real talent. I know it's a competitive field, but these are sellable. Painting ought to be more than just a hobby for you.'

'Talent's a subjective judgment,' he demurred.

'So, I'm the only one who's ever told you you have real talent?'

'No, but if you keep looking at the horizon, your feet are going to stumble.'

I told him he had an obvious problem with underachievement, probably rooted in either some kind of fear of failure or fear of success or both. I offered to obtain for him a medical release from his reassignment so that he could stay on post for us to work together exploring the roots of his problem. But he was adamant that it was his 'duty' to proceed to Germany. His symptoms were not sufficient for me to order him to do otherwise. I gave him the name of the chief psychiatrist at his new post in Germany and suggested that he use my name to seek substantial psychotherapy there for his difficulties.

I doubt that he ever did. I suspect that his resistance to his vocation was so great that he would never follow the calling. We did not have the time to understand the nature of his resistance. Fortunately, upon occasion, psychotherapists do have the time. Then they may discover that the resistance is rooted either in a false teaching from parents that the patient swallowed hook, line, and sinker, or else in a reaction to such teaching.

Abby, for instance, was a brilliant as well as beautiful young woman who had become pregnant in the eleventh grade and dropped out of high school. She initially came to see me because of marital difficulties. Once these were resolved, we began to discuss her future. Since she had wealthy and supportive parents and a wide range of interests, I found it strange that she gave no consideration whatsoever to going to college. When I pressed her on it, she balked. Over the course of three months, I would periodically readdress the issue, and each time she would fight back, even to the point of screaming at me that I was trying to 'play God,' and had no right to direct her life so forcefully. I began to doubt my methods. But I tried again one day, telling her she was as bright as anyone I'd ever met in medical school. Suddenly, Abby broke into sobs.

Very slowly, in between continuing sobs, the story came out: 'When I was about twelve I crawled into Daddy's lap one evening. I asked him, "What do you want me to be when I grow up, Daddy?" "A doctor," he answered. "But suppose I want to get married?" I asked. "Maybe *after* you become a doctor," he replied, "but until then you won't have time for marriage what with college and medical school." It was so definite. Suddenly I had a fantasy—no, it was more like a vision. I was walking down a long corridor wearing a starched white lab coat. I was powerful, but totally isolated. All around me were young students smiling at each other, couples walking hand in hand, laughing together, sometimes kissing, having fun. And no one even noticed me. Everything about me was stiff. I was an old man, no one cared about me, and I was so, so alone. I've had that vision ever since. It's haunted me. Not a week goes by that I don't think about it.'

In the sessions that followed, Abby and I worked on her 'negative fantasy.' We explored the reasons she had given her father so much authority over her. I explained how she was right, that I was not God; that I could challenge her on what seemed inappropriate for her, but I was not wise enough to determine the specifics; that I had mentioned her being a doctor just by way of example; only she was wise enough to decide herself upon her special calling. And we discovered the profound effect the fantasy had had upon her young life. We learned how, when she had just turned fourteen, she and the other ninth graders had to fill out a form expressing whether they wanted to go to college or take vocational courses, and she elected the vocational track. We learned the next fall her teachers told her she was too intelligent for vocational education and that they had decided, despite her choice, to place her in the college preparatory program. We learned how hard she had then tried to fail her courses, how her grades had dropped but she couldn't quite pull it off well enough for them to track her differently. And we learned how, finally, at the end of her junior year, in desperation, she had become pregnant to assure that she wouldn't go to college.

That was a long time ago. Today Abby is not only a competent mother of grown children, but also a highly respected litigation lawyer and a partner in a major New York City firm.

The discovery of a denied vocation is not necessarily so difficult, however. Angela had been seeing me for many years, first to work through a messy divorce and then through a very messy childhood. Curiously befitting her name, and despite all her troubles, she had a kind of light inside her that radiated out and naturally drew spiritual people to her. She was nearing the end of her therapy and we were discussing its termination, with all the uncertainties involved. One was her occupational future. She was a high school teacher, and a good one, but she had a nagging feeling there was something else she ought to be doing. Lying on the couch one session, she had fallen into a peaceful, contemplative silence. Then she abruptly broke the silence, saying, 'The last damn place you'll ever find me is a convent.'

I pricked up my ears. 'Why did you suddenly say that?'

'I dunno,' she replied. 'It just popped out of my unconscious.'

'Well, you'd better look at it then, hadn't you?' I responded.

With only slight reluctance at first, she began to do so. That was my only intervention. Four years later Angela was a nun. Sometimes you can sniff the existence of a vocation just from the resistance to it.

There is a success/failure flavor to the preceding stories that needs to be looked at more closely.

The fact that an individual is exercising his true vocation does not guarantee him happiness. One cannot doubt that Van Gogh was called to paint, but the fact that he frenetically followed his calling did not relieve him from his inner torment. Indeed, sometimes we suspect that such inner torment may be an essential ingredient of the calling. Even Picasso, who lived so exuberantly into a seemingly joyful old age, apparently suffered a degree of restlessness that few could tolerate for long.

But God does call each of us in our own way to success, although such success has little to do with the world's measurements. Picasso's wealth, power, and fame were not his success; his art was. Van Gogh's poverty was not a failure any more than Christ's execution as a petty, provincial, political criminal was. A person fulfilling a true vocation as a homemaker will raise his or her children to the glory of God while the life of a tycoon may look dismal in God's eyes.

The secular definition of vocation usually implies only income-producing activity. The religious meaning of the word—which is how it will be used throughout the remainder of this book—is infinitely broader. So we may speak not only of vocations to business and brick-laying, art and aviation, soldiering and science, but also vocations to celibacy, marriage, or the single life, to homemaking and retirement, to parenthood and childlessness, to gardening and globe-trotting—to any activity or condition at all, no matter how poetic or prosaic, that God means for us.

While the fulfillment of a vocation does not guarantee happiness—as in the case of Van Gogh—it does often set the stage for a kind of peace of mind that may result from fulfillment. It is, therefore, frequently a pleasure to witness a human being doing what she or he was meant to do. We delight when we see a parent who truly *loves* taking care of children. There is such a sense of fit. The man who promotes many of my speaking engagements likes to tell how 'even back in college I somehow always found myself the chairman of the program committee.' I myself have no taste for such things as negotiating with a hotel over the size of a ballroom, checking sound systems, laying out the coffee, or crating and uncrating books, but I enjoy seeing the enjoyment he actually gets from these activities. And he's good at it. That's why I do so much work with him. He's a good promoter, a successful organizer.

Conversely, there is always a sense of dis-ease when we see people whose work and life-style does not fit their vocations. It seems such a shame, a waste. The sergeant major I described was wasting his artistic talent and other abilities as well. It was despite himself that he rose to the rank he did (although he should have risen to a much higher one) just as it was despite herself that Abby didn't flunk out of high school. Bearing in mind that success is always relative, however, the denial of vocation invariably breeds a lack of success and personal misery. I have seen women who married into great wealth, for instance, who would be considered successful in the world's terms, whose jewels and position were the envy of multitudes, but who lived in despair because they were never called to marriage in the first place.

Since they are so accustomed to seeing people trapped in roles having nothing to do with their vocations, I do not know any psychotherapist—male of female—who has not been basically a supporter of the women's liberation movement. We have all seen women who married not because marriage was their vocation, but merely because it was what they felt was expected of them, and who had children not because they liked motherhood, but because they felt they had no other option. And who then, in their old age, berated themselves for causing their children's difficulties when they did the best they could operating out of pure duty. The women's movement is indeed one of liberation: it has freed women to not have children, to not get married; to be actresses, businesswomen, and construction workers when that has been their calling. It has also liberated men to follow their vocations, to—when appropriate—be homemakers and nurturing fathers without *having* to bring home the bacon.

Yet we still suffer from a lack of understanding of the individuality of vocation and from our tendency to stereotype. The one downside of the women's movement is that it has led a few women to feel uneasy with their calling to heterosexuality, marriage, and motherhood and some men to feel guilty over a lack of vocation to housecleaning and child raising. This is stated not to denigrate the movement in the least, but simply to warn that stereotypical liberation becomes its own variety of imprisonment.

So God's unique vocation for each of us invariably calls us to personal success, but not necessarily success in the world's stereotypical terms or means of measurement. Nonetheless, upon occasion, God does call us to positions the world also calls great. One of my relatives, distant family legend goes, had a clear calling to be a drummer boy in the Civil War—at the same time that Abraham Lincoln had what seems to me to have been a true vocation to both the presidency and to greatness. So I think there is a distinction to be made between 'humble' and 'grand' vocations. As I suppose fits the needs of society, most men and women have humble vocations. I do not want to imply that such humble vocations are less in God's eye than grander ones. Among us Christians, we sometimes speak of 'noisy Christs' and 'quiet Christs,' and we generally consider the role of the quiet Christ to be the nobler one. Indeed, the humble vocation, such as that of a blacksmith, may be *crucial*. As the old saying goes: 'For want of a nail, the shoe was lost; for want of a shoe, the horse was lost; for want of a horse, the general was lost; for want of a general, the victory was lost; for want of a victory, the nation was lost.'

But there is a special problem that afflicts the minority

who have grand vocations: a 'personal sense of destiny.' To my knowledge this problem—or condition— has never been adequately addressed in scientific literature or, for that matter, in any literature at all. Being deeply familiar with it both personally and professionally, I address it here because its mention may serve to relieve a certain amount of unnecessary suffering for some readers.

By sense of destiny, I mean the deep, but often inchoate, sense that perhaps five to ten percent of the population have, usually beginning in childhood or adolescence, that they are supposed to do great and glorious things in their lifetime. Perhaps a quarter of the time this sense is profoundly unrealistic. Indeed, it seems to be a particular characteristic of a variety of schizophrenia. Psychiatrists refer to it as 'grandiosity.' Such people feel as if they are—or at least should be— great and powerful when, in reality, they are utterly lacking the personal, spiritual, or intellectual assets that make for greatness. Perhaps because they are unable to bear the disparity between the reality and the feeling, they bridge the gap by plummeting into a realm of pure fantasy where they believe they have already achieved greatness. So they may sit, without any discernible talent at all, in the back ward of a psychiatric hospital, firmly believing that they are in that position precisely because they already are the 'messiah.' After all, what does the world do to messiahs but deny them by labeling them mentally ill and crucifying them with the meanest of treatment?[2]

The other side of the coin, however, is that I have never known a genuinely talented person who achieved 'greatness' without a sense of destiny—who did not, years before such achievement, experience an almost burning sense that she or he was called to grand and glorious achievements. An example of this phenomenon was Sigmund Freud. At the age of twenty-eight, a whole decade before the publication

[2] See Milton Rokeach, *The Three Christs of Ypsilanti* (New York: Alfred A. Knopf, 1964).

of the work that began to make him famous, he wrote to his
fiancée:

I have just carried out one resolution which one group of people, as
yet unborn and fated to misfortune, will feel acutely. Since you
can't guess whom I mean, I will tell you: they are my biographers. I
have destroyed all my diaries of the past fourteen years, with
letters, scientific notes and the manuscripts of my publications. . . .
Let the biographers chafe; we won't make it too easy for them. Let
each one of them believe he is right in his 'Conception of the
Development of the Hero': even now I enjoy the thought of how
they will all go astray.[3]

Freud was not always so confident. He frequently
worried during this same period that his ambition was not
paying off. For him and for most who have genuine grand
vocations, their sense of destiny may be a very significant
burden. Experiencing inklings they are destined to do
'something particularly important' in the world, they may
begin to doubt their sanity. As a psychiatrist, I have had to
assure some such men and women that they were quite
sane. Despite this reassurance they often began to wonder if
they were not doing something seriously wrong. Their
feeling was not that they would for certain do great things,
but that they *ought* to be doing great things. They feel guilty.
If God was indeed calling them to greatness, it certainly
seemed they were letting God down. Some of these patients
never have made seemingly great achievements, as far as I
know. But others have, and their greatest joy was then not
their fame, but their relief. Their destinies had finally,
finally begun to catch up with them.

I do not know you. If you have a sense of destiny, I cannot
certify that sense, sight unseen, to be perfectly sane. And
even if I met you, it is unlikely I could prophesy—no matter
how sane you are—that you will, in fact, do the great things

[3] Letter of April 12, 1885, quoted in Ernest Jones, *The Life and Work of Sigmund Freud* (New York: Basic Books, 1953), vol. 1, p. xii.

you feel you ought to be doing. I cannot relieve you of the burden. But I can tell you two things. One is that your sense of destiny is not necessarily a sign of mental instability; indeed, if you are past the age of twenty-five and not doing too badly, it is extremely unlikely. The other is that your sense of destiny may be a perfectly valid sign that you do have a grand vocation—that you are called to do great things, although that calling will likely be worked out in ways that you currently can't even begin to imagine.

Thus far, vocation has been spoken of as if it were a single, more or less lifelong choice. So it may be, but such responses hardly begin to exhaust the variety of ways in which God calls us. It is quite possible, for instance, for someone to have a number of different occupations within a single lifetime. While the writing of books may be my own 'grand vocation,' I believe I previously did have a genuine calling to psychiatry and to government service. Yet I believe those eighteen previous years were also a time of preparation. From both my personal and professional experience, I have concluded that God is quite capable of routinely killing at least two birds with one stone.

Because they do not understand the nature of sequential vocations, many people unnecessarily berate themselves for wasting time. Angela, who had said, 'The last damn place you'll ever find me is a convent,' and four years later entered one, five years after that left the convent. Does that mean that her vocation to be a nun was invalid? That those five years were wasted? Given the fact that she left the convent a considerably wiser woman than when she entered it, I do not think so. It was helpful to her to have this pointed out. I think Angela had a very genuine vocation to monastic life and five years later had an equally genuine vocation to leave it. As Ecclesiastes might have put it, 'There's a time to go to church and a time to leave the church.' And, I suspect, for some, 'a time to return to the church.'

The place I have found the understanding of sequential vocations most helpful is in counseling women and men who have become divorced after a twenty- or thirty-year marriage. They often think of themselves as failures. They berate themselves for having made the wrong choice of a mate. They feel all those years have been wasted. Occasionally this self-condemnation does seem partially justified. It seems that they did make the wrong choices and did waste decades. But often they leave their marriages with far greater psychospiritual maturity than when they embarked upon them, and have learned in the process to become loving parents to children with whom they maintain good relationships. To such as these I am able to say, 'Why regard these years as a waste when you have grown so far and accomplished so much? Just because your marriage was wrong for you at fifty doesn't mean it wasn't right for you at thirty. Don't you think it is possible for God to have called you into married life twenty-five years ago and now decide it is time to call you out of it?'

Indeed, the greatest problem with sequential vocations is people's resistance to them. The term 'mid-life crisis' has become deservedly popular these days; it is a very real phenomenon. The most common reason it is a time of crisis is that it is properly a time of vocational change. It is a time when God calls us to revitalization, and frequently that revitalization requires a radical shift in activity or focus. The more we resist such shifts, the longer the painful crisis is prolonged. And when the shift—the call—is refused, the crisis cannot be resolved and the human soul progressively decays. It is a sad thing to see a mother whose children have left home but who is too fearful to leave home herself, who refuses the call to adventure and to tasks other than mothering and thereby has no option left except to deteriorate in her empty nest. It is equally tragic to witness a bored bureaucrat reject a deep passion to be a landscape gardener for fear of losing his pension rights when stagnation is the greater price.

And then there is the final vocation of our lives on earth: our calling to grow old gracefully. This is particularly problematic for the secular-minded, like the four remarkably similar women I saw in the course of my practice. They came to me with exactly the same complaint: depression at growing old. Each was well educated and goodhearted. Each had married well. They had either made a lot of money themselves or else their husbands had. All of their children had turned out golden. Their lives had gone according to script. Only now, in their seventies or late sixties, they were suffering from glaucoma or emphysema or facing hip replacements, and they were furious. Early on I told each of them, 'All of us are actors in a marvelous, complex, cosmic drama. The most we can hope for is to get little glimpses of what the drama is about and little glimpses of how best to play our roles. But what I hear you saying is that not only do you want to be the best actor you can possibly be in this drama, but you also want to be the scriptwriter.'

Of course, all of us, impossible though it is, would like to be the scriptwriter, but for the secular-minded no other option is conceivable. I saw no way to help these women without pushing them toward a conversion in their worldview, toward a vision of old age as something more than a time to just watch yourself rot away—but rather as a period filled with opportunities for spiritual growth and preparation. In attempting to facilitate this conversion of attitude, I kept saying over and again to each of them, 'Look, it's just not your show.' Sadly, two of the four in short order left my ministrations, preferring to be depressed than to come to terms with the fact that their lives were actually larger than their own show.

In youth we are called from dependency to independence; in middle age to interdependence; and in old age, ultimately, back to dependency again. But to make this final transition, we must be willing and able to give up control. A sixty-five-year-old woman came to me for depression precipitated by detached retinas, which had rendered her

84

ninety percent blind. She was filled with rage at her condition and at the ophthalmologist who had failed to save her from it. By our second session the underlying theme had become clear. 'I just *hate* it,' she said, 'when they have to take my arm to usher me into the pew or help me down the church steps.' And shortly thereafter, 'I'm just plain bored stuck at home so much. Lots of people offer to drive me wherever I want to go, but I can't ask them to assist me all the time.'

Fortunately for us both, she was a religious person. 'It is clear to me,' I said, 'that in your life you managed to become a remarkably independent woman, and it is quite natural for you to have taken a great deal of pride in your independence. But, you know, it's a journey from here to heaven, and I suspect we can get there only when we travel lightly. I'm not sure you can make it carrying around all that pride. I can't fault you for thinking of your blindness as a curse. It is conceivable to me, however, that you might think of it as a blessing given to you to help otherwise, you've probably got another good fifteen years left. It's up to you whether you want to live those years under a curse or under a blessing.'

She made the right choice, and her depression quickly lifted. But a great many do not make the right choice and fight the calling to give up control until the bitter end. Dylan Thomas was a superb poet, but I'm not sure he gave us good advice (nor followed it himself) when he wrote, 'Do not go gentle into that good night; rage, rage against the dying of the light.' It is always sad watching people refuse their vocations. It has been particularly sad for me as a psychiatrist to helplessly watch so many elderly men and women clutch on to control over their money, their cars, and all manner of temporal power long after they have lost the capacity to decently exercise such control. It is so pathetic. God does not call us to be pathetic. A minority of us may be called to temporal power, but seldom to the end of our days. On the other hand, God calls all of us—and always—to spiritual power, including the power to surrender.

Thus far, I have been talking about occupational or other relatively long-term vocations. Of sometimes greater importance, I suspect, are the 'little' momentary vocations in our lives. Why might I feel strangely called to speak to the person next to me in an airplane when it is my custom on such occasions to bury myself in my work? It is at such moments that much of the civility or incivility of the world is exercised. I have a young friend who is rapidly going blind from juvenile diabetes. He is practically unemployable. He can't even drive himself to the places he needs to go. Yet on his travels he has a way of making virtually all the people he meets feel good about themselves. I think he is a saint.

God calls us to be ethical, to civility. Yes, this calls upon us to ask such big questions as, 'Is it right for me to be working in the weapons industry?' But ethics and civility are also very daily matters. Illustrating the interrelationship between ethics and civility and health, between psychopathology and theology, let me offer two examples of my own everyday sin.

There are a number of ways to define sin. 'Missing the mark' is the most common one in Judeo-Christian tradition. Disobedience to God or our Higher Power—as we may disobey, reject, a calling—is another. But the most useful definition for me is that of the mystical author Charles Williams. A central thesis of Williams was that we all live in what he called a 'web of exchange.' Sin, he held, is any blockade of this web, anything that unnecessarily prevents exchanges from being made.[4]

Sin and neurosis are not identical, but there tends to be a large area of overlap. One of my sins is a propensity for extensive independence. It has its roots in my childhood as the son of parents who were generally decent, but often overcontrolling. To have been significantly dependent on them would have been to place myself in a position where I would be steamrollered out of my own identity. For my

[4] See such novels by Williams as *Shadows of Ecstasy, The Greater Trumps, Many Dimensions, The Place of the Lion,* and *Descent into Hell,* all published by Eerdmans.

psychological survival I had to keep my psychic distance from them. I could do this only by the development of an unconscious motto of independence: 'Who needs them? Who needs anybody?'

Consequently, had you asked me when I entered psychoanalysis at the age of thirty whether I was a dependent sort of person, I would have answered, 'Scott Peck, dependent? Why, I don't have a dependent bone in my body!' Indeed, I was one of those men so terrified of dependency that I couldn't even ask for directions. 'You do it, honey,' I'd say to Lily whenever we pulled into a gas station. The primary reason my psychoanalysis was profoundly healing for me was because it put me in touch with my dependency. I came to realize not only that I did have quite a few dependent bones in my body but also that that was very much okay.

Neuroses, however, are not like little pebbles you simply kick out of your path once you recognize them. Rather they are like huge boulders one has to keep chipping away at for a lifetime. So it is today, twenty-five years later, I am still too slow in asking for help when I need it and in accepting it when it is offered—much, much better at it, but still handicapped. On a Sunday morning, not too many years ago when I was still in practice, I was coming out of church with a patient, Susan, after it had started pouring rain. Susan's car was parked close to the church; mine was a hundred yards up the road. When we reached hers, Susan said, 'Here, Scotty, take my umbrella. You can give it back to me at our appointment Wednesday.'

'That's all right,' I replied, refusing her. 'I don't need it.' And I didn't, really. I was but slightly drenched by the time I reached my own car. It was only when I had driven several miles toward home that I realized the significance of the event. 'You've done it again, haven't you, Scotty?' I said to myself. 'Dammit, you've done it again.' I had sinned once more. It was not merely that I did need her umbrella; more important, I had unnecessarily rejected Susan. It would have made her feel good to have made the loan, but I had blown the opportunity, that little momentary call. It was an act of incivility on my part. I had blockaded the web of exchange.

For me Jesus has been a useful tool whenever I have had a significant ethical dilemma and am trying to figure out my calling. At such times I simply ask, 'Hey, Jesus, what would you do if you were in my shoes now? How would you behave?' It is surprising how clear the answer usually is. And often how startling. An example is provided by another of my larger sins, previously mentioned. I still have a 'deep-seated tendency to want to be 'Mr Nice Guy,' as if life was nothing more than a popularity contest. The problem was literally brought home to me a decade ago before I had an unlisted phone number. I'd agreed to give a Friday evening talk to a public audience at a local church. At nine-thirty the preceding Wednesday evening our living-room phone rang, and I picked it up to hear, 'Are you Dr Peck?' The shrill voice on the other end was clearly that of an elderly woman.

'Yes, I'm Dr Peck,' I answered.

'Are you the Dr Peck who's speaking about sexuality and spirituality at Saint Michael's Church Friday night?'

'Yes.'

'Well, I'm coming to your lecture,' the harsh voice declared, 'and I'm bringing my husband. My husband says he's too old to have sex with me and I want you to tell him he isn't.'

'Well . . . uh . . . uh,' I stuttered in response, 'that's not what the lecture is really about. But there will be a question-and-answer period afterwards, and if you or your husband should ask a question about sexuality and aging, I'll do my best to answer it. I hope you'll find the lecture worth your while. Thank you for calling.'

I put down the phone with a bad feeling, irritated with both the woman and myself, but unsure of how I might have handled the situation differently. 'Jesus, how would you have answered that phone call?' I asked.

The answer came to me with certainty. What Jesus would

have said in essence was, 'Lady, where the hell do you think you come off, calling me at home on a Wednesday night, trying to tell me what to lecture about on Friday night? It's the most arrogant, self-centered thing I've ever heard of. Maybe if you were a little less self-centered your husband might be a little more interested in you. Good night!' And then Jesus would have hung up the receiver with a certain definiteness to emphasize his point.

Does it seem to you that this response of my imagined Jesus was lacking in civility? If so, remember the distinction has already been drawn between politeness (which is often not genuine) and genuine civility (which may be quite confrontational). And remember that while in the gospels Jesus was remarkably gentle with certain sinners and outcasts and importunate people, he also had a remarkable kind of authority with which he would openly berate the self-righteous.

Perhaps God's calling us to daily civility may come in the form of a literal call. My polite response over the phone to that elderly lady's unrealistic demand that I specifically address her particular issue in my lecture was, in fact, an act of incivility. It is typical—natural—for us to repond to incivility with incivility in turn. But how can I label my politeness as uncivil? The problem was that in my desire to be 'Mr Nice Guy' I was pretending to be in a web of exchange with that woman. But it was just a pretense. The reality is that not only did she give me nothing, but I also gave her nothing. There was no exchange at all. Had I been willing to be impolite I would at least have been able to give her honest feedback as to how inappropriate and annoying her behavior was. Whether she would ever possibly accept such feed-back is another matter, and really not my concern. It was probably a very small chance, but I never even gave her that chance. I met her only with a stony wall of meaningless politeness. Nothing was exchanged; nothing happened.

Many aspects of the matter of vocation are inherently obscure. In the process of psychotherapy, as recounted, I was often able to discern denied or hidden callings. But I also saw some rather aimless patients where no distinct calling emerged. Would things have become more clear had they stayed in treatment longer? If we had gone deeper? Or are there times when there actually is no calling at all? I simply don't know.

And what about those schizophrenics who have such a strong sense of grand vocation when they frequently seem to lack the personal assets to fulfill even minor callings? Schizophrenia is, for the most part, a biological disorder. Is the grandiosity of some schizophrenics a biological or psychological phenomenon? And if biological, does it seem cruel of God to create an individual with a sense of destiny who can never come close to meeting it?

Certain vocations are obviously genetic. There are dramatic instances of the inherited nature of musical genius or artistic talent. Yet there are also many instances where extraordinary genius seems to arise *de novo* from the most ordinary families. Are these cases of genetic mutation or is there something else going on? To what extent was I born to be a professional writer and to what extent was I trained to be one? In the next chapter we will discuss ways in which God speaks to us through the still small voice of the Holy Spirit and other graceful interventions in our lives. But we cannot neglect the fact that God also calls to us through our genes. The matter of vocation is multidimensional.

Americans tend to have great difficulty thinking multi-dimensionally. Sexuality is a striking instance. At lectures I am consistently asked simplistic questions such as, 'Should homosexuals be ordained?' as if homosexuality was just this or just that. In my experience some people are homosexual as a result of early childhood experience in dysfunctional families. Consequently their sexual orientation is theoretic-ally a condition treatable by psychotherapy, albeit only with great difficulty. It has been obvious in others that their orientation was purely a biological one—that God created them homosexual. And then there are those with all degrees of 'in-betweenness' whose sexuality is a matter of both nature and nurture. Sometimes it is the task of psychiatrists to assist homosexuals to come out of their closet in relation not only to others but also to themselves—to not only accept their calling to homosexuality, but, insofar as possible, rejoice in it. God loves variety; in variety he/she delights. And when we attempt to categorize something like sexuality as just this or just that, we are violating the subtlety of God's creation.

This subtlety and multidimensionality is merely one of the reasons Matthew Fox, in his selection of the six greatest mysteries of our existence, included 'the mystery of vocation.'[5] It has already been demonstrated that people have it in their power to accept or reject callings, but the degree—if any—to which they can actually choose their vocations is hardly demonstrable. It has been impressive for me to hear certain homosexuals, for instance, eloquently respond to their detractors: 'You act as if I chose to be homosexual. How do you know that to be the case? It is much easier to be straight than gay. If it were my choice, I would prefer to be straight. But I'm not; it's not me.' There are few gay women and men who have not asked the age-old question of vocation: 'Why me?'

As I have whenever, for better or for worse, I have been different or out of step. Why me? Why have I possessed—or been possessed—by the virtue or vice of being so outspoken? Why have I had a seemingly greater capacity for organizational consciousness than others? And on and on. Why was I born white and not black? Into wealth rather than poverty? Why did I write my books and not someone else? Why me? Occasionally there seem to be glimmerings of answers to such questions, but only glimmerings. At the

5 Matthew Fox, *On Becoming a Musical Mystical Bear. Spirituality American Style* (New York: Paulist Press, 1972).

most basic, radical level I am always left facing the inherently inscrutable mystery of vocation.

Still, I do believe some things and know some things. I believe that our vocations are rooted in the covenant that God has with each and every one of us. I believe that the callings we hear come from the 'mouth' of God in the context of that covenantal relationship. And while there are so many strange twists and turns in the mysterious will of God, I believe the calling in conformity with covenantal love is always to psychospiritual growth and ultimately to the One who calls. Schizophrenia may be a cruel twist of fate, but I have witnessed schizophrenics whose disease has not improved one iota gradually grow in the direction of sainthood. By virtue of our own free will, I do not believe such growth is guaranteed. On the other hand, I have never seen a variety of human affliction that made it impossible.

I know that most vocations are unconscious. We tend to feel the calling more in our blood than actually hear it in our minds. Either way we can accept or reject the call. But remember that civility has been defined as '*consciously* motivated organizational behavior that is ethical in submission to a Higher Power.' The more conscious we can become of our callings, the more we are able to consciously cooperate with God in her designs for us—the more we will be able to match our true vocations with our secular ones— the more civil we will be. So we turn now to a few guidelines as to how we can help ourselves become more conscious of the voice of God in our lives.

Before we do, however, it may be helpful to realize that these consciousness-raising procedures are more poignant than methodical. There is a constant theme that runs, one way or another, through the utterances of great prophets over the millennia—Moses, Isaiah, Jesus, Mohammed, and other prophets or martyrs since. Those truly called by God to speak Her Word (as well as many of the more ordinary of us who've also heard the call to service) have echoed the same refrain across the generations: 'Is it really You that I hear? Why me? I am not worthy. Can't you find someone else? Must I? I am faint of heart. Will You help me? Stay with me? I'll do it if I have to. But will You leave me out in the cold or hanging on a tree?'

8

How Not to Waste Your Time

Prayer (or Whatever You Want to Call It)

Since it is neither easy nor painless, civility does not come naturally. It takes some work, and that work takes time.

I have a very full and busy life and occasionally am asked, 'Scotty, how can you do all that you do?' There are multiple answers, including being blessed by a superb staff. But the most telling reply I can give is: 'Because I spend at least two hours a day doing nothing.' Ironically, the questioner usually responds by saying he's too busy to do that.

My two hours doing nothing are the most important hours of the day for me. I do not take them all in one gulp. usually they are distributed into three forty-minute periods: shortly after I first awaken, in the late afternoon, and again before I sleep. They are 'alone' times, times of quiet and solitude. I could not survive without them.

I refer to these periods as my 'prayer time.' During them I actually spend no more than five to ten percent of the time in what most people would call prayer: talking to God. And no more than five to ten percent in meditation: listening for God. Ninety percent of the time I'm just thinking. But if I called it my thinking or contemplation time people would feel free to interrupt it. So I call it my prayer time instead to make it seem holy, which it is. It's another one of the benefits of being a 'religious person.'

Even though I am an introverted, introspective person by nature, setting aside these prayer times did not come naturally to me. I had to have some outside help. Fifteen years ago, when I first asked her to fill the role, my new spiritual director immediately inquired about my prayer life. 'Oh, I've got a rich prayer life,' I informed her. 'I pray all the time. I pray when I'm out walking. I pray when I'm going to sleep. I often pray silently when I'm seeing a patient and I don't know what the hell else to do.'

'Do you set aside specific times during the day to pray?' she asked next, looking quite innocent in her nun's habit.

'No,' I replied. 'That feels stultifying to me. Kind of rigid and unspontaneous.'

'Maybe so,' she countered, 'but what I hear you saying is you communicate with God whenever *you* feel like it. That seems to me like a very one-way relationship. If you love God as much as you say you do—and I suspect you do, Scotty— why then I think you owe it to him to make yourself available to him at certain times whether you feel like it or not.'

So it was I began to carve out my prayer times. It took a little effort. It felt somewhat unnatural at first. But it is our glory as human beings that we have it within our power to change our nature when we need to. It also felt rigid and unnatural when my parents first demanded I brush my teeth, yet it has long since become 'second nature' to me. I would feel unnatural not brushing my teeth now. Just as it would feel unnatural not to take my prayer time. If you don't want to have time for prayer, fine. But please don't tell me you're too busy, because setting aside this time will shortly make your life all the more efficient. Don't let anything stand in your way. You don't have to get dressed up for these occasions. You don't have to get on your knees. All you have to do is be available. When I returned for my second visit with my spiritual director, feeling like the most depraved individual in the world, I asked her if it was all right for me to smoke when I prayed.

'That's a surprisingly common question,' she said with a smile, 'so common we have a standard answer: If you can pray when you smoke, then you can smoke when you pray.'

Spiritual directors tend to have a way of being tough *and* consoling.

Like God herself, prayer has never been adequately defined. And never will be. It is too large, too deep, too multidimensional and paradoxical.

It can be divided into types and subtypes, if you will: prayers of praise, of thanksgiving, of confession and contrition; petitionary and intercessionary prayer; formal and informal prayer; verbal and wordless prayer, and so on. Here only one type will be considered: contemplative prayer. Entire books have been written about contemplative prayer alone, so this book on civility must restrict itself to brief mention of only a few aspects.

Contemplative prayer may be looked at as a life-style. If so, it is a life-style dedicated to maximum awareness. Those who adopt it—contemplatives—desire to become as conscious as they can possibly be. To this end, they set aside vast amounts of time for quiet and solitude. After a while this requires little discipline; they need and yearn for such time.

They do not see this as time wasting. To the contrary, they feel it is the most efficient and cost-effective way to live. For them, as Plato put it in the Dialogues, 'the unexamined life is not worth living.' What we contemplatives do during our precious quiet times is to examine our lives. We enjoy experience, but only in relatively small doses. What we like to do is take a little bit of experience and, by contemplating it, milk it for all it's worth. We believe that in this way we can ultimately learn more—become more conscious—than those who lead more frenetic lives crammed with far greater amounts of unreflective experience.

One of the things I am continually doing during my prayer time is checking out my life with my Ideal Observer. 'Tell me, God,' I am asking, 'what I just did or what I am thinking of doing—how does it look through your eyes? Does it look civil?'

I have spoken about how a major function of psycho-analytically oriented psychotherapy is the development and exercise of our observing ego and, hence, our capacity to utilize an Ideal Observer. In fact, much of such therapy might be looked upon as a variety of contemplative prayer. It is both similarly and properly habituating. Psychotherapists are so frequently asked the question 'How do you know when it is time to leave therapy?' that they have come up with a fairly standard answer: 'When you have become your own therapist, so that therapy has become a way of life for you.'

Another similarity is the issue of time. Just as many will protest that they don't have time for a more contemplative life-style, so many complain that 'therapy takes so much time.' Yet in reality, as with other varieties of contemplation, it is often a profoundly cost-effective process. Another standard question is, 'Since we're all neurotic, how do you know when to go into therapy?' and, again, there is a standard answer: 'When you're stuck.' People who enter therapy frequently do so because of an accurate sense that they are spinning their wheels. And if therapy is successful, when they leave—when they are unstuck—they do so with a deep sense that all the time and money was well spent—a small price to pay for the increased efficiency and effectiveness of their liberated lives.

We contemplatives pay attention not only to our outward experiences but also to our inner voices. Indeed, those of us who are religious believe that God actually often speaks to us through such voices: that they may be revelations. We further believe that a contemplative life-style dramatically increases either the frequency with which God speaks to us or else our capacity to hear her.

For instance, both in psychotherapy and out, we pay attention to our dreams because they may be such revelations. I say 'may' be. I think only a small minority are messages from God and that most of our night dreams are dross. How then do you separate the gold from this dross? The same question arises with other internal voices. How do we know when that 'still small voice' is the voice of the Holy Spirit as opposed to simply that of our glands, or possibly even the voice of Satan? This is the issue—the problem—of 'discernment of revelation.' It is an enormously important issue. Were it not a distraction, the subject would deserve several chapters in and of itself. There are no formulistic solutions to the problem, but there are guidelines. Here I shall only touch upon three. I call them the guidelines of time, heart, and emptiness.

The first and most crucial guideline is to take *time*. It takes time—thinking time or contemplative time—to discern whether a dream is pregnant with hidden meaning or whether it is more likely a mere distraction resulting from random neuronal activity. It takes time to test all our inner messages (after we've taken the time to listen to them in the first place), to check them out against reality and reason and experience, to question their wisdom and creativity. Except in the rarest of circumstances, beware of instant revelations! Beware of them in yourself, and beware of others when their every thought or feeling is immediately ascribed the status of godly wisdom or origin.

In summary, it takes time to think. It takes time to become conscious. And since consciousness is the major root of civility, it takes time to be civil. Indeed, the desire to be as civil as possible is a deep motive for the contemplative life. Over and again it has been made clear to me that it is probably not possible for someone to be a deeply civil person without nurturing her or his contemplative side.

To my mind, the best of the works of the controversial theologian Matthew Fox is his early book about prayer, *On Becoming a Musical Mystical Bear*. Although not wholly adequate, his definition of prayer is still my favorite. It is a definition that doesn't even use the word *God*. Fox defines it as 'a radical response to the mysteries of life.'

Three things make this definition so meaningful to me. The first is the word *radical*, which comes from the Latin *radix*, for 'root.' It implies that prayer requires that we get to the root of things without being distracted by superficialities. We must think deeply about our lives, which, of course, takes time. It is a contemplative definition.

The second is the word *response*. It implies that through prayer we must not only think deeply but also translate our thinking into action. We need to behave out of deep thoughtfulness. Such behaviour is civility if we assume, as I do, that deep thoughtfulness will result in both consciousness and submission to a Higher Power.

Finally, it implies that life is an inherently mysterious business and that there are no easy answers or simple formulas. Even those answers we arrive at through our very best thinking will not necessarily be crystal-clear ones that relieve us from the burden of taking risks.

As mentioned, Fox designated 'the mystery of vocation' as one of the six greatest mysteries of life to which we need respond. So it is that to be civil, we must struggle with such questions already raised as 'Who am I meant to be?' 'What is God calling me to do in this instance, in this organization, in my career?' 'Why me?' And, after all our struggling, the proper response will still likely require some leap of faith. Furthermore, to be civil, we must struggle to discern not only our own vocations but also the vocations of others. The following sections on the family and business will demonstrate the need to assess the vocations of our spouses, our children, our subordinates, and even those of our co-workers and supervisors. And respond with the kind of faith demanded by 'submission to a Higher Power.' There are no formulas.

In regard to the discernment of vocation, however, theologian Frederick Buechner does offer a second guideline:

There are all different kinds of voices calling you to do all different kinds of work, and the problem is to find out which is the voice of God, rather than that of society, say, or the superego, or self-interest. By and large, a good rule for finding this out is the following: the kind of work God usually calls you to is the kind of work (a) that you need most to do, and (b) that the world needs most to have done. If you really get a kick out of your work, you've presumably met requirement (a), but if your work is writing deodorant commercials, the chances are, you've missed requirement (b). On the other hand, if your work is being a doctor in a leper colony, you've probably met requirement (b), but if most of the time you're bored and depressed by your work, the chances are that you've not only bypassed (a), but probably aren't helping your patients much either. Neither the hair shirt nor the soft berth will do. The place God calls you to is the place where your deep gladness and the world's deep hunger meet.[1]

This is what I call the guidelines of the *heart*. Eight years ago, at a moment of intense struggle over whether to take on a new task that the world very much seemed to need done even though I was feeling depleted of energy, I made my only emergency phone call to my spiritual director. 'God never calls someone to do something that doesn't feel *right* in his heart,' she told me. It was a piece of advice I have used a number of times since.

It is not, however, a simple piece of advice. Joseph Campbell's expression of the vocational guideline of the heart, 'Follow your bliss,' has recently become very popular. It is valid for many occasions, but not for some others. When Jesus, for instance, sweating blood in sheer terror in the Garden of Gethsemane, accepted his calling to go to the cross, he was not following his bliss. He did, I believe, choose the cross because it was the only alternative that felt right in his heart. But it was hardly a blissful alternative.

So, from time to time—not too often, mind you – we may be called to make some 'radical response' to life that is actually sacrificial. At such times, precisely because it is not blissful, the call, as it did for Jesus, may feel quite murky. Moreover, since life is continually changing and evolving, these murky 'judgment calls'—to use a play on words—may have to be made repeatedly.

[1] Frederick Buechner, *Wishful Thinking: A Theological ABC* (New York: Harper & Row, 1973), p. 95.

When I first began to lecture, I didn't know whether it was the right thing. Was it something God was calling me to or was I just on a narcissistic ego trip, eager for the roar of the crowd? I agonized incessantly over the question. A woman who sponsored my second speaking engagement, with whom I had shared my agony, sent me a poem she had written a month later. She had not written it with me in mind, but the last line of it provided me with the answer I needed—not the answer I wanted—to my dilemma. It read: 'The Truth is that I want It, and the price I must pay is to ask the question again and again and again.'[2]

I understood then the root of my undue agony. The problem was that I had been looking for a voice from God that would not only clearly tell me what to do, but also lift me from any burden of sequential vocation. I wanted a fail-safe formula, a revelation for all time, telling me, 'Yes, go speak, Scotty, always,' or else, 'No, Scotty, don't speak ever.' Instead, I realized what I would need to do each time I spoke, each month, each year, when I renegotiated my schedule, would be to ask the question again and again, 'Hey, God, is this what you want me to be doing?' The discernment of vocation—of what feels right in our hearts—frequently must be an ongoing process.

Meditation may be categorized as a subtype of contemplative prayer. Listening for God is my definition of meditation. It is not the way, however, the word is often used. The essence of Transcendental Meditation (TM), for instance, is attentiveness to a repetitive sound—a mantra —that one says silently to oneself, and not attentiveness to God. Similarly, in many varieties of yoga, the practitioner is taught to attend only to her breathing. These practices are effective techniques for relaxation. As such, I would refer to them as 'meditation aids.' They can be helpful— occasionally even required—for us to become sufficiently relaxed

2 Louise Magavern, unpublished poem.

that we can begin to meditate, but they are not meditation itself. I come now to the third guideline: *emptiness*.

Far closer to true meditation, from my point of view, is the Zen Buddhist meditative practice called 'No Mind.' Here the practitioner is instructed not to fill the mind, as with a mantra, but to empty it. This process of emptying the mind is of such importance it will continue to be a significant theme. It is not an easy process. Despite the fact that mystics through the ages have extolled the virtues of emptiness, people are generally quite terrified by it. It may help to remember, therefore, that the purpose of emptying the mind is not ultimately to have nothing there; rather it is to make room in the mind for something new, something unexpected, to come in. What is this something new? It is the voice of God. But God—or life—can speak to us in many ways.

My first day in the fourth grade was a traumatic example. It was not only a new school for me; in entering it I also skipped over the third grade. No sooner was I seated among strange classmates and the door shut than Mr Spicer, our austere teacher, instructed us to prepare to take dictation so that he might ascertain how well we students had retained our academic skills over the summer. The other boys all reached into their desks and extracted fresh pads and pencils. In imitation, I did likewise.

Mr Spicer then began to read a story entitled 'King Bruce and the Spider.' I was puzzled. I could not understand why he was reading it so slowly. Nor could I understand why my new classmates had started to write away so furiously. The problem was I had never heard the word 'dictation' before and had not the foggiest idea what it meant.

But no matter. Despite its painfully slow recounting, I rapidly became totally immersed in the story. It told of how Bruce, a Scottish tribal chieftain, had gone to battle six times in an attempt to unify the tribes of Scotland, and had failed each time. Following the last failure, he had retreated alone, deserted by his soldiers, to a small hut deep in the mountains. In the hut was a single piece of furniture, an old table adjacent to the only window. Bruce was sitting in a corner, huddled in his cloak against the cold, empty of hope, when his eye was caught by a spider as it made a leap from the windowsill toward the table. It missed and fell to the floor. Because he had nothing else to do, being a totally defeated man, Bruce continued to watch the spider scuttle across the floor, up the wall to the windowsill, and leap again for the table. Again it missed. But back to the wall it went. Bruce followed it through four more missed attempts. Finally, on its seventh try, it barely made it. It seemed to be resting on the edge for a minute, and then suddenly it darted through midair back to the windowsill. And back to the table. And back to the windowsill. Bruce realized the spider had began to spin its web.

Bruce contemplated what he had just witnessed. If the spider could have the pertinacity to keep trying, then he himself should not give up on his dream, his vocation. So emboldened, he shortly ventured forth to make the allies and the plans to go back into battle yet one more time. Only this time he won and succeeded in forging Scotland into a new nation with him, Bruce, as its first king.

Mr Spicer had stopped reading. The story was clearly over. But my classmates were still scribbling frantically. I looked over at the little red-haired boy to the left of me to try and figure out why. When he finished, he saw me peering at his paper, raised his hand, and exclaimed in a loud voice, 'Mr Spicer, sir, the new boy next to me is cheating.' Mr Spicer stood up from behind his desk, marched down the aisle, grabbed my pad, and pronounced, 'Why, this paper is empty!'

We stared at each other, he with astonishment, me with dawning horror. 'There isn't anything on it,' he said. 'What's the meaning of this?'

I began to cry, which was hardly the thing for a boy to do on his first day in the fourth grade in a new school. The year did not get off on a good start. But that is not the moral of the tale. I tell it because it is a tale of meditation.

First, it is a tale of Bruce's meditation. Ordinarily, an important, powerful, and busy man would not take time out from affairs of state to watch a lowly spider. Only because he was empty of hope, defeated with nothing else to do, did Bruce allow the spider to fully enter his consciousness. As a result, the very course of history was changed.

It is also a tale of my own unwitting meditation. How many of my fourth-grade classmates, do you suppose, still remember the story of King Bruce and the spider? Not many, I would venture. Yet precisely because I was not busy writing it down—because I was listening—because my paper was empty, blank, I was perhaps the only one who was truly able to hear the story, absorb it, and today recall it almost word for word. Just as something quite profound happened to Bruce, so something profound happened to me.

The goal of meditation, therefore, is not relaxation, but to relax, to slow down sufficiently to silence the chatter and empty the clutter of our everyday minds. The purpose of this silencing, this emptying, is to make room in our minds so as to let in either such indirect revelations as may come from spiders and stories or to more directly hear the voice of God calling in our minds and hearts.

But God does not always speak. Often she is a 'silent God.' While meditation and other forms of contemplative prayer will increase the frequency with which we hear her, they never guarantee it. There are many times when, no matter how desperately we yearn and assiduously pray, the desired revelation does not come. God does not operate according to our schedules. She is not a possession, an 'It.' It is a delight to have a clear calling. There is no longer any doubt, any uncertainty, when we are following our 'bliss.' But we all must also go through our own little 'Gardens of Gethsemane,' when there is no voice from God and the place feels utterly empty of God's presence. Frequently, it is not at all clear what the right thing is and the Truth that we want seems murky indeed, no matter how often or loudly we scream the question. Still, there is no alternative except to persevere, to seemingly go it alone and simply do the best we can in the dark.

For this reason, the most crucial form of emptiness is not just that of meditation; it is the emptiness of not knowing. This terrifying emptiness is the ultimate price of the contemplative life, of radically responding to the mysteries of life with full awareness of their mystery. It is also the price of civility.

To my mind, one of the best religious books to be published in the past decade is entitled *The Myth of Certainty*.[3] The 'illusion of certainty' might be an even better title. It would be a strange God who showered us with certainty, thereby relieving us from any need to exercise courage, initiative, and our capacity to figure things out for ourselves.

But, oh, how we still yearn for certainty!

Far and away the most common question I am asked at lectures is, 'Dr Peck, would you give me the formula so that I know that what I am doing is right?' It comes in a thousand different guises: 'How do I know when to blame somebody or blame myself?' 'How do I know when to intervene with my child and when to leave him alone?' 'How can you tell when to get out of a bad marriage or when to keep working on it?' 'How do I know when to challenge my boss?' 'Just where is the dividing line between being sacrificially loving and masochistic?' 'Where do you draw the line between trying to help someone and being codependent?' Note that these are all questions that pertain to issues of civility. And lest it need be endlessly repeated, please remember the answer: 'You don't know. You can never know for certain. But just asking the question is likely to bring you much closer to the right track. Only there are no formulas. Every situation is different. Consequently each and every time you will need to ask the question all over again.'

[3] Daniel Taylor, *The Myth of Certainty: The Reflective Christian and the Risk of Commitment* (Waco, Tex.: Jarrell, 1986).

So the guidelines offered for the discernment of revelation are merely guidelines, and not formulas to relieve you of having to go through empty deserts of uncertainty. Still, there is a sort of formula for the discernment process in general, although hardly a very consoling one. I have previously written an abbreviated version of it in discussing 'the emptiness of not knowing.'[4] The unconscious is always one step ahead of the conscious mind in the right direction or the wrong direction. It is therefore impossible ever to know that what you are doing is right, since knowing is a function of consciousness. However, if your will is steadfastly to the good, and if you are willing to suffer fully when the good seems ambiguous (which, to me, is about ninety-eight percent of the time), then your unconscious will always be one step ahead of your conscious mind in the right direction. In other words, the Holy Spirit will lead you and you will do the right thing. Only you won't have the luxury of knowing it at the time you're doing it. Indeed, you will do the right thing precisely because you have been willing to forgo that luxury.

If you are unclear about what this formula means, you might want to consider its opposite and remember that most of the evil in this world—the incivility—is committed by people who are absolutely certain that they know what they're doing.

Over the course of the first five chapters a redefinition of civility was developed. 'Consciously motivated organizational behaviour that is ethical in submission to a Higher Power' may be a mouthful, but it is a far more radical, meaningful, and useful definition than 'politeness.' It made possible the uncovering of the major cornerstones of real civility.

These past three chapters have further elucidated one of

[4] M. Scott Peck, *The Different Drum*, p. 220.

these cornerstones: the relationship of an individual in submission to God or a Higher Power. God convenantally cares for each of us whether we submit to her or not. Our free will as to whether to submit was examined in light of vocation—the concept that God actively calls each of us to make specific organizational choices. Such civil choices are not necessarily clear, risk free, or painless. They demand that we tolerate ambiguity. They are best made prayerfully within the context of a life-style that is at least somewhat contemplative so that consciousness can be maximized. Such a life-style requires us to routinely set aside time to be alone, quiet, and empty in order to be able to listen for the voice of God in our lives. This time is not wasted; it is the key to efficiency at the most radical level of existence. Remember that civility—painful though it may be—is healthy, healing behavior. Uncivil people, making the wrong choices, are always making a mess of their lives. Consequently, they are continually engaged in either picking up the pieces or compelling others to do so. It is incivility that is wasteful and inefficient.

The next two sections will proceed at a more leisurely pace as they flesh out the details through lengthier stories of family and business life. Often they will be stories of incivility, of men and women who did not take the time or effort to become conscious, to look at the larger system and listen for the voice of any Higher Power. Their primary focus will be on the relationship between the individual and the organization to demonstrate how individuals might behave more civilly within the context of marital, family, and business systems.

At the end, in the concluding section, or 'Epiphany,' the pace will pick up once again as much new information is introduced to provide a glimpse of a possible, more civil future society. There the primary focus will not be on the individual but the organization itself, and upon recently learned 'whole group' interventions that can facilitate the development of civil organizations. These interventions must be initiated, however, by already civil individuals. It is hoped the stories that follow will help us become such individuals.

Part Two

MARRIAGE
AND THE
FAMILY

9

For the Friction

Marriage and Narcissism

Like God and prayer, other things in this world are also too large to submit to any single, adequate definition. Marriage is one. If it is defined as a relationship of two, then what about group or polygamous marriages? If between a man and woman, where do long-term, committed homosexual relationships fit? If it is a legal entity, what about common-law marriage? If a religious union, what about the vast number of purely civil marriages? And what is a union? A merger? If it implies a sexual relationship, how do we regard all those couples who no longer sleep together? And, if not, what is the difference between marriage and partnership? And on and on.

One might think that because marriage is the smallest of common human organizations, it would be the simplest. The opposite is perhaps the case. For a variety of reasons—including the intimacy involved—in some ways it is the most complex. If this makes marriage sound like a mysterious business, you hear correctly. At its worst it can be a living hell, although often a strangely comfortable hell. At its best a long-term marriage is a mystical sort of phenomenon, rich beyond description.

And beyond formula. Remember the basic premise of organizations: contingency theory, which holds that there is no such thing as *the* best organizational structure. What is the best structure is contingent upon the size, purpose, age, location, and other characteristics of the organization. So it is with a marriage. Every human being is unique, as we have noted. As an organization of unique partners, every marriage is consequently unique. There are stereotypical bad marriages. There are *no* stereotypical good marriages. 'Goodness cannot be stereotyped,' as a theologian once wisely said.[1]

Still, there is, I believe, one clear feature that distinguishes good and bad marriages: the civility—or lack thereof—with which the partners treat each other. This section is not meant to be an exhaustive or scholarly treatise on marriage. I will simplistically define marriage as 'an organization of two people who have made a commitment to attempt to maintain that organization,' and I shall be using only traditional, heterosexual marriages by way of example. For my intent is not to talk about marriage in general; it is solely to discuss the issue of civility as it commonly relates to marriage.

Civility, like its ally, love, is often best defined by describing what it isn't. Consequently, to illustrate my points, I shall often employ examples of incivility in marriage and parenting. They will be examples of either men or women, but bear in mind that the sexes are virtually interchangeable in this regard. Although it may have slightly different flavors, the dynamics of incivility transcend gender.

Janet came to see me at the age of thirty-eight because of depression. Her depression had begun suddenly three months before, on the very day her husband, Ralph, had left their house to live in his own apartment. This separation was part of a divorce action that he had initiated a year previously. Their twelve-year marriage was virtually over; the court date was set for two weeks hence. She was very angry. 'He has no right to be doing this to me,' she stormed.

[1] Thomas Langford, in an unpublished talk, Lake Junaluska, 1986.

'And doing it to us.' By 'us' she meant herself and their nine-year-old son, Sean.

As depressions go, hers was moderate. She was still able to function relatively well in her demanding job as a regional sales manager for a cosmetics corporation and to care quite adequately for Sean. But she could barely sleep. Formerly a sound sleeper, now she tossed and turned until after midnight and then would be wide awake by 3:00 A.M. Usually she would get back to sleep by five, but would be up again before the alarm at seven. Her face was drawn and bitter.

When asked why Ralph was terminating their marriage, she almost spat in reply, 'I suppose for another woman, of course.'

'You suppose?' I echoed. 'Of course?'

'Well, he says it isn't. But I'm sure he's lying. There must be another woman.'

'If he says it isn't another woman,' I responded, 'then what does he say?'

'I don't know,' she replied. 'He just doesn't make any sense when he talks about it.'

I asked if she would object to my speaking with him. 'Of course not.' Janet's eyes lit up slightly. 'But probably he won't be willing to,' she added.

'The reason I would like to see him has nothing to do with trying to repair the marriage,' I hastened to explain. 'In my experience, when things have gone this far, it's almost always beyond repair. I have a standard policy of trying to see the spouse—even ex-spouse—of all my patients, if possible, just for information so I can get a full perspective. It's routine.'

Ralph was different when we met from what I had anticipated. Knowing him to be a successful executive at forty and prepared for him to be a ladies' man, I had somehow imagined him as tall and lithe. Instead, he was on the short side, with the beginnings of a paunch. While not physically prepossessing, he was articulate and spoke with a quiet kind of authority. 'Tell me about the marriage from your point of view,' I requested.

'It's very sad,' Ralph said. 'It's got to be hard on Sean. He says it isn't when I get him on the weekends, but I think he's just trying to be brave. And there's a part of me that still cares for Janet. I admire her intelligence and determination. I'd give anything for it to have turned out differently.'

'But you've fallen in love with another woman?' I suggested.

'Heavens, no. That's what Janet told you? I suppose she would. It's what she believes no matter how much I try to tell her otherwise.'

'Why did you initiate the divorce then?'

'To save my life.'

The starkness of his reply stunned me.

'It's not an easy thing to put into words,' Ralph began to explain. 'Maybe I don't do a very good job at it. Maybe that's why it's so hard for her to understand. You see, Janet is a very possessive kind of person. At least that's the way I perceive her. I feel she wants to own me. And I felt owned by her until I finally filed for divorce. And even then, until I got out of the house. I wish I could be a better husband, a different kind of person. But I can't stand being owned. It makes me feel as if I'm suffocating. Literally. Actually, I did get asthma shortly after we got married. Not bad, but annoying. And it does seem to be much better the past three months.'

I pricked up my ears at the psychosomatics. Was he lying? I wondered. On the one hand, it was rather pat. On the other, it was not the sort of thing a layman was likely to make up. 'You say she's possessive,' I asked. 'Do you mean she's jealous?'

'Yes, that and more. Of course, she's particularly jealous of any woman I know or talk about who's the least bit attractive. She was convinced I was having an affair within the first year we were married. It would flare up whenever I worked late. Speaking of which, even when she knows there's no woman involved, she's jealous of my work. She doesn't admit it, but I get all these little gibes from her whenever I get turned on by a project. It's as if she can't stand my being interested in anything but her. It's the same with my men friends. She denies it, but she resents them. Sometimes I even think she's jealous of my relationship with Sean.'

'Oh?'

'She's always nagging me to spend more time with him, telling me that a boy his age very much needs a father. Which I agree with. And I feel badly that I don't spend more time with him. But, you know, it's funny. When the three of us are together it's all right. Yet when Sean and I have been off alone and he comes back kind of high about it, the way nine-year-olds do, I can immediately feel her get irritable.'

'You've confronted her with her jealousy?'

'Many times. At least, as often as I can stand it.'

'Stand it?' I repeated.

'Yeah. It's always unpleasant,' Ralph elaborated. 'And it doesn't get us anywhere. She admits she's jealous of other women, but insists that's healthy and normal. She simply denies that she's jealous of my job or men friends or Sean. And whenever I press her on it, she goes wacko.'

'Wacko?'

'Well, not really wacko. She either gets up and leaves the room or starts shouting at me, telling me I'm immoral or demented. So I stop pressing. I have this feeling if I continued, I'd drive her over the edge.'

'That must be frightening.'

I had said it with empathy, but I was still surprised to see tears flood his eyes. There was a long moment of silence. 'It is.' He looked at me gratefully. 'Thank you for understanding.'

'So, you've given up and called it quits?'

'Yes, it's quits,' Ralph said with definiteness. 'But it was a long time coming. Six or seven years ago, I asked that we go into marriage counseling. She refused, saying it was all my fault. Then I saw a therapist myself. It didn't solve the problem—only helped me feel I wasn't imagining it all. I urged her into therapy. No way. Two years ago, I told her I intended to divorce her if nothing changed. It didn't. So I had her served a year ago.'

'Janet told me she became depressed only three months ago,' I commented, 'after you left the house. I wonder why that was?'

Ralph looked at me as if I was blind. 'She didn't believe me until then. Even with the papers and lawyers she didn't take me seriously. She has a way of not taking me seriously.'

Our time was almost over, but there was one loose thread I wanted to pick up. 'When I asked you whether Janet was jealous, you replied "that and more." What did you mean by more?'

'It's a bunch of little things,' Ralph answered. 'Like photographs.'

'Photographs?'

'Janet likes to take photos, particularly of me, and I don't like my picture taken much. Whenever we went on a trip she was always handing strangers the camera and asking them to take a picture of the two of us together. Five or six times a day. It probably shouldn't have, but it annoyed me. I asked her to cut it down, but she wouldn't. I felt she was always somehow trying to literally capture me with her on film. Finally, I put my foot down and insisted on being photographed with her only once a year. Otherwise, I just refused. Then she started snapping pictures of me whenever I was with Sean. Again, I tried to limit it, but there was nothing I could do. She sneaks pictures of us.'

'Sneaks pictures?'

'Yeah. Three or four times when I've been sitting with Sean at the kitchen table helping him with his homework, suddenly a flashbulb will pop, and I'll look up to see Janet with her camera again. It doesn't bother Sean, but it makes me furious, although I suppose I shouldn't get so upset over such a little thing.'

That was the only time I saw Ralph. My initial strategy with Janet was to be as supportive as possible. The closest I came to confronting her for a while was during her next appointment after she had said once more, 'He doesn't have the right to be doing this to me.'

'I'm not sure I understand what you mean.'

'I meant just what I said.'

'He does have a legal right,' I commented. 'Otherwise there would be no such thing as divorce court.'

She glared at me. 'But he shouldn't have the right.'

'Probably we're just haggling over the word,' I said consolingly. 'As a noun, right refers to a freedom. As an adjective, it refers to something that is morally correct. I imagine you're feeling what Ralph is doing isn't morally right.'

'Of course. But he shouldn't have the legal right either.'

I let the matter drop. When she was still just as depressed two weeks after the divorce, I suggested a trial of anti-depressant medication. Within two more weeks she was sleeping much better. Her depression, however, did not lift and her constant resentment remained untouched. I used the time to explore her background. It was one of poverty and abuse. Her father, a garage mechanic, had been an alcoholic who beat her and her siblings with regularity for little or no reason. Her mother had been chronically apathetic, as if the business of marriage and child raising were beyond her. In one sense, the most remarkable thing about this background was the degree to which Janet had succeeded in overcoming it. Washing dishes, waitressing, even milking cows, she had worked her way through college while maintaining an A average. Later, as a caring mother, she still managed to be such a successful salesperson that she'd been promoted to regional sales manager in her early thirties. Her brother and sister, on the other hand, had never finished high school. Janet kept only the most distant contact with them. Intelligent, hard-working, and competent, she had left them behind.

Like her husband, I admired her. But I found it peculiarly difficult to feel close to her. She could not remember her dreams. She was reluctant to recall her childhood. She had no belief in a personal God or desire to develop one. Despite my taking every possible opportunity to be supportive of her, she never warmed up to me. And her depression continued unabated. Her resentment of her husband was an unending litany that could be interrupted only briefly. Financially she had long since transcended the poverty of her childhood, but I sensed an impoverishment of her inner life. After three months, we had made no progress and I could not sense the possibility of progress unless I became less supportive and more confrontational.

The occasion quickly presented itself. 'He has no right to treat me this way,' she said yet again. Thus far, Ralph had been perfectly scrupulous with liberal alimony and child-care payments and highly cooperative in regard to his frequent attention to Sean.

'We've been through this before,' I responded. 'He had the legal right to divorce.'

'He still has no right,' she repeated it. It was as if she hadn't even heard me.

I took another tack. 'You said he has no right, using the present tense. You're speaking of the divorce in the present, as if Ralph was divorcing you now. But the reality is that the divorce is past. He did it to you. It's over. It's done. Yet you feel as if it's still happening. I can understand that. It's hard to shift gears. But that's also why you're still depressed. And I don't see how you can stop being depressed until we can help you put it in the past.'

'I don't want to put it in the past,' Janet stated without the slightest hesitation.

I was startled by her honesty, being accustomed to more labyrinthine neuroses. It was a long moment before I could respond, 'Yes, I can understand that also. But it places us in a predicament, doesn't it? There is a conflict between what you want and what is. Between your will and the reality of

118

the situation. That conflict is the "why" of your depression. And, obviously, you're going to stay depressed until you can accept reality—even to the point of forgiving Ralph.'

'I would rather stay depressed than ever forgive him,' she responded bluntly.

This time I replied instinctively, 'Somewhere in the Bible it's mentioned—I don't know where—"Vengeance is mine, saith the Lord." What do you think that means?'

'I'm not going to listen to that religious horseshit,' Janet proclaimed.

Better to go more slowly. 'Look,' I said, 'in this conflict between your will and reality, I think we may need to honor your will before going further. For instance, there is no way you could have worked your way through college and up to the position you hold without an extremely strong will. It was no small trick. You've reason to be proud of yourself. But I wonder if there wasn't some other time—maybe in your childhood—when your will got in your way, when you couldn't change reality and kept butting your head against a stone wall? Would you think about that between now and our next session?'

She did and she began the next session with a most touching confession. 'It was so embarrassing,' she said. 'In our last year of high school I took a physics course. One of our assignments was to draw an electrical wiring diagram of our home. I was ashamed that our house had only two rooms. So I made a diagram for an eight-room house. When the teacher gave us the assignments back, I was astonished he had given me an F. I asked him why. He told me he'd been torn over it. My diagram was excellent. I clearly understood the subject. But he knew where I lived and knew that it was only a shack. He failed me, he said, because I had not done the assignment. I'd drawn some-body else's house when the assignment was to do my house. It was a kind of lie, he told me, and he thought it was more important that I be punished for not being truthful than rewarded for understanding electrical circuitry. Physics is science, he told me, and science is ultimately about accuracy and truth.'

I was delighted and congratulated her. We got nowhere when I gently prodded her to remember similar material from the past, for we seemed to be encountering, once again, the strange impoverishment of her inner life. However, for the first time in our work together I felt truly hopeful.

It was all the more painful, therefore, when at the start of the following session she proclaimed the beginning of the end. 'I stopped taking the pills,' she announced.

'Oh, why?'

'They weren't helping me.'

'I thought they improved your sleep.'

'But they're not doing anything for my depression.'

'That's true,' I agreed, 'but wouldn't you rather at least sleep well while we're trying to straighten out the depression?'

'I don't care. I don't care about anything. He doesn't have the right to be doing this to me.'

We were back to square one, except that I finally realized she actually did believe Ralph had no legal right to divorce her. 'I suspect when you married you felt you had captured him for good, as if in taking the vows he had become your property.'

'Of course,' she said guilelessly.

'But people aren't property. They haven't been since slavery was abolished.'

'He took the vows, didn't he?'

'Still,' I persisted, 'the law makes it clear marriage is not slavery. And Ralph objected to feeling owned. He made that clear to you, didn't he?'

'He said something of the sort.'

'How many times?'

'How should I know? I hardly kept count.'

'And how would you respond when he raised the subject?'

Janet gave a large yawn. 'It didn't make any sense to me, so there wasn't any way to respond.'

120

'You're a smart person,' I said. 'What would you do if one of your salesmen told you something that didn't make any sense to you?'

'I'd ask him to clarify it.'

'Did you ask Ralph to clarify?'

'This therapy isn't working,' Janet declared. 'I've been seeing you for four months now and I'm as depressed as when I first started. I'm thinking of quitting.'

I made a desperate maneuver. 'You can't,' I said.

'Can't what?'

'You can't quit therapy.'

'What do you mean I can't quit therapy?'

'Just what I said. I've become interested in your case, and I've decided to work with you until you're cured, no matter how long it takes, no matter how many years, even decades.'

'That's outrageous!'

'Of course it is,' I admitted. 'But maybe you can understand now how Ralph felt when he talked about feeling owned.'

'I don't care how Ralph feels?'

'I'm sorry I played a game with you just then, Janet,' I told her. 'You are utterly free, of course, to leave therapy anytime you want. But even if you do leave, I wish at the very least you would keep our next appointment. And between now and then I'd like you to think about what you just said—that you don't care how Ralph feels.'

Somewhat to my surprise, she did keep our next appointment. Unsurprisingly, she began it by announcing that it was definitely our last one. 'So we've got only fifty minutes left?' I inquired.

'Yes.'

'Would you like me to refer you to another therapist? I may not be the best one for for. Perhaps I'm too impatient. There are some other fine therapists in the area.'

'No, thank you. I'd rather go it alone at this point.'

'As you wish. But don't hesitate to let me know if you change your mind. By the way, did you give some thought to your statement last week that you don't care how Ralph feels?'

'I did,' Janet replied. 'It was misleading. When I thought about it, I realized you were referring to the past and I was speaking in the present. To be honest, I'm so angry at him for the way he's treating me, I really don't care how he feels now. But back when we were married I cared a great deal about his feelings. I'd fix him special dinners. I was sympathetic when he had problems at work. I'd worry about him when he got sick or was overtired. No, I cared about him a lot.'

I gave it a last-ditch try. 'Ralph told me he disliked you taking pictures of him, and that he'd asked you not to without his permission. But he said you kept on sneaking pictures of him with Sean. He felt you didn't respect his feelings or take him seriously.'

'Oh, but that's such a little thing,' Janet retorted. 'How could anyone seriously object to such a little thing?'

I gave up. 'Would you like to hear my analysis of your situation before you leave?'

'Certainly. I might as well get my money's worth.'

'I only spent an hour with Ralph, and that's insufficient for me to make any decent judgment of either his relative goodness or badness,' I began. 'But you yourself have been consistently self-righteous in our meetings. You clearly cling to the notion that you have been the perfect one and Ralph the bad one in your relationship. That position holds precious little hope for you ever being able to forgive Ralph, and hence precious little hope for release from your depression.

'Forgive is an interesting word. It does imply a giving—a giving in or giving up. The most common cause of depression is when a person is caught between the need to give up something and their will to hold on to it or their anger at having to give it up.

'Often that something we need to give up is fantasy, a desire for things to be a certain way even when the reality is unalterably different. Sometimes, with a strong will and hard work, we can make some of our fantasies come true. So it is you succeeded in escaping from poverty.

'But we also need to give up those fantasies that cannot come true. Certain people become unable to do this. For them their fantasies are not only a possible reality; they *are* reality. Then they get in trouble just as you got into trouble in high school with your fantasy of living in an eight-room house.

'You see, when we cling to our fantasies at all cost, then we have to ignore the parts of reality that don't fit in. I'm afraid you tend to do this. I'm not saying Ralph is the good guy, but I am saying that in insisting that your marriage conform to your fantasy you did ignore him. You ignored the reality of him when it didn't fit what you wanted. There are ways in which you discounted him, and now you are paying a price for that discounting.'

There was a long silence. It had sounded so abstract. 'Are you done?' Janet asked.

'Yes.'

'Thank you. I know you tried your best.'

It was a strange accolade, but hardly a satisfying way for us to say good-bye.

There are only two valid reasons to get married. One is for the care and raising of children. When it works (which sometimes does not seem that often) we have not yet invented any institution better than the two-parent home for the care and raising of children. The only other valid reason to get married—there are lots of invalid ones—is for the friction.

When nuns and monks used to come to see me for consultation, ninety-five percent of the time the first thing they wanted to talk to me about was 'community.' And ninety-five percent of the time what they meant by community was something like 'Sister Suzie is driving me up a wall' or 'I'm about to strangle Brother Thomas.' Many have the fantasy that convents and monasteries are places of great holy tranquility, where the monks and nuns go about their days in unending, prayerful peace of mind. The reality is that they are usually places of great struggle and tension and friction.

But even though it is what they most frequently complain about, community is also perhaps the primary reason that nuns and monks join monasteries and convents. They know somehow, correctly, that they need the friction of community to polish them, to refine them on their journeys of spiritual growth.

This talk of convents and monasteries is germane because a pastoral counselor once used the metaphor of 'marriage as a monastery.'[2] It is the most proper model for marriage that I know. A marriage properly should be a marriage of two people gathered together for some purpose higher than the mere pleasure of being together: namely, to enhance each other's spiritual journeys.

Some years ago a book was published entitled *Living Together Alone* and subtitled *The New American Monasticism*.[3] What the title signifies is that even though monks and nuns live together in close quarters with a high amount of interaction, convents and monasteries can be lonely places. And so it is with marriage. Marriage is often a lonely place. One of the problems in our culture, which idolizes romantic love, is that people often have the fantasy that if they marry well, they will never again have to be lonely. It was, as I have said, my fantasy when I married Lily. Then, when the inevitable friction occurs and they feel isolated from their spouse, they often wonder whether their marriage wasn't a mistake even though the reality is that the friction and consequent loneliness are usually par for the course.

There are a number of more or less adaptive ways to deal

[2] Michael Dwinnell, 'Private Practice: A Three Legged Stool,' *Private Practice News* (575 Forest Avenue, Portland, Maine 04101), undated.
[3] By Charles A. Fracchia (San Francisco: Harper & Row, 1979).

with the friction of marriage. Perhaps the most remarkable thing about the case of Janet is that she didn't—or wouldn't—deal with the friction at all. She remained oblivious to the conflict—the friction—between her will and Ralph's until almost the very end. When she could no longer conceivably ignore it, she continued to refuse to deal with it by insisting that she had played no role in it. This clearly served her to avoid the pain of friction, but by what mental sleight of hand could she do so? How could she have been so oblivious? To answer this question we need to now turn to the subject of narcissism.

As Martin Buber suggested, narcissists are incapable of I-Thou relationships. Some narcissists do recognize other people as being different, but as soon as this recognition occurs, the other becomes one of 'them'—the enemy. Thus they have what have come to be called 'I-Them' or 'We-Them' relationships. It is an 'either you're totally with me or else you're against me' kind of psychology.

Sometimes narcissists seem unable to recognize the 'personhood' of other people. For them, others exist only to be used, as if they were merely mechanical tools or unfeeling pieces of property. These are what Buber referred to as 'I-It' relationships.

Finally, narcissists often seem unable to recognize the difference between themselves and others at all. They solely have what are now named I-I relationships, where they relate only with themselves. It may seem bizarre for someone to be incapable of recognizing others, but unfortunately, the condition is not uncommon. An example may help.

Typically, the one week course I attended on ethics at the Harvard Alumni College some years ago included two hundred or so alumni and spouses. And, typically, there were four or five men among them (this is a predominantly masculine style of narcissism—women have their own styles) who, right from the word go, got up and started asking incredibly long-winded questions. In short order the others of us realized that they were not so much interested in answers to their questions as they were in listening to themselves talk. By the end of the second morning of the course, a newfound friend who sat next to me had dubbed them 'the creeps.'

On the morning of the fourth day, Sissela Bok, cochair of the course, had arranged for a pediatrician from Boston Children's Hospital to present us with some cases of conflicts between the needs of children and those of parents in regard to confidentiality in a medical setting—conflicts that can raise some of the very thorniest of ethical dilemmas. The pediatrician was not familiar with the four 'creeps,' but by now Sissela was. So she began the two-hour block of time by announcing she wanted it to be a highly participatory session. 'Up until now,' she said, 'virtually all of the questions have been asked by a very small number of participants. Consequently, for the next two hours, if you are one who has thus far asked a question, I request you to refrain from doing so in order that the others can have a chance. I'm not talking about the whole rest of the course. I'm just referring to the next two hours. So please, just for the next two hours, if you've asked a question before, please hold back for the sake of the other participants.'

Within the first hour all four 'creeps' had asked another one of their long-winded questions. As we were leaving the session, my newfound friend implored in exasperation, 'How could they? How could they? I don't understand it!'

'That's because you don't understand narcissism,' I countered.

'What do you mean?'

'Sissela asked them to shut up so that the others could have a chance,' I explained. 'For those four men, there are no others.'

We can laugh at the 'creeps,' and indeed, they may experience less pain than the more healthy among us. But, my God, how lonely it must actually be, living in a world

where there are no others, where one has only I-I relationships, where one relates only to oneself.

While only a small minority of us are full-blown narcissists, it is essential to remember that we all have significant
narcissistic tendencies. For example, almost everyone has
fallen in love. And, as Buber enthusiasts have pointed out,
falling in love is a variety of the I-I relationship and a totally
narcissistic phenomenon. When we fall in love, we do not
fall in love with someone else; we fall in love with a *fantasy*
we have of that someone else. It is an I-I relationship
because we are merely in love with our own fantasy.

What happens then, after a couple of weeks or months, or
even a couple of years after we have taken marriage vows, is
that we wake up one morning to discover that our beloved no
longer conforms to our fantasy, that we are left stuck there with
a *You,* a stranger. That, of course, is when the work of real love
begins—transforming that stranger, that You, into a Thou,
despite the friction, with the friction, through the friction.

Janet's problem was clearly one of narcissism.

To what extent narcissists are born and not made is a
matter of debate. My own view is that we are all born
narcissists. What then happens if we are supported through
the natural humiliations of childhood by our parents and by
grace is that we gradually grow out of it. If the circumstances
of our youth are not so advantageous, however, there may be
considerable survival value in our retaining our innate self-
centeredness. In the face of chronic adversity, it may be
helpful to see life as we want it to be rather than as it is, and
maintain a continuing self-determination that would be
excessive under other circumstances. Generally speaking,
the more narcissistic my patients were, the more dramatically humiliating their childhoods seemed to have been.
Certainly Janet's father routinely violated—humiliated —
her, and her mother was too apathetic to protect her from
him and other particularly harsh vicissitudes.

In any case, Janet did not seem capable of an I-Thou relationship with Ralph. He was hardly beloved to her. Had he been she would have treated him with respect. But his complaint that, despite her professed love, she did not regard him seriously seemed quite accurate. Her attitude toward him had all the characteristics of an I-It relationship. He was more of a possession to her than a genuine person with rights and his own unique, individual desires and needs.

This denigration of the personhood of the other is characteristic of the master-slave relationship.[4] The slave is more property than person, and whenever his desires differ from those of the master, the master simply doesn't take him seriously. Slavery has been formally outlawed precisely because it has been judged as a grossly unethical form of organizational behavior. And while marital relationships of covert enslavement remain common (with the husband in the master position at least as often as the wife) they are neither healthy nor civil. However vague the guidelines otherwise, marriage is not properly a relationship of ownership.

The three types of narcissism tend to blend into one another. While the predominant flavor of Janet's marriage was that of the I-I relationship, she did on a certain level begin to wake up to the fact that Ralph was not 'ownable' when he finally left home. At this point he became one of 'them,' the enemy, and she became depressed with helpless rage. By the end it was something of an I-Them or I-Him relationship for her, in which she would not entertain the slightest notion that she herself might be at some fault. Yet throughout it was also a kind of I-I relationship. In her ability to ignore Ralph's desires and my own attempts at intervention, Janet stayed anchored not in the reality of marriage as an organization, but in a world of her own fantasy.

4 The very word *denigration* (which comes from the Latin *niger*, meaning 'black'—the same root as *negro*) implies the devaluation of persons as if they were black slaves.

Earlier, I defined marriage as an organization of commitment. Consequently, partners are entitled to expect commitment to the marriage from each other. Where does the realistic expectation of such commitment leave off and the false expectation of ownership begin? There is no clear dividing line. There exists a potential tension between commitment and ownership in every marriage—hence the potential for friction over these issues. A significant aspect of civility in a marriage is how the partners deal with this tension or friction. Janet, of course, did not deal with it at all. In her narcissism, she simply ignored it.

Narcissism is the principal precursor of incivility.

One way to look at narcissism is to regard it as a type of thinking disorder. Specifically, narcissists do not think clearly about other people—if they think about them at all.

Since civility is consciously motivated organizational behavior that is ethical in submission to a Higher Power, by definition it requires that we take our fellow human beings into account. How can narcissists do this when they cannot think well about others in the first place? It is simply not possible to humanistically see others as precious when narcissim allows them to be seen only as enemies ('one of Them') or an 'It' or simply nonexistent.[5]

Because their thinking of others is seriously flawed, the consciousness of narcissists is similarly damaged. We cannot be conscious of that which we don't think about. And if we cannot think about others, how can we think about groups of others or organizations? A lack of consciousness of other people inevitably leads to a lack of consciousness of organizations. This is a second reason narcissists are inherently uncivil. They are virtually incapable of

---

[5] It is possible, even common, for narcissists to espouse a humanistic ideology. I have known several narcissists who were confirmed intellectual 'liberals' filled with public concern for the poor and downtrodden. But their humanism was all in their head. In practice, they treated others like dirt.

consciously motivated organizational behavior. Their behaviour in organizations is remarkably unconscious and, hence, largely unconscious in its motivation. Consider the previously mentioned 'creeps.' They behaved as if they were not even aware they were in a class. They seemed oblivious to their prestigious instructor. And, of course, they were totally unaware of the effect of their uncivil behavior upon their classmates, including how they were making themselves into organizational laughingstocks.

One of Janet's striking features was her peculiar stupidity. By most measurements, she was an intelligent person—an A student in college, then a successful, responsible executive. But there seemed to be holes in her intelligence. This 'Swiss cheese intelligence' is characteristic of people with psychological disorders. They are able to function quite well in certain ways (psychiatrists refer to these as 'conflict-free areas of the ego'), while in others they fail abysmally. We all know of such people: powerful politicians who are impotent lovers; talented executives who are incompetent parents; warm, nurturing mothers who are frigid wives.

While she was perfectly conscious of sales figures, Janet was peculiarly unconscious of marriage as an organization. She was unwilling or unable to recognize how it might differ from the institution of slavery. She acted as if she were utterly unaware of Ralph's legal right to divorce, as well as oblivious to certain other aspects of his personhood. Along with—and, I believe, related to—this unconsciousness was that quality I referred to as an 'impoverishment of her inner life.' There was her failure to warm up to me, her lack of interest in religion, and her bland want of concern for my opinion.

In painting Janet as a villain of sorts, however, I do not want to mislead the reader into thinking of Ralph as the hero. Seldom, from the point of view of systems theory, is there such a thing as sole-fault divorce. I did not get to spend nearly enough time with Ralph for his own limitations to be revealed. So I am left with questions about him. Surely the impoverishment of Janet's inner life would have been perceivable in the course of their dating. Why, then, had he extended their premarital relationship into a marital one? What had attracted him to her in the first place? Almost never do we get to know the complete picture, the whole system. Still, there is no question in my mind that God calls some people to divorce. Ralph may well have been correct that divorce was the only way literally to save his life.

The earlier chapter on our customary lack of group consciousness—our astonishing lack of awareness of the organizations to which we belong—was entitled 'The Hole in the Mind.' In this chapter I have spoken of Janet's 'Swiss cheese intelligence.' Is there a connection? Indeed. I have stated my belief that we are all born narcissistic. Consequently, I believe we are innately stupid about the rights and needs of others and relatively unconscious of the organizations to which we belong. But I also stated that when the circumstances of our life are reasonably decent, we can and do routinely grow out of narcissism. As we butt against the reality of others—of the 'Yous' in our lives—we gradually learn to think of their needs. Similarly we can learn to think organizationally. But such learning is not guaranteed. Not all childhoods are decent, and grace, perhaps unfathomably, skips over some of us. In any case, Janet was one of us who did not grow in consciousness about her marriage or husband.

But both narcissism and incivility run deeper than mere unconsciousness. Civility has been defined not only as conscious organizational behavior, but also that which is ethical in *submission* to a Higher Power. The final reason narcissism is inherently uncivil is because of its characteristic lack of submission. We may think of a narcissism of the will as well as of the mind. When we get down to rock bottom, as in the case of Janet, it is usually unclear to what extent narcissists cannot think of others or whether it is more a matter that they *will* not think of others.

Society has outlawed grossly unethical organizational

behavior such as slavery, atrocious child neglect, spouse battering, and 'white-collar crime.' The law alone, however, is insufficient as a Higher Power. Aleksandr Solzhenitsyn criticized the culture of narcissism in American society, for its ethos of 'legalism,' by which he meant our unfortunate attitude that 'as long as it's legal, it's okay.'[6] It was an accurate and devastating criticism. The fact that an act is legal doesn't necessarily mean that it is ethical or civil. Janet did nothing illegal. But her subtly destructive—uncivil — marital behavior was characterized not only by its lack of consciousness but also its lack of submission.

For Janet there was no Higher Power. When I asked what was meant by 'Vengeance is mine, saith the Lord,' she snapped, 'I don't want to listen to that religious horseshit!' If we allow that reality can have an existence independent of our own will and fantasies, then even reality can be a Higher Power. Thus, I once defined mental health as an 'ongoing process of dedication to reality at all costs.'[7] By 'at all costs' I meant the cost of the pain we must bear when we give up cherished illusions in favor of what's real. Janet was unwilling to bear that pain or pay such costs. There was a willfulness in the way she repeatedly chose to ignore reality in favor of her fantasies, just as when she was a teenager, she had magnified her house fourfold on paper. Her 'I' never submitted to the reality of Ralph's 'You' or even to the reality of the breakup of their marriage. This lack of submission of the will to the world above and beyond itself is as characteristic of narcissism as is the lack of consciousness. No wonder our narcissism is the principal precursor of incivility.

It is not only possible for us to grow out of narcissism; it is essential. By essential I do not mean it has to be done for individual survival. The Janets of the world manage to

---

6 1978 Harvard Commencement address.
7 *The Road Less Traveled* (New York: Simon & Schuster, 1978), p. 51.

survive. But it is necessary both for our collective survival and for grasping the essence of what life is all about. For our lives have little, if any, meaning if they are not spiritual pilgrimages, and learning to grow out of narcissism is the core of the spiritual journey.

One morning, at the age of fifteen, walking down the main road of Phillips Exeter Academy, I spied a classmate fifty yards away. He was strolling toward me, and when we came abreast, we spoke to each other for five minutes and then went on our ways. Fifty yards further down the road, by God's grace, I was struck by a revelation. I suddenly realized that for the entire ten-minute period from when I had first seen my acquaintance until that very moment, I had been totally self-preoccupied. For the two to three minutes before we met all I was thinking about was the clever things I might say that would impress him. During our five minutes together I was listening to what he had to say only so that I might turn it into a clever rejoinder. I watched him only so that I might see what effect my remarks were having upon him. And for the two or three minutes after we separated my sole thought content was those things I could have said that might have impressed him even more.

I had not cared a whit *for* my classmate. I had not concerned myself with what his joys or sorrows might have been or what I could have said that might have made his life a little less burdensome. I had cared *about* him only as a foil for my wit and a mirror for my glory. He was a pure 'It' to me.

And then, by grace or God, it was not only revealed to me how self-centered and self-absorbed I was, but also how, if I continued with that kind of consciousness, it would inevitably lead me into a fearful, empty, and lonely 'maturity.' So it was at the age of fifteen I began to do battle with my narcissism.

It is not an easy battle. The tentacles of our narcissism are subtle and penetrating and must be hacked away one by one, week after week, month after month, year after year. A decade later, only after two years of marriage, did it really begin to dawn on me that Lily might be something more than my appendage, my 'It.' It was the friction of our relationship that opened my eyes. I found myself repeatedly annoyed at her for being away from home shopping at times when I needed her and equally annoyed at her for 'pestering' me at home when I felt in need of solitude. Gradually I began to realize that most of my irritation was the result of a bizarre assumption in my mind. I assumed that Lily should somehow be there for me whenever I wanted her and not be there whenever her presence was inconvenient. Furthermore, I assumed that she should somehow not only know which time was which but also know it without my having to tell her. It was perhaps another decade before I was able to fully cure myself of that particular insanity.

Marriage is not the only form of community and hence not the only vehicle for that friction that we can use to whittle away at our narcissism. But as the most common of human intimate organizations, it is generally the best vehicle for that purpose.

This is not to say we will use it for that end. Janet did not, and there are many men and women like her who choose to live in a narcissistic fantasy world rather than grow out of it by facing the friction of their marriage. Janet's refusal to wake up—to become conscious and submit to reality—highlights the fact that civility is a choice. It has been my burden as a psychotherapist to see many, like Janet, who have not made the choice, who have rejected what might be called 'revelation by reality.' On the other hand, it has also been my privilege to witness many wives and husbands who have made the choice to respond to the organizational friction of marriage by spiritual growth, by diminishing the narcissism. They have grown as a result in civility and holiness. It is a wondrous thing to watch people grow.

10

No Place to Go but Up

Marriage and Power

I was at home on a Sunday evening fifteen years ago when Bruce Bunnell, a local internist, phoned. 'Scott,' he said, 'I'm calling about a patient of mine, Martha Ann Moorehouse. She's the sixty-three-year-old wife of F. Clayton Moorehouse, who's chairman of the board of some big conglomerate. Also a major donor to the hospital. Anyway, they have a country place in the area. They were up here last weekend when she developed an intestinal obstruction. She was operated on first thing Monday morning. No cancer. Simple resection of the ileum with a perfectly good prognosis. The postoperative recovery has been fine, and the surgeons had been planning to send her home tomorrow. But because she's an old patient of mine I dropped by to see her on my rounds this afternoon, and I found her depressed as hell. I've got no idea why. I asked her if she was willing to talk with you. She was reluctant at first, but agreed. I sure wish you'd take a look at her as soon as you can.'

I told Bruce I'd see her around lunchtime the next day.

As with all hospital consultations, I began by reading the chart. It gave me no new information except that Bruce had already been in to see her again that morning and had written in the progress notes, 'Seems less depressed than yesterday. Dr Peck to see.'

I found her sitting up in her private-room bed, reading—or pretending to read. Mrs Martha Ann Moorehouse was a slender woman whose every motion exhibited taste and dignity. Her hair was neatly coiffed and she wore an elegantly simple robe buttoned to her neck. I had the sense she had prepared for my visit. She also looked at least five years older than her age. And no amount of preparation could disguise the slight droop of both sides of her mouth when she wasn't smiling or the lack of sparkle in her eyes when she was. She may have improved, but she was still a lady who was depressed.

She acknowledged the fact. 'Yes, I'm a bit off my feed,' she put it. But she was quick to add, 'It's nothing like yesterday. I had such a feeling of gloom and dread, even despair. Thank God I'm getting over it. But I'm afraid I gave poor Dr Bunnell a bit of a scare.'

No, she had no idea why she was depressed. She had never been depressed before. Or had to see a psychiatrist. It had come on all of a sudden. 'I would suppose that it's just some passing physical sort of reaction to surgery. But, of course, you would be in a much better position to know than I,' she hastened to say.

For the next twenty minutes we chatted about her life. She and her husband had three children—two daughters and a son. All of them were married and doing well. No, none of them had presented any problem when they were growing up. No need for psychiatry there. Oh, one of them, Judy, who lived in Denver, had seen a psychotherapist for a while a few years back, 'But not because she actually had any *problems*, as far as I know. It was a personal growth sort of thing. They seem to be into "growth" out there. I think it must be the mountains. Young people there seem to want to reach for the sky.'

There was little life to her tone. Some slight light came into Mrs Moorehouse's eyes only when she talked about her childhood. She had grown up with a younger brother on a huge sheep ranch in southwest Texas. Her parents, whom she adored, had both been killed in a small plane crash during her senior year at college and the ranch was sold. Here tears momentarily filled her eyes, but the light returned as she continued to tell me about those early years. 'It was a different world back then. We were the wealthiest people in the small town, of course, but it never seemed that way. Everybody knew each other. There was no one my brother and I didn't play with—Mexicans, whites, rich, poor, it made no difference. It was, well, a real sort of community. It's not like that anymore.' The light was gone from her eyes again.

'A while ago you said "Thank God," ' I said, 'when you spoke of how much better you're feeling today. Do you have a relationship with God?'

'What an odd question! I mean it's really not the sort of thing one talks about, is it? Certainly, I believe in God. A relationship? Well, I suppose you might say I have a relationship with him, but it's a very private thing, of course.' There was a hint of warning in her tone.

'Of course,' I agreed. 'You go to church?'

'Occasionally. But my husband likes to play golf on Sundays whenever we can. Besides, God doesn't live in a church, does he?'

I smiled. 'As a golfer myself, I also think he can be encountered on a golf course. But may I take it, then, that your husband isn't a believer?'

'A believer? Well, he would have to speak for himself on that score. But if I had to, I suppose I could say I'm the more religious one.' There was a note of finality in her voice. The subject was not to be explored further.

'Talking of your husband,' I asked, 'would you mind if I spoke with him? I can imagine he's quite difficult to get hold of.'

'Certainly you can speak with him. And no, he's not difficult to get hold of at all. No one could ask for a more attentive husband. He's probably in the visitors' lounge right now reading his *Journal*.'

I hoped so. But there was a hunch I wanted to follow up on first, although it wouldn't be easy. 'At the time of your surgery, you must have wondered if you were close to death,' I remarked.

'Naturally.'

'Did you feel ready to die?'

The silence was electric. Mrs Moorehouse clearly either could not or would not respond to the question. 'Often as we get older,' I went on, 'we become more ambivalent about life. Particularly after our children are grown and left. Many then feel that their job is done. It's not uncommon for people in that position who have emergency surgery, once they realize they are going to recover, to feel a certain sense of partial disappointment.'

'My job is not done.' Mrs Moorehouse had emphatically regained her speech. 'My husband has an extremely important position. Consequently, we have a very active social life. He needs all the support I can possibly give him.'

'I don't doubt it,' I said, getting up from the chair. 'And now I'll go looking for him. I'll be back to see you this time Wednesday, the day after tomorrow.'

'Oh, you don't need to go to that trouble.'

'It would be trouble, Mrs Moorehouse, only if you didn't matter. But you matter a great deal.'

'What if my surgeon discharges me before then?'

'I'm going to suggest to him that he not do so,' I explained. 'Your depression may well be very temporary, but I doubt if he would want to discharge you before we have a couple of days to make sure. It wouldn't be good medical care. Besides,' I added, 'I like you and I want to see you again.'

'Well, if you really want to.'

'Yes, I want to, Mrs Moorehouse.'

As she predicted, I found her husband in the visitors' lounge reading *The Wall Street Journal*. F. Clayton Moorehouse was obviously no ordinary man. Handsome, casually dressed, he looked much younger than his wife, though he was two years older. He exuded a vigorous sense of drive, of purpose and energy and confidence. 'It's gracious of you to come by, Doctor,' he said, laying down the paper.

'It has nothing to do with graciousness,' I answered, sensing the need to quickly cut through any pretense. 'It's my job. Your wife became seriously depressed, and they call me in when people become depressed.'

He appeared not the least discomfited by my bluntness. I guessed he was a man who actually enjoyed a good fight, enjoyed it because he could do it well. 'How can I help?' he inquired disarmingly, and proceeded to reveal nothing. He had no idea why his wife had become depressed, except to suppose it was some sort of physical reaction to her surgery. Certainly there were no inordinate stresses in her life. They were well off financially. No problems with the children. Their marriage was perfect. They loved to play golf together and liked to travel. They got to travel often and had the same tastes in the sights they wanted to see and the best hotels to stay in. There was no real action until I got up to take my leave. 'I'll be seeing Mrs Moorehouse again the same time the day after tomorrow,' I announced.

'I'm not sure I understand, Doctor, why you would need to see my wife again.'

I gave him the same explanation I had given her. 'But it's clearly such a temporary little thing,' he insisted.

'How do you know that?' I responded, dimly but uncomfortably aware of the stakes this man felt he was playing for. 'And what difference does another day or two in the hospital really make? Is there anything that makes you afraid of my seeing Mrs Moorehouse again?'

'I should think that hospital food would make anyone depressed,' he urbanely switched the subject. 'No offense meant to this hospital. It's excellent. But hospital food is hospital food, isn't it? Naturally, I just want to get her home. And naturally she wants to get home as soon as possible.'

'Naturally,' I agreed. 'But her depression, whatever the cause, goes deeper than hospital food. I'll be back on Wednesday.'

'We'll see, Doctor,' he said. 'We'll see.'

I had hardly begun with my first patient the next morning

when the receptionist informed me that a Mrs Judy Moorehouse Minton from Denver was on the line. It was apparently urgent, so I took it. 'I'm Martha Ann Moorehouse's daughter,' the caller informed me. 'I talked to both of my parents yesterday afternoon and evening. Daddy's going to try to prevent you from seeing my mother again. That's typical of him.'

'Oh?'

'Yes, Daddy's a nice man—a wonderful man, in fact—as long as he's on top, as long as he's in control. He's the most overcontrolling person you can imagine. He's utterly crushed Mom.'

'Crushed her?'

'They used to fight a lot when I was a kid. But then, twenty-five years ago, Mom just caved in. Ever since, she agrees with everything he says. She has no opinions of her own. He's made a child of her. He feeds her her allowance. I'm sure he's afraid that if you see her she might get out from under his thumb.'

I suspected what she was saying was true. Yet children can have their own neuroses and are often not the most accurate of observers. 'Your father seems a most attentive husband,' I commented.

'Oh, he's attentive whenever she's sick. That's another way he can be on top. But as soon as she's well, he goes bouncing around the country to all his board meetings and doesn't give her the time of day.'

Which could be another reason Mrs Moorehouse might be depressed by the prospect of her recovery, I thought. 'How do you think I can help?' I asked.

'If you could only get her to talk about herself, about her marriage. I'm afraid she may die if she can't. You're her last hope.'

It sounded dramatic, and represented a degree of responsibility I hardly relished. 'I'll see what I can do, Mrs Minton,' I cautioned. 'It may not be much. It may not be anything. It's usually impossible to interrupt these systems

140

when they've been going on much of a lifetime.'

Not unexpectedly, Dr Bunnell phoned me two hours later. 'Scott, Mrs Moorehouse wants to be discharged today. The surgeon doesn't see any reason to keep her. And her husband's convinced there's no reason for her to receive any more psychiatric attention.

'Really? That's interesting. I just finished talking with his daughter who called me because she thinks that psychiatric attention is her mother's last hope.'

'So, what do we do?'

'You can do what you and the surgeon want, Bruce. She's nowhere near ill enough for me to commit her. You can't hold her against her will. The only thing you can do—and I hope you've got the courage—is to tell the Moorehouses that if you discharge her, she'll have to sign out against medical advice—AMA. Her husband will be furious. On the other hand, I think he'll be a bit squeamish about going AMA. But pushing it may not help your relationship with him. So you have to do what you think best, all things considered.'

Bruce took the courageous course. Consequently, Mrs Moorehouse was still in the hospital for me to see the next day. 'I told you it was just a little physical reaction to surgery,' she exclaimed the moment I entered the door of her room. She was dressed in a svelte suit. Her eyes sparkled without a trace of depression. She had made a remarkably rapid recovery indeed. Maybe it had been 'just a little physical reaction.' On the other hand, a phrase well known to psychiatrists flitted through my mind: 'flight into health.' It referred to patients who made dramatic—but usually temporary—recoveries in order to avoid having to see a psychiatrist. 'Bags all packed, eh?' I smiled in inquiry.

She smiled in return. 'Yes, I'm champing at the bit.'

'Well, I'm sorry I held you back an extra day. It was all my fault, not Dr Bunnell's,' I said. 'And if you still want to, I'm sure you'll be able to leave here almost immediately after I do.' I fished a business card from my wallet and handed it to her. 'Here's my address and phone number. Would you like to come back to see me as an outpatient?'

She slipped the card into her pocketbook. 'What would be the point, Doctor, when there's nothing wrong?'

'But I suspect there is something wrong, Mrs Moorehouse. For one thing, I suspect you may have a difficult marriage.'

'What a thing to say, Doctor. You couldn't be more wrong. My marriage is perfect.'

I smiled to make the moment as easy as possible for her. 'Sometimes with a psychiatrist you can't win,' I told her. 'There's no such thing as a perfect marriage. Consequently, people who say they've got a perfect marriage are often out of touch with reality. Look, Mrs Moorehouse, I'm not a money-grubber. I've got a busy practice and no need for new patients. I'd like you to come see me because I think you need to tell your story.'

'My story?'

'Yes. The story of your marriage. The story of your friends. Of your accomplishments. Of your failures. Of your angers. Of your sacrifices. Of your loneliness. You're sixty-three now. You're a very private person and I doubt you have told your story to anyone for at least thirty years. At sixty-three I believe it is time that a human being should start to tell her story to someone safe.'

For a moment I detected yearning in her eyes, but within seconds it was replaced with dignified determination. 'I think there are some things that are better not talked about,' she announced.

I tried again. 'Seeing me would be a little bit like being back in southwest Texas, back before your parents died. Being in psychotherapy is sort of like being back in community again, back when you had real chums, back when you could still say what was on your mind.'

Once again the yearning look returned, and once again it fled. 'I don't see how I can ask my husband to pay for something he doesn't believe in,' she responded.

I was flabbergasted. 'To pay for therapy?'

'Yes, that's what I said.'

'Why couldn't you pay for it yourself?'

'Because I don't have any money.'

'You don't have any money?'

'Oh, I have a checking account which I use for my clothes and presents for the children and for household things. When it gets low, I just ask Clayton for more. He gives me virtually everything I want. Clayton is very generous.'

'You have no savings in your own name?'

'No.'

'But from what I understand, your husband must be quite a wealthy man. How much does he have in his name?'

'I have no idea.'

'No idea?'

'None. Clayton's not one of those men who goes around talking about money all the time.'

It was worse than I had feared. 'Tell me,' I asked, 'after your parents died and the ranch was sold, you must have inherited some money. How much was your inheritance?'

'Gracious, that was forty-two years ago. It's hard to remember. I think it may have been around a half a million dollars.'

'What happened to that money?'

'Oh, I think it was used up long ago. Clayton wasn't always wealthy, you know. He had to struggle quite hard when he was young.'

'If your inheritance hadn't been spent, if it had been kept in conservative investments, do you know what it would be worth today?'

'Good heavens, no. I've never had any head for figures.'

'About ten million dollars,' I told her.

'That seems a lot, doesn't it?' she said uninterestedly.

'Have you ever wanted to have some savings of your own, that you could manage yourself?'

'No, never. Clayton's good with money. I'm not. As I told you, I have no head for figures.'

I knew I had lost. 'It sounds to me as though you've made up your mind,' I said. 'You'd rather not look at your life, would you?'

'No, you're correct, Doctor. You've been quite kind, but I really am too old a dog to learn new tricks.'

'You've got my card,' I said. 'Feel free to call me if you should change your mind. Good luck.'

I called her daughter to tell her of my failure, and then I more or less forgot about Mrs Moorehouse.

Until four years later, when her daughter called me again. 'It's not about my mother,' she said. 'She had a heart attack and died six months after she saw you.'

'Your prediction was prophetic,' I remembered. 'I'm terribly sorry. She was a gracious lady.'

'Her death was mercifully quick. Now I need your help with my father. I wish *his* death could be mercifully quick.'

'Oh?'

'He did fine after my mother died. Stayed on as chairman of the board. Dated other women and was thinking of getting remarried. But ten weeks ago he had a stroke. His right side is paralyzed. That's doing well with physical therapy. He's quite ambulatory with a cane now. He needs help with his dressing. That's not the problem. We've got round-the-clock nurse's aides. The problem is the stroke also demolished the area of the brain which deals with numbers. He can talk almost as well as before and can read and understand perfectly, but he can't even add two and two. "Acalculia" they call it. The neurologists don't see any chance for significant recovery at this point. So, of course, he's been pensioned off the corporate board. And he's driving me nuts. He screams and throws things. No sooner do we get a new nurse's aide than he fires her. Or they quit because he's so irascible. It's kind of like he's become a lost soul in hell because he can't count his goddamn money anymore. Anyway, he needs psychiatric help in the worst way, and I will too if he doesn't get it.'

I told her I was too busy to take on new patients. Besides, I suspected her father did not remember me too kindly. I suggested Dr Jacob Weinberg, a most competent new psychiatrist in town. She agreed. I took her number and called Jake. He was grateful for the referral, and after briefing him on what I knew of them, I once again put the Moorehouse family out of mind.

Until two years later, when I was attending a quarterly case discussion meeting of psychotherapists in the area. Jake got the floor. 'Ordinarily,' he said, 'I would present either an extraordinarily juicy psychoanalytic saga or else a case where I was particularly at sea and needed your consultation. Instead, I have chosen to present a seventy-two-year-old male nursing home patient, Mr F. Clayton Moorehouse.'

Jake told the patient's history, including my assessment of his wife and marriage and the nature of his stroke. 'There are five reasons,' he said, 'that I would like—no, I need—to present the case.

'One relates to the nature of psychosis. His brain was remarkably unaffected beyond the motor strip and his acalculia. I'd read him complicated passages of philosophy out loud, and more impressive than the fact that he could practically repeat them verbatim was the coherent, even brilliant interpretations he would make of them. He loved to match wits with me. Yet he would scream at the aides when they would interrupt us with his medications and call them the foulest names. He twisted buttons off my jacket many times, trying to hold on to me to prevent me from leaving. He was terrified of being left alone and of dying. It was obvious to everyone. Yet whenever I raised the subject of his fear, he refused to talk about it. The one thing he most wanted to avoid was ending up in a nursing home, yet he behaved in just such a way as to force us to put him there. I happen to believe that he was insane, but there is no textbook of psychiatry which would help to justify my conclusion.

'The second reason I'm presenting his case relates to the

way some people get to nursing homes. His net worth was about thirty million dollars. Full-time nursing coverage at his house didn't even represent a luxury for him. There was no physical reason for him to require nursing-home care. But no private-duty nurses or aides would work with him despite total family support. He was too abusive and manipulative. No private psychiatric hospital would take him because he was chronic and untreatable. The family couldn't bear him to be in the back ward of the state hospital. So ultimately he was committed to the nursing home where, because he screamed so much, they placed him in a wing of comatose patients. Most of the time for the past two years he had to be restrained.

'The third reason I need to talk about Clayton Moore-house is simply to ventilate. You see, he was the most pathetic person I ever worked with. None of it had to be. After I committed him to the nursing home, the family requested that I continue to see him once a month on the off chance he would change his mind. They kept the house open for him to return to. All he had to do was change his mind and he could have been sitting at home, reading and enjoying sunsets, his needs perfectly well attended to, surrounded by children and grandchildren and interesting friends to talk with. Every month I tried to point it out to him. All he had to was to give up control and sit back and enjoy life. But that was the one thing he couldn't do: give up control. So he rotted away among the comatose, endlessly obsessing about his bowels because they were the only thing that he *could* control, screaming at the aides because he couldn't manipulate them or get them to dance to his precise tune, and tied down in bed yelling at closed doors in endless terror. It was so pathetic.

'The fourth reason I tell you about him is because he may have started me on the road to a religious conversion. In trying to help him give up control—which was the only way I could possibly help him—I realized he had to have some-thing to give it up to. Why surrender at all except to a superior power? So I found myself in the bizarre position, as an agnostic, of attempting to convince this man of the existence of God. But like everything else I attempted, it got nowhere. He seemed to have a compelling need to be his own god. Yet in trying to convert him I started listening to my own words. I still don't know if I believe in God, but I can tell you this: If I should ever be in his situation I'm going to choose to become a believer.

'And lastly, I present the case to celebrate. Clayton Moorehouse had a massive stroke on Friday and died the day before yesterday. Thank God the poor man is finally gone.'

The varieties of incivility, like those of sin, tend to blend into each other. Certainly F. Clayton Moorehouse was a study in narcissism. But moving deeper into the subject, I wish to use the Moorehouses to illustrate issues of power in marriage.

Perhaps the most effective way to avoid dealing with the proper friction of marriage is through the establishment of a pattern of dominance and submission. Couples frequently fall into such patterns very early—often during their engagement and sometimes even on their first date. Roughly two-thirds of the time in our culture it is the male who is dominant and the female the submissive one, but in a sizeable minority of cases the wife is dominant and the husband totally submissive.

It is not difficult to see how such a pattern is friction-avoiding. There need not be any friction at all when one partner is utterly comfortable giving all the orders and the other utterly comfortable taking all the orders. Indeed, many marriages survive well past the golden wedding anniversary on just such a pattern. The only problem with it (as the Moorehouses so sadly demonstrated) is that it is not good for the spiritual growth of the partners involved.

Consequently, what happens in healthy marriages that survive is that somewhere between the five- and ten-year mark the dominant partner becomes tired of having to make all the decisions and the submissive one becomes fed up with being bossed around all the time. Then the couple begins the difficult process of negotiating a more equitable power balance in the relationship. One of the not infrequent causes of divorce—and perhaps the most legitimate—in the first fifteen years of marriage is that one of the partners strives for a healthier balance while the other continues, year after year, to insist upon remaining totally dominant or totally submissive.

Based on her daughter's account, Martha Ann Moorehouse did make one attempt at creating a healthier system, but then 'caved in.' It would probably have been better had she gotten divorced. She might still be alive today. And possibly her husband, younger then, might have learned from his wife's leaving that not everything can be controlled.

Note I just referred to the power balance in marriage as a 'system.' Since marriage is an organization, it is inevitably also a system. And recall the basic tenet of systems theory: If you alter one component of a system, then the other components must also change for the system to survive. Martha Ann Moorehouse could have succeeded in assuming more power within the marriage only if Clayton Moorehouse had succeeded in learning now to relinquish power. I could have assisted her when I saw her only with her husband's consent. Without that consent, I was helpless, because my real patient was not so much an unhealthy woman as an unhealthy system. And systems are difficult to change even under the best of circumstances.

I know. Long before we married, Lily and I had slipped into the pattern of my being the dominant member of the relationship and she the submissive one. But within five years of marriage, I began to feel increasingly frustrated by Lily's dependency and she increasingly angered at me for being a male chauvinist pig.[1] So we set about trying to

[1] This was before the days of the women's movement. Lily invented the term 'male chauvinist pig'—accurately—for me.

change this state of affairs, although I'm not at all sure how well we would have succeeded had not each of us entered individual psychotherapy.

At the seven-year mark of our marriage, when we were both in therapy, we decided to take a course together in Southeast Asian politics. Initially the professor announced there would be no papers involved; just a simple answer exam. But halfway through the course he informed the class that he had changed his mind and assigned us two papers to write. Immediately Lily went into an absolute panic, and as the day the first paper was due grew closer and closer, her distress got worse and worse. Finally she confessed to me the reason she was so upset was that she had never in her life written a paper. The way she had made it through the numerous colleges she had attended, she told me, was by taking only those courses that required no papers.

'Gee, that's neat, honey,' I said, interested in becoming better acquainted with the You, the stranger, I had married. 'I didn't know that. But wait a minute; that's not true really. Back when we were engaged and you were at the Columbia University School of General Studies, you took that course on art appreciation for which you had to write several papers, if I remember correctly.'

And then I slapped my head. 'Oh, my God,' I exclaimed to myself in embarrassment, recollecting how, lovey-dovey, hand in hand on a Sunday afternoon, we would visit the Metropolitan Museum of Art, how we would just happen to wander up into the Monet room, and how Lily would ask me, 'Scotty, which one of these Monets do you like the best?'

I would look around and make my choice. 'I do, too,' Lily would say. 'But what is it you like about it?' I'd tell her, and she'd start to write on a little pad she kept in her purse. 'Anything else you like about it?' she'd continue. I would happily give her another dissertation and she would scribble away. 'God, Scotty, you've got such a wonderful way with words,' she'd praise me when I stopped. 'But is there anything you happen to not like about it?' Again, I'd be only too glad to provide yet one more homily. 'What a brilliant analytical capacity you have!' Lily would proclaim and resume her writing.

Which of us was the more crippled? Certainly you might conclude it was Lily, so into helplessness and avoidance that she couldn't write her own papers. But think of how blind and stupid I was—enjoying such a male ego and power trip that I could be manipulated into writing papers for her without even being aware that was what I was doing!

Systems are hard to change. The night before that first paper was due I had to lock myself in the bathroom. Lily was a good manipulator and I so much relished being the answer man! But change they can. She finally finished the paper at 4:00 A.M. and got a B minus. She finished the second paper before I completed mine, and got an A minus. And I had taken my first small step out of the role of compulsive caretaker toward learning a little something of the art of empowerment.

There are two types of power: political and spiritual.

Political power is the power to influence others through coercion. It is the power to hire and fire, to punish, to imprison, even to kill. Or to threaten such things. Political power has nothing to do with wisdom or benevolence. It does not reside in a person or her character. It resides solely in money or position. This is why it is often referred to as temporal power, because these things are temporary. They can be stripped away overnight, just as Clayton Moore-house's stroke stripped him of his position as chairman of the board and of the capacity to count his wealth.

Spiritual power is the power to influence others through one's own being—by example, by kindness, by humor, by widsom and love. It is exercised at least as often by the poor as the wealthy, by the lowly as the high and mighty. Indeed, its hallmark is humility. The more spiritually powerful people become, the more aware they are that their power is a gift from God and has little, if anything, to do with their achievements—that it is not theirs, but God's power acting through them. And usually they are surprised by the extent of their influence for the good.

Spiritual power is invariably civil.[2] Political power may be exercised with civility or it may be exercised with the grossest incivility.

People have an unfortunate tendency to think of political power and spiritual power as opposites. The reasons for this tendency are not hard to understand. Political power is achieved by ambition; spiritual power is not achieved at all; indeed, it often requires of its practitioner the renunciation of ambition. Political power has everything to do with control. Spiritual power has much to do with surrendering control. Political power is a matter of externals and spiritual power a matter of what is within. Political power enormously tempts its possessor to lose touch with her or his humanity and thereby forsake the path of spiritual power. It is no accident, therefore that there is something of a tradition within certain religions that political power is best avoided.

But this is simplistic, black and white, either/or thinking, which like all simplistic thinking can get us into trouble. Are we to leave the governance of our organizations and institutions to the spiritually infantile? At what cost to

[2] There are ambiguities here.

Hitler, for instance, was a charismatic man. That adjective comes from the Greek word *charism*, meaning 'a spiritual gift.' Can we not conclude that this spiritual giftedness, residing in his personhood, was uncivil? One the other hand, the question may be a red herring. For might we not more accurately conclude that he was so notoriously uncivil by virtue of his misuse of political power that the issue of his gifts is irrelevant?

A brilliant man may be a brilliant liar who swindles thousands, or he may use his brilliance as a professor who helps thousands to discern truth. Can we not look at such gifts or personality traits as a spellbinding speaking ability or intellectual brilliance as essentially neutral capacities? I believe it is our choice to use these gifts, these capacities, for either civil or uncivil purposes. For me, the will to make the civil choice—the will to love—is more radical than any *charism*. What I call spiritual power has much more to do with this mysterious will to love than any superficial talents.

Still, the ambiguity deserves noting.

society? Would not the most spiritually powerful people be the ones most likely to handle political power gracefully—to exercise such power without succumbing to its temptations, its corrupting influences? And how could someone grow into the further reaches of spiritual power without the experience of political power to learn from?

The problem with Clayton Moorehouse was not that he possessed political power, but that he refused to learn spiritual power. One of the great hazards of political power is that it can be used to insulate us from life, and hence from life's lessons. But it does not have to be that way. Clayton Moorehouse was an obviously intelligent man. He would have observed others struggling with the issues of old age. Surely he could have figured out that the central issue is one of learning how to give up control. But spiritual power is to some extent a choice, and the will is free to choose to remain stupid. So he refused the vocation to old age even though it meant living his last years in such pathetic torment.

The problem of Martha Ann Moorehouse was that in 'caving in,' in forsaking the quest for political power, she also forsook her spiritual growth. She not only settled for having no money of her own; she also settled for having 'no head for figures.' She virtually stopped thinking. The issue of the unbalanced control of money in their marriage was symbolic of the pervasive disease in the whole system. In abrogating all political power within the system, she had placed her soul in her husband's keeping, even to the point of rejecting the psychotherapy offered—rejecting psycho-spiritual growth and healing. The result of her choice of political impotence was, ultimately, that of spiritual and intellectual impotence.

Political and spiritual power are separate phenomena, but they may go hand in hand, and often should. I believe we are all *called* to spiritual power, and that frequently means to political power as well.

Since civility is organizational behavior that is ethical in submission to a Higher Power, and since God calls us to power, a major characteristic of civil women and men is their eagerness to help others grow into power. Civil behaviour is empowering behavior.

There are times in child raising and management and certain other situations when it is appropriate to hold on to control and political power. Had his wife been a compulsive spender, for instance, it might well have been the right thing for Clayton Moorehouse to keep her on an allowance. Since she was not, however, his treatment of her was uncivil. He discouraged rather than encouraged her independence.

Because civility is organizational behavior, the basic principles of civility in marriage will also be the basic principles of civility in families and larger organizations, be they business corporations or governments. It is the task of any good executive, for example, to make herself replaceable by empowering her subordinates through coaching, training, and other forms of staff development and through delegating to them the maximum responsibility they can handle. Conversely, one of the most common forms of incivility in large organizations is for executives to hold on to their power when they should be giving it away—just as it is when parents withhold power from children who have grown mature enough to asusme it.

While she might have once wanted power, by the time I met her Martha Ann Moorehouse no longer desired it. This lack was itself uncivil. It may seem strange to designate a lack of desire for power as a possible form of incivility, but remember its ultimate effect on her husband. By failing to stand up to him, she contributed to the living hell of his last two years. Remember also that as 'consciously motivated organizational behavior,' civility is characterized by consciousness and incivility by a lack of consciousness. Again we are confronted by 'the hole in the mind.' Although unusually intelligent people, both the

Moorehouses were remarkably unconscious of the obvious unhealthiness of the system in which they participated.

Since money is one of the two determinants of political power, it is inevitable that money and power issues in marriage should be inextricably interwoven. The role of breadwinner in traditional American sexist society, for instance, has tended to be of higher status than the role of homemaker, even though homemaking is usually the more complex and demanding job. But this kind of inequity—this incivility—can be combatted. If a division of labor is appropriate in a particular marriage, then (except under the most unusual circumstances) a division of income is also appropriate. There was no reason the vast Moorehouse savings should not have been half in his name and half in hers. To settle for the inappropriate was uncivil on both their parts.

For wives and husbands are called to enrich each other literally as well as figuratively. This same principle holds true in all organizations. People are called to empower each other whenever possible, and incivility always implies some failure to do so—some abuse of power within the content of an organization.

But all organizations, like all marriages, are different, and the civil use of power is contingent upon the particular situation and system. Moreover, since situations change, it is appropriate for systems—no matter how difficult it might be—to also change. The imbalance of power in the Moorehouse marriage was tragic in part because it became more rather than less rigid as the marriage aged. In the last chapter, Janet essentially said, 'I'd rather stay depressed than adjust to this system change.' In their own way, the Moorehouses said the same; each preferred to die rather than assume or relinquish power. Spiritual power may be exercised inwardly as well as outwardly. Consistent civility in the use of power in relation to others requires the timely exercise of the power to change ourselves.

11

Walking the Tightrope

Marriage and Separateness

This section began by speaking of the mystery of marriage, and underlying these pages has been the major theme of contingency theory—one translation being that there are no clear, fail-safe formulas or stereotypes to successfully govern organizations. Reality—in this case the mysterious reality of the organization of marriage—has a way of being disconcerting.

Many people are startled, for instance, to learn that for psychotherapists the greatest problem in treating marriages is not too much separateness but too much togetherness. When Lily and I were still in the practice of psychotherapy and working with couples, sooner or later we had to say to almost all of them, 'You're too much married.' In couples group therapy it was frequently necessary to separate the husband and wife and seat them apart from each other in the circle. When we would ask Mary, 'How do you feel about that?' John would often instantly respond, 'Oh, Mary feels this way.' We would have to instruct him, 'Hey, John, let Mary have her own feelings.' Or when we would ask John, 'What do you think about that?' Mary would immediately answer for him, 'John thinks such and such.' And then we would need to jump in again: 'Mary, let John think for himself.'

The point was also made that God covenants with us as individuals, but not with organizations. Since marriage is an organization, I do not believe there is anything inherently holy about it. Nor do I believe that God calls any of us to a marital relationship with any specific individual. The popular notion that there is someone special 'meant' for us in our 'stars' needs to be debunked. This is not to say there are no forces that attract one person to another. The most obvious force, however, is prosaic indeed. The stale adage, 'Birds of a feather flock together,' is still a lively principle of psychiatry. In psychiatric hospitals, for instance, one of the best ways of assessing the severity of a patient's illness is by the company he or she keeps. There is a profound tendency for the most ill patients to hang out with the others who are most ill, while the least disturbed generally associate with the other least disturbed. So it is with marriage. The personalities of marital partners are often strikingly different, but their level of maturity is usually strikingly similar. Thus, emotionally healthy individuals tend to marry other healthy individuals, emotionally sick people to marry other sick people, and the in-betweens to marry in-betweens. This pattern of choice is as predictable as it is unconscious.

A related and disconcerting fact is that the longevity or stability of a marriage is not necessarily an indicator of its organizational health. The Moorehouse marriage, for instance, was a lasting one of close 'togetherness,' but it was hardly a vibrant, creative 'monastery of two.' Indeed, the very sickest marriages psychotherapists see are often the most stable. They occur between partners whose psychopathology fits together hand and glove, who may murder each other daily though they cannot be pried apart with a crowbar.

I have referred to marriage as a vocation. A vocation to what? Virtually all young couples and most older couples don't have the foggiest idea what they are doing when they get married. Certainly at the age of twenty-three I had no understanding of either the realities of marriage or of Lily. Had I not been so blind, I might never had stepped down the aisle. Thirty-three years later I'm glad I did, and I do believe I had a vocation to marriage. But that vocation was hardly marked by the clarity of my vision, and I'm not sure that Lily and I entered matrimony with a level of consciousness any higher than that of the most misbegotten of couples.

If a vocation to marriage is not a conscious calling to a state of intense togetherness with a particular person, then what in God's name is it a calling to? A part of the answer, I believe, is contained in the definition of marriage with which the section began: 'an organization of two people who have made a *commitment* to attempt to maintain the organization.' A vocation to marriage is a vocation to commitment.

I was so nervous at the time that afterwards I could remember literally nothing of our marriage ceremony beyond the shaking of my knees. Why was I so terrified in that little chapel, surrounded by a small group of close and supportive friends? It was because I was making a commitment. I had no idea of what kind of commitment. We didn't have the option of writing our own vows back in those days. What did it mean 'to have and to hold from this day forth'? Yet I am not sure that our children, who chose their own vows, have any more idea than we how those vows would become fleshed out—incarnated—over the years. Indeed, being in the dark was a part of my terror. All I knew was I was making a commitment to something and that commitment was very, very serious.

Yet there is a certain ambiguity inherent in commitment. The basic law of contracts is that they are binding, but the reason there are all those thick books in lawyers' offices is that most of them are filled with exceptions: contracts are binding except in the circumstances of Smith v. Jones or Harris V. Harris or Garcia v. Mendoza. The *ideal* of marriage is that of a covenantal relationship whereby I commit myself to stay with you regardless of what I might think or feel. When we make the marriage vows, the most conscientious of us are dimly aware that we are committing ourselves to strive for that ideal. Is the ideal attainable? Yes. Is it always attainable? No.

It feels attainable when we are in love. But it has already been indicated that the 'in love' relationship is a narcassistic

I-I relationship of fantasies rather than of real human beings. Romantic love is illusionary. The reality is that two human beings cannot fulfill each other or meet all of each other's needs. Just as I had the narcissistic fantasy that Lily could be with me whenever I wanted and absent whenever I didn't want her, so she also had her own unrealistic expectations. It would have been nice for her if I could have been detached and objective whenever she needed a cool head for advice, dedicated to my work only when she was dedicated to hers, playful whenever she was playful, passionate whenever she wanted passion. But I just couldn't pull it off.

So what are we to do with our unmet needs in marriage? Suppress them? Yes, certainly, sometimes. But not always. It is one of the characteristics of a healthy marriage that both partners over the years develop a complex and evolving system for meeting some of their needs together and some of them separately. There is a balance of togetherness and separateness in the relationship. Maintaining—and, when necessary, shifting—this balance is a bit like walking a tightrope. There are no formulas for this tightrope walking, since the best balance is going to be quite different for different marriages and at different times. So we cannot commit ourselves beforehand to a specific pattern of togetherness and separateness. What the vocation to marriage is, then, is a calling to specifically commit oneself to deal with the friction of unmet needs in the manner of walking a tightrope.

There are limits to tolerable separateness. Lily and I have survived all manner of separation and friction. Yet were she to tell me she would return home by 5:00 P.M. Monday and then not show up until 10:00 A.M. Wednesday without offering any explanation, it is quite possible that by Friday morning, I would be consulting with either a lawyer or a psychiatrist in response to such incivility.

The point is that there are degrees and kinds of incivility that render walking the tightrope absolutely impossible.

Some marriages, by virtue of excessive separateness or excessive togetherness, are literally killing. People would die—and often have, like Mrs Moorehouse—if they could not, for whatever reason, get out of them. As I believe that God calls some to marriage, so I also believe that God calls some people to divorce. Actually, I am quite hard-nosed about the matter. The other side of the coin is that the only valid reason to divorce is that there is very clear evidence that that is exactly what God is calling you to—and not just because you and your spouse happen to be in faintly different spiritual stages or suffering a modicum of friction that makes the grass look a bit greener on the other side of the fence. Evidence that the time has come to quit can usually be accumulated only after years of agonizing over not knowing the right thing to do.

It is secular as well as spiritual wisdom to beware of divorce. If you do not come to deeply understand and fully accept your own personal responsibility for 'irreconcilable differences' in marriage number one, it is quite probable you will discover the very same sort of insoluble problems in marriage number two. And marriage number three. Many psychiatrists, myself included, have seen a woman who divorced her husband because of his alcoholism only to marry a second man who also turns out to be an alcoholic— and perhaps even a third. Divorcing one spouse to remarry another frequently means a leap from the frying pan into the fire.

Still, there is no point to a marriage where all togetherness has been lost and none is retrievable. And even less point to one where togetherness is so mandated as to be suffocating unto death. Besides our mutual capacity to keep our day-to-day promises and commitments, there are other reasons our marriage has survived. Preeminent among them has been our evolving capacity to allow each other 'space.' Gradually, I was able to stop thinking of Lily as my appendage, to respect her often independent schedules and honor her own need for privacy. Similarly, she became able to modify her natural possessiveness, allowing me sufficient freedom to be my unique and separate self. One of the most joyous moments of my life occurred in 1979 after I had delivered my first sermon. We were at the back of the church, and the real minister was introducing us to some of the parishioners. An old, retired priest turned to Lily, saying, 'So he's your man, is he?'

'No,' Lily replied, 'he's God's man.'

Ronald Vankampf, a highly successful middle-aged manager, phoned to request help with his thirty-year marriage. 'I don't know what's wrong with it,' he said. 'As far as I'm concerned, it's fine. But my wife, Gloria, thinks there's something wrong. Only she's not telling me what. So I suggested we try to get an appointment to see you together, and she agreed.'

I explained that I saw new clients only for consultation and no longer did ongoing work. They were welcome to have a session with me, but it was likely that I'd be referring them on to another therapist for actual therapy. The conditions were acceptable and an hour appointment was set up.

It was a remarkably unproductive hour. Ronald had indicated he was happy with his marriage, and he looked it. Handsome and boyish, he appeared to have great zest for life. And, as he had also indicated, Gloria was clearly unhappy over something. She was a physically attractive woman, but her face suggested she had been feeling sad for a long time. She readily acknowledged she'd been depressed for several years. However, she could be no more specific about the reason for her depression except to reiterate, 'I'm sure it's the marriage.'

Because she was unable to offer any complaints about her husband, I attempted to explore with Gloria other possible reasons for her heaviness of spirit. Their two children were grown and had left home. Might it be possible, for instance, that she was suffering from the empty-nest syndrome? But every avenue of inquiry was met with the same refrain: 'No, I'm sure it's the marriage.'

I was perversely intrigued. I had frequently been bored in working with slow-to-change patients over the long haul, but this was the first time in twenty years of practicing psychiatry that I found myself bored in the first interview—and with not one but two clients to boot. *Something* must be going on. I also felt uneasy referring them to any particular therapist without having the slightest handle on what that something was. They took me up on my offer to return for a second hour of consultation. Just before they left I said to Gloria, 'It's our experience that patients' instincts about their own symptoms are usually correct. I suspect you're right that something about your marriage is causing you to be depressed. It may help you to be more specific, Gloria, to realize that depression literally always has to do with anger. When you come back next week I want you to be prepared to tell me something—anything—about Ronald that you're angry over. You've got to do that homework.'

She did do it. She began the next session by stating. 'What makes me angry about Ronald is *his* anger.'

'*My* anger?' Ronald was clearly surprised. 'But I don't get angry.'

'You never get shouting, screaming angry,' Gloria retorted, 'but you're often very irritable. And irritating.'

'Really?' Again Ronald seemed genuinely surprised. 'Like when? I always thought I had an equitable disposition.'

'Like last month when we went to *Figaro*. You were cursing at the cars all the way to Manhattan. You were impatient with the service at the Russian Tea Room. I could hardly talk to you during the intermission. And then you were cursing the cars all the way back to Connecticut. You were absolutely no fun to be with.'

'Well, I was a little bit out of sorts that evening,' Ronald admitted.

'You're almost always irritable when we go to the opera,' Gloria challenged him.

'Is that so? I wasn't aware of it.'

The tension was rising. Ronald looked uncomfortable. 'Do you go to the opera often?' I asked.

'Oh, about six times a year,' Ronald replied.

'So you're really something of opera buffs?'

Gloria nodded in assent. I noted that Ronald did not nod. 'How do you decide when to go to the opera?' I inquired.

Ronald was quick to respond. 'Well, it's a complex of things. We don't have season tickets because my schedule's unpredictable. I often have to go out of town on business. So Gloria just decides which opera she would particularly like to see and asks me if I want to go. If my schedule's clear, then we go.'

'If you want to go,' I repeated. 'Do you like opera, Ronald?'

'Oh, sure, I like opera.'

'Really? You say it as if everyone liked opera. Actually there are many people who find opera tedious.'

Ronald looked profoundly uncomfortable now. 'Well, I'm not exactly sure I like opera quite as much as Gloria,' he said.

'Have you ever been tempted, when Gloria asked you if you wanted to go to an opera, to tell her that no, you didn't want to go, and suggest she go by herself?'

Ronald's obvious discomfort continued. 'No, I couldn't do anything like that.'

'Why not?'

'Well, that's just part of marriage. I mean, I owe it to Gloria to be available to be with her whenever I can.'

At this point Gloria pounced. 'I've often suspected that sometimes you've scheduled your business trips just so you wouldn't have to go to the opera,' she said.

'What would you do, Gloria,' I confronted her, 'if Ralph were to tell you he didn't want to go and proposed you go by yourself?'

It was Gloria's turn to be discomfited. There was a long silence before she answered, 'I don't know.'

There was another long silence before I went on. 'I don't know how many problems the two of you might have in your marriage,' I finally said, 'but it really doesn't matter. In a way, a marriage is made up of problems. But at least we've been able to start clarifying one problem. There is a significant difference between the two of you in regard to your liking of opera. You have not been honest about this difference, Ronald. You've dealt with it by trying to pretend it didn't exist. You've not been up front about it at all. For Christ's sake, you're quite entitled to not like opera. At this point I can't begin to tell you what the right way to deal with this difference is. But I can tell you that it's the wrong way to try to cover it up. Of course you're going to be irritable every time you go to the opera if every time you're making a sacrifice you don't want to make. Your time is valuable and you don't have to sacrifice it every time Gloria might want it, and Gloria's equally entitled to like opera and to do things you don't want to do. There's a better way than the way you both have been doing it, and the two of you need to figure it out.'

Niether Gloria nor Ronald looked the least bit happy.

I referred them to Marsha Morales, a skilled marriage therapist in their locale. 'I'm a little concerned about Mrs Vankampf's depression,' I told her. 'Right now it looks pretty mild and all psychological, but if it gets worse you might want to have your psychiatric consultant check her out again. For the moment, however, her dissatisfaction may be the best thing they've got going for them.'

The practice of psychotherapy would not only be the most enjoyable but also one of the easiest professions were it not for a single reality: resistance.

Personality has been defined as a 'consistent pattern of intergration (or system) of psychic elements.' The key word is consistent. There is a consistency to the personality. It need be so. Our marriage survives in part because I'm pretty much the same old Scotty from week to week and because I do not wake up to find a different Lily every morning. I'd just as soon not be married to someone with a multiple personality disorder. But the dark side of this consistency is that the personality inherently resists change. People who come to psychotherapy do so saying they want to change, and then from the moment therapy starts they usually begin acting as if the last thing on God's earth they want to do is change.

I was delighted to finally get a handle on some of what was going wrong with the Vankampf marriage. A naive onlooker might have expected both Ronald and Gloria to be equally pleased by this initial progress in laying the groundwork for improvement in their relationship. But they did not look pleased. Why? Because at that moment of clarification it dawned on both of them that they would need to change. And that their system of her expectation of togetherness and his superficial compliance with it would also need to change for the marriage to grow.

The personality resists change because it is an entrenched system or organization of psychic elements. As has been pointed out earlier, if a component element changes, then the whole system must change, whether subtly or dramatically. Conversely, if the system changes, the component elements must also change. And all systems resist change. Just as an individual person or personality is a system that resists change, so also a marriage is a system with a personality of its own that tends to struggle against any alteration. By law a coproration is often considered a 'person' in its own right. And, indeed, still larger organizations or systems such as business corporations also have unique personalities of a sort. They too resist change.

Because resistance is such a barrier to organizational health and growth, some of the most advanced business corporations in very recent years have initiated a program of routinely scheduled periods of self-examination. Every two or three years, for instance, they make a practice of 'revisiting their mission statement.' This statement is a crucial document. It sets forth the basic purposes or aims of the organization, and managers are often surprised by how rapidly these can change unawares. They have found it valuable, therefore, at regular intervals to look formally at whether the aims of the business have fallen out of 'sync' with its mission statement, whether these aims need to be brought back into line, or whether the statement itself needs to be rewritten to reflect current realities. At the same time they will often also reanalyze their own 'company norms,' readjusting those that are outdated or dysfunctional. The equivalent in marriage would be for a couple every few years to repeat, revise, or renegotiate their wedding vows. Such a practice might have kept the Vankampfs from falling into difficulty.

Like a corporation or any other organization, the Vankampf marriage had norms. Most of these—their sexual norms, for instance—I never had the chance to discern. But it was a norm for Gloria to initiate requests to go to the opera. It was a norm that Ronald's business trips were an adequate reason to reject the request. It was a norm for him otherwise to comply. It was a norm that they should go to the opera together or not at all. To assist them to better walk the tightrope, as they were leaving my office for further treatment with Marsha Morales, I handed them a copy of Kahlil Gibran's immortal lines on marriage:

> *But let there be spaces in your togetherness,*
> *And let the winds of heaven dance between you.*
> *Love one another, but make not a bond of love:*
> *Let it rather be a moving sea between the shores of your*
> *souls.*
> *Fill each other's cup but drink not from one cup.*
> *Give one another of your bread but eat not from the same*
> *loaf.*

*Sing and dance together and be joyous, but let each of
you be alone,
Even as the strings of a lute are alone though they
quiver with the same music.
Give your hearts, but not into each other's keeping.
For only the hand of Life can contain your hearts.
And stand together yet not too near together:
For the pillars of the temple stand apart,
And the oak tree and the cypress grow not in each
other's shadow.*[1]

I did not have the opportunity to follow up on this case. I
hope the Vankampfs were able to develop a more vibrant,
creative marriage. But I am not necessarily optimistic that
either Gibran or Marsha was able to assist them in doing so
because it had taken them almost thirty years to even begin
to consider their organizational norms. It would be helpful
for couples to apply some of the more advanced business
management practices to marriages earlier in the game.

Ronald Vankampf had never told Gloria he did not like
opera or suggested she go by herself because he felt that to
do so would have been uncivil. His notion of civility
required the pretense that he enjoyed going to the opera
with Gloria. Yet his desire to be civil backfired on them
both, since he ended up actually uncivil during those
outings.

The problem was that he was operating according to a
false definition of civility. His pattern of behavior was largely
unconscious. Despite being a manager himself, he had
never given sufficient thought to his marriage as an
organization to realize that it did not necessarily demand
that he 'owe' Gloria such togetherness. His desire to avoid
conflict with her over their separate tastes was not 'ethical in

[1] Kahlil Gibran, *The Prophet* (New York: Alfred A. Knopf, 1955), pp. 15–16.

submission to a Higher Power.' Gloria was not a higher power; she was a partner. There was no inherent reason her desires should take precedence over his. Moreover, the maintenance of a significant pretense (which his compliance was) is never ethical, and hence never an act of civility.

The hallmark of civility then is *not* conflict-avoiding pretense and politeness. The hallmark is, to the contrary, the commitment to *deal* with the significance of organizational life. Many of these are issues of togetherness and separateness. Issues cannot be dealt with by avoidance. They cannot be dealt with painlessly or dishonestly. Ronald Vankampf got into trouble precisely because in his desire to avoid hurting his wife's feelings, he was evading through pretense a significant issue in their marriage. But un-addressed issues in organizational life, like neuroses in our individual psyches, become ghosts that invariably come back to haunt us, just as they haunted the Vankampfs who had failed for so many years to walk the tightrope.

By now it should be clear that true civility in marriage leads to an early and honest surfacing of issues to encourage their conscious and creative resolution. I deliberately use the word *resolution* instead of *solution*. In a great many marriages there are one or more differences—sexual, religious, philosophical—that cannot be 'solved,' no matter how civil both partners may be. Usually the most civil resolution of such insolvable differences is mutual acceptance and forgiveness. Or an agreement to disagree.

Fourteen years ago my marriage with Lily hit bottom—not quite the rocks, but bottom. At the time I was leading an overnight retreat for ten participants at a small convent. Sister Lucia, who was the guest mistress in charge of the tiny retreat house where we were staying, was eighty-seven if she was a day. That night, after dinner and after I had been lecturing all day, several of the retreatants pulled out bottles of whiskey. Because I'd had a couple of drinks under my belt, because I was in a good deal of emotional pain at the time, and because she had such a kindly old face, I found myself sitting at Sister Lucia's feet telling her that I was feeling badly since I had failed at my marriage.

Sister Lucia beamed. 'Oh, that's just wonderful,' she exclaimed.

'Lord, Scotty,' I thought, 'get a couple of drinks in you and you go shooting your mouth off simply because this nun's got a kindly old face when the reason it's so kindly is probably because she's got no brain left behind it.' I spoke to her again, more loudly now, the way one does to the senile. 'No, no, you didn't understand me. I was telling you I've failed at my marriage.'

Again Lucia beamed. 'Oh, I'm so glad for you,' she answered.

By this time I was becoming seriously annoyed. I practically shouted at her, 'No, no, you haven't heard what I've been saying. Probably you've got a hearing problem. You're quite entitled to have a hearing problem at your age, my dear. But, anyway, you haven't understood anything that I've said, so let's just drop the subject.'

'I've heard and understood you perfectly, young man,' Sister Lucia responded, looking at me keenly. 'You've been telling me that you have failed at your marriage, and I'm so glad for you. Do you know how terrible it would be never to fail? Oh, that would be dreadful!'

I recollected certain people I'd known who felt they had never failed and thought of just how insufferable they were, and I began to think that maybe she did have some gray matter left behind those intelligent eyes. It also occurred to me it was perhaps no accident that both Sister Lucia and I were attempting to follow a Lord of Failure, a man executed at an early age in the standard manner of the day as a petty provincial political criminal, spat upon by his enemies and betrayed by his friends.

It is also, I think, no accident that my marriage with Lily began to considerably improve along about that time. For what happened after I'd concluded I'd failed at my marriage was that, on a certain level, I gave up trying to make it work. And that meant I gave up trying to change Lily. It was also around that same time that Lily decided she too had failed at the marriage, and also stopped trying to make it work and trying to change me. Furthermore, I suspect it is no accident that since that time, both she and I seem to have done a good deal of changing.

This tends to be a pattern in those marriages that survive past the twenty- or twenty-five-year mark: somewhere between fifteen and twenty years of marriage the partners begin to figure out how to stop trying to change each other. Isn't it remarkable how rapidly we human beings learn?

Still, there are some gulfs too wide to be bridged and some disagreements so devastating that they should not be tolerated. How is one to discern those differences that are probably acceptable and those that should be judged unacceptable? Between those with which we should hang in together and those that are not only so irreconcilable but also so vast as to call us out of our marriage commitment? Once again there is no formula. Yet I think that irrevocably unacceptable marital behavior can be discerned on the basis of its chronic incivility. Conversely, while there is no set definition of a good marriage, I believe the essential feature of long-term marital success is sustained, genuine, mutual civility. And that a vocation to marriage is a vocation to civility.

Lily and I have been married for thirty-three years now—much more than half our lifetimes—and it begins to look as though we will make it together until death do us part. We are ever-more conscious of that impending death as more and more we are called to support and encourage each other in facing our separate, different, increasing aches and pains. It's very nice to know that someone's there. There is little that is innocent about us anymore. As I look back on our early love, it was filled with demands and expectations and all manner of unconscious manipulations.

What we have today seems infinitely more compassionate
and respectful of our unique differences.

12

Bows and Arrows

Child Raising and Vocation

On the twenty-third of April, two weeks after his seven-teenth birthday and in the spring semester of his junior year, Seth Crompton walked into the auditorium of his prep school and sat down to take the Preliminary Scholastic Aptitude Tests (PSATs). An hour later he was observed by one of the faculty monitors to have his head down, lying across his examination paper, apparently sound asleep. The monitor shook him awake. He opened his eyes, but they looked glazed. When asked what was wrong, he responded with speech that was slurred, almost unintelligible. Another monitor was summoned. When they helped Seth to his feet, he swayed, and it required both of them to lead him stumbling out of the auditorium, across the quad, and into the infirmary.

The school nurse asked him whether he'd taken drugs. He acknowledged taking four 'pills' but denied knowing what they were. Over the course of the following three hours his speech became progressively less slurred and his gait steadier. He was kept in the infirmary overnight. The next day, facing a faculty committee, Seth continued to deny knowing what kind of pills they were, but with the hint of a smile, said, 'I guess they must have been downers.' Despite serious pressure from the committee, he insisted upon maintaining that he had 'just found the pills on a windowsill of the dormitory bathroom,' and that he had no idea how they'd gotten there. When the committee asked why he'd chosen to take them at that particular time, he blandly told them that he'd been anxious about the exams and had thought he might score better on the assumption that the pills would 'relax him.'

Drug abuse was ordinarily a cause for expulsion from this private boarding school. But because he had been at the school for almost three years, had an above-average academic record, had apparently not been involved in drugs before, did not have a reputation as a troublemaker, and because the committee members intuitively suspected there was something significant about the timing of the incident, the committee broke with tradition. It recommended to the headmaster that Seth not be expelled but be placed on strict disciplinary probation on the condition that he also receive psychiatric care. His parents agreed to this condition. Such were the circumstances under which Seth was referred by the school to me for evaluation and presumably 'treatment.'

My first and overwhelming impression of Seth was that he was *average*. He was of average height and build for a seventeen-year-old, well-fed, prep-school boy, with an average kind of handsomeness (even beauty with his just postpubescent sexuality). He was neither withdrawn nor voluble, and like average adolescents, he was formidably noncommital. In other words, he was not easy to relate to.

'I'm going to make an appointment to meet with your parents,' I informed him. 'I am obliged to tell them what I think *about* you. But by law I cannot tell them—or the school—anything you say to me. Your confidentiality is protected. Do you understand?'

Seth understood. But the guarantee did nothing to either change his story or loosen his tongue. The school was 'fine.' His family life was 'fine.' Everything was 'fine.'

His parents, Henry and 'Buffy' Crompton, a wealthy and neatly manicured couple in their early forties, also assured me during their appointments that everything was 'fine.' Except for one thing. 'I'm worried that by missing the PSATs Seth may have seriously jeopardized his chances of getting into a good college,' Henry said.

'How about you, Mrs Crompton?' I asked. 'Is there anything that worries you?'

'Only what my husband said,' Buffy answered, crossing her well-tanned, shapely legs. 'Seth's been a very stable boy. I'm sure he's not really a psychiatric case.'

'Well, he *is* a psychiatric case under the conditions of his probation,' I commented. 'I honestly don't know whether you have anything more serious to worry about. Seth hasn't opened up to me yet, not that I would have expected him to. My task is to build a relationship with him so that he can feel safe with me. On the outside, he doesn't look depressed or suicidal for the moment. Of course I'll let you know if you do have something to worry about, although I can't let you know anything specific that he does tell me. I must say, however, that I am seriously concerned about *why* he took the pills in the first place and *why* he took them at the particular time he did.'

I chose not to confront them with another worry: their own apparent lack of concern as to the whys of their son's behavior, as if the only thing to worry about was its effect upon his potential college career. There was no point in challenging them unless I had to.

Seth missed his next two appointments with me. This was a common problem with boarding-school patients in a rural area. Transportation services were poor, and their academic and sports schedules were complex. Often reluctant to see a 'shrink' in the first place, they had a host of ready-made excuses. I called the school dean to make sure that Seth would be hand-carried to an appointment so I could at least see him once more before his summer vacation.

When he finally showed up and had given me the usual excuses, I explained that confidentiality did not extend to his behavior, and I had to inform the school when he wasn't keeping his appointments. Ordinarily I would also inform his parents that they were being charged for missed visits. To help get our relationship off to a good start, however, I told him I'd keep quiet about it for the moment. But for the moment only. I made it clear I'd expect things to be different in the future.

Then we talked about his summer plans. He had a job set up painting and repairing sailboats in the pleasant Massachusetts coastal town where the Cromptons lived. He liked sailing and looked forward to working on the boats. I asked him what he thought about coming to see me once a week over the summer. 'I don't see how I can,' he responded. 'I'll be working.'

'Lots of people work during the week,' I countered. 'That's why I see patients all day Saturday. It's my busiest day.'

'I don't think my parents would be willing to drive me all this way.'

'Why are you so sure?'

'Well, they're really into tennis and golf. It would cut their weekends in half.'

'How about driving yourself?'

'I don't have a driver's license yet.' Seth seemed un-embarrassed by this admission.

'How come?'

'I just haven't gotten around to learning how to drive.'

'Your parents haven't tried to teach you?'

'Nah, they're awfully busy. But that's another thing I plan to do this summer. Take a driver's ed course and get my license.'

'Why do I have the feeling, Seth, you just made up that plan on the spur of the moment?'

He didn't look angry at this confrontation. 'Nah, I've been thinking about it for a long time' was his bland response.

I was in a bind. Intuitively I felt that Seth *needed* to see me over the summer. But there was nothing tangible I could base that intuition on in attempting to explain it to parents, who, as he had already suggested, would probably be resistant to the notion. And he too would be resentful at such a major incursion into his summer vacation. So I simply made an appointment to see him again three days after the beginning of the fall term of his senior year. He promised me he would keep it.

He 'forgot,' of course. So it was back to the dean for him to be brought to another appointment. He apologized perfunctorily for missing the first. He looked tan and well. It had been a good summer, he told me. He'd enjoyed his job. He had a girlfriend. He felt happy to be back at school and wanted to work hard to get into a good college. Everything was 'fine.'

'You got your driver's license?' I asked.

'Nah, I kept forgetting my appointments with the instructor. There was so much else to do what with my job and my girl and all.'

Seth missed his next session again. So it was back to the dean. It was the beginning of October now. Time was running out if I didn't start to move. 'Seth, you have a style of relating to the world that we call passive-aggressive,' I began. 'Let me explain what we mean by that. When a passive-aggressive person is angry at something or some-body, he doesn't say it; he just goes and does things to screw it up so he doesn't do what is wanted or expected of him. In other words, he shows his anger only in passive or indirect ways, rather than standing up for himself and fighting back directly. Does that make sense to you?'

'Yeah. But I don't see that it has anything to do with me. I'm not angry about anything.'

'Bullshit,' I responded. 'Everybody's angry about some-thing. For one thing, you're angry about coming to see me. That's natural. Who wants to see a shrink when they're seventeen? You're forced to see me by the school. But rather than being up-front about not wanting to see me, you just forget about your appointments. That's the name of the game, isn't it?'

'Yeah. Seeing you wasn't my idea,' Seth acknowledged.

'So of course you're resentful about it,' I continued. 'I also suspect you didn't want to take drivings lessons. But you weren't able to be upfront about that either. So you forgot about those too.'

'I'd kinda like to drive,' Seth protested.

'Kind of,' I mimicked him. 'Sure, you'd kind of like to drive, but if you really wanted to drive you would have made your appointments, wouldn't you?'

'Well, it wasn't on the top of my list of priorities.'

'I also think you're angry as hell at your parents,' I persisted.

'No, I'm not. Why would I be angry at them?'

'Well, I'm guessing a bit here, Seth,' I began, 'but I hear they don't have much time for you. You told me they're too busy to teach you themselves how to drive. You told me they would be too busy playing golf and tennis to bring you up here on weekends to see me over the summer.'

'Nah, I'm not angry about those things.'

'And, above all,' I continued, seemingly ignoring him, 'I think you're angry at them for trying to force you into a mold. Do they care about you or do they just care that you goose-step off to college according to their schedule?'

'I'm not angry at them,' Seth insisted.

'Do you want to go to college?' I asked.

'Sure, I want to go to college.'

'Then why'd you get zonked out at the PSATs last year?'

'I told you: I was nervous about them and needed to relax. I wouldn't have been so nervous, would I, if I didn't want to go to college?'

I pressed on. 'You said, "Sure, I want to go to college," as if it were obvious, as if there were no other alternative in the world.'

'Well, it's not exactly like I have anything else in mind.' There was a strong hint of sarcasm in his tone, yet simultaneously the hint of a suggestion of wonderment.

'You could drop out and get a job for a year or two,' I countered. 'You could do a postgraduate year. Lots of kids do postgraduate years because they don't feel ready yet to go on to college. They've got a postgraduate program at your school, don't they? I bet even you seniors look up to the postgrad students. I mean, they've got it made. Most of them have already been accepted at collage. They can pretty much personally design their own academic and sports program. Of course, you wouldn't have to do it at your school; you could do it at some other prep school if you wanted a change of scene.'

Seth did not respond. There was a long silence. 'Would you like to do a postgraduate program?' I finally asked.

'I wouldn't mind.'

There was another long silence. 'To be honest, Seth,' I began after I'd collected my thoughts, 'I'm not sure you'll be ready to go on to college next year. Oh, you're intellectually ready. But maybe not emotionally. I think you have a bit more growing up to do, and I think it would be good for you to have another year, a year that would be largely fun and not in lockstep with some rigid, formulistic schedule. What I'd like to do is to see your parents again before our next appointment and recommend a postgraduate year to them. How do you feel about me doing that?'

'I wouldn't mind' was Seth's answer.

Mr and Mrs Crompton had not changed over the summer except, if anything, to look even more well-tanned and self-assured. Everything was still 'fine.' 'Seth did wonderfully at his job and he has a girlfriend. She's a sweet young thing,' Mrs Crompton told me benevolently.

'I understand he didn't get his driver's license,' I commented. 'Does that concern you?'

'Not really,' Henry said. 'It's not as if he needs it at school where he can't have a car anyway. And he can get it next summer, although again there's no particular reason he'll need it in college either. Kids who drive are just more likely to get into trouble.'

'So it didn't bother you a bit?'

'Well, it bothered me that I had to pay for a bunch of missed appointments at the driving school. At first I felt he ought to pay for them out of his own earnings, but then I thought, "Why make a big deal out of it?" I suppose you'd call us rather liberal as parents go.'

As I had expected, it was not going to be easy. 'Getting a driver's license is a major rite of passage for an adolescent in our culture,' I said. 'It's a sign of being grown-up. Adolescents who want to grow up will get their license as soon as possible. On the other hand, when an adolescent hasn't obtained a license by the time he or she is seventeen —or seventeen and a half at the latest—just about invariably it is a sign that they don't feel ready to grow up yet. And I don't think Seth is ready. Of course, since Seth is your oldest child, there's no way you could have been expected to know this sort of thing,' I added, letting them off the hook as far as possible.

'Isn't that interesting, darling,' Buffy asked rhetorically. 'I suppose it must be more difficult to grow up these days as the world gets more and more complicated.'

'It is.' I nodded in superficial agreement. 'Another rite of passage is entering college. I would guess that the reason Seth took drugs at his PSATs last spring was because he didn't feel ready to start the whole college application process. It frightened him. I suspect he didn't want to be that old that fast.'

'You suspect?' Henry inquired. 'Did Seth tell you that?'

'No, it's just a suspicion,' I admitted, 'but so likely to be correct that I want to recommend to you we go slow on this college entrance process. It's not the only way, but one of the best ways for a kid like Seth is to do an extra year of prep school between graduation and college. Oh, they can go ahead and apply to college and get accepted; they just don't have to go quite yet. In fact, colleges like their students to do postgraduate years. When I told Seth I was going to recommend a postgraduate year to you, he was quite amenable. That's another sign. If he was eager to move on, he wouldn't have been.'

'And I suppose you would like to continue to treat him at seventy dollars an hour each week during this so-called postgraduate year?' Henry asked, his voice dripping with hostility and suspicion.

'No. First of all, as I already suggested to Seth, he might want to do a postgraduate year at a different school. That's a common practice. At other times it's better for a kid to stay where he's comfortable. I have no idea which is which in Seth's case yet. Secondly, I also have no idea yet whether Seth will need psychotherapy beyond this year at all. But look,' I added, trying to defuse Henry Crompton's anger, 'I know it's a major recommendation, and one I'm sure you'd like to think about. Why don't you think about it for a couple of weeks and then come back to talk it over with me some more?'

'Another appointment?' Buffy was genuinely aghast. 'Doctor, you're acting as if Seth has a major problem when he's a very well adjusted boy.'

'It's probably not a major problem now,' I said, 'but I think it will be a major problem if you push him faster than he needs to go.'

'It's also a major problem to shell out twelve thousand dollars more than we'd budgeted for his education,' Henry countered.

'You can't afford it?' I asked.

'We can afford any necessary expense for our children. As I said, we're liberal parents. But we cannot afford unnecessary expenses. And you've told us nothing which would certify this to be a necessary expense. You acknowledge it's only a guess, Doctor.'

I fought back my anger for one last try. 'I really believe you're rushing this major decision, Mr Crompton,' I said calmly. 'Surely you know that many things can't be certified. Best guessing is often what child raising is all about. It's not that different from business, is it? Any company that didn't go along with its best guesses would soon be out of business. So why don't you take a couple of weeks to consider it?' I thought the business analogy might appeal to his money-oriented mind.

But it didn't. 'And any business wouldn't even make a

best guess without a great deal more data to go on. You give us more data, Doctor, and then we'll consider your proposal further.'

'How about you, Mrs Crompton?' I asked, aiming for the possibility of some feminine softness. 'Would you be willing to take more time to consider such a sensitive issue?'

'My husband's approach seems very sensible to me,' she replied coldly.

I grew cold in turn. I'd lost, and all that was left was to play the dance out to its disharmonic conclusion. It was psychiatry at its most unpleasant. 'I have another suspicion,' I said. 'I suspect that Seth is very angry at the two of you. He doesn't say so, so it is, indeed, just a suspicion. I'd feel better about him if he were angry, as healthy adolescents usually are at their parents. For me to help him, I need to help him get in touch with his anger toward you, and the best way for me to do that would be family therapy.'

'Family therapy?' Buffy echoed. She was again aghast.

'Yes, where I would see Seth together with the two of you for a series of appointments. And maybe, after a while, bring in your younger children.'

'In order to have our other children angry at us as well?' It was Buffy's turn to be sarcastic now. 'What a novel approach, Doctor!'

'And one which doesn't interest you, I gather?'

'Doctor, I've told you, Seth's a very well adjusted boy. You're making a mountain out of a molehill.'

I continued with the final inexorable moves. 'I have one more recommendation then. Since you are unwilling for family therapy, I recommend that the two of you get into some kind of psychotherapy, separately from Seth. It should obviously be with a therapist other than myself. There's something wrong when parents don't even seriously consider a recommendation their child's therapist makes to them. I think you need to look at that.'

It was Henry's turn. 'Do you try to order everyone who disagrees with you into therapy?'

'Not everyone. No interest again, I gather?'

'None.'

'You realize, of course,' I came back, 'that I will need to tell Seth you have rejected my recommendation for a postgraduate year and for any involvement of your own in his treatment beyond paying his bills.'

'Speaking of which,' Henry asked, 'what happens if I refuse to pay your bills or request the school to refer Seth to a more mature therapist?'

It hurt even though I was quite prepared for this. 'I don't really know,' I responded. 'I would need to give the school my recommendations and my judgment that you haven't seriously considered them. I honestly cannot tell you whether that judgment would propel them to seek another therapist for him or to expel him for violation of their probation agreement with you.'

'What gives you the right to sit in judgement of us?' Henry fought back. 'When we're paying you and we're paying the school? When we're the ones who are paying and you're not? When we're obviously committed to his success in life?'

'How do you define Seth's success in life?' I asked.

'By his getting into and through a good college as expeditiously as possible, so that he can then get a good job and have a good career.'

'What does that have to do with his happiness or goodness as a person?'

The Cromptons were clearly at a boil. 'I'm not going to get into useless word games with you,' Henry shot back.

And Buffy added on, 'Frankly, I resent it, Doctor, that you would make a major recommendation to Seth without consulting us first.'

'I've noticed, Mr and Mrs Crompton, that you both have a significant concern with time and money,' I replied, standing up to signal that our meeting had come to a close. 'Had I made a recommendation to you which was unacceptable to Seth, I *really* would have been wasting your time and money. Because what's acceptable to him is what really counts. You see, he's the number one player in this game. Because, whether we like it or not, he's got a will—and a soul—separate and independent from any of us.'

Surprisingly, the Cromptons did not make a move to fire me, and more surprisingly, Seth showed up unprompted for our next appointment. I told him that his parents had rejected my recommendation of a postgraduate year for him out of hand. 'Does that make you angry?' I asked.

'Nah, why should it?'

'Because, without any serious consideration, they closed off a possible option in your life.'

'I'm not angry,' Seth insisted.

'Well, it pissed *me* off,' I confided. 'They only seemed interested that you proceed along the fastest course possible. It seemed to me very one-dimensional thinking—so much so that I also proposed they get more involved here with your therapy or they get some therapy themselves. But they refused again. They don't even take your need for therapy seriously. They're only going along with it because it's a condition of your probation. How does that make you feel?'

'I'm sure they know what's best for me,' Seth replied, adding, 'I don't even know myself why I need therapy.'

'Good. At least you can tell me that. Do you want to know why I think you need therapy?'

'Yeah.'

'It may sound pretty farfetched to you.'

'Go ahead.'

'Do you remember me telling you last time that you have a style of relating we call passive-aggressive? That you have trouble being up-front with your desires and your anger so that you get your way through means that are indirect and passively underhanded?' Seth nodded. 'Well, that's a common style for young people,' I continued, 'but by the time they're your age they've usually started to grow out of it. If they don't grow out of it, then this style becomes so entrenched in adulthood that they can't respond any differently. It becomes a sort of compulsion. They no longer have the freedom to be up-front. When it gets to that point, it's no more just as style; they have what we call a personality disorder, and it causes them—and others—all kinds of difficulty. I think you need therapy so that you won't end up in such a fix.'

I didn't expect Seth to understand this, but a strange thing happened: he began to keep all of his appointments with me. They were not exciting appointments. In fact, he had so little to say we would spend the first half of each of them playing a series of ongoing chess games. We were evenly matched: neither of us was good and neither terrible. The second half of the hour we would talk, and I would tell him at least as much about myself as he about himself. He would tell me about his girlfriend, about how he took the SATs and scored quite well, how he finished his college applications, the essays he'd written in them, and finally how he was accepted by a mid-ranking college—which seemed to please him. Meanwhile I told him about some of my activities in peace work and my belief in God. He declared himself to be an agnostic. He didn't know about this God business but, to my surprise, seemed to be particularly interested in why I had specifically become a Christian. So I told him gospel stories of Jesus, focusing on ones about how few people understood him, how hurt he was at not being understood, how much of the time he was frustrated and angry, and how on occasion he would let people know how angry he was and would really blast them.

I worried about how little seemed to be happening during these sessions, but there is a general rule in psychotherapy — one particularly true in treating adolescents—that if the patient keeps showing up for his appointments, *something* worthwhile must be happening. I did take the risk in stirring up the waters in late April, after he'd been accepted at college, by pointing out, 'You know, you're still on probation. It's been over a year now, and you've not been in any more trouble. I'm sure if you asked about it, the dean would take you off.'

'Yeah, I'll do that.' Seth seemed enthusiastic.

'I wonder why you didn't think of it yourself?'

'I dunno. I guess I just assumed it had to go on until the end of the year.'

'There is one possible little problem, though,' I went on, curious as to what his reaction would be. 'If you get taken off probation, you'll no longer have to see me, and then your parents might not want to pay for you to see me anymore.'

Seth smiled conspiratorially. 'Well, I guess I'll just have to stay on probation. These visits have become sort of a habit. I'd miss them.'

'I'd miss them too,' I acknowledged. 'But, you know, we've only got about five left. So it looks like you're going to have to miss them anyway, sooner or later. How do you feel about that?'

'I'll get along,' Seth said.

'Yeah, I will too,' I responded. 'But I'll still miss you.'

The phone rang on the Saturday evening before our last appointment. 'You son of a bitch!' the voice said on the other end of the line. It was a man's voice.

'Who's this?' I asked, all my muscles tensing.

'You know goddamn well who it is. This is Henry Crompton, you son of a bitch.'

'What's the matter?'

'You mean you don't know? They've kicked Seth out. One week before graduation.'

'*What? Why?*'

'Cheating. The little bastard cheated on one of his final exams. Plagiarized or something.'

'Oh, my God!' I was stunned. 'How is he?'

'How is he? I'll tell you how he is. He's out of school. He's out of college. We spent all that money on him for nothing. And you, you goddamn son of a bitch, we spent all that money on you for nothing. You not only didn't do anything; you turned him against us. "Dr Peck cares for me more than you do," he tells us. Well, I tell you what I'm going to do, you son of a bitch. I'm not going to pay your last bills.

184

Furthermore, I'm going to report you to the medical society for malpractice and alienation of affection. And I damn well may sue you.'

'Where's Seth now?'

'Where is he? He's at school, of course. We're picking him up Monday. Why?'

'Because I want to see him before he goes.'

'To alienate him some more, is that it?'

'Would you like to see him with me?'

'I'm never going to set eyes on you again, you son of a bitch.'

'Why did you call me, Mr Crompton?'

There was a long pause. As I suspected, he'd called without thinking. 'To let you know I'm going to get your ass,' he finally said.

'Yes, I think you called because you're angry,' I responded, 'and I don't blame you for being angry. It must be one hell of a disappointment for you and Mrs Crompton. I can really understand. But I'm also going to see Seth tomorrow, if it's at all possible. Because I suspect he's feeling pretty awful also. And because I need to say good-bye to him. I won't charge you for that visit. But I will be charging you for all his other visits. If you don't pay my bill, then I'll just have to send it to a collection agency. Whether that would hurt your credit rating, I don't know. You are free, of course, to complain about me to the medical society or even sue me, if that's what you want. But I remind you that you rejected each of the recommendations I made to you, so I hope when you calm down you'll think better of it. I also hope you'll be kind to Seth. Much as he's disappointed you, he needs your support at this time. Not your financial support, but your emotional support. I've gotten to know him pretty well. Despite what he's just done, inside he's really a very good kid. I know. And if there's anything I can do for any of you at any time, please give me a call.'

'I told you, I'm never going to set eyes on you again, you

son of a bitch,' Henry Crompton said just before he slammed down the phone.

I drove over to the school the next morning to bring Seth back to my office. It would have been simpler just to see him in his dormitory room, but I sensed it would be best for him to say good-bye not only to me but also to the office we'd shared. When we got settled, I thought I detected a slight quiver in his lower lip. It would probably be easy to help him cry, but was that what he needed? I didn't know yet. 'Well, I guess I really blew it, didn't I?' he began.

'Maybe, maybe not,' I answered noncommittally. 'Was that what you wanted to do? To blow it?'

'I don't think so.'

'What happened?'

'It was an essay exam. We'd been told beforehand we could write on any one of three issues. I went to the library and dug up one of the references mentioned in the textbook. I read it over a few times and then paraphrased it for my answer on the exam. I guess the teacher must have read the same reference and I guess I didn't paraphrase it well enough. He went to the library and found I'd checked out the reference. So I was caught.'

'Okay, but why?'

'I dunno. It just seemed easier than making up my own answer. I'm lazy, I guess.'

'I don't buy it, Seth,' I came back at him. 'It's not ordinary laziness. You're not a lazy person. The past eight months you've come for every one of your appointments when it would have been easier to just forget about them, the way you used to. And it probably took more effort to look up that reference than it would have to make up your own answer. I think you wanted to blow it. I think it has to do with this passive-aggressive thing.'

'Well, I wasn't conscious of it,' he said. 'But I have been thinking about it. It was really stupid. Even if I'd never answered the question at all, even if I'd gotten an F on the exam, I still would have passed the course for the year, and would have graduated. I did blow it, didn't I?'

'Do you think you could have blown it because you didn't want to go to college?'

'I told you, not consciously. Maybe unconsciously.'

'So what happens now?'

I'd expected Seth to say passively, 'I dunno.' Instead, his whole carriage suddenly became decisive. 'I learned Friday morning that I'd been discovered and would probably be kicked out. I called the navy recruiting office that afternoon. It sounds like they'll be able to take me in a couple of weeks. I have an appointment with the recruiting officer Tuesday morning. I'm going to enlist in the navy. Four years.'

I whistled, partly in surprise and partly in admiration. 'Wow, that's brilliant!' I exclaimed.

'You mean you approve of it?' It was Seth's turn to be surprised.

'Sure. I think it's a very smart move. Among other things, you like boats.'

'But I thought you were a peacenik.'

'I am. But that doesn't mean I'm a total pacifist or against the military in all respects. I spent almost a decade in the army, remember?' I reminded him. 'In many ways I admire the military, and one of the healthy functions it fulfills is to serve as a moratorium for young people just like yourself?'

'A moratorium?'

'Yes. It means a kind of time out, a time when major decisions don't have to be made. Many people your age need such a time, a space to grow when great things are not expected of them. That's why I'd proposed a postgraduate year for you, because it would be such a time, such a space. But a hitch in the navy could serve you just as well. Yes, I think it's probably a very smart move.'

Seth practically beamed.

'I hear you told your father that I care for you more than he does,' I moved on, knowing how much we had to accomplish in this last hour.

'Yes. I guess I shouldn't have, should I?' Now Seth was

blushing. 'But he was so angry at me—I mean it was a tirade where I couldn't even get a word in edgewise—somehow I just felt like fighting back.'

'Congratulations. I'm really proud of you.'

'Huh?'

'To my knowledge, it's the first time you've ever fought back against your parents. That you've ever stood up to your father, and he's not an easy man to stand up to. For once you weren't passive-aggressive. You spoke your mind. Congratulations.'

'I was really pissed off. I mean, I *am* pissed off at them. All they care about is college, college, college. They care more about me going to college than they care about me. You care about me.'

'I do care about you, Seth, and I think you're full justified in being angry at them. They *are* rigid. But I'm not sure they don't care about you at all,' I added. 'You see, it's pretty easy for me to care about you, above and beyond the fact that I find you likable. I'm trained to know how to care for people. I get paid for it. I generally do it by appointment. So in some ways it's much simpler to be a psychotherapist than a parent. Still, it's also not easy to be a son either, and you're perfectly entitled to be angry at your parents' shortsightedness.'

We fell silent for a long moment before I went on to tie up another loose end. Seth needed more than just congratulations. 'Whatever your motives, no matter how unconscious they were, the fact remains that you cheated on an exam. How do you feel about that?' I asked.

'It was stupid' was Seth's reply.

That wasn't good enough for me. 'You're going to do lots and lots of stupid things in your life,' I said. 'It's human to make stupid mistakes. Does that mean you're going to cheat again?'

'I hope not.'

'Oh, why?'

'Well ... well, I don't want to be a cheater. I mean, cheating's not just stupid; there's something not right about it.'

'Yes, that's why they kicked you out, wasn't it? But now that they've punished you, do you feel badly about it?'

Seth looked crestfallen. 'You know, I really didn't when I came here. Mostly I was just angry and feeling sorry for myself. And I'm glad I'm going into the navy and not going to college. But I wish I could have done it in an honest way. I guess it was easier to cheat than stand up for myself. Shit.'

The expletive signified real contrition. 'Feeling that way makes it easy to forgive you,' I said, standing up. 'And for God,' I added. 'It's also easy because I like you. I suspect God likes you too, Seth. I'm going to miss you. As for God, he'll be moving right along with you.'

Then I drove him back to school to face his parents in the morning and the navy recruiter the day thereafter. It so happened the Cromptons did pay my bill and did not make a complaint against me to the medical society, despite the fact that they no longer had a perfectly average son.

The varieties of cruelty parents can inflict on their children are endless. But in considering the nature of incivility, we are looking at only the more subtle examples. The Cromptons did not beat, starve, or maim Seth. It might seem they were wicked in their insensitivity, but I suspect I saw them at their worst. They would never have treated him illegally. They did support him well financially. In their own minds, and according to their own lights, they truly wanted what was best for him; the only problem was that they were utterly thoughtless about it. It is this kind of everyday thoughtlessness or everyday incivility that we are examining.

I spoke of how *average* Seth seemed when I first met him, and I have used this story precisely because his was such an average case. I doubt there are many psychotherapists who have not seen similar cases. A reason for this is that one of the more common forms of subtle incivility in child raising is the failure of parents to significantly attempt to discern the vocations of their children.

The corollary is that it is an essential task of parenthood not only to provide for children but also to try to sense who they really are. Narcissists cannot do this. Since they are unable to appreciate the 'otherness' of people, they are unable to envision their own children as unique individuals with differing destinies. Instead they think of their off-spring as narcissistic extensions of themselves, who are 'bad' whenever they do not conform to parental expectations. The Cromptons seemed to be treating Seth as such an 'extension' or 'It.'

It is no accident that the most beautiful words I know on the subject of child raising—again those of Kahlil Gibran —address just this issue:

> *Your children are not your children.*
> *They are the sons and daughters of Life's longing for itself.*
> *They come through you but not from you,*
> *And though they are with you yet they belong not to you.*
>
> *You may give them your love but not your thoughts,*
> *For they have their own thoughts.*
> *You may house their bodies but not their souls,*
> *For their souls dwell in the house of tomorrow, which you cannot visit, not even in your dreams.*
> *You may strive to be like them, but seek not to make them like you.*
> *For life goes not backward nor tarries with yesterday.*
> *You are the bows from which your children as living arrows are sent forth.*
> *The archer sees the mark upon the path of the infinite, and He bends you with His might that His arrows may go swift and far.*
> *Let your bending in the archer's hand be for gladness;*
> *For even as He loves the arrow that flies, so He loves also the bow that is stable.*[1]

[1] *The Prophet*, pp. 17–18.

To analyze more fully the Cromptons' parental incivility, recall the definition of civility as 'consciously motivated organizational behavior that is ethical in submission to a Higher Power.' First of all, their behavior was thoughtless. Thoughtfulness takes time, and they wouldn't even take the time to think about my questions or recommendations. Their response to Seth was narcissistically instinctive rather than conscious.

They were also unconscious of the true nature of that organization called the nuclear family. They had apparently never given significant consideration to the proper ethical relationship between children and parents, between bows and arrows. They therefore shot carelessly, missing the mark.

Finally, the concept of Higher Power so central to Gibran's lines seemed absent from Buffy and Henry Crompton's notions of the responsibilities of parenthood. In attempting to discern their children's separate vocations, civil parents must ask not so much, 'What do I want from my child?' as 'What, from the broader viewpoint of an ideal observer, does this God-given child most need that we can offer?'

The failure to adequately discern a child's vocation takes two forms. One is to misread that vocation entirely. Most of us know parents who have done this, who have pushed their violinist children to become athletes or their naturally athletic children to be scholars. It causes great, unnecessary suffering.

The other, more subtle form is to misjudge the timing of a vocation. This was the Cromptons' sin in spades. It was not so much that they were blind to Seth's eventual needs as they were to the pace that he required. They not only wanted him to become an educated adult; they wanted this to occur according to a schedule purely of their making, an inflexible schedule lacking in any imagination or room for his own movement.

It is crucial to note that children usually have a far better sense of their own vocation than do their parents. Consequently, when we ask how parents can best discern the vocation of their children, the first answer is, 'Listen to them.' Observe them. It was my impression of Buffy and Henry Crompton that they were sufficiently narcissistic and overcontrolling that they not only couldn't listen but that Seth probably couldn't safely talk to them. This is why he was essentially forced into a passive-aggressive style of expressing his needs through the indirect actions that psychotherapists call 'acting out' behavior. And, even then, they weren't willing to listen to the message in this seemingly self-destructive behavior.

In defense of parents it must be said that it is no easy matter to discern a child's vocation. The problem was clearly stated by Saint Thérèse of Lisieux, who was a novice mistress (a parental equivalent) of her convent. At the age of twenty-three she wrote, in effect, 'One of the most difficult things about being a spiritual director is to encourage people along paths you would not choose for yourself.'[2] How true! (I wonder how Thérèse could have figured that out at twenty-three when I was still trying to figure it out at forty-six?)

The difficulty is compounded by the reality that much of the time our children may not have a particular vocation or, if they do, are quite likely to misidentify it themselves. How do parents know what to do then? How do you know when to push them into colleges or jobs when they seem to have no desire to move at all? Even after prayerful consideration, we usually have no certainty whether to intervene in the life of a child who *seems* to be following a false call. Or whether to leave children alone to flow as they will. And how do you know what to do when you have no reason to believe they will learn from their mistakes?

You don't. A vocation to parenthood is a vocation to live with enormous uncertainty. The problem with the

[2] Saint Thérèse of Lisieux, *Story of a Soul*, trans. John Clarke, Q.C.D. (Washington, D.C.: Institute of Carmelite Studies Publications, 1976), p. 238.

Cromptons was that they had such definite plans for Seth when they were actually in the dark. They were unwilling to wait in the 'emptiness of not knowing.' To fulfill the role of parent with true civility is to play a role of glory. It requires us, on occasions when we are utterly unsure whether we are doing the right thing, to act with vigor—even in the certain knowledge it will incur our beloved child's wrath against us. Mostly, however, it requires us to do nothing except exist in helpless prayer. The holy agony of it was once described in a poem of parenting:

For Julia, in the Deep Water[3]

The instructor we hire
Because she does not love you
Leads you into deep water,
The deep end
Where the water is darker.
Her open, encouraging arms
That never get nearer
Are merciless for your sake.

You will dream this water always
Where nothing draws nearer.
Wasting your valuable breath
You will scream for your mother—
Only your mother is drowning
Forever in the thin air
Down at the deep end.
She is doing nothing,
She never did anything harder.
And I am beside her.

I am beside her
In this imagination.
We are waiting

[3] John N. Morris, *The New Yorker*, October 25, 1976, p. 158.

Marriage and the Family

Where the water is darker.
You are over your head.
Screaming, you are learning
Your way toward us,
You are learning how
In the helpless water
It is with our skill
We live in what kills us.

Saint Thérèse, as a novice mistress, was a 'child raiser.' The role of parent can be filled by many who are not the actual biological parents. As a psychotherapist I have seen dozens of women and men who, as children, were victims of brutal incivility from fathers and mothers, but whose souls were literally saved by a conscientious and loving aunt or uncle or grandparent. It is no accident that the head of a convent is so often referred to as as the 'Mother Superior.' Or the leader of a monastery as the 'Abbot' (which is derived from the same word as *Abba*, or 'Daddy'). This chapter has focused upon examples of incivility. It is proper for contrast to offer at least one instance of civility. The most touching example of discernment of vocation by a person in a parental role was provided me (as its beneficiary) by my high school teacher, Mr Lynch.

At the age of fifteen, in the middle of my junior year, I quit Exeter, one of the most highly regarded preparatory schools in the nation. As I look back on that turning point in my life, I am amazed at the grace that gave me the courage to do it. Not only was I dropping out of a prestigious prep school against my parents' wishes, but I was walking away from a golden WASP track that had all been laid out for me. Hardly aware that it was what I was doing, I was taking my first giant step out of my entire culture. That culture of 'the establishment' was what one was supposed to aspire to, and I was throwing it away. And where was I to go? I was forging into the total unknown. I was so terrified I thought I should seek the advice of some of Exeter's faculty before finalizing such a dreadful decision. But which of the faculty?

The first candidate who came to mind was my advisor. He had barely spoken to me for two and a half years, but he was reputedly kindly. A second obvious candidate was the crusty old dean of the school, known to be beloved to tens of thousands of alumni. But I thought that three was a good round number, and the third choice was more difficult. I finally hit upon Mr Lynch, my math teacher, a somewhat younger man. I chose him not because we had any relationship or because he seemed to be a particularly warm sort of person—indeed, I found him a rather cold, mathematical kind of fish—but because he had a reputation for being the faculty genius. He'd been involved with some kind of high-level mathematics with the Manhattan Project, and I thought I should check out what I was considering with a 'genius.'

I went first to my kindly advisor. He let me talk for about two minutes and then gently broke in. 'It's true that you're underachieving here at Exeter, Scotty, but not so seriously that you won't be able to graduate. It would be preferable for you to graduate from a superior school like Exeter with lesser grades than from a lesser school with better grades. It would also look bad on your record for you to switch horses in midstream, Besides, I'm sure your parents would be quite upset, so why don't you just go along and do the best you can?'

Next I went to the crusty old dean. He let me speak for thirty seconds. 'Exeter is the best school in the world,' he harrumphed. 'Damn fool thing that you're thinking of doing. Now you just pull yourself up by the bootstraps, young man!'

Feeling worse and worse, I went to see Mr Lynch. He let me talk myself out. It took about five minutes. Then he said he didn't yet understand, and asked if I would just talk some more about Exeter, about my family, about God (he actually gave me permission to talk about God!)—about anything that came into my head. So I rambled on for another ten minutes—fifteen minutes in all, which was pretty good for a depressed, inarticulate, fifteen-year-old. When I was done, he inquired whether I would mind if he asked me some questions. Thriving on this adult attention, I replied, 'Of course not,' and he queried me about many different things for the next half-hour.

Finally, after forty-five minutes in all, this supposedly cold fish sat back in his chair with a pained expression on his face and said, 'I'm sorry. I can't help you. I don't have any advice to give you. You know,' he continued, 'it's impossible for one person to ever completely put himself in another person's shoes. But insofar as I can put myself in your shoes—and I'm glad I'm not there—I don't know what I would do if I were you. So, you see, I don't know how to advise you. I'm sorry that I've been unable to help.'

It is just possible that that man saved my life, and that I'm able to be sitting here writing this today because of Mr Lynch. For when I entered his office that morning over forty years ago, I was close to suicidal, and when I left I felt as if a thousand pounds had been taken off my back. Because if a *genius* didn't know what to do, then it was all right for me not to know what to do. And if I was considering a move that seemed so insane in the world's terms, and a genius couldn't tell me that it was clearly, obviously demented, well then maybe, just maybe, it was something God was calling me to.

So it was that that man, who didn't have any answers or quick formulas, who didn't know what I should do and was willing to be empty, who was the one who provided the help I needed. It was that man who listened to me, who gave me his time, who tried to put himself in my shoes, who extended himself and sacrificed himself for me, who loved me. And it was that man who healed me. It was an extraordinary act of civility.

I have focused on the issue of children's vocations in this chapter on parenthood because that is where even relatively civil parents have trouble. But I hardly mean to imply that the discernment of vocation is all there is to parenting. Even more important is the whole matter of the character development of children. I give it short shrift, however, for two reasons. One is that it could fill a whole volume in itself. Paradoxically, the other is that it is a simple matter: Behave the way you would want your children to behave. Parents are the most important models that children have. With relatively few exceptions, civil parents automatically raise civil children, and uncivil parents uncivil children. Such modeling is primarily wordless: 'Handsome is as handsome does,' my grandfather used to quote. So it is that 'Do as I say, not as I do' parents will be the progenitors of boys and girls who, when they grow up, will likely be telling their own children in turn, 'Do as I say, not as I do.' And so on down through the generations.

Still, from time to time, it is necessary for civil parents to verbally instruct their children in moral development. My own parents had a great deal of difficulty when it came to my vocational choices, but many of the even more important things they handled quite well. I am particularly grateful for the graceful way in which my mother and father worked together in scolding, teaching, or disciplining me. I have spoken of the tightrope wives and husbands should walk between extremes of separateness and togetherness. There is, however, one area in which I come down foursquare in favor of togetherness in marriage: It is extremely important for parents to come together sufficiently so as to speak to their children with a 'single voice.'

Nothing can be more destructive for children (at least until they are well into adulthood—say, past thirty-five) than to have Father telling them one thing and Mother telling them another. It literally tears them apart. Indeed, one of the few legitimate reasons for divorce occurs, in my judgement, when parents are consistently unable to communicate sufficiently with each other to reach any coherent agreement on how to address their children. Divorce is a terribly painful thing for children. Perhaps the chief value of school grades is as an indicator of a student's emotional health. Consequently, it is common when a child's parents get divorced to see his or her grades plummet. Occasionally, however, when parents divorce, one can watch the child's grades go shooting up because he or she no longer has to live in the midst of that terrible confusion and chaos of mixed messages.

I have said there are only two valid reasons to get married: for the care and raising of children and for the friction. Nowhere has the civil friction between Lily and me been more constructive than in our child raising. There are innumerable times when I would have been too harsh with the children had Lily not gentled my judgment, and quite a few when I would have been too gentle had not Lily said, 'Hey, Scotty, I think this is a time for tough love.' And vice versa, I to her.

But this coming together to reach agreement on how to speak to children with a single, considered, conjoint voice requires time—high-quality time. One of the most important tricks that we have learned in the thirty-three years of our marriage has been how to make appointments with each other. Initially, this seemed stultifying and unromantic. Should you have to make an appointment just to talk to your wife or husband? But the problem, you see, was that in our earlier days I would raise some complicated issue about our marriage in the kitchen when Lily was in the midst of preparing dinner for a party of twelve. Or I would come home after a long day, stretched to the limit, and as soon as I crossed the threshold Lily would hit me with an incredibly complex problem about one of the children when there was no reason the problem couldn't have waited an hour or even a day or two.

So, what each of us has learned is to say these days, 'Hey, honey, there's this particular matter I want to talk with you about. When would be a good time?' And we will make an appointment for later in the day, or later in the week, or even later in the month. It is a time to which we come not only after having seriously contemplated the issue but also when we are able to be totally available to each other—not just to talk but even more to listen. I am amazed at how few couples have learned this trick. The vocations to marriage and to child raising are too important to be fulfilled haphazardly.

Having, I hope, struck a strong blow for togetherness, let me return to the necessity for separateness in family life. For in Western industrialized societies it is our number one task as parents to encourage and enable our children ultimately to separate from us.

Early in my psychiatric career I observed a strange pattern. Children who grew up in warm, loving, nurturing homes usually had relatively little difficulty in leaving those homes, whereas children raised in cold homes filled with hostility and incivility often had great difficulty leaving them. Logically, the opposite should have held true. It seemed to me that children growing up in warm, nurturing, loving homes would want to stay there, while those in cold and hostile homes would want to get the hell out.

But gradually it dawned on me that the experience of their home life tends to shape children's visions of the world. If they grow up in a warm, nurturing home, they tend to envision the world as a warm, nurturing place and think, 'Hey, I want to move out there; I want more of this.' Children raised in cold and hostile homes, however, tend to see the world as a cold, hostile place and think, 'I don't want to go out there. At least here I know what the rules are and how to keep myself safe.' Parental civility, then, provides the springboard from which children can leap into a separate, independent adulthood.

Even under the best of circumstances this leap, this separation, is a difficult task. Remember how terrified I was in leaving Exeter, which was the beginning of my leap, and how Seth at seventeen was not even ready to make that beginning. Indeed, from being able to observe our own three now-grown children over the course of their lives, I have come to believe this process of separation is the central theme—the overriding dynamic—of our adolescent years and even our twenties and thirties.

It goes way beyond a matter of simple geographical separation; it is a deep psychological and spiritual process. Carl Jung labelled the process 'individuation' and held it to be the very goal of psychological development. As previously stated, this is a goal most of us fail to reach fully. Most people never become true individuals, wholly able to think for themselves. To a greater or lesser extent they remain until death emotionally or intellectually, if not geographically, tied to their parents' aprons strings, unable to completely liberate themselves from the out-dated values of family and clan.

The failure of parents to realize that the essential function of the nuclear family organization is to encourage the individuation of children is a root failure of civility. And parental narcissism is the essential ingredient of this failure. Severe narcissists cannot see others, including their own children, as even being separate from themselves at all. Such total blindness is obviously going to interfere seriously with—if not demolish—the process of their children's separation from them. Lesser narcissists will recognize when their children start to become separate individuals, but then they 'hostilize' them: the children become one of *them*, the enemy. Obviously, this lack of respect for the otherness of their children will also impede the separation process.

We saw considerable evidence of narcissism in Henry and Buffy Crompton's treatment of Seth. They would not even contemplate the possibility he might have a timetable or goals different from the ones in their own minds. Because he sensed the narcissistic rage and rigidity with which they would react to any overt adolescent rebellion, he had to insist that everything was 'fine.' This necessity to deny normal anger forced him into self-destructive, passive-aggressive behavior.

But sometimes things work out. Almost four years to the day after I had last seen him, Seth phoned me asking for an appointment. He had just been released from the navy, he told me, and was in no difficulty. He simply wanted to see me again to 'catch me up,' and would be happy to pay for the appointment himself. I told him that such follow-up was at least as much to my benefit as his, and there would be no charge.

My first impression on seeing him again was paradoxical. On the one hand, physically he hardly looked a day older. On the other, there was something indefinable about his carriage and presence that made him seem even more mature than his twenty-two years.

'For the most part I liked the navy,' he told me. 'A year and a half ago I was even thinking I might make it a career. But it was sort of like I was saying to my parents in my mind, "Screw you, I'm damned if I'm going to go to college, since that's what you want me to do so much." Yet gradually I realized that I was basically smarter than most of the people in the navy, even many of the officers, so it started to feel like a dead end to me. And whether my parents wanted me to go to college was irrevelant to whether I wanted to go.

'So I'm off to U. Mass. in the fall. I could get into a more prestigious college if I wanted, but then I'd be older than almost all my classmates. U. Mass. has a more mature student body, and besides, it's cheap. My GI bill will pay for it. My parents have been good to me financially. All the time I was in the navy they put money in a trust fund for me, so I've got a nice little nest egg. I may use it to go to medical school.

'Speaking of my parents, we get along pretty well on the surface. I'd come home whenever I got leave, and they'd go their way and I'd go mine. But it's a real superficial relationship. In fact, they're superficial. I mean, Jesus, it's like the country club is their whole life. Why can't they grow up?'

I complimented Seth on how *he'd* grown up and how far he'd managed to emotionally separate himself from his parents. Just before he left I told him, 'Maybe, somehow, your parents will grow, and maybe they won't. If they don't, you may find one day that you will need to forgive them for not growing if you're going to be totally separate from them in the healthiest sense. But not now. That's for the future.'

I didn't tell him that even the healthiest of us don't usually manage to pull off that final trick of separation until we're in our forties.

13

Karass or Grandfaloon?

The Family as Organization

In agrarian societies the extended family or clan is likely to be an economic as well as social unit, with a relatively stereotypical—indeed, often rigidly prescribed—form of organization. In industrialized, culturally diverse societies such as the United States, however, it generally no longer serves much of an economic function. Its members are often geographically dispersed. Consequently, the forms of its organization are so variable that it is difficult to generalize about them. Still, a few important things can be said—and need to be said—about the 'modern' family as an organization.

First, even when it no longer serves an economic function, the extended family can serve many invaluable social purposes. I have already mentioned the legions of children from abusive nuclear families who have been literally saved by a relationship with a loving aunt or uncle or grandparent. If actively present, grandparents provide children with a sense of history and rootedness. Grandchildren, in turn, may give their grandparents a sense of meaning in their old age and a connection with both the present and the future. Cousins, if they discover each other, broaden each other's horizons.

But families can also be oppressive, sterile institutions. Although family was a more important organization in first-century Palestine than it is today, Jesus took pains to make it clear that he was no great family man. He announced that he came not to bring peace, but a sword, that dealing with him would set children against their parents and brothers and sisters against each other.[1] When a disciple asked for a delay in order that he might attend his father's funeral, Jesus coldly told him, 'Let the dead bury the dead.'[2] Jesus needed repeatedly to make it clear that one's primary calling is to God, not one's family, and that vocation takes precedence over family loyalty. He needed to do this because he was fighting against the idolatry of family of his day.

Two thousand years later millions upon millions of individuals must continue to struggle against it. The idolatry of family occurs whenever family togetherness becomes an idol, when it becomes more important to do or say what will keep the family matriarch or patriarch happy than it is to do or say what God wants you to do or say. This idolatry has posed a problem with which the majority of my patients have had to wrestle in the course of psychotherapy. Remember that Christian theology holds that God covenants with individuals, and not with organizations, including families. But it is not necessary to speak of this in religious terms. Secular psychotherapists for decades have been instructing their patients that allegiance to their own personal growth properly supersedes allegiance to family norms.

One reason for the idolatry of family is the old misconception of civility as a kind of invariable politeness that never makes waves. Consequently, many who dare to disagree with parents, grandparents, uncles, aunts, or siblings feel guilty, as if such disagreement by definition makes them uncivil. So again it must be repeated that true civility has only something to do with politeness and *nothing* to do with not making waves when waves are called for. Rather, it has lots to do with honesty and openness and challenging unrealistic family or other organizational norms. It is civil to oppose others when one is doing so in submission to a Higher Power. Conversely, to reject a vocation in favor of a

[1] Matthew 10:34–36.
[2] Matthew 8:21–22.

show of family tranquility is a decision of cowardly incivility and a betrayal of God.

Another reason the idolatry of family is so common is that the abuse of power by authority figures in families, as in other organizations, is so common. In a sense, parents are God's representatives to children. Many parents, in their narcissism, go way beyond appropriately humble representation by believing and acting as if they were God. They suggest that the wrath of God will be called down if they are defied. And temporal power may also be inflicted by the fist. When such parents become elderly they may still maintain their power through what I call 'the tyranny of the aged,' conveying the blackmailing message, 'You'd better do or say what I want you to do or say, or else I will probably have a heart attack and die.' To reject a vocation in favor of family tranquility is cowardly; the converse is that defiance of the family matriarch or patriarch in order to follow God's will is often an act of considerable bravery.

A third reason for the idolatry of family is the fifth of the Ten Commandments: 'Honor your father and mother that your days may be long upon the land.' From the standpoint of psychiatry, it is probably the only thing in the entire Bible that needs rewriting. Radical rewriting. For the most part, children naturally want to honor their parents. The problem comes when their parents are, in reality, dishonorable people. All manner of self-destructive mind control—self-lying—has been practiced by children through the generations in the attempt to respect reprehensible parental behavior in the name of such biblically misdirected 'civility.' Untold neuroses have resulted. I do not think it an oversimplification to state that twice as many psychotherapeutic hours are spent attempting to deal with the ill effects of the Fifth Commandment as are spent on any other psychological problem.

A fourth reason is that families, like all other organizations, are systems. Systems resist change. Break with a family tradition and no wonder the system will fight back.

You have upset the balance of things, and the family norms may have to change.

Finally, perhaps as a holdover from our agrarian past, there still remains an ethic in industrial society that family loyalty is a great value. 'Blood is thicker than water,' we say, implying thereby that it *should* be thicker. Taken literally, for instance, it would mean we should never marry anyone our families disapprove of. It also implies that we should like our family more than others and enjoy their company more than that of 'strangers.' As a psychotherapist I have had to assist many who were not only struggling with their anxieties about making family waves but also with great guilt over the simple fact that they often did not feel comfortable with their families.

In this psychotherapeutic work I have been greatly assisted by Kurt Vonnegut, who in his novel *Cat's Cradle* coined two neologisms: 'karass' and 'grandfaloon.' By grandfaloon he meant a meaningless group. He used the example of Hoosiers. The stranger sitting next to me on a flight to Paris asks me where I'm from, and when I tell him 'Muncie,' he slaps my thigh and exclaims, 'Wow, no kidding! I'm from Gary. We're both Hoosiers. We gotta get together in Paree.' I would not take too kindly to his suggestion, since as Vonnegut pointed out, Hoosiers are a grandfaloon—a meaningless grouping. The fact that we might both live within the geographical confines of the state of Indiana is a matter of chance that fails to imply that we have or should have any relationship. It is a nonexistent connection.

By a karass, on the other hand, Vonnegut meant a distinctly meaningful grouping of human beings. It is not so simple to categorize as a grandfaloon. Superficially, the members of a karass may not have much in common, such as geography or age or race or socioeconomic status. For instance, the nonprofit organization board of directors on which I sit currently consists of eleven members: myself (an author), a psychotherapist, a retired company president, a nun, an artist, a business executive, a lawyer, a homemaker, a clergyman, a flight attendant, and a school principal. Most of us are Christians, but some are not. We have known each other anywhere from two to thirteen years. We are six men and five women. We range in age from thirty-five to sixty-five. Three of us are relatively wealthy, but eight of us have little money to spare. We dwell in seven different states. But what we all do have in common is that each of us, by one route or another, has been *called* to assume the responsibilities of trusteeship of this rather unusual organization and, hence, to serve closely together as a unit with the utmost civility that we can summon. Wc arc a karass. We have been brought together not by superficial commonalities but by invisible forces that seem distinctly mysterious, if not at times a bit cosmic.

That which was originally a karass may become a grandfaloon. I am reminded how, when Lily and I first moved into a large military housing area on Okinawa, a lady from a house across the street greeted us by saying, 'Oh, we'll have to have you over for tea. We're neighbors.' She undoubtedly felt she was being genuinely civil and was probably astonished at our seeming incivility when Lily and I responded, 'No, you don't *have* to have us over for tea. If we come to like each other, great. But simply because we live on the same block doesn't mean that either of us has any obligation to socialize with the other.' In the wilderness, when they had to band together for self-defense and help each other build barns, neighbors were definitely a karass, a meaningful group and concept. Today, however, in many areas, 'neighbours' has become a meaningless concept, a grandfaloon, with no more significance than 'Hoosiers.'

A family may be either a karass *or* a grandfaloon. The fact that you are a member of a particular family may be of great significance. Or it may be a matter of mere biological accident with no significance whatsoever. Also your family may be a karass for you when you are young but become a grandfaloon when you're an adult. Finally, the same family may be a grandfaloon for one member while it is a karass for another.

'I don't know what's wrong with me,' psychotherapy patients often say. 'I don't want to visit my parents. All they do is watch TV or talk about some bridge game they played thirty years ago. Who cares? Well, my sister does. She seems very comfortable. She has the TV on all the time at her house too. But I'm bored. And whenever I try to talk about something that interests me, they immediately change the subject. They don't even really know what I am. I feel like I'm a total stranger when I'm over there. I know I shouldn't feel that way, but I do. I feel like I'm an alien. But they they're my family, for God's sake!'

It can be a real relief for such a patient to be introduced to the concept of a grandfaloon. 'Look,' I would say, 'there's no reason you should feel at home in your parents' home. Their ways are *not* your ways. The fact that they happened to give birth to you doesn't mean you've got anything in common with them or need to feel close to them. You didn't choose to be born into your family, and even if you had, it wouldn't meant that you've got anything in common with them today. The fact that they are your biological family doesn't mean that they're your true family, your karass, the place where you really belong. Families can be grandfaloons, you know. Whether you do need to put up with the awkwardness of your visits is a matter for you to decide, but there's no need to feel guilty about that awkwardness.'

And, finally, the extended family can be partly karass and partly grandfaloon at the same time. Joel, a fellow psychiatrist, was seeing me for analysis. In his late thirties, he and his wife, Ingrid, also a physician, had two preteen sons. He also had a wealthy father who customarily took his 'clan' to the Caribbean for a ten-day annual family reunion. It was late November. Joel was recounting a lengthy family Thanksgiving dinner. 'Jesus, it was boring,' he exclaimed. 'It's got both me and Ingrid dreading the damn reunion in January. I wish to God we didn't have to go.'

'*Have to* go?' I echoed.

'Okay, you got me. I don't "have to" do anything.' Joel became more reflective. 'It's just that I'm so ambivalent. I *believe* in family reunions. I like seeing my parents—*briefly*. I don't even mind seeing my sister and her stupid husband —*briefly*. And it's good to see their kids once in a while. Our boys love it. They get along well with the cousins. Ingrid and I are happy to get some sun and a brief change of scene. But ten days? I mean, Ingrid and I are ready to kill them all— except the kids—after five days. We have zero in common with them. Ten days! That's like three percent of our year every year to feel like climbing the walls. We've got better things to do with our time.'

'As I hear you, the problem isn't the reunion,' I commented, 'so much as its length.'

'You're right. That's clarifying,' Joel said appreciatively. 'If it was four or five days it'd be okay. That's plenty. Except for the boys. They'd be happy if it was twenty. But for Ingrid, and me, ten days is like forever.'

'I wonder if there isn't some way that everyone could get their needs met—some win/win solution?' I queried.

'Theoretically, there is. The boys are old enough to fly by themselves. We could send them down for the whole ten days. Then Ingrid and I could fly down for the last five. But that's only a theoretical possibility.'

'I'm not sure why it's only theoretical.'

'Well, the mechanics of it are possible. But my father would have a real fit. I can just hear him now: "What's the point of my paying all that money on airfare for you to come down here for just five days?" he'll scream. Of course, I could tell him we'd pay for the tickets ourselves. That might shut him up. And I'd be quite willing to do that—spend one day's earnings to save us five days of agony. But money isn't the real issue. They'd want to know why: why do we want to come only for five days? I'd tell them that we're just too busy with our practices to take off ten days. But that won't wash. Both my mother and father would be upset. They'd realize that we don't care enough, that we don't love the family that much. And that's the truth. My sister and brother-in-law would gloat, and rub it in that I'm the uppity, ungrateful son. I don't want to spend ten days, but I also don't want to screw up our relationship with the whole family.'

'It may be the truth that you don't care for your family as much—or at least in the same way—as your sister seems to,' I said. 'But it is also the truth that you are both, in fact, very busy and that your time is valuable.'

Joel was silent for a long time. 'Well, I just don't know,' he finally mused. 'It's not like it would be the first time I've ever bucked the family. But there's always a price, and I'm not sure it's worth it. It's also not just my decision, thank God. It's Ingrid's too, and right now I have no idea what she'd think the best way to play it would be. But her judgment's damn good in these sorts of things. I'll talk with her this evening. It's an intriguing possibility. Thanks for suggesting it.'

'I didn't suggest it,' I told him. 'I only suggested you might consider all the alternatives.'

'True,' Joel acknowledged. 'But it's pretty stupid of me to need you to suggest I explore alternatives.'

'There you go again, expecting yourself to be perfect,' I reminded him. Joel's chronic chagrin was a problem on which we'd been working for some time. 'It's not easy to be objective about your own family, even for a psychiatrist.'

The next session Joel was close to exuberant. 'Ingrid thought it was worth the risk,' he told me, 'so I called my father to explain that we'd like to send the kids ahead of us, but we ourselves were too busy to take ten days off. He was furious, just as I'd expected, but he grudgingly agreed to it when I told him we'd pay our own way if necessary just to have a brief reunion. That backed him into a corner. I'm sure my mother and he think we're weird and rude, but then they don't understand anything that Ingrid and I do anyway.'

I suspect Joel was correct that his parents considered

him rude and ungrateful. For my own part, however, Joel seemed to me a family man of exemplary civility.

All organizations have norms, mottoes, and myths. These are primarily established by the organization's leaders. While they may upon occasion be established deliberately, more often than not they come into being and are maintained unconsciously. Whether conscious or unconscious, they are necessary. They are what gives an organization its personality or character and much of its definition. Because norms, mottoes, and myths may be realistic or unrealistic, civil or uncivil, sane or insane, they are the primary determinants of the health of the organization—or its lack of health.

Joel's parents sent the norm that there would be an annual family reunion as well as the norm that it would be ten days in duration. Joel was quite aware he was violating the duration norm. He and his wife made the judgment that they could probably get away with it, but he was right to be anxious about it. There is often a high price to be paid for violating an organizational norm—not infrequently expulsion from the organization.

Among the myriad ways organizational norms are reflected or manifested is through the use of titles. How, for instance, do children in a particular family address their father: by first name, nickname, Daddy, Dad, Father, or sir? Norms may or may not bespeak the larger culture. In the southern United States children are more likely to address their parents as 'sir' or 'ma'am' than in northern families, but this does not mean these titles are always used in the South and never in the North. What might it signify about the family if the children call their father 'Sir' but their mother 'Mom' rather than 'ma'am'? Or if the sons call their father 'sir' while the daughters call him 'Daddy'? These norms are pregnant with meaning.

But the meaning is variable. In families where children

address their parents as 'sir' or 'ma'am,' it is generally also a norm that they should not 'talk back' to their parents. Occasionally, however, talking back in such homes is permissible, while in families where 'Mom' and 'Dad' are the titles, unquestioning obedience may be expected from children.

One way in which norms become conscious is through mottoes. 'Children should be seen and not heard' is a motto typical of homes where 'back talk' to parents is not allowed. While I am always in favor of making norms conscious, this does not invariably mean that an unconscious norm is unhealthy or a conscious one inherently good. 'Children should be seen and not heard' may be fully conscious, but it makes for a profoundly uncivil and unhealthy norm. It not only requires unquestioning obedience, but suggests that children are inferior beings in relation to adults—not just different but inferior—as if they are not worth listening to but adults automatically are. It is the converse of an empowering motto. Civil leaders, including parents, as has already been stated, are called to give away or share their power just as quickly and widely as they can within the constraints of organizational integrity.

The opposite extreme of 'Children should be seen and not heard' might read 'Children should be encouraged to talk back and interrupt adult conversations, no matter how disrespectful their behavior might seem.' This is not a healthy norm either. 'Nothing in excess' was the motto of the Athenians who constructed the gracefully proportioned Parthenon. Generally speaking, extremist norms will be unhealthy whereas healthy norms are characterized by moderation and balance. Certainly the pleasantest, liveliest homes I've been in were ones where the parents welcomed back talk up to a point and discouraged it beyond that point. Theoretically one might think that such 'tightrope' norms would be more difficult for children to handle than simpler (and simplistic) absolutist parental positions. But I have been impressed in these homes by how skilled the children

212

had become at a relatively early age in discriminating between appropriateness and excess, between rightful assertiveness and rudeness.

Teasing in families is another illustration of these principles. In some homes it is customary—normative—for the members to tease one another without restraint. It is miserably uncomfortable to watch children viciously poking 'fun' at each other while their parents sit placidly by or even join in the process of supposedly amusing humiliation. On the other hand, I have also visited households where the atmosphere was so constrained and proper that I felt oppressed myself. Wondering about that suffocating deadliness, I came to realize one of its characteristics was a total absence of teasing. As with talking, the liveliest of families in my experience have been those where parents teased their children, the children teased them back, and everyone teased one another—in moderation. Each member seemed to know when to stop and how to keep it gentle and genuinely humorous rather than scornful. Norms of flexible moderation are not only the most civil ones; they also teach civility.

This healthy flexibility should not be confused with inconsistency. Lily and I once had cocktails with a couple who had a six-year-old son. The boy started bouncing a tennis ball in the corner of their living room. After a few minutes the ball hit a wall and careened off into our midst. 'Don't play with the ball,' his mother told him. 'You know you're not supposed to play with the ball in the house.' A minute later the child started bouncing the ball again. Inevitably, it careened into our midst again. 'I told you not to play with it,' the mother screeched. 'Now stop!' Shortly afterwards the boy started to bounce it again. As his parents ignored him, Lily and I helplessly waited for the minor tragedy to play itself out. When the ball interrupted us for the third time, the boy was slapped by his father and sent off to his room crying. Leaders who repeatedly ignore the violation of norms (in this case, 'You're not supposed to play

213

with the ball in the house') except when they are personally inconvenienced are not practicing moderation; they are operating out of a lack of organizational consciousness and they are practicing incivility. Inconsistency can wreak great harm. Lily and I were not surprised a decade later to hear that the boy—now in his mid-teens—had severe behavioral problems.

Closely related to mottoes and norms are organizational myths. These are attitudes, shared by the leaders of the organization, based on selectively remembered history. They serve not only to give the organization identity but also usually to enhance its collective pride. 'There's something special about us because *we* came over on the *Mayflower*,' is a particularly well known family myth in the United States. Note that the attitude is at the center of the myth. The historical fact that one of the family's sixty or so great-great-great-great-great-great-grandparent's grandparents happened to emigrate to North America in 1620 is remembered (while virtually all other family history has been forgotten) because it supports the attitude that there is 'something special about us.'

As deep-set values or attitudes, myths are more basic than norms—a kind of foundation that often gives rise to the organizational norms. The traditional duration of ten days for the annual reunion was a norm for Joel's family. Underlying that norm was the assumption, or myth, 'We're a close-knit family that enjoys being together.' Joel was correct in his realization that the greatest danger in seeking to change the ten-day norm was that his doing so represented a challenge to this family myth. He was doing something *radical*. And, like radical surgery, it did cause his parents pain. It threw the whole system into question. Yet such psychospiritual pain is often healthy, and in the end I suspect that not only Joel and his wife but the entire family was the better for it.

Organizational myths are frequently illusionary, but they are still building blocks that contribute to family cohesiveness. Neither I nor other students can imagine an organization that survives for long without myths and subsequent norms. But while myths are necessary, they may, like norms, be oppressive. Arthur Mitchell came to see me at the age of twenty, quite depressed over his low grades in his second year of college. He readily acknowledged his lack of motivation to study, adding, 'But that's just the point: I should be better motivated, like Uncle Ted.'

'Who's Uncle Ted?' I inquired, and learned how this relative's legs had been blown off by a mine during the invasion of one of the Japanese-held Pacific Islands in World War II. 'He crawled, literally on his belly, hundreds of yards through the jungle to get back to his unit,' Arthur recounted.

'That's impressive,' I commented, 'but what does it have to do with you not liking to study?'

'Well, when we want to get somewhere, we Mitchells are going to get there even if we have to crawl,' he explained.

So it was in the very first session we were confronted with a family myth. 'I hear that you come from a very determined family,' I said, 'but where is it that you want to get?'

'To graduation, of course. And I'm not going to get there at the rate I'm going. I'm not pushing myself the way Uncle Ted did.'

We were coming close to the end of the hour. I made an appointment to see Arthur the next week, but before we concluded I said, 'There are three possibilities. One is that you simply lack your family's—or your uncle Ted's — determination. A second is that something we don't even begin to understand yet is interfering with your determination. A third, however, is that graduation from college is not where you really want to get. Between now and when we see each other again I'd like you to seriously consider each of those possibilities.'

Arthur began the following session by stating he wished he didn't have to *get* to graduation. He had always loved auto mechanics, and while college had seemed like a good idea at

215

first, now he wished he could just drop out and work on cars. 'Well, why can't you?' I asked.

Here he hemmed and hawed, and I kept pressing him as he continued saying, 'I just can't,' 'I have to graduate,' and 'It's a trap I can't get out of.' It wasn't until mid-session that we made progress when, close to tears, he exclaimed, 'My parents have always told me, "Don't start something unless you're going to finish it." So you see, I have to finish college.'

A family motto to reinforce the family myth! I suggested to Arthur that mottoes were only guidelines, and not rules, and that 'Even rules are made to be broken,' fighting a motto with a motto. We agreed to have a meeting with his parents where I would explain to them that he seemed to have a vocation to auto mechanics, and it might be better for him, to fulfill his vocation than to stick it out in college in blind obedience to a motto.

The meeting went well. Arthur's parents turned out to be reasonable people who loved him too much not to be able to put aside rigid formulas. He dropped out of college with their blessing.

The Mitchells were an upwardly mobile family. Their myth and motto of determination expressed the kind of values and attitudes that make for upward mobility. And there is nothing inherently wrong with these. In fact, in remarkably short order Arthur fulfilled the family myth. Within eight years he had gained a national reputation as as mechanic uniquely expert with antique autos. He traveled extensively, receiving astonishingly high fees for his services, and was probably far more successful than if he had stayed in college. The only problem with the myth was that it had been interpreted too narrowly.

Unfortunately, many myths are not so healthy and most psychotherapy cases not so successful. Family myths are just as likely to support downward mobility. 'You boys are no-goods just like your father and his father before him.' 'We Jacksons have always worked in the mills. We're ordinary folk. We don't put on airs the way rich people do.' One of the deep sadnesses of my life is that I have seen six separate adolescent patients, all intelligent, sensitive, and artistic, who were in turmoil over their attempts to pull away from the poverty of their families. Not one was I able to help. Each was pulled back by 'Don't you get uppity on us' and 'We aren't the kind of people who go for fancy education' and 'You go off to college and you better not come back here with any big ideas or spouting big words.' As with the violation of norms, there can be a devastating price to pay for the 'betrayal' of family myths. Try to be 'better than' in a culture of poverty and there is a fair chance you will end up the family scapegoat.

While family myths supporting downward mobility are obviously destructive, it should not be assumed those that support upward mobility are inherently healthy. I grew up with a myth that my father was a man of extraordinary intelligence and competence. After all, the historical data were obvious. Had he not graduated first in his class from Harvard Law School at the age of twenty-two? Had he not been the youngest full partner of his firm? Had he not been a self-made man who brilliantly managed money?

My father was an only child. My mother had a single older sibling, 'poor old Uncle George.' What little money George had he hadn't really earned, my parents hinted. He got it by going into his wife's father's real estate business, and then when he inherited the small business, he hadn't made anything of it. How could he when he mostly just fished and boated in his little boat in the waters around his slightly seedy Long Island home so many miles away from my father's important world of Wall Street? Yes, he'd graduated from Princeton, but he'd never put his degree to any use. He really wasn't very bright, my parents suggested. Even when I was little and my parents were in their early forties and he not yet fifty, he was referred to as 'poor old Uncle George.' I saw no reason to consider this quiet, unassuming man worthy of my attention.

217

When my parents were in their late sixties and George in his early seventies, his wife died. Shortly thereafter Lily and I returned to New York City for a visit after years away. My parents were going to take us out to an extremely elegant and expensive restaurant. 'Would you mind if we also asked poor old Uncle George to come along?' my mother inquired. 'What with his wife dying we need to do what we can for him.'

'Of course not,' Lily and I replied. We were more interested in the fine food than my parents' conversation, which we had long found pretentious and boring. Even poor old George might add some spice. And he surely did. We had hardly been seated when Lily and I glanced at each other with amusement over the pompous manner in which my father was dealing with the fawning headwaiter. Then we happened to note that Uncle George was looking on with the same kind of amusement. It was the beginning of an extraordinary evening. The conversation floated on three levels. The most verbal one was controlled by my parents, with their standard questions and opinions. But weaving in and out was another level on which Lily and George and I explored one another and gently teased my parents—so gently they had no idea they were being teased or that there was any significant conversation other than their own. Finally, there was a level of nonverbal communication on which Lily and George and I expressed our immense mutual enjoyment of all these interactions, so much richer than the usual conversational fare with my parents. It was clear that my uncle George could run intellectual circles around my mother and father.

In retrospect I know now that within my nuclear family, George had been used as a kind of scapegoat by my parents to bolster their self-esteem. It probably didn't bother him in the least, but I think I lost something thereby. For that dinner was the last time we got to see him. Lily and I returned to our busy lives and a year later he had a stroke and died. I wish I'd been encouraged to get to know him better much earlier in my life. Had I done so, I suspect there was a lot I could have learned from 'poor old Uncle George.'

The problem—the unhealthiness—of this myth was its exaggeration. The basics of the myth were accurate: my father was, in fact, an unusually intelligent and competent man. But to support materialistic upward mobility and my parents' pride, it became a myth that my father was the *most* intelligent of men and extremely competent in the *only* significant way. The fact that George, although less narrowly focused, was at least as intelligent as my father and more spiritually competent represented a threat to this nuclear family myth. Consequently, he had to be scape-goated as 'poor old Uncle George.'

Exaggeration is not the only form of distortion. Since they are based on 'selectively remembered history,' myths may exclude more reality than they include, to the point where they become serious distortions. Lily and I participated in the initiation of one such family myth that fortunately was nipped in the bud. Our parents were extremely over-controlling couples. Had they been given the chance, they would have selected each of our spouses and careers for us. After so many years of keeping them at bay, once we were married Lily and I vowed not to be controlling parents ourselves. And in one sense, we did keep that vow. From the moment of their birth, we were scrupulous in giving our two daughters the maximum amount of reasonable latitude.

When they were six and seven, an older psychiatrist, Bob Anderson, came to visit us on Okinawa and stayed in our home. Idly chatting the last night of his visit, I commented to him, 'We're not pushy parents.' Lily nodded her head in agreement.

'You're not *what*?' Bob retorted in obvious disbelief.

'We're not pushy parents, 'I repeated emphatically and with a touch of annoyance. 'I mean, we're very careful to not lay trips on the girls. We don't push any particular expectations on them. We want them to be free to choose their own paths.' Lily nodded again.

'Well, you may be right that you're not particularly specific about what you want the kids to do,' Bob acknowledged dubiously. But then he went on. 'I've been observing you for four days now and I think you're good parents, but I sure as hell wouldn't say you're not pushy. The message I've seen you give is, "We want you to do whatever you want to do as long as you girls are excellent." You may not have specific expectations of them, but you have an expectation of excellence, and I sure wouldn't call that "not pushy." '

Thank God for the Bob Andersons of the world. Perhaps we too can take some credit for listening to him and allowing our fallacious myth to be exploded. I think we would have done the children considerable harm had we gone on expecting excellence of them while blithely believing ourselves not to be pushy. Ever since then it has been out in the open. 'We're not as controlling as our parents,' we say now, 'but otherwise we are a family in which there is a great deal of subtle pressure to succeed or excel in some way or another. One of the problems you children have is to figure out how each of you can best deal with that pressure.'

Our myth, 'We're not pushy parents,' was a conscious one. What we were unconscious of, however, was the distortion involved. And that is why it was potentially so uncivil. Conscious or unconscious, distortions subtract from the light and add to the darkness and the confusion in the world.

Although uncivil—unhealthy and destructive—such unconscious distortions are so common as to be accepted as 'normal.' Rarely, however, they can be so bizarre that they are considered insane. Psychiatrists occasionally see a psychotic delusion that is shared among family members. This is most likely to occur when a very dominant member goes crazy, placing a submissive or dependent member in a dreadful dilemma. He must either buck the dominant one or else come to agree with the insanity, and the choice may well be the latter.

The most flamboyantly crazy individual I saw during my

psychiatry training was 'Queen Frederika,' a strikingly beautiful, twenty-six-year-old American woman whose real name was Elizabeth Martin. The day before we met she had been apprehended leaving an elegant San Francisco department store with an armload of furs and dresses for which she had not paid. She denied shoplifting, insisting she was the queen of Sweden and that the Swedish government would naturally pick up the tab. The police were called. Her imperious manner and story were so outrageous that they brought her to the hospital. It did not take me or the staff long to realize she was not pretending to be a queen; she truly believed, without question, that she was Queen Frederika. Her treatment was difficult. Several months of hospitalization and high doses of major tranquilizers were required before she came back to earth.

More intriguing to me than this biologically impaired schizophrenic woman, however, was her husband, Barnaby Martin, a successful young lawyer. He and Elizabeth had been married nine months previously. The trouble started three months later when Elizabeth told him she had seen a radio transmitter in their landlord's apartment and believed the man to be a Nazi spy. She wanted to report him to the FBI. It was 1964. Barnaby thought she was unreasonable, but took what he thought was a civil way out. He suggested she did not yet have enough evidence to support the accusation but volunteered to help her find it. Every evening for weeks, when he came home from work, Barnaby would join her in rummaging through their landlord's garbage searching for 'evidence.' Elizabeth then became convinced that the landlord had become aware they were onto him and had placed hidden microphones in their apartment. Now each night Barnaby would join her not only in sorting through the trash but looking under the cushions, mattresses, and other furniture for 'bugs.' Two weeks before her admission, Elizabeth had begun telling him that she was of royal blood. Barnaby had doubts, but he loved her so much he kept them to himself.

It was a relief for him when she was finally hospitalized and formally designated as 'ill.' It was something he had suspected all along. But it was discomforting for him to acknowledge that in joining her searching through the garbage and under sofas, he had been behaving as crazily as she. A skeptical lawyer quite capable of confronting people on the witness stand over subtleties, he had been unable to confront his own wife's obvious delusional system. Indeed, he had caved in to that system and by doing so had become part of the system itself. Moreover, we pointed out to him, his pain-avoiding, seemingly 'civil' acquiescence had quite possibly delayed her treatment by as much as six months, permitting her delusions to become fixed and all the more difficult to combat.

Usually such delusions are shared between pairs: a husband and wife, as in the case just outlined; two close siblings; a mother and daughter. First described in the French psychiatric literature, the phenomenon came to be known as *folie à deux*, or 'folly of two.' But it has been since noted in larger family groupings, and I myself have seen a *folie à quatre*—a complex psychotic delusional system held by a husband and wife and both their adult children.

True *folies*—shared family delusional myths or psychoses—are actually quite rare. They would not have deserved even this relatively brief mention were it not for the fact that organizations much larger than families will shortly be considered. Might it be possible for an entire church or a business corporation or even a nation to succumb, through similar dynamics, into folly? Are there such things as mass delusional myths and corporately shared insanity? I believe the judgment of history must be that there are.

Somewhat different from organizational myths, norms, and mottoes are organizational lies and secrets. These are conscious, deliberate falsifications of reality that do not serve to give the organization an identity; they serve wholly to give it misidentification. Individuals often lie or keep secrets, but here we are speaking of falsifications initiated by the organization's leaders for the purpose of misinforming the organization itself. Even if well meaning, they are acts of incivility invariably destructive to the organization's health.

Mildred Cernicke was referred to me by the school system because, in the course of a single year, the grades of her two children, Cynthia and Robert, ages twelve and ten, had dropped from A's to D's. The precipitant seemed obvious. A year earlier her husband, Harry, the children's father, had begun to serve a three-year prison term for embezzlement. 'It must have been a terrible shock for them,' I commented, 'not only learning that their father was guilty of a crime, but also losing his presence and having to witness a devastating decline in your financial life-style.'

'Yes, that's why I've done my best to soften it,' Mildred said. 'At least they don't know their father's in jail.'

'How can they not know?' I asked.

'I've told them that Harry was sent to Vietnam to work over there for the government helping the people. With the AID program. That's what Harry and I agreed to say before he went to serve his term. He'll probably get parole, so he'll be back in another year, thank God. The kids love him, and this way they'll keep their respect for him.'

It took me the better part of an hour to convince her that the children needed to be told the truth. 'I know that you've told them a lie in order to protect them. But a lie is still a lie,' I said. 'They're obviously hurting and need help, and I can't work with them without dealing with the truth. They may know the truth anyway. It's hard to keep secrets from kids. And it would be better coming from you than from me.' She reluctantly agreed finally to confess she'd lied to them, but only during a session with me there to pick up the pieces.

They were nice-looking children. It was very painful for Mildred as she haltingly began. 'I have an apology to make to you. I told you that Daddy is in Vietnam, but the truth is that he is in prison. He took some money from his company

223

that he wasn't supposed to. It was a crime. But he's not a bad man. He did it because he just wanted us to be able to live in a big house with lots of toys. I'm not saying it was right. But he's paying for it and he'll get out of jail in another year or two and then we'll all be together again. Both Daddy and I love you very much. I'm sorry I lied to you. I shouldn't have. But it's very important to me that you love your daddy, and I didn't want you to think he is a bad man.'

I had been watching the children closely as their mother made her confession and was surprised to see them start grinning before she was halfway through. By the time she finished they were jubilant. 'Why do you look so happy?' I asked them.

'Because we thought Daddy was in jail for murder,' Cynthia said.

It turned out that they hadn't bought the lie from the beginning. The other kids at school had teased them about their father being in jail. They had seen the mail from the Department of Corrections. They had known what their mother was doing when she went off to visit him. But they had been unable to talk to her about it. 'We didn't want to upset her,' Robert explained.

I had a hunch. 'What does the word "embezzlement" mean?' I asked.

'We figured it was some kind of murder,' Cynthia answered. 'The other kids at school kept using it. But I guess now it means a kind of stealing, doesn't it?'

It did, I told them. We spoke briefly about their feelings for their father, about what he had done, about their mother's lie and the teasing they received at school. But their feelings about these things at that point paled before their overwhelming relief that 'Daddy's not a killer and he'll be coming home soon.' They had assumed that he would be in jail for life. They promised that they would be able to talk about everything with their mother now. By this time Mildred was also jubilant.

That was all the intervention needed. Relieved of the

burden of their misapprehensions, the grades of both children went shooting up within the month.

The moral of this family story can serve as a bridge to the next section of this book, where we consider business organizations—often very large organizations—in which fallacious myths, lies, and secrets may be mass forms of incivility.

Carl Jung used the term 'Shadow' to designate that part of our mind containing those things that we would rather not own up to: traits that we are not only trying to hide from others but also from ourselves, that we are continually trying to sweep under the rug of consciousness. He ascribed the root of individual human evil to one's 'refusal to meet the Shadow.' As individuals can have Shadows, so can groups. The father's crime and imprisonment was the Cernicke family Shadow, its collective skeleton in the closet.

Such skeletons soon begin to stink. Why? It is literally as well as figuratively the stench of decay. The Cernicke children's school performance had dramatically deteriorated. Individuals or families or larger institutions held in the grip of their own Shadows are dying organizations. The decay has begun.

Isn't it interesting that decay does stink—that we perceive its smell as bad rather than good or neutral? Could it be that God (or evolution) has given us noses with which to sniff out lies and distortions and the ensuing rot they cause? And might not society's greatest problem be that the sense of smell of the majority of its citizens has grown dulled to the odor of spiritual decay, to the uncivil everyday dishonesty and deception pervasive in our institutions?

In any case, Light and Truth are synonyms for God. As potentially godly creatures, we are called to face ourselves and expose our Shadows, individual and collective, to the light. We are called to consciousness. God does not desire us to be in the dark or to attempt to keep others there. We are called to genuine civility as opposed to the pretense of politeness. Like medicine, like surgery, the truth may hurt, but in the long run, as it was for the Cernicke family, it is always healing.

Beware even of little white lies. There are no absolute formulas. Civility may, upon occasion, require that we withhold from others the full truth of our desires—albeit only with trepidation. Its general rule, however, is that of disclosure, of self-honesty and interpersonal honesty. Never has the vision of a truly civil society been more clearly expressed than by the glorious prophecy: 'And the hidden shall become known.'[3]

---

[3] Matthew 10:26.

Part Three

YOU GOTTA KNOW
YOUR BUSINESS

14

Who's There?

Roles and Transference

The summer I was sixteen I worked for Lionel, a weather-worn New England farmer and gentle teacher. Whenever I made one of my frequent mistakes or expressed my admiration for his expertise, he would clap me on the shoulder with his giant hand and exclaim, 'You gotta know your business.'

Lionel, who ran a one-man show, was referring to the technical expertise of farming: the proper way to lift a full milk can or to hold sheep for the shearing, the timing of mowing and planting, the methods for moving a boulder or constructing a root cellar. Very few people are one-man shows anymore. Most of us today exercise our technical expertise in the employ of large and complex organizations. But I have learned that Lionel's motto remains more true than ever. For in such settings, 'You gotta know your business,' means you not only have to know the job for which you've been hired, but you had also better know the organization of the business in which you work.

From now on I will use the word *business* in its generic sense: that which keeps us busy. It has become customary in our specialized society to restrict the word *business* to a particular kind of commerce, so in our universities we have graduate schools of business separate from our schools of law, medicine, education, government, and so forth. Similarly, we divide the work world into the private, public, and nonprofit 'sectors.' But for the purposes of this book, such separations are arbitrary and unnecessary. The principles of organizational behavior hold true across the board whether you are in the business of commerce, the business of government, the business of teaching, and even if your work is voluntary.

'You gotta know your business' does not actually mean you *must* know your business. While the vast majority of people are technically proficient, only a few know much about the organization for which they work. Our organizational consciousness is usually dramatically deficient, yet most of us get by. 'You gotta know your business' means, among other things, that you've got to know the organization if you're going to do more than get by—if you're going to be as happy and effective as you'd like to be.

There are many textbooks and other excellent works on organizational behavior in business. It is not my purpose to duplicate or replace them. Rather, it is my intent to focus solely on the relationship between organizational issues and civility, with particular focus on those relevant issues other works have generally overlooked.

I have already touched upon some of the primary principles of organizational behavior in our consideration of families. For instance, myths, mottoes, norms, and often secrets and lies are common not only in families but also in virtually all businesses. Yet there is a basic principle that huge numbers of people in their lack of organizational consciousness need to learn: *A business is not a family.*

For one thing, businesses hire and fire. A person is born into a family, not chosen or hired into it. Even if someone is disinherited by his parents, this does not mean he no longer has parents, brothers or sisters, or aunts and uncles. The distinction between family and business was agonized over by a farmer and his wife in Robert Frost's poem 'The Death of the Hired Man.' The hired man, who had quit his job in the midst of haying season the year before, now has a fatal illness and returns 'home' to the farm to die. In discussing his very questionable right to do so, the husband says, 'Home is the place where, when you have to go there, they have to take you in.' His wife describes home slightly differently: 'I should have called it something you somehow haven't to deserve.'

Regardless of this couple's charity and all the Equal Employment Opportunity legislation, a business does not *have to* hire you or take you in. And regardless of all employee protection legislation, one does not automatically *deserve* continued employment. Even in the most charitable of businesses, if you do not demonstrate at least a minimal sustained level of competence, you will, in fact, deserve to be fired.

The other crucial distinction between family and business organizations is the issue of roles. The primary role of a family is to nurture its members. No matter what other roles it might play, a family that does not nurture its members (as is often the case) will essentially be a failure as a family. The primary role of a business is to produce a marketable product above and beyond itself. No matter how much it might nurture its own employees, a business that fails to market an effective product—that is, to serve customers effectively—will in relatively short order become obsolete and be demolished.

Since the roles of business and family are different, the roles of members of a business are substantially different from the roles of family members. But one consequence of our lack of organizational consciousness is our profound tendency to confuse business roles with family ones. The essence of this confusion is the problem of transference. This problem has not received adequate attention in business circles. It is the cause of mountains upon mountains of unnecessary, neurotic suffering for workers and the workplace.

Jennifer Guglione, a twenty-five-year-old clerk-typist, was referred to me by the EAP (Employee Assistance Program) of the large corporation for which she worked. She had been

231

hired six months earlier to work in a typing pool for the marketing division. Initially she seemed to do well, but for the previous three months was reported to be unproductive, sloppy, contentious with her supervisor, and often tardy. Most companies would simply have fired her, but this one placed a high premium on personnel relations. 'Retention pays' was both a corporate motto and a policy.

Three things were remarkable about Jennifer from the start. One was that she was overqualified for her position. She was a college graduate who read widely in her spare time. Indeed, for two years after her graduation she had worked in a low-level management position in a distant city. A second feature was Jennifer's vagueness. She was frustratingly vague as to why she had left this higher-paying job for the low-status one of a clerk-typist. She was also vague about her parents and family. Finally, despite this, there was something remarkably pleasant about her. I liked her and looked forward to our few visits.

Those visits were few because after the third one, the EAP administrator called me to report an astonishing improvement in Jennifer's work performance. 'You've pulled off a miracle,' he told me. 'The problem's solved.'

'If I've pulled off a miracle,' I countered, 'I've no idea what it was. I don't even know what the problem was. But when you say it's solved, I get the sense you'd just as soon not pay me to keep seeing her.'

'Well,' he cautiously answered, 'of course we wouldn't want to pay for therapy if she doesn't need it. If there's some reason she actually needs it, well, then . . .'

'Got the picture,' I replied. 'When she comes next week, I'll explore it with her. If nothing emerges, I'll let her go, but I need to warn you we psychotherapists tend to distrust "miracle cures." '

Nothing did emerge in that next session. Jennifer was customarily vague as to the reasons for her dramatic improvement and expressed no desire to keep seeing me. We parted on pleasant terms.

Two months later the EAP administrator phoned me once more. 'Jennifer's work has gone to hell again. It looks like you were right about miracle cures and you need to see her longer.'

'Okay, but while I've got you, tell me what you can about her supervisor,' I requested.

'Woman in her mid-fifties. No ball of fire. She's been with the company for twenty-two years and demonstrated no desire to climb any further. But she's been a fine supervisor. She really cares for the employees under her. "Her girls," she always calls them. The morale's always been high in the steno pool, and this is the first time EAP's ever had to be called in on one of her supervisees since we began the program ten years ago.'

This time I warned Jennifer that I was going to be relentless in countering her vagueness, and so began to 'pull teeth' out of her. It emerged that she was extremely angry at her mother, a 'neurasthenic' woman bedridden much of the time by a host of indeterminate illnesses. She said her mother seldom lifted a finger around the home and was utterly inattentive to her children, except occasionally to fly into a rage when they failed to perform their assigned household chores. Jennifer's father was an entirely different matter. He was a 'doer,' who not only held down a responsible middle-management job but seemed tireless in doing the lawn mowing, repairs, shopping, and housecleaning. All this homemaking he somehow managed to turn into a game he played with his three daughters. 'Daddy's the greatest father a girl could ever have,' Jennifer proclaimed.

I also wormed out of her that she disliked her supervisor. 'A lazy bitch!' Jennifer pronounced with uncharacteristic vulgarity.

'Lazy? What do you mean, lazy?'

'She sits around on her fat ass talking, talking, talking. All she does is boss us girls around. Even when there's a crisis with rush work to be done, she hardly ever even lifts a finger to the keyboard herself.'

233

'How many of you "girls" are there in the steno pool?' I asked.

'There's an even dozen of us.'

'How about your supervisor?' I asked. 'Is she one of the girls?'

'No. She doesn't even ever go out to lunch with us. She hangs around with management, the snotty bitch.'

'Well, she is a manager, isn't she?' I commented mildly. 'Supervising a dozen women is a pretty big responsibility.'

'It wouldn't be big if she'd just leave us alone. But she's always evaluating us. "Performance objectives," she keeps saying. Always evaluating us, all the time.'

'But isn't that her job?'

'Well, she'd get more work out of us if she just left us alone,' Jennifer insisted.

Another 'tooth' I pulled out of her was that she seldom dated. 'I'm not a lesbian and I'm not a virgin,' she explained. 'It's just that I hardly ever meet a man I respect.' But she did not seem to regard this as a problem, and my probing could get me no further. It also remained unclear exactly why she had left her previous, more challenging position. I did learn that in it, too, she had worked for a woman. Meanwhile, I found it intriguing that despite my tooth pulling, she continued to be pleasant toward me and enjoyable to work with.

This time it was six sessions before the EAP administrator called me. 'Well, you've done a miracle again,' he announced. 'Jennifer pulled herself back together as soon as she returned to you. But I've waited five weeks to see if her improvement is solid, and it is.'

'I'm not at all sure it's so solid,' I replied. 'I know enough about her now to understand that she's got some pretty big dynamics going on. I'll tell you what, though. If she's not eager to continue working with me, I'm willing to do an experiment and let her go again. But only under one condition.'

'What's that?'

'If she relapses once more, that you're prepared to subsidize her in getting some long-term psychoanalytic treatment with a different therapist— specifically a woman. We're talking at least a year and maybe two. I need a promise from you on this. Otherwise it wouldn't be fair for me to stop seeing her at this point. Also, I need to warn you her improvement may well not be as rapid the next time.'

'That's a pretty big promise. My instinct is to say okay, but let me run it by her supervisor and the people in personnel and get back to you tomorrow.'

He did, and the promise was made. I began my next session with Jennifer by telling her about my conversation with the EAP administrator in full detail. 'Why specifically a woman therapist?' she asked.

'Because I think you've got your supervisor and your mother mixed up.'

'That's ridiculous!' The reaction was instant and emphatic.

'Why so ridiculous? You're very angry at both of them. Both of them you speak about in the same language. Each you repeatedly call "lazy" and a "bitch." '

'But they're not the same at all. My mother isn't really lazy. She's ill. You know that.'

'And you've correctly distrusted your mother's many illnesses,' I countered. 'Deep inside you've known your mother's used illnesses as a disguise for her laziness. I think your poor performance at work has been a way of trying to fight back against your mother.'

'But I'm not performing badly anymore,' Jennifer protested. 'EAP just told you so.'

'Is that because you don't hate your supervisor anymore or because you're trying so hard to please me?' I asked.

Jennifer looked distinctly confused. 'Why do you think it is that you've done so much better at work twice now,' I continued, 'the very moment you began to see me? Even though your feelings toward your supervisor haven't changed? You've never been able to explain that, have you?

235

Well, I think that just as you've got your supervisor and your mother all mixed up, you've got me and your father all mixed up. Because you love your father so much you want to please him desperately. Similarly, you start doing well at work the minute you start seeing me because you want to please me so much. It's like the company is your family and your supervisor is your mother, and you hate her. But you start doing well because I'm like your father and your desire to please me is even greater than your desire to get back at your mother—just as it was when you were a child at home and you did your chores most of the time because you were a good little girl, good for your father's sake, not your mother's.'

But it didn't work. 'That's stupid!' Jennifer protested. 'I know perfectly well you're not my father.'

I made a last-ditch attempt. 'Consciously, intellectually, you know I'm not your father. Just as you know on a conscious level that your supervisor isn't your mother. But that's not the way it is at the level of your unconscious. Can you recognize that you may be reacting on an unconscious level, that your unconscious may be what is really determining your behavior?'

'It's all a bunch of bullshit,' Jennifer pronounced.

And then there was a long silence. Finally, I broke it. 'What would you like to do? Do you want to keep seeing me or do you want to try an experiment of seeing how it goes at work without me?'

Jennifer's pleasantness returned. 'I like you,' she said. 'I like you a lot. But it is a hassle for me to drive all the way up here each week. And there really isn't any reason now I'm doing fine at work.'

'But if you relapse?'

The question hung for a long moment. 'If I relapsed couldn't I come back to see you?' Jennifer tried to negotiate.

'No, a woman.' I was firm. 'You'd need to see a female therapist.'

'I could quit my job.'

'Of course,' I agreed. 'But that wouldn't solve the problem would it? I have a very good woman therapist in mind. I'd feel much more comfortable stopping seeing you now if I knew you were willing to see her instead of running away from the problem.'

'All right,' Jennifer said, likely out of her need to please me. 'If I relapse again I'll see your woman friend.'

And, of course, she did relapse. I referred her to Nadine Goldschmidt, a well-known Freudian analyst. In doing so, I requested Nadine to send me a progress report when her work seemed terminated. Two years later Nadine scrupulously honored my request:

Dear Scotty:

I am grateful for you referring Jennifer Guglione to me. It has proven a most satisfactory case, although I must admit a twinge of professional jealousy over the accuracy with which you called the shots. What with her negative maternal transference she was at my throat by our third session.

Very gradually her work performance improved as she continued to transfer her rage from her supervisor onto me. Angry as she was at me, it was difficult for both of us to keep seeing each other twice a week. But we hung in there, and at nine months we had one of those breakthroughs (I won't bore you with the details) where she suddenly *saw* how inappropriate her feelings for me were. Then, of course, we were really able to get down to work.

The hardest part of that work was her coming to the realization that her father was, in many ways, a weak man who not only subsidized but encouraged his wife's psychopathology. So we were able to resolve the good parent/bad parent split. Since Daddy is no longer so wonderful in her mind, she has become able to look at men more realistically and is now dating regularly.

She has also had a good relationship with her supervisor for well over a year, and with the woman's blessing is in the process of applying for a marketing position where she will be using the steno pool instead of working in it. We have just terminated, and I expect her to do well, although I've left the door open for her to return if she has difficulty.

It's always nice, isn't it, to get a case that works? Thanks again.

Best,
Nadine

Who's there? Consciously, Jennifer proclaimed, 'My supervisor, of course.' Yet, locked in the grip of transference, her behavior shrieked a different answer: 'My mother.'

Transference has been defined as 'those ways of responding to the world, developed in childhood and usually appropriate to the childhood environment (indeed, often life-saving), which are inappropriately transferred into the adult environment.' I have referred to it as 'the outdated map.'[1]

Jennifer's anger at her mother was inappropriately transferred onto her supervisor and later onto Nadine. Because her anger properly belonged to her mother, we speak of it as a *maternal* transference. Since it made her difficult in relationship to older women, it was specifically a *negative* maternal transference. Her manner with me, however, was so pleasing by virtue of the fact it was determined by a *positive paternal* transference. She didn't so much see *me* as she was seeing *in me* the good father she wanted so much to please.

While it can be pleasant to work with a patient or subordinate who sees you as a good mother or good father, such positive transferences can get in the way of effective relationships just as much as negative ones. In the case of Jennifer, for instance, her inappropriate desire to please me caused her to improve her work performance, but *only as long as she was seeing me*. It did nothing to heal the problem; in fact, her sudden improvements simply removed her

---

[1] *The Road Less Traveled*, pp. 44–51.

motivation to work on it. This is why what the EAP administrator referred to as my 'miracle cures' are what we psychotherapists call 'transference cures.' Such cures occur when a person's behavior improves because her situation has changed in such a way as to 'fit' with her transferences, and not because *she* has changed to any degree.

Sometimes it can be tempting to use transference cures. In Jennifer's case I actually considered the option of advising the EAP administrator to shift her to a different position where she could have a male supervisor. Such a shift would probably have taken care of the problem temporarily. Sooner or later, however, there would have been another female authority figure in the picture, and the superficial solution would simply collapse, perhaps to both Jennifer's and the company's even greater detriment.

More important, there is a common way that positive transferences are subtly destructive in the business world. It is seductive indeed for an executive to have an adoring assistant who is unfailingly pleasing and compliant, as people in the grip of a positive transference are likely to be. It feels nice to be regarded as the good mother or good father. But the best executives are those who are willing to forgo such adulation in favor of an assistant who can criticize them or disagree with them in an appropriate fashion. Positive transferences deprive the supervisor-supervisee relationship of the valuable energy of creative friction.

Because subordinates with a positive transference are so pleasant, they are also frequently promoted to positions above their level of competence, where far more is called for than pleasantness and compliance. Finally, it is not unlikely that the employee with a positive transference will also have a negative transference that may be affecting some other part of the organization. This is the good parent/bad parent split of which Nadine spoke. As a female director of marketing, for instance, you may be most pleased by an endlessly helpful young woman deputy, but you are also having trouble with the accounting department. Your deputy refers to the male head of accounting as 'that skinflint SOB,' and you are inclined to agree. But might it be that your deputy's negative transference is precipitating the conflict with accounting and you are inadvertently being caught up in her good parent/bad parent split?

Still, while positive transferences are subtly destructive, it is negative transferences that most bedevil organizational life. One does not have to be a supervisor or executive for long before one finds oneself the unwitting victim of some fierce antipathy from an employee that seems to come out of the blue or, as Jennifer's supervisor experienced, some unfathomable pattern of noncompliance from a subordinate. Freud discovered the concept of transference, and psychotherapists are the experts on the subject. But I used to tell my psychotherapist students, 'On one level you'll never really know what tranference is until you become an executive.'

Parental transferences are the most common. This is why executives, who like parents are in positions of authority, are so often their targets. But there are also child transferences, where executives react to their subordinates as if they were their own children. Jennifer's supervisor referred to the women in the steno pool as 'her girls.' It may be that she had a transference of her own that played into Jennifer's.

I once worked with the chairman of a physics department who became inappropriately enraged at one of his Ph.D. students when she requested a leave of absence. Only gradually did it emerge that she was his best student, his 'fair-haired girl,' whose performance enhanced his self-esteem. It took much effort to convince him that his appropriate role of mentor was significantly different from the inappropriate role of father. There was a long struggle before this childless man could confess how deeply he had always yearned to have a daughter.

Not only are there child-to-parent and parent-to-child

transferences, but also sibling transferences. Shortly after Jennifer Guglione's case had been resolved so satisfactorily, the EAP manager of her company called to say the president had asked if I would come down to see him at the corporate headquarters. 'I have no idea what it's about,' he explained. 'It's all hush-hush. I only know he's heard about the good work you've done.' I was withdrawing from practice at the time, but was so curious about this summons from on high that I couldn't resist responding with alacrity. It turned out the president wanted help with a long-standing conflict between Ernie, his vice-president for sales, and Angelo, the vice-president of marketing. While the problem intrigued me, I immediately realized I didn't have the time to deal with it. Consequently I referred him to my friend, Jack Withers, an expert industrial psychologist and management consultant.

Jack began by meeting for two hours with the president, inquiring about the four different sessions he'd spent with the two men, unsuccessfully trying to help them resolve their conflict. Next he reassured the president that it was hardly remarkable he'd been unsuccessful, since conflicts between sales and marketing departments are notoriously common and difficult. 'They're so closely related areas,' he explained, 'yet they require such very different people.' Then he explored what the president had failed to do. 'Have you ever told them it is their job, their role, to figure out how to cooperate with each other?' With some embarrassment the president acknowledged that he had not done this 'in so many words,' assuming that because such cooperation was specified in their job descriptions, Angelo and Ernie already understood it. Jack then asked him to bite the bullet. 'If either or both of them are unable or unwilling to fulfill their roles of cooperation, are you prepared to fire either or both of them?' Reluctantly, the president agreed that he had no other choice. Finally, Jack asked him to meet with the two together, be very specific with them about their role of cooperation and the fact that they would be let go if they couldn't succeed at it, and explain how they were being referred to an industrial consultant as a kind of court of last resort.

Within the week, Jack met with each of them alone for an hour. As expected, he found them to be competent, energetic men in their mid-forties, Ernie slightly the older. Angelo reported that Ernie was 'sadistic—always pressing me, always demanding, always nit-picking about schedules.' Ernie described Angelo as a 'wild-eyed money-grubber, concerned only about himself, always trying to get a bigger piece of the pie for marketing.' Yet neither in any way coveted the other's position. Jack gave each of them a Myers-Briggs Personality Type Indicator test to complete within forty-eight hours, asking them to return it by courier.[2] He explained the tests would be scored and analyzed independently by an associate and the results given to both of them. Finally, he made an appointment to see the two of them together in ten days.

Jack began that appointment by simply handing each of them a copy of his own and the other's test report, asking them to spend fifteen minutes in silence reading the reports and thinking about the results. Angelo's report described him as an intuitive, somewhat introverted man, an intellectual who liked to think in terms of the big picture, preferring to leave details to others, comfortable in the company of artists. Ernie's, on the other hand, described him as a highly extroverted man, comfortable with all kinds of people, well organized, with a superb eye for detail, and someone who enjoyed developing formulas.

Jack finally broke the silence. 'Well, what do you think?'

'Sounds right,' Ernie was quick to respond.

'The test is amazingly accurate,' Angelo said with obvious appreciation.

'You're two very different people, aren't you?' Jack commented.

[2] Trademark of Consulting Psychologists Press, Inc., Palo Alto, Calif., copyright 1976, 1987 by Isabel Briggs-Myers.

Angelo immediately recognized that Ernie's personality ideally suited him to be not only a salesman but a manager of salespeople. Ernie, in turn, easily acknowledged that Angelo was the type of person who was a born designer, who intuitively knew how to lead advertisers and packagers. 'That's why neither of you covets the other's job,' Jack remarked. 'Judging from those reports, which of you would you say is the better person?'

Both agreed that while the reports described vastly different men, there was nothing to indicate one was superior or inferior to the other. 'We have no idea what makes for such different personality types,' Jack elaborated. 'What we do know is that different types of jobs require different personalities. Generally speaking, the more different personality types you can have working in the same organization at an executive level, the healthier the organization is likely to be—that is, if the different types can learn how to work together.'

Ernie and Angelo both laughed. Jack told them he wanted to see them together again as soon as possible, and they set up an appointment for three days later. 'At that time I'm going to want each of you to talk about your childhoods. I'd like you to be thinking about how you might do so with color and accuracy.'

In the next session, Angelo reported that he was a middle child, with an older brother and a younger sister. 'My brother was always bearing up on me,' he said, and proceeded to describe several situations in which he was the victim of quite outrageous brutality. 'I don't know why. Maybe he was just a born bully. I can see traces of it in him still. He tends to gang up on people. It's almost as if he likes to hurt them.'

Ernie was the oldest of two brothers. 'My parents were tough on me, but they seemed to ease up by the time he came around. In fact, he took advantage of them. He was always manipulating them, getting away with things, getting more than his fair share.' Like Angelo, Ernie was able to provide some touching examples of the inequality with which he'd been treated.

'Now comes the tough part,' Jack announced. 'Each of you in your first session with me described each other in the same terms you've used for your brothers. Angelo, you referred to Ernie as a sadist. Ernie, you spoke of Angelo as always selfishly trying to get a bigger piece of the pie. This is going to be uncomfortable, I know, but I want each of you to sit in silence for the next minute, looking straight at each other with open eyes.'

After the minute, Jack said softly, 'Angelo, your brother was—and probably still is—a real sadist. Who are you looking at now? Are you looking at your sadistic older brother?'

'Well, Ernie is older,' Angelo answered uneasily. 'And I have felt that he's picked on me. Although I can't recall him doing so lately. Maybe not. I don't know.'

'Ernie,' Jack said, 'there's no question in my mind that your brother was a self-centered, manipulative, greedy little twerp. Who are you looking at now? Who's there? Are you looking at a younger brother who's always trying to take advantage of you?'

'I dunno,' Ernie replied. 'I'm not sure. I've watched the statistics. Angelo's budget and mine have risen in proportion to each other since we've been at headquarters together, but maybe that's because I have been watching them. I can't really tell what would have happened if I hadn't been keeping score.'

Jack gave them a lecture on the nature of transference. Then he made an appointment to see them again together in another three days. 'If you happen to see each other, I want you to ask yourselves, "Who am I looking at? Who's there? Is it someone like my brother or is it just someone who's quite different from me and who's doing his best to do his job?"'

When they returned, each of them was still cautious. 'I can't tell yet,' both said. 'I'll have to see how it goes.' But each spontaneously acknowledged that 'there might be something to this transference stuff,' and that it was 'interesting.'

Jack decided that it would need time, so he went on to the next aspect of his agenda. He set up a flip chart and asked them to brainstorm their hobbies, pleasures, and interests while he wrote their answers down in a column for each. It emerged that while neither of them knew much about the sport, both of them occasionally liked to fish, Angelo in streams for trout and Ernie off the dock in the bay for flounder.

'Okay, here's the plan,' Jack announced. 'I want each of you to keep asking yourselves when you meet, "Who's there? Who am I really talking with?" I'm going to make an appointment to see you again in two weeks, and every two weeks after that until it's clear that you're out of the woods and you no longer need regular checkups. In the meantime, if anything even *starts* to go sour between the two of you, I regard it as the responsibility of each of you to call me up immediately and initiate an emergency appointment. Clear?'

It was.

'Okay,' Jack continued. 'You are also to set aside one full working day each month to go fishing together. Unless you decide otherwise, you will alternate between stream fishing and bay fishing. If it's winter and the weather is too unpleasant or it's not the fishing season, you will travel elsewhere to where you can and would like to fish. Such travel will be on company time and at company expense.'

'How come you insist that it be on workdays?' Ernie shot back.

'Yeah, and what's this about travel on company time and company expense?' Angelo immediately added.

Despite their differences, as company men Ernie and Angelo were now operating in obvious accord. 'Look,' Jack responded, 'cooperating with each other is perhaps *the* most important part of your goddamn job description. It's part of the job. So treat it as if it's important! That means you take time to do it. High-quality time. Company time.'

'But what if the president doesn't feel that way?' Ernie, the older, asked for both of them.

'Talk to him. If he doesn't support it, then call me instantly and I'll be on his back within the hour. This is important, damn it!'

The plan worked. No emergency appointments were required. Within two months the regular checkups were discontinued. Ernie and Angelo went fishing once a month together for a bit over a year, and then the arrangement petered out. Being so different, they were not natural best buddies. But they had become natural coworkers, coexecutives who deeply respected each other and now cooperated without giving it a second thought.

Ernie and Angelo were setups for transference reactions. The more different people are the more difficult it is for them to empathize with each other. And, in the absence of empathy, the easier it becomes to project—transfer—onto the other whatever distrust or hate is lurking in one's mind. Add to this the fact that sales and marketing are so closely related, yet require such different skills, placing the two men in an organizational configuration that commonly breeds conflict. Finally, it so happened that their age, sex, and some of their personality traits mirrored the systems of their families of origin. Yes, it was a setup.

Jack's intervention was quick and relatively superficial. In a sense, Ernie and Angelo were not 'cured'; only their relationship was. Many transference reactions are not so easily treated. My suggestion to Jennifer that she was in the grip of a transference had no effect whatsoever. Her condition could not be healed until she developed a similar transference to her therapist and had 'worked it through' in the context of a therapeutic relationship. This takes much time. It is possible that Angelo and Ernie might once again fall into the trap of transference, though in their case it is also doubtful, since their difficulties were so specific to the setup.

While his 'therapy' was superficial from a psychoanalytic

point of view, Jack intervened with all the precision of a surgeon. Indeed, at one point he even used the 'medical model,' speaking of the need for regular checkups and possible emergency appointments. But rather than treating an individual patient, he was treating an organizational system. Not all industrial psychologists and management consultants (or psychotherapists) are equally competent, but Jack's intervention demonstrates something of what a truly skilled organizational 'physician' can accomplish. He knew exactly what he was doing.

The cost-effectiveness of such expert treatment is also dramatic. I would guess Jack charged the company $5,000 at the most for his services. The company might have spent as much as another $5,000 on Ernie and Angelo's fishing trip expenses. To have fired and paid off either or both of these long-term ranking executive employees, then searched for and trained equally competent replacements with loss of productivity in the meantime, would probably have cost the company a million dollars or more. Yet many businesses (like many individuals with problems) are often amazingly reluctant to seek such help.

It is also possible for an individual to transfer onto an organization as a whole.

Claude came to see me, after some psychiatric research on his own, for what he called 'generalized anxiety.' His self-diagnosis was correct. His hands shook, his voice quavered, and he was one of the most timid men I ever saw. He was also a very bright, creative mechanical engineer.

One root of Claude's anxiety was clear from the start. He had grown up in the backwoods of French Canada, the oldest son of impoverished parents. His father was a brutal disciplinarian, a truly terrifying man who beat him mercilessly for the most minor of infractions. Talking back to him was a *major* infraction.

Money was very much one of Claude's innumerable

worries, and rightly so. His wife did not work, and they had a five-year-old daughter. Even then, twenty years ago, his salary of $20,000 a year was modest for a thirty-year-old man with a very marketable master's degree. I soon learned he had not received a raise in the three years since he had joined the company. Yet he was routinely assigned more demanding projects than other engineers of similar age and experience who were earning more. When I inquired about this inequity, he simply told me that he had asked for a raise a year before and had been flatly rejected. He didn't feel up to asking again.

As he continued to complain about money, increasingly I began to point out to Claude that it was his own fault. 'I know you're scared,' I told him, 'but I doubt that therapy is going to make you any less scared until you start *acting* less scared. If you're too frightened to ask again for the raise you deserve, then you ought to get out. It's clear the company's screwing you over. If they're not willing to pay you what you're worth, it's a dead-end job. Start hunting.'

He balked with all manner of rationalizations: he didn't know how to prepare a resume; he couldn't phone for job interviews on company time using the company phone; he couldn't afford to move and there was no other good company in the area. But I escalated the pressure on him, and finally, after six months, he began to send out resumes and let acquaintances in other companies know he was looking for a new position.

Two months afterward he began his session saying, 'Now I've *really* got a problem. I got a job offer from another company for twenty-three thousand. That's a better salary, but it would mean a move, and a move would eat up at least three thousand. Besides, I don't want to move, and I'm not sure how stable this other company is. And I also doubt the work is as interesting. I like what I'm doing now. Still, a three thousand increase is nice. I don't know what to do.'

'How about going to your company and telling them your dilemma?' I asked. 'Tell them you've received an offer of a fifteen percent salary increase, that you'd really prefer to stay where you are but you simply can't unless they at least match your offer.'

Claude was visibly aghast. 'I couldn't do that.'

'Why not?'

'I don't know why. I mean I just couldn't.'

'Well, if you could, whom would you talk to about it?'

'I don't know. I suppose maybe my boss. More likely his boss, who's head of engineering. But maybe it would be the director of personnel. I don't know.'

'So you're afraid, but it's not a particular person you're afraid of. It's as though you're afraid of the company hierarchy in general.'

'Yeah, that's what it's like.' Claude nodded miserably.

'But what is it about the company hierarchy that makes you so afraid to simply tell them the reality of your situation?'

'I don't know.'

'Well, think, damn it!' My voice had risen. 'What's so frightening?'

Claude looked like a cornered rabbit. 'I mean it would be like negotiating,' he blurted out.

'And what's so frightening about negotiating? That you might be turned down, that you might lose?'

'No, that's not it, I just can't. I just can't.'

Finally, the obvious dawned on me. 'Could you negotiate with your father?' I asked.

'No.'

'Why not?'

'You just didn't.'

'What would have happened had you tried?'

'He would have hit me.'

'If you negotiate with your company, will they hit you?'

Claude looked dubious. 'I guess probably not,' he answered.

'Why not?'

'Well . . . I suppose . . . I guess it wouldn't be legal.'

'Why would it be illegal?'

'I mean, people aren't allowed to hit each other.'

'You mean,' I corrected, 'they're not allowed to unless it's a brutal father hitting his child in the backwoods without breaking too many bones. Intellectually you know the company's not going to hit you if you negotiate. But what do you *feel*?'

Claude's eyes lit up for the first time in our work together. He knew we'd made a breakthrough. 'I feel as though they'd hit me,' he said.

'Even though you know they can't?'

'Yes.'

So we spoke about transference, how unrealistic yet emotionally powerful it could be. Claude *saw* that he had made a paternal transference onto the company. 'Companies are not families,' I told him. 'It's not their role to treat you like a son. They can treat employees well or badly, but they never treat them as badly as children are treated in the worst of homes.'

It hardly removed his terror, but the insight into its origin and unreality was sufficient for him to overcome it. Claude did present his situation to his boss and the director of engineering three days later. Within the week he was offered $25,000 a year to stay on.

Claude terminated therapy after another six months, having grown about as much as he could at the time, still a chronically anxious man. But less anxious. Indeed, he had even begun to develop a certain affinity for job hunting and salary negotiating. When I last heard from him four years later, he had made two more job changes and was vice-president for research and development of a small specialty company at a salary of $45,000 per annum with a good stock option plan to boot.

Subordinates are not the only ones who can develop a transference onto an entire organization. There are numerous instances where a top executive has come to regard an organization as a child, as his or her own 'baby.' It is most likely to occur in the case of enterpreneurs who have started a business from scratch or taken over a small one and turned it into a giant. Yet I have seen the same phenomenon in chief executive officers or chairmen who came into already successful businesses. This type of parent-child transference in executives who come to regard the organization as their particular, personal offspring has caused the demise of or seriously jeopardized many an otherwise fine institution.

Several matters deserve brief clarification at this point.

One is that certain types of business organizations are more likely to foster transference problems than others. In the interest of brevity, I will mention only the most obvious such situation: the family business.

There are many types of family businesses but, again, for brevity's sake, I will offer a single glaring example: our own, M. Scott Peck, M.D., P.C. The initials P.C. stand for 'professional corporation.' By law, a corporation must have officers or directors, and we have the minimum number of two: myself as president and Lily as secretary. As well as being directors, the two of us are also employees in managerial roles. I am the product manager, and Lily is the general manager. The corporation has three additional employees, each with demanding responsibilities but no supervisory role. Lily and I are the supervisors. Although the two of us have different, albeit overlapping, functions, it is impossible to tell which of us has the greater organizational power. Titularly, she is the more powerful at the operational level and I at the director leve. In reality, the two of us make all major executive decisions consensually.

A year after we had assumed this organizational configuration, significant conflict erupted between the two of us and the staff of three. Only then did it dawn on us that we had, without forethought, created a structure identical to that of a nuclear family, with three 'children' and a 'mommy and daddy.' That structure is not, in itself, bad. To the

251

contrary, depending on the nature of the business and our lives, it remains the best possible structure. The primary problem was that we'd been unconscious of what an organizational setup it was for encouraging transference. Most of the difficulty was resolved when we did become conscious of it. We then developed a norm that it is incumbent upon each of the five of us employees to be aware of family dynamics and spot them as quickly as possible, nipping them in the bud as we remember that we are a business and not a family.

All managers, whether in a family business or not, are well advised to think of how their organizational structures might be conducive to transference behavior and be alert to the possibility of family dynamics in the workplace.

Another loose end needing to be tied up is the clarification that not all transference is 'pure.' While transference feelings, by definition, are inappropriate and unrealistic, they may be mixed with quite appropriate ones that are neither neurotic nor unconsciously motivated.

A major reason I entered psychoanalysis twenty-seven years ago was that I was experiencing extreme anxiety and conflict in my relationship with the commanding general of the army post where I was stationed. Let me call him General Smith. I hated General Smith's guts with a passion I had begun to recognize was almost crazy. Although I seldom even had to encounter the man, I would lie awake at night obsessing over his faults, what I saw as his wickedness, his own downright evil. By the end of my therapy, I was able to discern that in some of the instances where I thought he had behaved despicably, he had simply been doing his job, decently filling his clearly assigned role. I was able to come to this discernment only after the psychoanalytic process had unveiled a depth of resentment toward my father of which I had previously been unconscious. This in turn allowed me to see how I had General Smith and my father all mixed up in a level of my mind deep beneath awareness. Despite my intelligence and my own psychiatric training, I had developed a classic negative paternal transference onto the man.

But while he was not my father, it so happens that General Smith was, in fact, a mean-spirited and often despicable person. It was not inappropriate for me to have disliked him. What was inappropriate was the intensity of my feelings. Many others in positions similar to mine disliked the general, but I was the only one who lay awake at night twisted into knots over him. Transference is as neurotic and uncivil distortion of reality, but this does not mean it is necessarily only distortion, without any elements of reality to add fuel to its fire.

All transference may be regarded as a type of role confusion. Jennifer Guglione had her supervisor's role mixed up with that of her mother. Ernie and Angelo had each other's respective business roles as vice-president of marketing and vice-president of sales confused with those of their brothers. Sometimes I was confusing General Smith's appropriate executive authority with my father's inappropriate domination. A third clarification, however, is that transference is not the only type of role confusion. Conversely, not all role confusion is transference.

For instance, the higher one moves in a business hierarchy, the more roles she is likely to accumulate. Indeed, one of the primary characteristics of a top executive position is the multiplicity of roles involved. As a member of the board of a nonprofit organization, my clearest role is that of director. Additionally, however, I also serve at different times as a fund-raiser, educator, marketer, and product development consultant.

As a director, it is generally appropriate for me to attempt to avoid interfering in staff operations. As a fund-raiser, however, I may need to solicit a donor who is pressing for a particular change in those operations. Despite such con-flicts, an executive is usually conscious of her varying roles—to a degree. The problem occurs when two execu-tives, each with multiple roles, are communicating with each other. In the aforementioned instance, the chief of staff may resentfully feel I am interfering with operations when I am speaking to him as a fund-raiser and not as a director. It is helpful—sometimes essential—to preface my communica-tion by specifying, 'I'm calling you in my capacity as fund-raiser,' or switching the subject, 'Now I'd like to speak as a consultant on that new training program.'

This type of specificity to avoid role confusion in communication requires a high level of consciousness. I know. I myself am just beginning to learn how to do it decently. But even when I don't, while the resulting confusion may be uncivil, it is hardly neurotic. It is not transference. There is no mix-up between business and family roles, and no resistance to clarification when the confusion is elucidated.

Negative transference produces conflict. Jennifer was in conflict with her supervisor, Ernie in conflict with Angelo, and I in conflict with General Smith. As we conclude this chapter, it behooves us to *begin* to look at the subject of conflict more broadly.

There are many frames of reference from which to examine conflict. All of them are valuable, particularly if we can keep our wits when the frames overlap—as we shall shortly see they often do.

One frame is simply to consider the entities involved. From this reference point, there are five types: intrapersonal conflict; interpersonal conflict; conflict between an indi-vidual and an organization; intraorganizational conflict; and interorganizational conflict.

Pure intrapersonal conflict is that which exists solely within one's own mind. For instance, I would like to finish writing this chapter before dark, yet I would also like to take a walk while it's still light out. Such a conflict doesn't affect anyone else. But it is not always so pure, because intra-personal conflicts will often spill over into interpersonal ones. There was a conflict in Jennifer Guglione's mind between her feelings for her mother and for her father, which was referred to as the 'good parent/bad parent split.' This conflict played itself out, however, in her struggle with her supervisor. Indeed, many instances of transference may be analyzed as *projections* of intrapersonal conflict onto another person and into the interpersonal arena.

In the case of Claude, we were considering a conflict between an individual and an organization. The case of Ernie and Angelo was primarily analyzed as an inter-personal conflict. Just as intrapersonal conflicts may spill over into interpersonal ones, so may interpersonal ones spill over into intraorganizational ones, such as that between their marketing and sales departments. Finally, inter-organizational conflict was occurring between Ernie and Angelo's company and several competing companies.

Conflict may also be divided into that which is normal, necessary, healthy, and civil, as opposed to that which is abnormal, unnecessary, unhealthy, and uncivil. It is vitally important to bear in mind that certain types of overt conflict are highly healthy and civil, while either covert conflict or the absence of conflict may be most unhealthy and uncivil. Claude was in covert conflict with his company when it was failing to give him the raise he both deserved and needed but for which he was too terrified to ask. Only when he brought that conflict out into the open could it be handled in a civil manner with beneficial results. His transference prevented him from bringing it out into the open for such a self-destructive period of time. Transference may prevent healthy conflict as well as produce unhealthy conflict.

Conflict resulting from transference is invariably un-healthy and uncivil by virtue of the fact that transference is inherently unconscious and distorting. Yet another way of looking at conflict is in terms of its dynamics—only one of which may be transference. While all transference conflict is unhealthy and uncivil, not all unhealthy conflict is transference-motivated. Examining the phenomenon of adversarialism in some depth in chapter 18, we shall see that other types of unhealthy, uncivil dynamics may be involved. We have only begun.

With all these caveats in mind, let me conclude *this* chapter by examining role conflict at an organizational level and looking at how essentially normal, healthy, and civil conflict can merge into unnecessary, sick, and uncivil behavior specifically as a result of transference dynamics.

Not only may individuals have transferences to organizations, but organizations themselves may transfer onto each other. There are often elements of transference involved in the conflictual relationships between organizations. When Jack, the industrial psychologist, was dealing with the interpersonal conflict between Ernie and Angelo, he pointed out that conflicts between the sales department and the marketing department of business are quite common. This kind of *intra*organizational conflict is seldom solely a matter of transference. Businesses are traditionally set up in such a way that departments must compete with each other for their slices of the budgetary pie. One or two top executives usually make the final decision as to which department gets pared and which gets beefed up. Yes, conflict is built into the system, but when one observes department heads maneuvering with each other, it is not difficult to understand some of their behavior as that of siblings squabbling for Mommy and Daddy's attention.

Again, it is natural for there to be friction between labor and management within a company, and labor-management disputes are often institutionalized forms of intraorganizational conflict. But even when labor is being quite reasonable, it is common to hear some management people complaining, 'Look at all we do for them, and they still want more, the greedy, ungrateful little buggers!' We need then to wonder whether these management representatives are viewing labor realistically or whether they haven't slipped into a parent-child transference relationship. On other occasions it may indeed be labor that is guilty of distortion. It has sometimes wanted more from a company that honestly and obviously lacks the assets to pay more, and the result may be disastrous. In a different vein, labor may complain about 'executive perks,' and such privileges may be excessive at times. At other times, however, I can hear the whining voice of a child in these complaints: 'It isn't fair that Mommy and Daddy stay up late and get to go out all the time.'

It is partly because issues of power can so easily hook us into old sibling rivalry or outdated parent-child patterns that intraorganizational conflict is so common. Consider board-staff conflicts. These may occur even in nonprofit organizations, where staff members are adequately paid and board members unpaid. It is obviously more than a matter of money. The board has the defined responsibility of making policy decisions, and the staff the defined responsibility of implementing those decisions. Yet the staff may consistently fail to do this. Such undermining is occasionally conscious, as when the staff concludes, sometimes correctly, that the board's policies made from on high are simply inappropriate to the reality of the situation in the trenches. More frequently, though, the undermining is unconsciously motivated. It is like the mischief of children rankling under parental authority purely because it is authority. Conversely, board members may inappropriately interfere with purely operational matters out of an unwarranted assumption that the staff is comprised of potentially unruly children not to be trusted and in need of tight parental supervision.

A common example of *inter*organizational role conflict is that between a government and many businesses. Like it or not, government at all levels has at least some regulatory role in relation to business. In a poll I once took of two hundred managers for a large interstate public utility company, over half of them expressed varying degrees of resentment at government interference in their work. As far as I could ascertain, the degree of this interference was neither excessive nor inappropriate to the roles involved, yet many of these intelligent executives had difficulty seeing it as simply the proper order of things. I was reminded of adolescents chafing under parental authority: 'Leave me alone. I don't need any supervision anymore. I'm grown up enough to totally manage my own life.'

The most dramatic example of interorganizational conflict is that of war between nations. Wars are complex phenomena. They are also uncivil. In order to become more conscious of our international behavior, it is incumbent upon us to discern whether transference is an element involved. Even on this grand scale, we should bear in mind the question, 'Who's there?' Are we seeing another nation as it is, or might we be looking at it through the distorted lenses of sibling, child, or parent? Among the *many* ways in which we analyze such matters, should we not include such concepts as U.S. paternalism in Vietnam, sibling rivalry in the Middle East, and adolescent rebellion in the Baltics?

15

Selling or Saving Your Soul

Vocation and Business

I believe that God calls each and every human being to civility. This means we are all under the obligation to become more conscious, to grow in spiritual competence, and to strive to be ethical in our behaviour. I do not know why so many choose to reject this calling or refuse to take its obligation seriously. What I do know, however, is that in making the choice to accept this primary vocation of civility, one's life becomes very different—much more constructive, more rich, more fulfilling. But it will not, as far as I can ascertain, be any easier. It would seem that in this regard, virtue is indeed its own reward.

I referred to civility as our primary vocation because in business we simultaneously have a number of secondary vocations. One of these, the most obvious, is a professional vocation. Am I called to be a homemaker, a lawyer, a scientist, an advertising executive?

Less obvious, perhaps, is the issue of one's vocation to a product. As a scientist, am I called to work on weapons development? As a lawyer, am I called to defend someone I suspect is guilty? As a gynecologist, do I or do I not peform abortions?

Less obvious still is the vocation to a particular organizational culture. Would it be a better 'vocational fit' for me to work in a business that is extremely hierarchical and structured, where there is little room for initiative but will always let me know where I stand? Or would I be better off with a company with a more 'lateral' structure, where creativity is encouraged but ambiguity is rampant?

Then there is the vocation to money and security. Am I being called to a lower-paying, more interesting job, or am I more called to support my family at a reasonable level of financial comfort? On the other hand, if I'm happy in my work, should I bypass an opportunity to make more money so that I can either save or give it away for the benefit of society?

These four different types of business vocations will be considered in turn, and it will be seen that they are often at odds with one another. Role conflict was touched upon in the last chapter. Here we shall see that, for the individual, vocational conflict is the greater problem.

And if all this were not enough, there is yet another vocational issue involved: the question of whether one has a calling to political power, to a leadership position in business. Some groundwork will be laid in this chapter with a brief discussion of management, but the vocation to power is such an important matter that it will be the entire focus of the next chapter.

Finally, underlying all these considerations will be the theme of our *primary* vocation to civility, with its emphasis on ethics. Both this chapter and the next will be filled with examples of ethical dilemmas the individual needs to face in his or her business life. There are no easy answers to these dilemmas. Wrestling with them raises a question: Is ethics the sole responsibility of the individual in the business world, or do business organizations themselves also have an ethical life? In other words, does God just call individuals to civility, or are organizations called to it as well? The answer is both. My belief is that organizations as a whole also have an obligation to be ethical. To understand the mechanics of how organizations can best fulfill that obligation, however, requires a deeper exploration of group dynamics and the different styles of behavior of collectives. This will be a subject for the concluding section, 'Community in the Workplace,' where the themes of adversarialism and ethics will be examined at a corporate level, that is, the level where organizations are considered in their functioning as a corpus, or single 'body.'

Most of what needs to be said about the issue of professional vocation was covered in chapter 7: the role that God may play in vocation in its literal sense; how individuals may resist a professional vocation: how society may force us into professions to which we are not called; humble as opposed to grand vocations, and the burden of a sense of destiny; the waste of vocational mismatches and the beauty of a true vocational fit.

The major subject not covered was the relationship between personality or temperament and professional vocation. The relationship is never cut and dried, but different types of people *tend* to go into law rather than medicine, just as there *tend* to be differences between those who seek MBAs and those who get M.Ed.'s. Such differences are generally even more striking within those broad professions. Psychiatrists *tend* to be a very different breed from internists, and internists from orthopedic surgeons. Someone who chooses the specialty of estate law is not likely to resemble the average professional litigation lawyer.

All this has given rise to a significant new career field: vocational testing and counseling. Such testing has become increasingly scientific and discerning, and vocational counselors more experienced. That said, as in my field, there are incompetent vocational counselors, moderately competent ones, and those who are truly excellent. The best are skilled psychotherapists. This is necessary because many who seek their services have a major underlying problem or resistance that has prevented them from discovering their proper vocations on their own. Moreover, as in the case of those who visit psychotherapists, many are looking for a 'magical' solution: they believe they will take a simple test that will point them to just the right job, and then they will be effortlessly happy ever after. It's not that easy. While they may misuse it in such a manner, I do not mean to imply that vocational counseling is overutilized by the general public. It is my impression, however, that good vocational counselors are *under*utilized by organizations. I believe they have a lot to offer managers in relation to issues of hiring, firing, promoting, and supervising employees.

So much for the individual engaged in the psychospiritual process of seeking her own vocation. What needs far greater focus at this point is the process of determining the vocation of others. I have already made it clear that this is a major responsibility of parents in relation to children. Now we will begin to see it as a major responsibility of executives in business. Much more than vocational counseling is required. For just as their narcissism so often interferes with parents' ability to assess their children with civility, so it also wreaks havoc in the world of business. For insofar as we fail to overcome our narcissism, it will preclude us from civilly appreciating how different we humans are and how much we need one another's different callings.

One of my teachers in this regard was a decade younger than I. Peter was a young enlisted man, a 'psych tech' who served under me in Okinawa. When I arrived at my new assignment, I found there were not nearly enough trained psychotherapists to meet the demand; yet a dozen of those twenty-year-old techs were sitting around. So I told them to start doing psychotherapy and I would provide them with on-the-job training. It was quickly apparent that half were not up to the job, and I set them to other tasks. But six had a natural talent for the role. One was Peter. For two years he served with distinction as a therapist. Then his enlistment was up and it was time for him to return home to the United States. As we were saying good-bye, I asked him about his plans. I was aghast when he told me he intended to start a milk distribution business. 'But you're a fine psychotherapist,' I exclaimed. 'I could help you get into a good master's program. Your GI bill would pay for it.'

'No thanks, my plans are set,' Peter firmly replied. But I persisted, outlining all the advantages of a career of a practicing psychotherapist. Finally, with an understandable edge to his voice, Peter silenced me by saying, 'Look, Scotty, can't you get it into your head that not everyone is like you, that not everyone with the opportunity *wants* to be a psychotherapist?'

As well as illustrating my own narcissism, the story demonstrates that just because someone has a talent for something doesn't mean she has a vocation to it. Secular vocational counselors know the best occupations for people are those in which their aptitude and interest coincide. But God is generous to many and bestows on them multiple gifts—interests as well as talents. The pattern of such gifts, however, is always unique to the individual. Each of us is created differently. I have gifts that you do not have. You have gifts that I do not have. And this is why we need each other.

Our common narcissistic failure to appreciate the separateness, the differentness, of others bedevils business life every bit as much as our family lives. I've already recounted how Ernie's and Angelo's failure to value each other's uniqueness fueled not only their transference but the costly conflict between their entire departments. Now let me give an example of the same sick dynamic at work in an even larger setting, creating a hateful and destructive schism within an entire profession.

I was tentatively asked not long ago to consult about a conflict between the two governing bodies of one of America's medical specialties. The 'American College' primarily represented the practitioners in the field while the 'American Academy' primarily represented its researchers. The memberships of both were composed of highly intelligent, extremely well educated, and supposedly civilized physicians. Yet the relationship between these 'sister' organizations had degenerated into marked incivility for over a decade.

I quickly learned that the practice of this specialty, on the frontiers of medicine, was much more of an art than a science. Those who belonged to the college and were treating patients on the front lines had to operate mostly by guesswork and intuition. It was no accident, therefore, that they were men and women not only accustomed to ambiguity but actually excited by it. Medical research, on the other hand, like all scientific research, requires extreme precision and clarity. By virtue of the ground-breaking nature of the specialty, this requirement was even more stringent than in other fields. Consequently, the members of the academy were women and men who hated vagueness and regarded ambiguity as their enemy.

After just two phone calls, I was able to ascertain that the major source of the conflict between the two organizations was the difference in the personality of their members. This extended even to their communication styles, which beyond any matter of substance seemed almost designed to antagonize the other. Failing to even acknowledge their different predominant personality types—much less appreciate the need for them—each body had come to assume that the other's hostility was malicious in intent. Unfortunately, both made the decision to not pursue reconciliation. Once hooked on conflict, many organizations, like individuals, would rather fight than switch.

Had these separate organizational bodies been willing to proceed with the consultation, they would have discovered that we now possess a distinct educational 'technology' to heal such unnecessary organizational conflicts. This technology will be the subject of the concluding section, 'Epiphany: Community in the Workplace.' For the moment, let me simply say it is a system of group learning techniques that cut through people's everyday narcissism, allowing them not only to see one another's differences but also to accept them. It is not painless learning, but it is effective. Through it people actually experience their mutual interdependence upon one another's gifts. They learn in their hearts what the Apostle Paul meant by 'mystical body' when he said:

Now there are diversities of gifts, but the same Spirit. . . . For to one is given by the Spirit the word of wisdom; to another the word of knowledge by the same Spirit; to another faith by the same Spirit; to another the gifts of healing by the same Spirit; to another the working of miracles; to another prophecy; to another discerning of spirits; to another diverse kinds of tongues; to another the interpretation of tongues . . . . For as the body is one, and hath many members, and all the members of that one body, being many are one body . . . for the body is not one member, but many.
   If the foot shall say, 'Because I am not the hand . . .' is it therefore not the body? And if the ear shall say, 'Because I am not the eye . . .' is it therefore not of the body? If the whole body were an eye, where were the hearing? If the whole were the hearing, where were the smelling? But now hath God set the members of every one of them in the body, as it hath pleased him. And if they were all one member, where were the body? But now are they many members, yet but one body. And the eye cannot say unto the hand, 'I have no need of thee'; nor again the head to the feet, 'I have no need of you.' . . . But God hath tempered the body together, having given more abundant honour to that part which lacked: that there should be no schism in the body; but that the members should have the same care for one another. And whether one member suffers, all the members suffer with it; or one member be honoured, all the members rejoice with it.[1]

Is it an accident, do you suppose, that we humans are created in such variety and called in so many divergent ways? How else should there be a society? We, the collective race, the body of humanity, need our practicing physicians and researchers, our executive and legislative branches, our marketers and salespeople, our farmers and steelworkers, priests and plumbers, authors and publishers, athletes and entertainers, prophets and bureaucrats. Yes, occasionally the threads may become a bit unraveled, but what a wonderfully variegated fabric we are!

[1] I Corinthians 12:14–26.

While nothing more need be said about professional vocations in general, much more deserves to be said about one profession in particular. This is the profession of management. There are many reasons to single it out for special attention.

First, it is generally the most powerful of professions. Indeed, it might be referred to as 'the profession of professions.' It is the manager who generally manages the other professionals. It is the manager whose decisions and behavior generally affect the most lives—thereby either enhancing or damaging those lives. Far more than anyone else, it is the manager who determines whether the organization will be a civil or uncivil institution.

Take the example of a hospital administrator. Although probably not as highly paid as the physicians, he is the one who does more than anyone else to manage them. And the nurses. And the laboratory technicians. And the physical therapists and respiratory therapists. And the cooks and the aides and the janitors, as well as interfacing with the cost commissions, the quality-of-care commissions, the certificate-of-need commissions, and so on. More than dozens of other people put together, he will be the one who determines the morale and quality of patient care within the hospital, and these factors will save or destroy more lives than any others.

The role of manager is the most complex and demanding of professions. Take it from someone who is on the inside. I can assure you that it is infinitely more difficult to be a good hospital administrator than it is to be a good physician.

Yet the profession of management is strangely denigrated in such settings. The demands and criticality of management are recognized within the private—for profit—sector in terms of salary and perks. But cross the line into the public or nonprofit sector and you'll find not only good hospital administrators paid less than mediocre physicians but also dedicated state commissioners of education paid less than mediocre lawyers—and forget the perks.

It is also denigrated in terms of training or education. Looking back on it, I am aghast at how the army could have sent me directly from my psychiatric training, where I had never managed anyone, to be the chief of a department where I had three dozen subordinates to manage without teaching me a single word about management. Yet my experience was not uncommon. Most people 'drift' into management, a fact to which we shall shortly return.

There is an explanation for this state of affairs. Management is the youngest of professions. Over a hundred years ago the traditional professions of medicine, divinity, law, and education were well established. But in a predominantly agricultural society most people worked alone or in small groups. There were very few large organizations to manage. A mere century later the vast majority of people were now employed by significant-sized businesses. Consequently, schools of business began to be established at most major universities. Nonetheless, there is still debate as to whether business should properly be considered a profession, and in these schools the teaching of management is, in my opinion, underplayed in favor of teaching marketing, accounting, production design, and similar subjects. To this day management not only continues to be considered more of an art than a science; many would question whether there is a science of management to teach at all.

They are wrong. As a tiny but telling example, I served a few years ago on a committee chaired by Will Clarkson, a retired corporation president, to search for a new president of a nonprofit organization. After we narrowed our field of candidates from two hundred to three, the time had come to check the references of those three. 'Of course, you know all about how to check references, Scotty,' Will said, 'but if you wish, I might offer a few suggestions.' As a psychiatrist, a student of human behavior, who had hired a few people and checked a few references in my time, I imagined myself sophisticated, but Janice, the other member of the committee, had never been in a position to hire. 'Sure, Will,' I said tolerantly, mostly for her sake, 'I'd be happy to hear any suggestions you have.' A half an hour later I'd taken two full pages of notes. I had not only learned, to my surprise, that there is a whole little science of ethical reference checking; within a few days I discovered just how well this science works.

It was not until the late 1940's that students of industry began to suggest that management might be recognized as a profession. They pointed out that skilled managers could competently lead a business regardless of its product. In other words, a successful chief executive officer of an airline might also make a successful CEO of a steel company. In earlier years top managers were those who had risen up through the ranks within a particular company or, at the very least, within the same industry. It had been assumed that the manager had to know the product from the ground floor up. But as the demand for talented top managers exceeded the supply, companies began to 'steal' them from different industries. Moreover, as companies began to diversify into multiple product lines, it became increasingly clear that management was more about managing people than products. Since this is so, the role of management requires complex skills that are transferable from one industry to another in 'the new industrial state.'[2]

Despite the fact that management is now at least something of a profession and a science, there is not much agreements as to what makes a great manager. Three reasons explain this state of affairs. One is contingency theory. Just as the best organizational structure is contingent upon the nature of the business, so is its leadership style, and a great manager of one company may not be able to switch her style that easily when she moves. Another reason is that management does remain an art as well as a science, and it is difficult to scientifically measure the softer, artistic talents of management such as vision or the capacity

[2] John Kenneth Galbraith, *The New Industrial State* (Boston: Houghton Mifflin, 1967).

to inspire. The most important reason, however, is that there is not yet any agreement as to what a business ought to *be*, beyond an organization that successfully markets a product. Does a business have an obligation to nurture its employees? This basic question has never been answered, much less the question of whether some ways of nurturing employees are superior to others. These are questions of 'corporate culture.' We shall see that the top manager is the primary determinant of the organization's culture, but our society to date encourages variety in business cultures far more than it does setting standards for them.

While there is no certified 'best' management style, nonetheless management is sufficiently a science, art, and profession as to represent a true vocation as well as occupation. In other words, God calls some people to be managers and definitely does not call others. A few of us are ideally suited to be managers. Most of us are ill-suited. And nowhere is the issue of vocation as critical as here.

It is so critical for two reasons. One is that management is a position of so much power. As indicated, the great manager can beneficially influence the lives of tens to tens of thousands of people. Conversely, the ill-suited manager can wreak havoc with similar numbers of lives. The position of management is a particularly potent locus of either civility or incivility.

The second reason is that management more than any other position is likely to draw the ill-suited into it simply by virtue of its power. One way this occurs is when, as is so often the case, people with an unbridled lust for political power seek positions of management for which, beyond their naked ambition, they are otherwise totally unqualified. Rather than being a profession they are called to, it is a position they abuse.

The even more common way is through mindless promotion within the organization. Most people drift into management as a consequence of seniority. Occasionally, it turns out to be a good fit. Usually, however, it tends to be a poor fit and one that is destructive not only for the business but also for the individual involved. This is the basis for the famed Peter Principle, which says that people are promoted to the level of their incompetence.[3]

The best thing that ever happened to Frank Francetta was the heart attack he had at age thirty-eight.

Frank and Rochelle had married young when they were both seniors in college. Rochelle immediately became pregnant and Frank went on to the state university to get a master's degree in electrical engineering. Although not wealthy, their parents supported both these decisions by taking out loans. They correctly discerned that Frank had a vocation to engineering and Rochelle to motherhood.

After he got his degree, they and their two children came to Connecticut, where Frank had lined up a job in a moderate-sized communications company. They were happy with their family life, their modest life-style, and his work. Loving this work and being very good at it, Frank rose to the position and title of senior engineer at the age of thirty-two, well ahead of his contemporaries.

But four years later things began to go sour. As the children entered their teens, Rochelle started to look ahead. 'Within five years both the kids will be ready for college,' she pointed out. 'We're in the income range where it will be hard for them to get scholarships or student loans. Yet it's the same range where it won't be easy for us to either get loans or pay them off. We've got to start saving more. Soon.'

She was right, of course. Frank assessed the situation. His salary was $41,000. Without a role change, the best he could hope for was to keep up with inflation. For a person in his position there were only two ways to move ahead. One would be to attempt to become a private technical consultant. The very best such consultants could make well over $100,000 a year. But most that he knew were scrambling—

[3] L. J. Peter and R. Hull, *The Peter Principle: Why Things Always Go Wrong* (New York: Bantam Books, 1969).

and ruining their family lives—just to stay even. Others had bombed out totally. The few who succeeded were not only those of high initiative but also gregarious types who seemed instinctively to know how to market themselves. Being on the shy side, Frank didn't think that he could make it.

The only other way was to move up into management. It was just sitting there waiting for him. Frank's boss, the director of the electrical engineering group—a gray, innocuous-seeming little bureaucrat past his prime—was retiring in nine months. The position was about to be posted. The salary began at $55,000. Even in the unlikely event he'd be turned down, Frank knew that at his young age he could get a similar position with another company. Just one thing held him back. His boss. The morale in the group was fine, yet the man seemed so colorless, just interested in pushing papers. But Frank set his doubts aside, applied for the job, and got it. He was about to begin his climb up the corporate ladder.

Within two months in the new position everything was a mess. The morale in the group plummeted. He couldn't make sense out of their complaints. Productivity dropped. The VP for engineering was hounding him daily. Deadlines and then more deadlines. Endless paperwork, which bored him to tears. The only pleasure was the challenge of understanding the technical details of the new projects assigned to the group. This took a mere hour a week, highlighting his yearning to be back actually working on those details. He envied the people he was now supposed to supervise. Frank was miserable.

The vice-president called him in for a conference. This time it was not about deadlines; it was about Frank himself and how poorly he was doing. The VP asked him all manner of strange questions for forty minutes, then leaned back in his chair with a pained expression. 'It's impossible for me to tell whether you're lacking talent for management,' he said, 'because it's clear that you don't even know anything about it to begin with. It's high time you went to school.' He set

Frank up for a weeklong course in St. Louis at the end of the month called 'Management; An Overview.' 'And that may be just the beginning,' the VP concluded. 'You'll probably need to take more focused and then more advanced courses.'

It was the most uncomfortable week of his life. Compensation and benefit packages. Competition, teamwork, inter-group rivalry. Strategic planning. Goal—and objective — setting. None of it had anything to do with engineering. It wasn't so much that he couldn't understand the material intellectually as it held absolutely no interest for him. From the beginning of the morning he had to struggle to keep his eyes open. He missed Rochelle and their home. But it was the final day on career development that took the cake. The professor lapsed into sermonizing, with an endless talk about how Jesus had said, 'Come with me and I will make you a fisher of men.' Frank had an antipathy to religion. He no longer even cared to understand. He felt lost in a fog at sea. That night, alone in a bar, he got seriously drunk for the first time in his life.

He lied to the vice-president when he returned, saying he'd enjoyed the course and would be attempting to put a number of the things he'd learned into action. But he was honest with Rochelle, confessing his boredom, his frustration and anxiety, even his despair. She tried to be consoling. 'Don't worry, honey, you're smart,' she said. 'I'm sure you'll get the hang of it before long.' That hardly helped. While he couldn't admit it yet, deep in his heart he knew that he really wanted out. Still he tried. He tried to do some 'team building' with his group, but it was a dismal flop, the morale dropping further. He knew the vice-president would be hearing their complaints.

Then, four days after his thirty-eighth birthday, Frank awoke at dawn with crushing chest pain. Rochelle, seeing his pallor and perspiration, instinctively knew what had happened and called the ambulance. Because of his age, modest cholesterol levels, and lack of family history of heart attacks, his internist queried him about stress. Frank acknowledged that he had been feeling under enormous tension. That was when I was called in. There was really nothing I need to do. I was concerned how Rochelle would respond to the financial aspects of the situation, but she'd already made the adjustment. 'If the kids want to go to college, they can go to State,' she said. 'They can get jobs if they're motivated enough, and maybe our parents can help out. It's not like we're starving. A heart attack is a heart attack, and I'd much prefer Frank to live doing what he likes than to die putting us in a higher tax bracket.'

Six weeks later Frank returned to work in his same company, but back in the position of senior engineer with a $13,000 salary cut. Not only his life but his soul was saved. He had no idea why anyone would ever *want* to be a manager except for the money, but thereafter he never envied a manager's income. And while he couldn't understand what made managers tick, he was now aware that management called for something more than ambition to get ahead. It obviously required mysterious talents he himself did not possess but which were clearly needed in the world.

Created differently, human beings are called to different professions or combinations thereof: law, medicine, engineering, management, and so on. But businesses are more than the professions involved. Lawyers, for instance, do not just work in law firms; many also work in government agencies, manufacturing corporations, and even in the nonprofit sector. Consequently, we not only have professional vocations but also have a calling (or lack of calling) to the product of a business. And just as some may sell their soul by working in a profession for which they do not have a vocation, so some tell their souls by working in a business that manufactures a product to which they have no calling.

Perched halfway up a mountainside, overlooking the vast expanse of the Rio Grande Valley, backed by pine forests and surrounded by sandstone canyons of glorious color, the town of Los Alamos, New Mexico, is one of the most beautiful places on earth. The climate is delightful. It may also be the best-educated little town in the world. Most of its many Ph.D's are scientists, and they have available to them the finest research equipment imaginable. Finally, as well as their own educated company, its citizens enjoy nice housing, good public education for their children, excellent benefits, and extraordinary job security. There is only one hitch: Most of them are in the business of manufacturing nuclear weapons of mass destruction.

They deal with the nature of their product in a variety of ways. A few deeply believe that the United States is the bastion of democracy, chosen by God to defend freedom in the world, and that the development of nuclear weapons is essential, even godly. For these people, thefore, the product is good—or at least good by virtue of being a necessary evil. A larger number more or less succeed in not thinking about the matter, at least not in ethical terms. For them nuclear weapons are neither good nor bad; they just are. Besides, it's not their role to pass judgment on a product that the government has adjudged worthy of manufacture. Others are uneasy with the product but believe their first loyalty is to their families. They have concluded that the evil of depriving their families of their satisfying life-style outweighs the evil of making nuclear weapons. Moreover, if they didn't do the job, somebody else would. Still others are attracted to the 'lab' to work with its superb equipment on research projects either unrelated to nuclear weaponry or focused specifically upon the peaceful uses of atomic energy. Weapons are just one of the lab's products, and because they work there on a different product they feel they have no relation to these weapons. In times of cutback, however, not a few such scientists have found themselves reassigned to bomb projects. And some decided they had to leave Los Alamos to save their souls.

I do not mean to imply that all—or even most—of those

who work at the lab in Los Alamos (or the laboratories at Oak Ridge or Livermore) are either unethical or uncivil. Nonetheless, there *are* ethical issues involved in nuclear weapons manufacture, and the level of rationalization in that place of seductive beauty does run high—not only among the employees, but also in the minds and souls of their spouses and their children.[4] And it is encouraged. Remember that civility and politeness are often at odds. One of the striking features of the Los Alamos 'community' is its orderly politeness. There is remarkably little talk about the ethics of the mission of the lab—indeed, remarkably little mention of 'the bomb' at all. Such talk, which would automatically challenge the rationalizations, is generally considered impolite, not in good taste. It is a sort of gentle, informal conspiracy of silence that encourages uncon- sciousness. 'You let me keep my rationalizations and I'll let you keep yours' seems to be the predominant unspoken norm of the culture.

I use Los Alamos simply because it is such a clear example of 'product vocation.' The same issues, the same dynamics and polite conspiracy, are rampant in the defense industries, defense-related businesses, and the government that spawns them. Nor is it simply a matter of weapons production. Similar dynamics are present in any industry with a questionably ethical product, and within any 'com- munity' supported by such an industry. Take the gambling industry, for instance. You would not be too kindly received by most of the citizenry of Las Vegas, Nevada, or Atlantic City, New Jersey, were you to initiate a discussion of the ethics of organized gambling.

[4] I also do not want to imply that no one at Los Alamos and similar sites deals with the issues in depth. J. A. H. Futterman, who works on the design of nuclear weaponry at the Livermore laboratory, for instance, has looked at them more squarely than anyone else I know (in an exciting, as yet unpublished manuscript currently entitled 'The Bomb and the Cross'). Indeed, it is my experience that people overtly in the public- sector business of war, such as those in such laboratories or in the military, tend to be relatively honest and open with themselves and their organizations, in comparison to those private-sector executives in the 'defense-related' part of the military-industrial complex.

I do not come at this matter from a high-minded position of moral superiority or with any sense that the ethical dilemmas involved are clear-cut. In 1962, entering my final year of medical school, I had to choose where to go next for training. At the time interns and residents in good civilian programs were paid a fraction of the minimum wage. The only decent training programs with a livable salary were offered by the military services as a trade for 'payback' time. Lily and I already had two young children. Even if I could have succeeded in begging sufficient support money from my parents, there would have been very thick strings attached. I was not a pacifist, but I did have real reservations about my country's potential to misuse war in fighting communism. McCarthyism was long since dead, however, and the truce in Korea had been stable for years. Vietnam, as far as I knew, was only an unimportant tiny country on the other side of the globe. Because I was a responsible family man, there seemed to be only one reasonable choice. Easily stilling my reservations, I entered the U.S. Army Medical Corps.

And I received excellent training. The only problem was that in 1965 I began to become seriously concerned about the inexorably escalating Vietnam War, and by late 1966, with a four-year army obligation ahead of me, I had decided that U.S. involvement in that war was evil. According to the criteria of those days, I could not obtain conscientious objector status. If I had refused my contractual obligation, I probably would have gone to jail. A few brave souls had already done just that, but they were simply hidden away and their voices lost. They also tended not to have families dependent upon them. Recognizing that it might be a cop-out, I nonetheless decided to be one of those who 'worked from within' against the war and for a military that would be more sane.

I did work hard within the system, even remaining in the army for more than two years beyond my obligation in order to do that work. I refused to buy 'voluntary' war bonds, fought against military racism, initiated a last-ditch attempt to forestall the all-volunteer army, sat on conscientious objector review boards, encouraged dissent among officers, pushed for a serious examination of My Lai, and occasionally 'blew whistles' or 'leaked' information to Congress. I also learned a good deal about administration and politics, about the inner workings of Washington, about the use and misuse of power, and about the 'psychiatry of government.'

By late 1972 I decided that the war in Vietnam was clearly coming to an end and there would be no further opportunities to be effective working from within. So I resigned. I look back on those years with gratitude for my training and all that I learned. It was a most valuable time in my development. But there is no way I can tell you with any certainty that it was not all a cop-out or that I had not sold at least a portion of my soul.

There are three types of relationships between vocations and business products: some have a vocation *to* a product, some a vocation *away* from a product, and some deal with a product that is 'vocation neutral' by virtue of the fact that it inspires neither a calling to it nor a calling away from it. The fact is that most people work for a business whose product is ethically or vocationally neutral. I have a friend, for instance, who is a top salesman for a company that manufactures electrical switches. Gregarious, intelligent, and energetic, I believe he does have a vocation to sales, but he would be the first to say he has no calling to the hardware he sells. 'Who the hell can have a calling to an electrical switch, except maybe the engineer who designed it?' he once asked rhetorically. 'I mean, it's useful, but it's not the only switch in the world. Three other companies manufacture ones that are pretty much the same as ours. If we went out of business, they'd happily produce more, and the world would be no worse off.'

Still, the fact that a product is ethically neutral does not relieve one from struggling with ethical issues. Let's say that my friend sells his switches not only to a manufacturer of pizza ovens but also to a manufacturer of intercontinental ballistic missiles. Or that the company that makes his switches also manufactures sighting mechanisms for machine guns that are exported to two nations currently at war with each other. Should my friend then have absolutely no ethical concern about his business?

Another type of problem arises when someone rejects a positive calling to work in a business with a vocationally neutral product. Suppose my switch-selling friend, also a dedicated hiker for many years, has been peripherally involved in the ecology movement. He is well educated about environmental issues. Knowing this and the fact that he is an accomplished public speaker as well as a forceful salesman, the Sierra Club seeks to employ him as a full-time environmental lobbyist at half his current salary.

My friend, at age fifty, is torn. 'I'm hardly essential where I am now,' he tells me. 'Any good salesman can sell switches just as well as I. If I quit, people would be battering down the door to get my job. The Sierra Club, on the other hand, does need me desperately. Not only that; I'd love to work for them. I'm sure I'd enjoy it much more than pushing switches. Besides, it would give me a deep feeling of satisfaction doing something I feel is so terribly important. But, my God, I'm averaging well over a hundred thousand dollars a year now. I'm paying alimony. I've just finished paying for the kids' college, so I've got no savings. I love my house. I love the swimming pool and the hot tub. The real estate market's down. If I went with Sierra I'd have to sell the house, and maybe even take a little loss on it. I've got enough in the company pension plan to take care of me in my old age. But if I quit now, I won't have a thing to leave my children. And I'd also have to quit a life-style I'm just beginning to be able to enjoy. I've worked hard. At my age I feel I'm entitled to have a little luxury in life.'

What should my friend do?

This has been a hypothetical example. I do not actually know the financial status of the Sierra Club. But if it is like most tax-exempt nonprofit service organizations dependent on charitable donations and membership dues, it probably has severely limited resources. Yet such organizations can get by paying lower salaries than the private sector just because there are some competent people willing to work in them for a monetary reward far below what their skills could otherwise command. This is because nonprofits usually deliver an ethically positive product, a product to which people feel actively called. Indeed, research shows that workers in the nonprofit sector demonstrate more satisfaction in and commitment to their jobs than those in the other sectors. Nonetheless, these competent men and women may have to make great financial sacrifice in responding to their calling.

As do families, businesses have myths, mottoes, and norms, secrets and lies, patterns of togetherness and separateness, and patterns of power. These are the interrelated organizational characteristics that in business are referred to as corporate culture. The culture of a business organization is less contingent upon its product than upon the personality or personalities of those few at the top.

I have had the opportunity for some years to observe simultaneously at close hand two businesses that manufacture and market the same type of product and hence are competitors within the same industry. I will call them Company X and Company Y. Having the same product, the structure of both companies is virtually identical. Yet their cultures—their organizational flavors, if you will—could hardly be more different.

At Company X one person's name is spoken far more frequently than the name of God, albeit with similar adulation or curses. It is the name of the president. He is the center of all power in the company. It would be impossible to imagine an organization being any more of a one-man show. Typical of such centralization of power, his management style is what is called 'autocratic.' He is more likely to consult with his lawyers than his own vice-presidents. Very seldom does he meet with any of his subordinates, singly or in groups, to be informed. His role with subordinates, as far as he is concerned, is to inform *them*. Often by criticism. Very seldom by praise. He secretly delights in the fact that his subordinates are afraid of him and openly subscribes to a philosophy of management by fear.

I have often thought of this company as having a corporate culture of sheer terror. The fear that pervades it has numerous effects. One is the extraordinary amount of politicking that goes on among the senior and junior executives as they jostle with each other for power and the president's favor. A second is the pervasive and subtle lying that the personnel seem to have developed almost into an art form in their effort to cover up mistakes. Once during a phone conversation, a junior executive apologized to me for the fact that a project would be delayed for two weeks because he was shortly going on vacation. Five minutes later I called him back. 'I want to thank you,' I told him. 'In nine years of working with Company X, this is the first time anyone in it has assumed any responsibility whatsoever for anything going even slightly wrong. It's not only clarifying, but it makes me feel good to know where things actually stand. Thank you!' He confessed how terrified he had felt in making the admission. Finally, Company X works largely by formula. There is little room for initiative. This is natural, since in an atmosphere of terror people *need* formulas to hold on to, to diminish the risks and to blame when things do go wrong. 'Well, we did it the way things were supposed to be done,' they can always say.

The corporate myth of Company X is 'We're the best in the business,' and its motto is 'Quality at all costs.' You can feel, even see, these in operation. The executives in Company X are known to be the highest paid in the industry. Its sales conferences are held in the most elegant of hotels. Office social events are catered by white-coated waiters with the best champagne flowing freely amid the popping of camera flashes. Even on the most ordinary of days there is a subtle sense of drama within the head-quarters' corridors, and people walk them quickly.

Although the architecture of the headquarters is identical, the atmosphere at Company Y is quite another matter. It gives off a 'laidback' feeling. People move more slowly. One does not have a sense of inefficiency, but the personnel are often working late. Indeed, they are frequently expected to work late—sometimes very late when there is a special project—even though their pay scale is just about average for the industry. Its sales conferences are conducted at hotels that are quite ordinary. Social events at the head-quarters are frequent but small and intimate—a group sitting around a table with their feet up and chicken sandwiches brought in from the local deli. There are never any photographers. It's quite relaxed.

The president of Company Y is seldom dramatically in evidence and not talked about as much as one might expect, although when he is, it is usually in terms of mild affection. His management style is primarily one of consultation, although at meetings he tends to take a backseat role to facilitate a high degree of participation. While he is a quiet man, slow to criticize, no one would call him a wimp. He can be quite firm at times, and he makes it clear that he expects loyalty. And generally he gets it.

The myth is 'At Company Y we're a community,' and its motto is 'Initiative will win out.' Both are observable. Relationships among coexecutives are friendly, usually comfortable, and remarkably uncompetitive. Although the whole industry tends to work by formula, Company Y is more likely than any other to deviate from the formulas and take risks. Sometimes these risks pay off dramatically. Others are mistakes, but mistakes are tolerated as an inevitable price for initiative and creative risk taking. The personnel of Company Y are far more honest and open, both with themselves and with the public, than those of

Company X. They readily and comfortably assume responsibility for things going wrong.

Which is better? Company X or Company Y? Frankly, at this point the question is unanswerable. Perhaps over the next decade the results will become more clear, but for the moment the profit margins of both are essentially the same. A significant number of talented executives desert Company X for Company Y, more than willing to accept a lower salary for a relaxed and companionable workplace. Yet an equally significant number of talented executives leave Company Y, attracted by the higher salaries and glamour of Company X.

While the answer to the question 'What is the best corporate culture for the production of a particular product?' is unclear, what is clear is that there can be vastly different cultures within the same industry, and that some individuals feel called to one type and some to the other. This means that as organizational creatures we human beings are not only called to particular professions and to identify ourselves with a particular product, but that we also have (or do not have) a vocation to the particular culture of the business in which we work.

How do we decide what kind of culture we are called to? The question is important. By the age of seventeen adolescents need to make decisions about which college they wish to attend. The rightness or wrongness of those decisions will be determined by the culture of the college of their choice. Often that choice is wrong. For the most part, our choices of cultural vocation are made by trial and error over the years. In fact, it may not be possible to adequately assess the culture of a particular institution, either as a student or an employee, until well after you have chosen to immerse yourself within it, even though the choice will make the difference between whether you will flourish or whether you will be miserable.

Still, there is the guideline of civility. If civility is of no importance to you, forget it. But if it is, remember civility has much to do with consciousness, with awareness as well ethics. A civil institution would not consciously promote myths or mottoes that substantially deviate from reality. Of the two businesses I described, Company X, while not necessarily any less successful, is, I believe, the less civil. It is not merely a matter of fear versus trust. It also has to do with honesty and the integrity of its myths and mottoes. The myth of Company X, 'We're the best in the business,' is not borne out by reality. Company Y's profit margin is equally good. Indeed, should Company Y's profit margin begin to exceed it, then if Company X continued to proclaim a myth of 'We're the best in the business,' it would be proclaiming an arrogant delusion. 'Quality at all cost,' the motto of Company X, is also questionable. Although the more ostentatiously lavish, no evidence supports the claim that the quality of its products is any higher than that of Company Y. The myths and mottoes of Company Y, on the other hand, do seem fairly realistic. It does encourage initiative among its employees, and its coexecutives do relate to one another with an unusual degree of friendliness and lack of competitiveness. Even here, however, there are faint discrepancies. Although the myth of Company Y is 'We're a community,' I have observed that there is a substantial social gulf between the senior and junior executives, whom the seniors in Company Y treat as underlings just as much as they do in Company X.

One can examine the degree to which a company's myths and mottoes conform to reality as opposed to the extent to which they are just so much 'hype.' If someone becomes practiced in doing so, it can actually become a rather simple matter to pick up quickly on the myths and mottoes of a business and assess their integrity with an interview or two before accepting or rejecting a company change. It's a nice skill to develop. It's very unpleasant—and sometimes impossible—to be a vocational cultural misfit. On the other hand, when one moves into just the right corporate environment, she will likely find her soul flowering, as if she were literally in the sunshine.

Frank Francetta moved into a management position for which he was not suited because he wanted to start saving money for his children's education. My friend, the switch salesman, was rejecting a hypothetical calling to environmental work because of the loss of money it would entail. I silenced my doubts about military policy in accepting army training for a livable wage. Executives often leave the friendly culture of Company Y for the higher salaries of Company X. Money, money, money!

It's a huge issue, this frequent conflict between vocation and money. The great story about it is that of the rich young man whom Jesus called to be a disciple saying, 'Sell all that you have, give it to the poor and follow me.' But the young man rejected the call because he had 'great possessions.'[5]

This story has been taken by some as a vocation to radical financial poverty. And there is no question in my mind that God does indeed call some people to a poverty of possessions. Albert Schweitzer and Mother Theresa are the most famous examples in this century.

I do not believe, however, that God calls everyone—or even most of us—to radical poverty. If I am wrong, I have certainly missed the boat. Perhaps it has been another copout on my part, but as time and again I have searched my heart in this regard, I have not heard within it any vocation either to personal poverty or to poverty work. To the contrary, the still small voice inside me seems to be saying, 'Do not feel reluctant to enjoy fine hotels and resort vacations. Celebrate these gifts. They nurture you in the work you do. Otherwise, live modestly as you communicate with the upper middle class. Don't try to work with the poor. You don't know how to do it, and you're no good at it. Leave it to others who were made for it. You were designed to speak to the well educated who labor under the burdens of their estrangement or selfrighteousness.'

The story of Jesus and the rich young man is often

[5] Matthew 19:16–22.

284

interpreted not so much as a message about the virtues of poverty as a statement about the dangers of security. In this interpretation the young man was unwilling to relinquish his great possessions because of the security they represented. And here I feel myself on firmer ground, for I am deeply familiar with the dangers of security and they are enormous.

I use the word 'dangers' rather than 'evils' because we *need* a certain amount of security. Children must have a steady supply of basic goods and services and stable emotional support if they are not to grow up with debilitating scars. As adults, we must have the same if we are to venture forth beyond a simple survival mode. In 1974 my father made us a gift that allowed us to pay off our mortgage and have some savings to boot. It is, I suspect, no accident that the very next year I began to cut back on my practice of psychiatry so as to begin work on my first book. Had it not been for the security he had given me, I am not at all sure I would have had the freedom to follow my vocation as a writer.

The problem, however, is where to draw the line. Security can become an addiction, and there are many for whom enough is never enough. I have a friend, Bart, a highly successful businessman whose net worth is close to fifty million dollars. Yet he is a poor philanthropist. He gives away very little of his wealth, and then under stringent conditions. His life-style is frenetic as he continues to make deals around the globe to amass an ever-greater fortune. It was some time before I realized that as far as he was concerned, in his mind the wolves were always at the door. 'Stagflation,' Bart would exclaim to me, 'it's likely right around the corner. It would wipe you out within a month.' You may think this laughable. You may think that if only you had just one million dollars in the bank, you would feel totally secure. Yet I can virtually assure you that were you fortunate enough to get to that point, questions would continue to arise. What about my old age? What if I became ill right now? What about the children's future? What if the bottom should fall out of the economy?

I do not think there is anything wrong in making money. Indeed, I think God calls some people to make great sums. Like Bart, who is a born businessman and deal maker. My criticism of him relates only to what he does with it once he's made it. He is not alone in his stinginess. The wealthiest segment of Americans gives away to charity a smaller portion of their income (approximately 2.1 percent) than does the middle or working class (approximately 2.8 percent). Because of their great wealth, the total they donate is greater, but the percentages are a telling commentary on the spiritual impoverishment of most who are financially rich. They mean that, on average, those for whom it is the easiest, the least painful, to give are the least likely to do so. The statistics are even more telling when one considers the fact that some of the very wealthy routinely give away half of their income. When you figure this into the averages, it means that most of the wealthy don't give away anything at all.[6]

If we come into money, God calls us to manage it. And the management of money is almost as complex and demanding a task as the management of people—and often related. One needs to learn about investing. The soul needs to be searched as to motives, as to just how much security is enough. Hard decisions must be made as to what to reinvest and what to give away. And then, if you become a significant philanthropist—a wonderful calling—you will find your problems have only begun. To whom and what should you give your money away? With what kind of strings? How do you give it in a manner that will empower rather than sap initiative? What are your responsibilities to assist in the management of the charitable organizations to which you make larger donations? When and how do you withdraw your support? I believe my multimillionaire friend's behavior lacks civility because he has largely ducked these hard issues. There is infinitely more to management than

[6] Douglas M. Lawson, *Give to Live* (La Jolla, Calif.: ALTI Publishing, 1991), p. 11.

hoarding. Good management, whether it be of people or money, always requires giving and serving. I do not believe Bart has been the good manager of money that God has called him to be.

Whole books can be written about the dangers of addiction to security—emotional, intellectual, and social as well as financial security. One, in fact, has specifically been written about it in relation to business, *The Addictive Organization*.[7] In it the authors only touch on an issue that I believe needs far more serious examination in our society: pension plans. There are a large variety of such plans, and often they are very sensible and appropriate. Many government agencies and other businesses, however, 'give' their employees only plans that require from them an extraordinary amount of service time before they can ever collect any of their vested monies. These plans are deliberately designed to encourage employee retention. The problem is that they also frequently encourage employee stagnation.

At age forty-five, Sarah is a top-level 'career' program designer for a large state department of education. She has been in the department for fifteen years and currently earns $53,000 a year. Divorced and raising an adolescent daughter, she needs almost every penny of it. The executives above her are all political appointees. For the most part she has been happy in her highly creative job and has won some national recognition in the field. Recently, however, there has been a political change in administration. Her new managers have a conservative philosophy that leaves little room for innovative program design. They are also threatened by Sarah's competence and popularity and have responded by burdening her with bureaucratic red tape. The situation is certain to continue for the next four years and probably for at least eight. Knowing she has begun to feel highly stifled, colleagues in other state education departments have offered her jobs at a similar salary that

7 Anne Wilson Shaef and Diane Fassel, *The Addictive Organization* (San Francisco: Harper & Row, 1988).

would make use of her creativity. Sarah is quite willing to move. There is only one problem: her pension plan. The plan of her state pays a pension of fifteen percent of base pay for those employees who retire with between ten and twenty years of service, fifty percent for those who retire between twenty and thirty years of service, and seventy-five percent for those who put in thirty or more years. If she moves to another state that can use her talents, Sarah will receive a pension of approximately $600 per month. If she can stick it out in her dead-end job for another five years, she'll get roughly $2,000 per month. Amortized to age seventy, the discrepancy in total benefits received over the years is between $180,000 if she leaves now and $480,000 if she waits. Essentially, by moving where she is more needed and would be happier, she would probably be throwing away $300,000—the equivalent of six years' earnings.

Because she is painfully aware of these figures, having consulted a reputable accountant, Sarah has decided to stick it out. Only her soul seems to be shriveling. And her body. Her periods have become irregular. Probably it is just slightly early menopause, but in checking on it her gynecologist tells her for the first time that she has a highly questionable Pap smear. She has also developed eczema, a highly uncomfortable, itching rash on her hands and forearms, a condition she has never had before. Sarah is determined to believe she has undergone an attitude change, that she has a more mature outlook in relation to her work and is comfortable now simply putting her hours in. Yet her friends tell her they are worried about her, that she seems to have lost her customary liveliness. In fact, for some months she has not been sleeping well.

What would Sarah do? You might say it is her problem alone. And I do think it is proper that one should exercise a certain amount of risk in responding to a vocation. The willingness to take a risk is one of the tests, the criteria, of a true vocation. But this much risk? I also think Sarah's problem is society's problem, that something is wrong with a society that creates organizations that routinely practice such subtle economic enslavement.

Certainly there needs to be a balance between the needs of the individual and those of the organization. The organization may say, 'Look, the fact that we have a pension plan at all indicates our concern for the individual employee and his security upon retirement.' But there is an enormous difference between an early- and a late-vestment plan. The latter costs a business nothing in the short run. It encourages the heinous but common practice of laying off employees just prior to the point that they become vested. Finally, it is actually not in the best interest of the business itself. Yes, late-vestment plans can encourage retention of employees such as Sarah, but it is a sick kind of retention. Do you want to retain employees who are called to thieir work or simply those who are economically trapped in their position? Are there not more creative means of retention such as sabbaticals, career development plans, and, above all, the kinds of caring personnel management that create attractive work environments where people stay because they enjoy their work, they enjoy the culture, and they feel useful?

Late-vestment pension plans, for the most part, not only oppress the individual employees involved but also the organization as a whole by encouraging the retention of 'deadwood.' It is a responsibility of managers to look at this problem. What might be done to change the system? Quite possibly the lawyers will say that it is next to impossible to change. But managers have to decide when to be dictated to by lawyers and when to use their lawyers to discover the way to accomplish management's vision. The best management is the difficult art of system change; the worst management is the easy acceptance of system stagnation. I believe that the development of civil 'portable' pension plans and options is possible. Conversely, I believe that late-vestment plans are a variety of institutionalized organizational incivility.

I do not mean to imply that the responsibility for such

system change belong solely to the business and its management; it belongs equally to even the lowest-paid individual employee. The individual either has or does not have a vocation to a particular corporate culture, and the company pension plan is part of that culture. Ideally, one should understand that plan before he accepts employment if he has any notion of a career within the organization. Certainly, once he has joined, he should quickly make it his responsibility to learn about the plan in depth. He shouldn't wait fifteen years, as so many do, and then suddenly wake up to the fact that, like Sarah, he is trapped. I am not saying one should never join a business with a late-vestment plan — only repeating, in a very specific way, the rule that 'You gotta know your business.'

And I do strongly suggest that if your employment is hooked into a late-vestment plan, you should start early to adjust your life accordingly. Save as much money as you possibly can so that your pension is not your only nest egg. Vow to forsake it if you are called elsewhere. You have no power if you are not free to quit your job. Don't find yourself in a position where you feel financially compelled to betray yourself, if not God. Remember that your primary vocation is to yourself and what God wants of you; it should not be to your pension.

16

May God Have Mercy on You

The Civil Use of Power in Business

Power—the capacity to influence others—is almost by definition the most *potent* factor in organizational behavior. Incivility might simply be described as the misuse of power. Indeed, the ultimate goal of this book is to promote the civil use of power.

The distinction has been drawn between spiritual power —the capacity to influence others by the loveliness of one's being—and political power—the capacity to influence others by one's memory or dominant organizational position. This chapter is about key aspects in the integration of these two types of power. It focuses on managers, the ones who possess the bulk of political power in business. Its thesis is that the spiritually incompetent manager will, inevitably, abuse her power. Consequently, its subject, the civil use of power in business, is the subject of management as a high spiritual calling.

There is debate these days about when and whether to employ the term 'leader' in place of manager. Without going into the various pros and cons, I will use the terms interchangeably. But Robert K. Greenleaf has been one of the most influential writers on the subject of management over the past generation through his elaboration of the concepts of 'the servant leader' and 'servant leadership.' He describes the servant leader as he who primarily serves and leads secondarily. Or she who regards the essence of her leadership role to be one of servanthood. Greenleaf and I are in agreement that the civil manager must be a servant leader, and that the art of civil management is that of servant leadership.[1]

While Greenleaf doesn't do this, his term servant leadership calls up the Christian notion of 'the sufficient servant.' What he does do, however, is distinguish between two types of servant leaders. Both feel called to power and fulfilled by its exercise. Beyond this they differ. One enjoys crises and the experience of living on the brink of exhaustion. The other finds crises sapping and lives in fear of the depletion of his or her own emotional resources. Without making any distinction between their effectiveness, it is clear that the latter type suffers the more in her leadership role. Insofar as I myself am a servant leader, I clearly belong to this latter type. I have no doubt that my personality affects what follows in this regard. For while I see glory in the role, it does not seem to me an easy glory, and I shall consistently speak of the suffering the civil manager needs to bear in the exercise of her vocation. May God have mercy on you.

I shall use the words *power* and *authority* synonymously. Defined as the capacity to influence, power is therefore the capacity to make things happen. Authority is literally the capacity to author matters, that is, also to make things happen. To have political authority is to be in charge, in a position on top, where one can make things happen.

There are those who have a naked lust for power, who yearn for authority for its own sake, without any desire to serve. As noted, they will abuse power. Since God calls us to civility, can we think of such people as having a vocation to power? Possibly, but then we must ask whether their calling might not come instead from the devil. More likely, however, it is not a calling but a compulsion to compensate

[1] See *The Servant Leader* and other literature available from The Robert K. Greenleaf Center, 1100 West 42nd Street, Suite 321, Indianapolis, Indiana 46208 (telephone and fax 317/925-2677).

for some deep impotence, some hidden wounds from their childhood, some terrible deprivation they once suffered.

Then there are others who may have a genuine vocation to civil power but reject the calling from fear of exercising authority. In my practice of psychotherapy I saw two types of such fear—sometimes in the same patient.

One type is rooted in the fear of arrogance. It is quite common. At least ten percent of my patients had to struggle to come to terms with their superiority. Jane was a typical case in point. She was a brilliant and beautiful young student in the second year of business school who had come to see me because of irritability. Her dates were dull. Her professors seemed pompous. Her fellow students, even the women, struck her as remarkably limited and unimaginative. She had no idea what the problem was, but she was smart enough to know that something was wrong about living in a state of constant annoyance. After several sessions going over the same old ground, she exclaimed in exasperation, 'I feel that all I'm doing here is whining. I don't want to be a whine.'

'Then you'll need to learn how to accept your superiority,' I retorted.

'My *what?*'

'Your superiority.'

'What do you mean?' Jane was dumbfounded. 'I'm not superior.'

'All your complaints—your whining, if you will—center around your probably accurate assessment that your dates aren't as smart as you, your professors aren't as humble as you, and your fellow students aren't as interesting as you,' I pointed out. 'In other words, all your unhappiness relates to the fact that you feel—and probably are—superior to most people.'

'But I don't want to feel superior,' she exclaimed with a touch of desperation. 'That's the point. I shouldn't feel superior. Everyone's equal.'

'Are they?' I arched my eyebrows. 'If you believe everyone

293

is equally as smart as you, then you're bound to be chronically irritated when people prove themselves not to be as smart. If you believe everyone is equal, you're going to expect everyone to be as intelligent, as humble, as adventurous, as ambitious as you yourself are, and then you're going to be constantly disappointed with them when they don't live up to your expectations.'

The weeks that followed were ones of excruciatingly hard work for Jane, although tinged with the excitement of grudgingly sensing she was on the right track. It was so much easier being ordinary. It was so safe. How could she accept her superiority and not succumb to arrogance? Not become mired in self-righteousness? If she really was superior, was she not then doomed to a life of loneliness? And if she was not ordinary—if she was, in fact, extra-ordinary—why? Why her? Why was she singled out, chosen or cursed?

I never answered these questions for her. But it was reassuring for her that I acknowledged that they were very real and very important questions. Gradually, she came to accept that she was not ordinary, that she was both chosen and cursed, blessed and burdened.

Had Jane stayed my patient, it is likely that in a few years, civil person that she was, she would have consulted me with a slightly different set of fears. This set most normally occurs in those who have accepted their superiority in some major dimension and have already specifically felt the call to power, but are afraid to follow it for fear of abusing their authority. Knowing that power tends to corrupt, it is a fear for their own souls. Also knowing the strength of their wills, it is even more the fear of the harm they might cause by making the wrong decisions affecting others.

There is a famous and remarkably condensed story about these fears and their reality. It demonstrates, among other things, how realistic it is for those with a true vocation to civil power to feel reluctant:

And Jesus, when he was baptized, went straightaway out of the water: and lo, the heavens were opened unto him, and he saw the Spirit of God descending like a dove, and lighting upon him: and lo a voice from heaven, saying, 'This is my beloved Son, in whom I am well pleased.'

Then was Jesus led up of the Spirit into the wilderness to be tempted of the devil. And when he had fasted for forty days and forty nights, he was hungered. And when the tempter came to him, he said, 'If thou be the Son of God, command that these stones be made bread.' But he answered and said, 'It is written Man shall not live by bread alone, but by every word that proceedeth out of the mouth of God.'

Then the devil taketh him up into the holy city, and setteth him on a pinnacle of the temple, and saith unto him, 'If thou be the Son of God, cast thyself down: for it is written, He shall give his angels charge concerning thee: and in their hands they shall bear thee up, lest at any time thou dash thy foot against a stone.' Jesus said unto him, 'It is written again, Thou shalt not tempt the Lord thy God.'

Again, the devil taketh him up into an exceeding high mountain, and sheweth him all the kingdoms of the world, and the glory of them; and saith unto him, 'All these things will I give thee, if thou wilt fall down and worship me.' Then saith Jesus unto him, 'Get thee hence, Satan: for it is written Thou shalt worship the Lord, thy God, and him only shalt thou serve.'

Then the devil leaveth him, and behold, angels came and ministered unto him. . . . From that time Jesus began to preach.[2]

To me it is clear that Jesus went into the desert to wrestle with the problem of authority. In being baptized by John, he is essentially told by both John and God that he is the Messiah. 'Me, the Messiah?' he must have asked himself. 'Where do I come off being the Messiah? I'd better go off alone and think this one over.'

So into the wilderness he went to face the issues. They were three. The first was the temptation to use power for food—for money and security. The second was to use it for what I call 'spiritual flashiness.' The third was to use it for the pleasure and glory of rulership. And then, having

[2] Matthew 3:16–17; 4:1–11,17.

rejected these temptations, having *emptied* himself of all ambition, he immediately came out of that empty place to preach *full of* godly authority.

There are many morals to this story.

Having been designated as the Messiah, Jesus could have gone right to work. Instead, he immediately went off on a spiritual retreat. I believe the civil manager will do likewise in some form or fashion. She will accept any promotion with sufficient trepidation to ask from the start, 'What will be the temptations, the issues, that I will need to deal with in this new position?' One of the requirements for the conscious-ness civility demands is that we face the issues as quickly as possible, and hopefully before taking action. Granted that not all the issues can be predicted in advance, I suggest that one of the characteristics of the uncivil manager is that he will remain oblivious to the issues well past the point they could have been discerned. I have already linked civility with contemplation, pointing out that the contemplative life-style is one dedicated to maximum awareness or consciousness. As the stakes escalate with power, such awareness becomes all the more critical. The civil manager must be something of a contemplative.[3]

It will be recalled that in Chapter 8 the essence of contemplation and contemplative prayer was designated as emptiness. There it was explained that the reason for the contemplative to empty himself was not to have a perma-nently empty mind but to make room for the new to come in. So I just spoke of Jesus emptying himself of ambition so that he could be, depending upon how you look at it, either full of godly authority or an empty vessel for God's spirit and wisdom. In any case, another moral of the story is that the

---

[3] Thomas J. Peters and Robert H. Waterman, in *In Search of Excellence* (New York: Harper & Row, 1982), found in studying managers that they tend to have a 'bias' for action, but Donald Schon supports my thesis in his book, *The Reflective Practitioner* (New York: Basic Books, 1983).

civil manager must ultimately empty himself of ambition. This is tricky. Those who have a vocation to power are naturally ambitious people. God would not call someone to leadership without giving him at least some taste for power. But before he can assume a position of leadership with full civility, the manager must refine this taste mightily. Defining ambition as the thirst for power for oneself, for one's own sake, he must then strip it away until all that if left is the thirst to be of service to others. Only then will the manager have become a true servant leader.

Still another moral is that the temptations Jesus faced nearly two thousand years ago in the desert are temptations universal to power. In order to be civil, the manager of the late twentieth century—and for every century to come — must efficiently resist each one of them. Indeed, they are so specific, so very real, as to form the framework for the bulk of this consideration of power in business. I now turn to them in their biblical order.

The first of the temptations was to turn stones into bread. Why on earth should Jesus have refused to do so? After all, he was hungry. What is wrong with a hungry man feeding himself? In fact, I don't think the story makes much sense unless it is interpreted symbolically. I see the issue here not as mere relief from the pangs of hunger, but total relief from the fear of starvation. The fear of starvation is very primitive, very basic. Remember my friend, Bart, whose net worth was close to fifty million dollars and yet who felt that the wolves were at the door, that starvation was potentially around the corner. Money for him clearly represented security that he would not starve, that he would never have to be out in the cold, that he wouldn't be without. But for Bart, as for all of us on some level if we admit it, the temptation of security is that there can never be enough of it. Bread, or food, is a symbol for money, which is a symbol for the sense of security that can come from power. In refusing to turn stones into bread, I believe that Jesus was symbolically rejecting security or his attachment to the illusion of security.

The subject of the temptation of security was addressed in the previous chapter in relation to money, and it was seen to be filled with ambiguity. We need a certain amount of security of some kind as a springboard from which to venture forth. Sarah's dilemma of whether or not to reject her pension was painfully real. I did not propose any easy answers. But here in this chapter, focusing on political power, I can be unambiguous. There is a profound tendency when one attains a position of high power in business to be terrified of losing it and, hence, a profound temptation to sacrifice one's integrity in order to hold on to it. As far as I am concerned, a prime rule governing the civil use of power in business is: 'Forget about job security!'

It is a strange rule in much of the world's eyes, but then Saint Paul essentially referred to Satan as the ruler of '*this* world.'[4] The majority would see the essence of 'the power game' as being a kind of popularity contest in which it is more important to do what is popular or 'politic' than what is right. The point of the game is to keep your position against competitors or, better yet, win an even higher one. The point is power for its own sake. The point of civility, however, is power for the opportunity to be of service.

In saying I am unambiguous in this regard, I do not mean that the civil manager should give no heed to popularity or never even make the slightest compromise in the interest of the greater good. But the capacity to rise above temptation is the essence of freedom. One is simply not free to serve, to do the right, when one gives in to the temptation to stay in power; that is, when it becomes a compulsion to do whatever is most popular. In order to be free to do the unpopular upon occasion, the civil manager must be prepared to quit her position or be fired at any moment.

[4] Ephesians 6:12

In a similar vein, the good manager must be an expert at collaboration, at working gently with other managers and other departments toward consenus. On the other hand, on relatively rare ocasions, the civil manager must be prepared not only to stand up and be counted, but to stand up alone, to take the minority position even to the point of starting very clearly and dictatorially, 'This is the way it's going to be.'

Let me use a hero and mentor of mine, Major General John Milton 'Micky' Finn, as an example. It was 1968 when he was the commanding general of Okinawa. Just as I was leaving my office one evening, the clinic secretary came running to say, 'General Finn wants you down at the stockade immediately. Now. There's some kind of emergency there.'

I arrived to find Micky sitting at a makeshift desk in the entrance hall of the stockade surrounded by a horde of clamoring officers, most of whom outranked me. A group of firemen and a SWAT team were waiting to the side. Five black prisoners were holding a white prisoner hostage in a cell. The leader had managed to embed a razor blade into a toothbrush and was holding it at his white cellmate's throat, threatening to cut it if his demands weren't met. No one seemed clear what the demands were.

Gradually, the situation was clarified. Six weeks before, there had been a massive riot at the Long Binh Jail (the LBJ) in Vietnam. The army tried to keep secret the fact that it had primarily been a racial riot. Okinawa had been directed to receive a shipment of sixty 'overflow' prisoners from the LBJ but had not been informed that these men were all black and mostly militant ringleaders of the riot. Unprepared for the problem, discipline had rapidly deteriorated in the stockade after their arrival. The stockade commander tried to take care of the problem himself without asking for help. His stereotypical response had been to place the troublemakers in disciplinary segregation. But as of the preceding evening, the dozen segregation cells were all filled and there were still more troublemakers to be dealt with.

Overnight, the stockade administration had obtained ten Conex containers and placed them in the exercise yard to serve as extra segregation cells. These were six-by-six-by-ten-foot metal boxes used for shipping furniture and other kinds of nonperishable goods. The stockade guards had punched holes in the sides of the containers so the prisoners would have sufficient air and had placed a mattress at the bottom of each. Over the course of the day, they had begun to put some of the black prisoners into them.

It emerged that the demand of the blacks was the removal of the Conex containers. They stated that the containers were for things, not people. They also believed the guards would pump poison gas into them, that the use of the containers was the first step in a program of racial extermination. The prevailing reaction of the authorities present was disbelief and distrust. Everyone knew there was no plan of racial extermination. It was absurd. The prisoners had to have some other, hidden agenda. As the psychiatrist, I pointed out that the unrealistic nature of this belief was no reason to question its intensity, that their vision of extermination was real for them and their paranoia should be taken seriously. Someone made a joke about how psychiatrists were known to be weird. There was a moment of levity.

It also emerged that there were regulations governing the size, ventilation, temperature, and lighting of disciplinary segregation cells. The Conex containers did not conform to any of them. For most, this seemed a minor issue indeed. The real issue to them was the maintenance of control. Giving in to the prisoners' demands would totally undermine the authority of the guards and their officials. The commander of the SWAT team opined a ninety percent probability that his men could shoot the ringleader, and any of the other blacks if necessary, without harming the white hostage.

Micky asked for recommendations.

The only black present at the meeting—a low-ranking

young sergeant—jointed me in my prophecy that if General Finn were to give in to the demands he would immediately have to deal with a rebellion on the part of the guards. Nonetheless, the two of us advised that he accede and remove the Conex containers from the stockade. The thirty others there—mostly senior officers—advised that the issue of maintaining control was paramount. They recommended the SWAT team be used to crush the insurrection.

Micky looked around the room. 'Get rid of the containers,' he ordered.

It was ten-forty in the evening. At eleven, the time of their change of shift, a delegation of sixteen guards requested permission to address him. He gave it. The delegation spoke of the abuse the guards had been receiving for weeks, of the fear that they had to live with, and of how his caving in to the prisoners had now made their extremely difficult job impossible. They were eloquent.

Then, very quietly, Micky talked to them about courage and honor, about leadership and loneliness, duty and responsibility, about good and evil, right and wrong, about liberty and American history, about strength and weakness, and the risks and the costs of being humane. Just before midnight the delegation saluted him smartly and returned to their posts.

The weeks that followed were difficult, but no blood was shed and further crises were averted. Had that not been the case, however, what might have happened to Micky Finn for taking the advice of two and rejecting that of thirty?

To 'catch-22' situations psychiatry has given the term 'double bind'—situations where you're damned if you do and damned if you don't. The implication is that these situations shouldn't occur. Indeed, one of the tasks of civil parents is to be sufficiently conscious that they don't put their children in such predicaments just as it is a job of civil managers to see to it that double binds are not created by a mindless bureaucracy. But life has a way of creating double binds, as it did that evening for General Finn. While children and employees should be protected from them as far as possible, parents and middle managers must face them from time to time. And they are the bread and butter of top management. Top managers are not paid to make easy decisions; they are paid to make the difficult ones, those that put their jobs on the line every day. The higher you rise in the power structure, the more double binds you are asking for.

There are two ways to play these agonizing situations. They cannot be played successfully with the intellect. All the intellect will see is the double bind, and paralysis—not leadership—will be the result. They need to be played according to the heart. By the time a person reaches a position of top management, her heart will either belong to her personal ambition or to a Higher Power. If to ambition, then her primary consideration will be the politics of the situation, her popularity, and what is most likely to make her look good so as to preserve or enhance her position and its power. If her primary allegiance is to a Higher Power, it will be to what is 'right.' This does not mean she will give no consideration to politics or that what is right will be clear; it is a matter of the primary orientation of her instincts. Micky Finn retired with two stars on his shoulders. I know enough about his lengthy career to believe he would have retired with four had he been a little less good, a little less civil.

The story of Micky and me illustrates another minor point. In even the most hierarchical of organization, there is always an invisible power structure of some sort as well. It may be a kingmaker in the background, some seemingly anonymous person behind the scenes. In this case, for a year and a half I was perhaps Micky's closest adviser, even though a hundred higher-ranking officers were between him and me in the hierarchy. Our relationship gave me, a very young major, extraordinary influence on the affairs of Okinawa. But when Micky was reassigned to the United States a year ahead of me, I became persona non grata overnight. All those other officers, naturally jealous of my unofficial power, immediately closed ranks against me. I couldn't even get through the new commanding general's door. My power was very temporary.

Which is as it should be. In contradistinction to spiritual power, which is an attribute of the immortal soul, we refer to political power as 'temporal'—time linked, temporary, fleeting. It is proper that we should concern ourselves with bread and see to it that our families have the security of food on the table and a roof over their heads. But to be civil, we need also look to our spiritual lives. And anyone who has come to identify political power with his security, who must cling to it at all costs, has become addicted to power and fallen into a spiritual trap. It is a trap that is devastating for both the individual *and* the organization. The old man trying to cling to his position well past his prime is a pathetic sight. And innumerable organizations have been deeply harmed by executives whose primary motive has been to attempt somehow to make their temporary power permanent.

Satan said to Jesus on top of the pinnacle of the temple of the holy city, 'If thou be the Son of God, cast thyself down: for it is written, He shall give his angels charge concerning thee: and in their hands they shall bear thee up, lest at any time thou dash thy foot against a stone.'

To most this seems like a strange temptation indeed. Why would anyone even want to jump off a tall building? Why would it be a temptation at all? But somebody who has a grand vocation, a calling to greatness, should recognize upon slight reflection what is going on here. For in talking about such vocations, I pointed out that the greatest burden they impart is the sense of self-doubt. I have never known such a person who did not for years have to harbor in her heart the question, 'How can I trust this feeling that I am supposed to be great when there is so little, if any, evidence of my greatness?'

What Satan is saying to Jesus here is 'Prove it. Prove your

greatness to me. Prove it to yourself and to others.' Oh, what a temptation this is! If I could only prove my greatness, then I would no longer need to doubt myself. I would be free from this burden of self-skepticism. Not only that, but the public would recognize my greatness and admire me!

I recounted how many schizophrenics seem to be cursed with a grand vocation, a sense of destiny, while lacking the psychological assets to fulfill it. Here the problem in psychotherapy is the opposite of helping the patient to accept his superiority; it is to help him accept his ordinariness. I was working with one such young man who spent much of his energy trying to look like Jesus. He had a beard and liked to wear robes. He spent hours before the mirror practicing a beatific facial expression. He frequently meditated in public not only so that others would observe him doing so but also in the vain hope that he would come to radiate a kind of inner peace he did not actually have. Much of our work centered on this second temptation of Jesus, but it was slow and tedious. Indeed, it was so tedious that he left my ministrations at one point to seek those of a priest who was famous as a spiritual director. This priest was deserving of his fame. At the end of a single session with my patient, he pronounced, 'You'd sell your soul to be holy,' and advised the young man to return to me. It was a magnificent assist.

The desire to prove oneself to oneself and the desire to prove oneself to others are closely related. It is difficult to have much self-esteem unless others demonstrate that they find us estimable from time to time. Conversely, to have high self-esteem when there is no external evidence to support it can be a most dangerous condition. Yet another dynamic involved occurs when people frantically seek power or status to compensate for a poor self-image or repair a lack of self-worth. These dynamics may be intertwined with those of narcissism. But it is important to remember that not all of our natural narcissism is bad, that God has a way of using our sins as raw material, and that there are rich permutations in human development. My hero, Micky Finn, can serve again as a case in point.

As soon as I arrived on Okinawa, the psychiatrist I was replacing said, 'Boy, wait until you meet the commanding general of this island! He's the damnedest phallic narcissist I've ever seen. He goes around with a swagger stick all the time and actually pokes people with it.' By phallic narcissist my colleague meant a type of man whose predominant and unconscious motive in life is a desire to be admired for the size of his penis. It is a dynamic that frequently drives men toward high and famous positions.

Had I not just emerged from my own psychoanalysis with its resultant healing of my authority problem, I doubt that General Finn and I would have hit it off. But we did, and over the course of the next two years, I had the opportunity to observe him poke a number of people with his swagger stick. I also observed his uncanny accuracy in poking only those men who were such mental sluggards they wouldn't otherwise budge spiritually. He himself moved quickly and, typical, of him, he kindly came to my office the day before he left the island to say good-bye. I used the occasion to satisfy my curiosity. 'You know how much I've come to love you, Micky,' I said. 'You're an extraordinary man. What do you think is the secret of your success?'

Contemplative that he was, he sat back in the chair for over a minute in silence. Finally, with a grin he answered, 'I would say it is that the greatest desire in my life has been to be admired.'

So Micky was able to squarely put his finger on his own psychodynamics. And from this there are two points to be made. One is, as I knew from many previous observations, he had long since given up a compulsive need to be admired by people. His primary desire had come to be that of being admired or pleasing in the sight of an ideal observer. In so doing, God had used his narcissism for a transmutation, with the result that Micky had become for me and many others an extraordinarily admirable human being.

The other key to the secret was his consciousness. Had he been unconscious of his narcissistic dynamics, there might have been no end to the havoc he could have wreaked with his political power. But he was able to use his power with such civility precisely because he was so conscious of his own motives, as well as being so closely in a relationship with his Higher Power.

With the exception of his use of the swagger stick, General Finn was not a particularly flash leader. The single word that came to my mind to characterize his leadership at the time was 'sane.' Was it an accident that the first two years I was there, the American military community on Okinawa was a remarkably healthy society? Or that in the next year after Micky had departed, the health of that society had visibly begun to deteriorate? I think not.

Earlier I noted that it is the top executive who, more than any other factor, determines the culture of the organization she leads. In fact, it is usually the single greatest power she has. In terms of decision making, she may often have little room to maneuver, but her personality—whether she likes it or not—will do much to set the tone for the whole business. In some ways it is a spiritual sort of phenomenon. Her spirit will permeate the organization, as did Micky's civility and spirit of sanity.

When I myself left Okinawa it was to move to Washington, D.C., where this aspect of power was again dramatically driven home to me. My new position was in the army surgeon general's office, where I worked closely with and ultimately under the Nixon administration from 1970 to 1972. I do not believe (as some do) that President Nixon was evil. In almost all respects he was, I believe, one of the most effective administrators to occupy the White House. But he had a fatal flaw: a virtually total blind spot in regard to civil liberties. It was not just the Watergate breakin. When people became upset about the break-in of Daniel Ellsberg's psychiatrist's office, Nixon simply couldn't understand what the fuss was all about. Why shouldn't the administration have the right to steal the files of the psychiatrist treating the man who leaked the Pentagon Papers? Why would the public make a big deal over such a minor action taken in the routine course of government affairs?

The men Nixon appointed as his top administrators generally had exactly the same blind spot. I know. I had to deal with their astonishing disregard of civil liberties on several occasions. But the matter goes deeper than the power of appointment, than 'Like selects like' or 'Birds of a feather flock together.' It is also a matter of example, which seemingly unleashes demons or encourages angels within the souls of the affected. Most of the people I worked with were not political appointees, yet they too had begun taping meetings, shredding documents, and taking a strange joy in sneakiness. The 'Spirit of Dirty Tricks' seeped down from the Oval Office and pervaded the entire executive branch, if not the entire government.

This particularly great power of the top manager to determine culture, to set the tone of a whole organization —small or huge—is usually exercised unconsciously. She doesn't even have to think about it any more than Nixon deliberately set about to create a culture of dirty tricks. It just happens. Whether she likes it or not, her personality will become a template for the school, the department, the hospital, the corporation, or the entire business she manages. But as management increasingly becomes a profession, managers are growing more conscious and self-conscious about this power. And in this consciousness they are faced with the temptation to throw themselves off the tower of the temple, the temptation of what I have called 'spiritual flashiness.' There are three ways they deal with this temptation.

One is to avoid the temptation by attempting to deny their power, or at least to hide it. Knowing that in their own personality they embody—incarnate—the vision of the organization, fearful of the power and temptation, they

307

shrink from the limelight. They do not walk the shop floor. They retire to back rooms under the illusion that they can somehow manage the organization through pure intellect, making key judgments solely through the inspection of balance sheets without ever having to show their faces. It doesn't work. Their fear becomes that of the organization, and all that their facelessness accomplishes is to create a faceless bureaucracy where no one knows where he stands. I have seen this devastating effect in several corporations.

The opposite way is to succumb to the temptation to become a seducer. 'Since I embody the culture of the business,' this type of top manager strategizes, 'let me dramatize my personality.' She not only walks the shop floor but takes every possible opportunity to be a flamboyant public figure. This is the consciously charismatic, 'spiritually flashy' leader. Ultimately, she too does not succeed. There are too many traps. She becomes prone to exaggeration. She tends to overidentify her true self with her persona or public mask. She loses sight of her private life and own spiritual development. She begins to think of herself as the business. She stifles the personalities of subordinates lest they detract from her act, her stage presence. She has become a prima donna.

What is the right way then? It is the way of tension. The truly civil top manager will neither flee from the temptation nor succumb to it; instead, she will live with it on a daily basis. She will go down to the shop floor, but more to listen than to show off. She knows how to orchestrate her personality to fit the organization's needs—to serve it—but she does so carefully, ever conscious of the temptation to go overboard. When it is occasionally called for, she can be flamboyant and forceful enough, but she will also retire into the background as soon as dramatic leadership is no longer required. She realizes she is both more and less than the business she manages. Less because its success is also dependent upon the optimal functioning of many others and she herself is its employee. More because she knows that her loyalty to her own spiritual life is even greater than that to the organization.

If all this sounds like a complex balancing act, that's because it is. It has repeatedly been noted that the way of civility is a way of tension. The civil use of power is not an easy exercise; it is the most difficult. But this is a constant theme. Ease and painlessness are not the point. The point is the health, competence, and effectiveness of organizations and organizational behavior.

Lastly, Satan took Jesus to a mountaintop and showed him all the kingdoms of the world, and the glory of them, saying, 'All these things I will give thee if thou wilt fall down and worship me.' The key word here, I believe, is 'glory.' The temptations of power are interrelated, but each appeals to a particular motive. The temptation just discussed, that of spiritual flashiness, caters to our desire for self-esteem, moving us to abuse power to maintain a high self-image. The first, to turn stones into bread, would satisfy our desire for security and push us to hold on to a powerful position long beyond any real need of our own or the world's to do so. This final temptation is the desire to seek power for its own sake, for the pure glory of it, or at least for the illusion of immortality such glory might weave. It is not the desire to be in a position to serve, to be a servant leader; it is the desire solely to be a leader.

Why might Satan have saved this temptation for the last? Was there something particularly appealing about it? I believe so. I believe it was so tempting paradoxically because Jesus had such a deep desire to serve. Think of how well he could have served as a king of kings, as the emperor of the world! Think of the brilliant and loving things he could have made happen with such power, could have authored with such great authority! He could have created social systems to serve the poor. Done much to equalize wealth. Established universal public education. Instituted civil liberties.

Brought peace to warring nations. He could have done all this and, through such service, even enhanced the glory. He would have gone down in history as not only the most powerful but also the most wise, the most just, the most beneficent, and the most humane king that ever was!

That ever *was*. The 'was' is the kicker. What would have happened when he died? What successors would have filled his shoes? Would not the nations be likely to resume their wars? The rich hoard their wealth again? The poverty programs collapse?

So we arrive at the great paradox of power: The only civil reason to seek power is to lose it, to give it away. The one mark, above all else, of the true servant leader is that she empowers others. The first duty of the civil manager is to train successors—not a successor, but as many successors as possible as quickly as possible. Use your power to seek and find people with a potential to lead even greater than your own, nurture their potential with all you've got, and then get out of the way.

Management has become enough of a science for there to be a few terms now used to describe different ways that managers may use their power—ways that power may be distributed within organizations. For instance, four management decision-making styles have been labeled: authoritarian, consultative, participatory, and consensual. Moving toward an ever more civil society, it is important for us to become familiar with these terms and understand the simple concepts behind them.

The most traditional and still most common style is authoritarian. The authoritarian manager makes all the decisions alone and merely informs his subordinates of what has already been decided. Or, if he is a mid-level manager, he is informed of decisions made by his superiors, then makes those within his purview, and passes the collection down the hierarchy. The direction of communication is entirely downward. This can be illustrated by the following diagram, where communication direction is signified by directional arrows and the ultimate decision-making authority located in that individual designated by an X, as opposed to subordinates, who are designated by an O.

AUTHORITARIAN

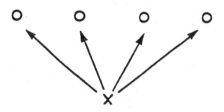

Almost as common is consultative management. Here the manager consults with the subordinate most concerned before making her decision. Sometimes multiple subordinates are concerned, so multiple consultations are required for a single decision. Generally these are accomplished on a one-to-one basis. In this style, communication goes both ways, and the subordinate has the power, the authority, to advise his supervisor. This authority is limited, however, to the issues clearly within his purview. Moreover, such advice is customarily offered only in response to the manager's request for it. The manager retains the initiative.

CONSULTATIVE

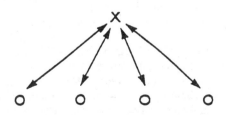

A less common, but still more empowering style is participatory management. Here subordinates communicate not only with their supervisor but also with each other in the decision-making process. Now the diagram begins to radically change.

PARTICIPATORY

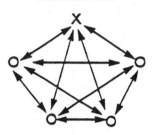

If this begins to look more like a circle, that's because it is. The work is done in a group as a collective. There are many new implications.

One is that the subordinate now has the authority not only to communicate and advise within her purview but also within the purview of all the other subordinates present. Imagine the top manager here to be a national sales manager and the four subordinates regional sales managers. The regional managers have the opportunity to receive input from and give it to each other, as well as to the national manager. National sales are no longer the concern of just the national manager. The regional managers now have a degree of responsibility for national operations. There is more sharing of responsibility, and hence power. The turfs are less clear.

As the density of the diagram suggests, in moving to a participatory management situation, there is a geometric increase in the amount of communication—and a similar increase in the amount of information available. Being more informed, the participatory manager will make better-informed decisions. Subordinates will similarly be enabled to make more informed decisions within their own regions. Furthermore, by virtue of being informed about nationwide operations, they will be in a better position to replace the national manager if necessary. With greater information and responsibility they will usually become more motivated in relation to the business as a whole and will develop a vision beyond that of their own turf. Obviously, participatory management also provides an excellent opportunity for an executive to select and groom her potential successors.

With all these advantages, why isn't participatory management the norm rather than the exception? The answer is that it is more difficult than the previously described styles for several reasons.

The least of these reasons is that it requires more time. Increase the communication, and you increase the time needed for communicating. Actually the increase in time is relatively small in relation to the enormous expansion in shared information and the richness of the ideas generated. Nonetheless, subordinates almost standardly complain, 'Oh, no, not another meeting!'

Yes, subordinates complain. Why? Why would they complain when they have more opportunity to participate, greater involvement in the organization, and broader responsibility for its operations? The plain answer is that many, if not most, people don't want greater responsibility. They want their job to be as simple and undemanding as possible. Those who like to lead are generally born 'high participants,' and they will take to participative management like ducks to water. But others may resist it mightily, even at the middle-management level. The situation might be impossible were it not for the fact that many of these resisters can be trained to like it. Low participators can learn to become high participators—some of them, some of the time. Some leaders can be made—not just born—to their own and others' delight. But such learning is often gradual, and the training demands skill and patience from the top manager.

Participatory management, then, is harder still on the top manager. Because it is a distinctly empowering style of leadership, the manager must want to share her power. Right away this requirement eliminates the many executives who have been ensnared by the temptations of authority. Indeed, she must want to share it even with those who don't want it, actually to the point of attempting to teach them to want it. She must know how to lead meetings well. This requires a very different kind of skill from that of decisiveness. It requires that she be a facilitator, a role in which she must often take a backseat—something quite impossible for the spiritually flashy leader. Being a natural high participator herself, she may have to work hard to train herself to be a low participator on appropriate occasions. Many top managers need to go back to school to learn facilitative skills. Occasionally such skills are so alien to her personality she must appoint a subordinate to facilitate her meetings in her stead. This requires that she actually authorize that subordinate to tell her, the top manager, to shut up when appropriate.[5]

Note that while the participative manager works hard to share power as much as possible, she still retains for herself the final decision-making authority. The four-hour meeting Micky Finn chaired in the entrance hall of the Okinawa stockade on that spring night was an example of participative management in action. He asked for everyone's advice. He sought information from many sources. He encouraged disagreement, argument, and debate among all those present. He himself said very little. But in the end, it was he—and he alone—who made that excruciating and highly unpopular decision. Participative management is not democracy.

There is a fourth and final style of decision making in business that transcends democracy: consensual management. It is the ultimate in empowerment. Here the top

[5] See Michael Doyle and David Straus, *How to Make Meetings Work* (New York: Berkeley Publishing Group, 1974).

314

manager gives away her 'topness,' assuming no more and no less decision-making authority than any other individual in the group. Consequently, there is no X in its diagram. Instead, after a most thorough discussion, the necessary decision is made without voting by the group as a whole through a process called consensus.

CONSENSUAL

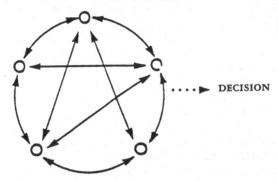

. . . . ▶ DECISION

By virtue of the fact that the decision making is totally shared and everyone involved maximally empowered, in certain circumstances consensual management is far and away the most effective. It is also the most time-consuming and the most difficult. Indeed, it is sufficiently difficult that the whole group must have significant training before it can be done successfully. A description of the nature of such training will be deferred until the final section of the book, where it can be discussed in relation to the subject of community.

No one of these four managements styles is 'the best.' I have extolled the virtues of participative and consensual management, yet my autocratic assignment of offices to my subordinates on Okinawa was just the right managerial move under the circumstances. We return here to contingency theory. The effectiveness of a style is contingent not only upon the nature of the business but also the particular decision-making situation. Generally speaking, the time required should be proportional to the importance of the decision. In other words, the smallest and easiest of day-to-day decisions in an organization can best be made autocratically. Anything more than a minor operational decision should at least be made with consultation. The most significant decisions are better made through participative management if the participants are trained for it, or, ideally, by consenus.

The truly competent manager, therefore, will have all four of these styles as her command. Moreover, she will know which style to employ at which time. This means that a major part of the art of management is a sense of timing. It includes the capacity to wait. With participative and consensual management, the leader must be willing to sit back and wait for the decision to evolve out of the group. It is a common error of managers to simply watch a problem, hoping it will go away when it actually deserves decisive action. An equally common and serious error, however, is to jump into action when a more thoughtful and discerning collective decision is called for. I believe an entire book could be written on the relationship between power and the discipline of waiting.

The process of sharing power is frequently termed collaboration. Thus far, it has been described in situations in which the managers shares power—collaborates—with subordinates. But managers also need to collaborate with their peers and superiors. There is collaboration sideways and upward as well as downward, and organizational dysfunction frequently occurs when a manager is good at one while being poor at the other. There are executives, for instance, who curry favor with the board of directors but fail to collaborate with their own staffs. Some may collaborate well both upward and downward, but out of competitiveness behave adversarially in their lateral relationships. Finally, there are those who may collaborate well with their staffs, with those under their authority, but are subtly or openly antagonistic to their superiors. Career civil service managers, for example, have been known to attempt to undermine the political appointees above them, or executive directors to subvert their own boards.

The notion of a top manager collaborating upward or at times relinquishing her authority to subordinates returns us to a concept discussed at the beginning of this chapter: servant leadership. The thesis has been fleshed out that the civil manager is, by definition, a servant leader. His primary motives are to serve God, his organization, his superiors, and his subordinates, and the primary means of his service are those of empowerment. Whenever constructive, he seeks to give away his power rather than retain it. But one fine additional point needs to be made. Giving away your power may, on occasion, mean something deeper than sharing it with another; the service may require actual submission to the other. The civil group leader must not only be alert to the possibility that any member of the group may come up with the best solution to a given problem but also then be prepared to follow that person's lead. For some years I have been deeply involved in teaching the art of group leadership. In developing this course of instruction, I have found it necessary to include a small section that teaches managers the art of 'followship.'

There's an old saw that it's lonely at the top. This loneliness poses a temptation associated with power that has not yet been considered. The temptation is to seek relief from that loneliness in a form that can be destructive. It is no accident that we hear so frequently of famous men who have developed romantic extramarital relationships. The phenomenon may be particularly common for people in positions of high power because they look to such relationships for some surcease of their dreadful loneliness. Unfortunately, these relationships may be either unethical or self-destructively indiscreet, or both.

There is an even more common and more destructive way that executives succumb to this temptation of loneliness. It is to form an alliance within the organization. This may be the root cause of those failures of collaboration just mentioned. The executive who collaborates with the board but not with his staff may do so because he has found his 'cronies' there and identified himself with them. Or he may form destructively 'entangling alliances' with coexecutives on a lateral level. Or he may seek friendship with his staff and so identify himself with them that it becomes him and them against the board. The lonely reality is that the civil executive cannot identify himself with any part of the organization; his loyalty must be to what is right for the organization as a whole.

But how does he decide what is right? Think of General Finn that night in the entrance hall of the stockade in Okinawa. Thirty men suggested that what was right for the U.S. Army in that situation, from their point of view, was to maintain authority and discipline. Only two saw it otherwise. Yes, the Conex containers were against regulations, but he could get rid of them after the insurrection was subdued. The point, they advised him, was to quell the insurrection first, even at a possible cost of several lives. To meet the prisoners' demands would reward insurrection and thereby so undermine authority that even more lives might be lost in future, probably larger insurrections. But it was Finn's decision, and his alone. He alone, at that moment, in that instance, had to decide what was right for the army, for the entire military, for the government, even for the nation as a whole.

I have known people in similar positions of power for whom that would not have been a difficult decision. By virtue of a lack of ethical sensitivity (Nixon's blind spot in relation to civil liberties, for instance), or prejudice, or narrowly dedicated allegiance to a part of the whole, or some other form of *unconsciousness*, the right course of action in that situation would have seemed obvious to them. But they were all leaders deficient in civility.

I simply do not believe it is possible for a civil leader to tolerate the loneliness of such a position. Forgoing the companionship of destructive alliances, the leader then has only one option: he must have the companionship of God; he must be in a personal relationship with a Higher Power at the time. In order to be civil, such decisions must be made prayerfully. I do not mean this metaphorically. I mean it literally. In those agonizing moments the civil leader will be praying—hard. He or she will be in active dialogue with God, even if the fact of that dialogue is not remembered afterwards.

I will go one step further. Responding to the three temptations, Jesus replied, in order, 'Man shall not live by bread alone, but by every word that proceedeth out of the mouth of God'; 'Thou shalt not tempt the Lord, my God'; and, 'Thou shalt worship the Lord, thy God, and him only shalt thou serve.' In other words, for Jesus there was only a single response to the temptations of power: God.

I think this implies something even deeper than the requirements for a civil leader to have a spiritual center and active prayer life. Beyond a certain point, as the stakes get even higher, I believe such a leader will increasingly recognize that God is the sole source of civil power. God is love; God is light: God is truth. To these great synonyms I add another: When it is civil, God *is* power. Increasingly, the civil leader or manager begins to sense that the power of her position is not hers. It is not her possession; it is not hers to possess. The power belongs to God, and the proper role of the civil leader is merely to be a conduit and to steward that power as God's agent. Merely! What a paradox! To exercise temporal power with civility is to undertake a role of great glory, and it can only be undertaken with genuine humility.

Part Four

EPIPHANY

Community in the Workplace

17

A Sum Greater Than Its Parts

Community: The Civil Organization

Thus far, our primary focus has been the individual: the characteristics of a civil individual and how such a person behaves in the context of an organization. In this concluding section the primary focus now switches to that of a group as a whole. How does a group become a civil organization? What does a civil organization look like?

From the minimal formal training I received in the practice of group psychotherapy, I can remember only a single instruction. We psychiatry residents were told that the competent group therapist must be able to focus his or her consciousness on two separate levels: the level of the individual patient and the level of the group as a whole. It was a valid instruction, but not one easy to follow. Perhaps it is impossible to fully attend to any two issues or questions simultaneously. I cannot listen wholeheartedly to my patient, wondering how best to respond to him, and at the very same time ask myself how the entire group is functioning, examining what its group dynamics are at that particular moment. The best we therapists can do is to vibrate relatively rapidly, switching our level of awareness from the individual to the group, and then from the group back to the individual, and then from the individual back to the group again until the meeting is over. Good group therapists earn their money.

During the first few years that I exercised my vibratory

323

capacity in this regard, I found it considerably easier—more natural—to focus my attention on my individual patients than on the groups as a whole. Over and again I would become so engrossed in what a particular patient was saying and what I might do to help her that I utterly lost sight of the group dynamics that were occurring. I would repeatedly fall into this trap even though, as a person, I already had a relative gift for group consciousness. Gradually, however, with some effort I became increasingly able to attend to group dynamics without ignoring the individual patients. My vibratory capacity became more balanced; my group consciousness *improved with practice.*

In 1980, I began to work with larger groups of thirty to four hundred at a time, groups of people who assembled not for the purpose of psychotherapy, but for an experience of spiritual education. As their leader, I now switched my vibratory frequency to focusing my attention almost totally on the group as a whole and only very occasionally on the members as individuals. Over the next two years I became fairly adept at leading such groups into 'community'—a way of being together with both individual authenticity and interpersonal harmony so that people became able to function with a collective energy even greater than the sum of their individual energies. I started to name these events 'community building workshops' (CBWs).

I would begin these CBWs by emphatically informing the participants that our sole task in being together was to build ourselves into a community. But even though the purpose was not psychotherapy, an astonishing amount of psycho-spiritual healing would occur in the course of these workshops, particularly after the participants had learned how to stop playing therapist with each other.

One of my techniques of leadership was to repeatedly point out how the group was behaving as a whole and then gradually ask the participants to contemplate themselves the health of the group. It worked! The majority became increasingly adept at thinking in terms of the group as a whole. Moreover, a substantial number of participants returned again and again to other CBWs, and as they did, I had the joy of witnessing them often become truly and consistently expert at spotting group dynamics without any help. The community building workshop is the most effective means I know for raising group consciousness.

By mid-1984 the demand for me to lead CBWs exceeded my capacity to supply it. Joining with others, I began to develop a corps of well-selected and trained community building leaders to replace me. When they are functioning in their role as leaders, these men and women are all adept at keeping their consciousness focused primarily on the groups for which they are responsible—on these groups as organisms, or whole systems.

Once a year these leaders gather for what is called a Leaders' Roundtable to rebuild themselves as a community and receive updated training. They are sacrificial people on the cutting edge of society. They lead workshops in their spare time for minimal fees. The rest of the time most of them work in demanding jobs in positions of high responsibility. They are on the front lines. Consequently, when they come back together for these roundtables, it is like coming home. Children, no matter how grown, have a tendency to regress when they come home. So it is even with these experienced leaders. We routinely joke about how immaturely we can behave at roundtables, as if we were squabbling sisters and brothers, dependent and demanding, rather than the true adults we usually are.

The primary dynamic of this immaturity is that we 'forget' how to use our capacity to keep our minds on the group as a whole. At one roundtable a relatively junior leader said something to me that was literally guaranteed to throw the group back into chaos. Later he apologized to me outside the group for the turmoil his remarks had caused. I suspected they did not constitute 'consciously motivated organizational behavior.' 'What you said was quite appropriate in relation to me, Hank,' I told him. 'But when you said it, were you thinking of just you and me, or were you also thinking of what effect your remarks would have upon the group?'

'I was only thinking of you and me,' Hank confessed.

'Supposing you'd been one of our designated leaders, instead of Peter or Joyce,' I asked. 'Would you have said the same thing?'

'I might have said it to you in the parlor, just between you and me, but, no I certainly wouldn't have said it in the group.'

'Well?' I waited.

'Do you mean I ought to *always* behave as a leader in group, even when I'm not the designated leader?'

'Sounds tiring, doesn't it?' I responded.

That was some years ago. Today Hank is one of our senior—and most powerful and experienced—leaders. I'm not sure it is possible anymore for him to be in any group—even a roundtable—and say anything without first considering the effect of his words upon the group as a whole. So it is for our other senior leaders. Their group consciousness is operating from the very second they step into every meeting of any kind. For them group consciousness and civility have become a way of life.

Few ever think objectively about the groups in which they are involved. But from the experiences just recounted, I can make hopeful claims. Virtually all people do have a potential capacity for such thinking. They will use that capacity when they are trained to do so. The community building process is an ideal form of such training. However, it is natural for them to forget this training unless it is repeated. If it is repeated often enough we know it is possible for many people's group consciousness to become so practiced as to be instinctive, natural, and no longer forgettable. The hole in his mind can be filled!

Over the past fifty years, psychotherapists, management

consultants, and other students of group behaviour have come to discern that when groups evolve, they tend to do so in certain somewhat predictable stages. This is not to say that all groups evolve in wisdom, maturity, effectiveness, or civility. Most, in fact, do not. But when they do, there is an order and lawfulness to the process. These stages have been given various names. My preferred ones are pseudo-community, chaos, emptiness, and community.

For many groups or organizations the most common initial stage, pseudocommunity, is the only one. It is a stage of pretense. The group pretends it already is a community, that the participants have only superficial individual differences and no cause for conflict. The primary means it uses to maintain this pretense is through a set of unspoken common norms we call manners: you should try your best not to say anything that might antagonize or upset else; if someone else says something that offends you or evokes a painful feeling or memory, you should pretend it hasn't bothered you in the least; and if disagreement or other unpleasantness emerges, you should immediately change the subject. These are rules that any good hostess knows. They may create a smoothly functioning dinner party but nothing more significant. The communication in a pseudo-community is filled with generalizations. It is polite, in-authentic, boring, sterile, and unproductive.

Over time profound individual differences may gradually emerge so that the group enters the stage of chaos and not infrequently self-destructs. The theme of pseudo-community is the covering up of individual differences; the predominant theme of the stage of chaos is the attempt to obliterate such differences. This is done as the group members try to convert, heal, or fix each other or else argue for simplistic organizational norms. It is an irritable and irritating, thoughtless, rapid-fire, and often noisy win/lose type of process that gets nowhere.

If the group can hang in together through this un-pleasantness without self-destructing or retreating into pseudocommunity, then it begins to enter 'emptiness.' This is a stage of hard, hard work, a time when the members work to empty themselves of everything that stands between them and community. And that is a lot. Many of the things that must be relinquished or sacrificed with integrity are virtual human universals: prejudices, snap judgments, fixed expectations, the desire to convert, heal, or fix, the urge to win, the fear of looking like a fool, the need to control. Other things may be exquisitely personal: hidden griefs, hatreds, or terrors that must be confessed, made public, before the individual can be fully 'present' to the group. It is a time of risk and courage, and while it often feels relieving, it also often feels like dying.

The transition from chaos to emptiness is seldom dramatic and often agonizingly prolonged. One or two group members may risk baring their souls, only to have another, who cannot bear the pain, suddenly switch the subject to something inane. The group as a whole has still not become empty enough to truly listen. It bounces back into temporary chaos. Eventually, however, it becomes sufficiently empty for a kind of miracle to occur.

At this point a member will speak of something particularly poignant and authentic. Instead of retreating from it, the group now sits in silence, absorbing it. Then a second member will quietly say something equally authentic. She may not even respond to the first member, but one does not get the feeling he has been ignored; rather, it feels as if the second member has gone up and laid herself on the altar alongside the first. The silence returns, and out of it, a third member will speak with eloquent appropriateness. Community has been born.

The shift into community is often quite sudden and dramatic. The change is palpable. A spirit of peace pervades the room. There is more silence, yet more of worth gets said. It is like music. The people work together with an exquisite sense of timing, as if they were a finely tuned orchestra under the direction of an invisible celestial conductor. Many actually sense the presence of God in the room. If the group is a public workshop of previous strangers who soon must part, then there is little for it to do beyond enjoying the gift. If it is an organization, however, now that it is a community it is ready to go to work—making decisions, planning, negotiating, and so on—often with phenomenal efficiency and effectiveness.[1]

In our customary language the word *community* is applied to virtually any group: a neighbourhood, town, or city; a church, college, university, or social club. This is so even when its members may be total strangers to one another or, if they are acquainted, their knowledge of each other is utterly superficial.

By now, it is clear my usage is far more precise. Specifically, for me, community requires communication —and not the mere exchange of words, but high-quality communication. The quality of group communication is so poor in our typical business and social organizations that I designate them as pseudocommunities or pretend communities. For the most part, keeping their interaction both light and polite, their members are only pretending to communicate. A genuine community, on the other hand, is a group whose members have made a commitment to communicate with one another on an ever more deep and authentic level. There are very few true communities.

When a group does make such a commitment, however, it will evolve through the stages just described and wonderful things will begin to happen. The members transcend their narcissism, coming not only to respect but to appreciate their differences. Long-buried resentments are surfaced and resolved. Enemies are reconciled. Hard eyes become soft, and swords become feathers.

After I had spent three years of leading groups into

[1] The characteristics of true community and the stages of its development are described in much greater depth in *The Different Drum*.

community, frequently assisted by Lily and a few others, it dawned on us that we had stumbled upon a pearl of great price. Knowing nothing at the time about how to design, much less manage, a decent organization, we did at least know that this pearl needed to be shared as widely and quickly as possible. With little more in common than a passion for peacemaking, eleven of us gathered together in December 1984 to establish a nonprofit, tax-exempt, public educational foundation: The Foundation for Community Encouragements, Inc. (FCE). It is to (FCE) that this book is so properly dedicated. Most of what follows is a condensation of what we have learned working with it and through it over the past eight years.

As an educational foundation, it is the purpose of FCE to teach the principles of community—that is, the rules for healthy and civil communication in groups. We did not arrive at these principles in a vacuum. Just as over the past sixty years we have developed a military technology to annihilate ourselves from the face of the earth, so — unbeknownst to most—we have quietly and unobtrusively developed a technology of peacemaking that we call community building. Various pieces of this technology have come from such diverse sources as Christian monasticism, the Quakers, Alcoholics. Anonymous and the Twelve Step programs, the sensitivity group movement, the Tavistock Institute in Great Britain, and the work of management consultants.

One reason we often refer to the principles of community as a technology is because they are analogous to software. Software is a system of rules that are fed into the hardware of a computer to teach it how to operate effectively. The principles of community are similarly a set of rules that can be given a group of human beings to teach them how to work effectively as a group. Any group of people willing to submit themselves to this system of rules will quickly learn to function together with remarkable efficiency and civility.

A system of rules to which one submits may also be called

a discipline. Depending upon the circumstances, I shall be referring to the principles of community as either a technology *or* a discipline. In any case, it is something that must be practiced. You cannot learn much about computers from a lecture or reading a book about them; you become truly knowledgeable about them only by using them. Consequently, FCE fulfills its educational mission primarily by teaching the principles of community through highly *experiential* group workshops, or CBWs. Its current philosophy and mission statements read:

PHILOSOPHY STATEMENT

There is a yearning in the heart for peace. Because of the wounds—the rejections—we have received in past relationships, we are frightened by the risks. In our fear, we discount the dream of authentic community as merely visionary. But there are rules by which people can come back together, by which the old wounds are healed. It is the mission of The Foundation for Community Encouragement (FCE) to teach these rules—to make hope real again—to make the vision actually manifest in a world which has almost forgotten the glory of what it means to be human.

MISSION STATEMENT

The foundation for Community Encouragement (FCE) encourages people, in a fragmented world, to discover new ways of being together. Living, learning, and teaching principles of community, we serve as a catalyst for individuals, groups, and organizations to:

- communicate with authenticity,
- deal with difficult issues,
- bridge differences with integrity,
- relate with love and respect.

FCE's approach encourages tolerance of ambiguity, the experience of discovery and the tension between holding on and letting go.

As we empower others, so are we empowered by a Spirit within and beyond ourselves.

331

I have already alluded to the fact that FCE's first task was to select and train leaders to conduct its community building workshops, or CBWs. It has been a major endeavor, since the selection has needed to be discerning and the training ongoing. Currently, FCE has some sixty-five such selected and trained leaders who, working in pairs, have to date conducted over three hundred workshops throughout the United States, Canada, Great Britain, and Australia—and even one thus far in Russia.[2]

In its early years, the vast majority of FCE's workshops were conducted for the general public. People, mostly strangers, would come from all across a region, individually pay their modest fee, build themselves into a community over the course of two or three days, and then, the experience over, depart for their individual homes. If the workshop was a particularly local one, approximately half the time some of the attendees would later form themselves into a local support group. Such groups have lasted anywhere from months to years. Other attendees have returned to one or more additional public workshops, and some have gradually worked their way into being active members of the FCE organization. For the most part, however, the participants not only came as strangers but returned to be strangers to one another once again. Unlike a standing organization, beyond their few days as a group they generally had neither a history nor a future together.

Many things we learned from these workshops, however, are applicable to building community within standing organizations. On their third workshop day, for instance, FCE sometimes has the participants—whether they previously be strangers or old cowokers—go through a series of exercises entitled 'Obstacles to Community.' The exercises are designed to assist people to clearly identify the

---

[2] FCE has recently spawned similar but independent community building organizations in Great Britain and Australia.

personal barriers they brought with them to the workshop and are likely to carry into future group situations: a need to look witty or wise, difficulty being in a receiving as opposed to a giving role, terror of being out of control, a compulsive tendency to organize, always being busy as a way of maintaining distance, and so forth. For the most part, these exercises are highly enjoyable, accomplished with considerable hilarity as the participants poke fun at themselves. But the most striking thing about them is that they are conducted *after* the group has become a community.

In other words, the obstacles are insufficient to prevent community. They have already been overcome, without any didactic training, in the process of building community. The purpose of the exercises is simply to cement the learnings for future reference.

The majority of personal obstacles relate to the familiar ethic of rugged individualism. This ethic holds that we are called to become individuals and think for ourselves, that we are called to independence and autonomy, to learn how to stand on our own two feet, and to be captains of our own ship, if not necessarily masters of our own destiny. If this sounds like a series of clichés, it is because they are so true. We are indeed called to these things. But the problem with the ethic of rugged individualism is that it neglects the entire other side of the coin. For we are also called to come to terms with our own inevitable sin and imperfection, our woundedness and brokenness, our human limits, and our natural interdependence. Consequently, we are programmed from early childhood on to look as if we've got all together when none of us actually does. We are pushed into a continual pretense of intactness and self-sufficiency and forced to hide behind masks of composure. So it is that one of the aforementioned exercises is entitled 'Personal Masks.'

But while the most common obstacle to community is the ethic of rugged individualism, it is hardly an impenetrable or fatal one. It must be broken through before community can occur. The old tapes must be reversed. I can neither love a mask nor trust a 'perfect' person. While people are frightened of the 'confession of brokenness' that community requires, it is amazing how rapidly they can relinquish the old tapes in the right situation with proper leadership. And how joyful they feel, individually and collectively, when they have been liberated from these oppressive, unrealistic tapes of rugged (as opposed to soft) individualism.

If these pages make it sound as if everyone can overcome his or her obstacles to community and break out of hiding, this is almost correct. On the average, two to three percent of attendees at FCE's public workshops depart before their completion. Half do so during the difficult periods of chaos or emptiness. Surprisingly, the other half leave after the group has reached community. It is as if, for some reason, they cannot bear all the love in the room. We do not know the reason. Occasionally they offer explanations, but these seem spurious. More often they simply depart, and we do not hear from them afterwards. Only once have we received valid feedback. Two men left a workshop independently. Later one of them informed FCE: 'You didn't know it, but we are partners in a profitable, long-standing business. There are many painful and difficult issues between us that we've avoided dealing with. I left—and I suspect my partner did also—because we realized that if we stayed we would have to bring these issues to light, and we were too frightened to do so.'

I imagine there are various reasons that the few leave. The only thing I can state for certain is that they are unrelated to ordinary mental illness or overt psychiatric disease. Many people who have been significantly disturbed have not only stayed, but often contributed mightily and lovingly to the group. My guess is that the few who depart have only one thing in common: something they feel they *must* hide—from themselves, if not from the group.

One other uncommon phenomenon deserves mention.

Several times toward the end of a public workshop, as the group is enjoying its sense of community, a previously silent individual has suddenly criticized the group with a devastating, extremely hateful precision. In these instances, the FCE leaders have felt that the individual had deliberately stayed around for the sole purpose of attempting to destroy the community. Regardless of what motives might underlie such unusual destructiveness, it has never succeeded; indeed, the groups involved took these incidents in their stride. Once in community, people are strong. They seemed to recognize these individuals as deliberate 'spoilsports,' and have responded to them by saying, 'We're truly sorry you're so unhappy, but frankly we have no intention of letting you ruin the experience for the rest of us at the last moment.'

I also need to make it clear that in the estimation of the FCE leaders, perhaps one in six of these public workshops never seems to arrive at a deep level of community. The reasons are obscure. Each group is different, and the problem seems to reside not in the individuals present but in some particular configuration of group dynamics—a configuration that is not necessarily the same for these 'failures.'

I have labeled them failures in quotes because they do not seem to be failures in fact. As many such workshops eventuate in ongoing support groups as do the seemingly more successful ones. 'Failed' workshop participants return to successive FCE public workshops as often as those who have had an ecstatic experience. There is remarkably little correlation between the leaders' assessment of workshop quality and that of the members.

Moreover, even when a group achieves an obviously deep level of community, there are always a few members who do not feel it—who do not feel 'in community' with the rest. Yet their postworkshop surveys are generally as favorable as those of the majority. It would seem that *under the right circumstances* people can benefit as much from their failures as their successes. In fact, with that qualifier, we know this to be the case. Frequently, toward the end of the third day, FCE leaders will employ a 'Dots Exercise.' Each participant is given six large dots to color either red or blue—red for a moment when they experienced intense community and blue for a moment of intense frustration, resistance, or isolation. Breaking into smaller groups to discuss their dots with each other, most quickly come to realize that while they enjoyed their red dot moments, they actually learned more from their blue dot ones. Indeed, they will often start recoloring them to end up with dots that are both red and blue. FCE tries to avoid developing its own special lingo, but one of the phrases that has crept into its culture is 'the Blessing of the Blue Dot.'

Be that as it may, ninety percent of those who attend FCE's public workshops at considerable effort and expense consistently evaluate the experience afterward to have been at least well worth their time and money. These statistics hold up over time. Indeed, the limited research FCE has been able to conduct in this regard indicates remarkably little 'fade effect.'

By virtue of the modest tuition but not so modest time and travel expense required, it is not surprising that attendees at FCE's public workshops have primarily been Caucasian, upper-middle-class, college-educated men and women. They have generally had a Christian orientation. Still, over time, there have been substantial numbers of Asians and blacks, Jews and Muslims. Adding to this experience with 'special workshops' comprising high percentages of Native American, Hispanic, or poor people, we know that neither race nor religion, nor cultural tradition, nor income, nor education represents a barrier to building community. Nor does any mixture of these factors. To the contrary, FCE's repeated experience has been that it is easier to build a highly diverse group into community than a homogeneous one.

In summary, approximately one person in twenty seems

incapable of participating constructively in the community building process. This incapacity seems to be solely the result of individual psychodynamics and to bear no relationship whatsoever to demographies. It is sad that there is this five percent, and I wish we knew more about them. But, for my own part, I find the converse statistic exhilaratingly hopeful: Ninety-five percent of humanity is routinely capable, when led to do so, of joining to form genuine community.

I have been using FCE's public workshops to introduce aspects of community building. Our overall subject, however, is organizations and not temporary groups of strangers lacking a previous history and an extended future together. The family is the most basic organization, and frequently I am asked, 'Can the principles of community be applied to the family?' But this concluding section is subtitled 'Community in the Workplace' because the answer is yes and no. It is an answer so filled with ambiguity that, after a brief consideration of the issues, we will restrict our consideration to the business world.

Many of the attendees at FCE workshops have reported that the experience vastly improved their marital and family relationship. This is hardly surprising, since families are groups and the principles of community are those of healthy group communication. What is reported is improved communication. 'I listen better,' a man will typically tell us. 'It's the most dramatic with my wife. We've set aside more time to talk to each other. I'm not as quick to judge her or as quick to respond. And it seems to have rubbed off on her. We're both less afraid to deal with our issues. There are periods of thoughtful silence now instead of raised voices when we struggle over those issues. It's less dramatic with the kids, but I listen to them better too. I'm more conscious of when I'm cutting them off or talking down to them, and sometimes I catch myself at it quickly enough to apologize to them for it. It's not as though everything's easy now, but it's hard to imagine what our family would be like if I hadn't gone to the workshop. Sometimes I think it actually saved my marriage.'

But there are other ways in which some of the principles of community cannot and should not be applied in families. While many of the patterns of organizational behavior hold true for both family and business organizations, as previously noted there are some fundamental differences in purpose and nature between a business and a family. It is because of such differences a family cannot be a true community in the fullest sense of the word.

A true community is 'a group of all leaders.' A nuclear family that attempted to be a group of all leaders would self-destruct. Children are inherently dependent upon their parents. Until at least mid-adolescence, 'quitting' the family is simply not an option for them, whereas it is virtually always an option for someone to quit a job. The authority of parents over their children is a life-and-death matter. The question of whether a three-year-old should or shouldn't run out into the street is not an issue for consensual decision making.

This does not mean children should have no voice in family affairs. However, the nature of that voice is a subject for subtle discernment, and the power of such discernment resides almost entirely with the parents. It is common and perfectly normal to hear a rebellious abdolescent vociferously demanding greater freedom on the one hand while desperately, nonverbally seeking limits and parental decisiveness on the other. It would not be civil to say, 'Figure it out for yourself, dear.' In different ways at different times and stages, children *need* their parents to exercise authority over them and make the hard decisions for them.

Business at its best is a cooperative venture, and it is quite civil for a business executive to expect, even demand cooperation. Parents who expect or demand cooperation from their children (as they so often do) are being blindly uncivil. It is not the task of children to cooperate; it is their task to grow. In nurturing that growth, it is proper for parents, in certain circumstances, to require obedience from their children. But obedience is something quite different from cooperation, and parents who do not understand the difference are unconscious. It may be civil to expect a child, under threat, to obediently take out the garbage. It would be stupid to expect a child to freely and consistently volunteer to do so. In fact, civil parents with a child who consistently volunteered to take out the garbage would have reason soon to be consulting a child psychiatrist about it.

Community requires its members to honestly and openly speak their minds, to risk intimacy, to confess what is appropriate, to make the hidden known when doing so is helpful. These kinds of requirements would often do violence to children within the context of their family. One of the enormous tasks of children is to develop their identities, and to accomplish this task successfully they need a significant amount of privacy. They need to have some secrets of their own, some psychological distance between themselves and their parents or siblings.

The bedrock of community is commitment, a willingness for people to 'hang in there' together when the going gets rough. But a child's proper commitment is not to its family. When the going gets rough in a family, children often need to escape to their rooms or run out of the house. While the commitment of community is never absolute, it is a force for togetherness and continuity. Family togetherness, however nurturant, is not a healthy goal for children. Their ultimate goal is to separate from their family, and whenever they assume significant personal responsibility for family togetherness, children do damage to themselves.

For these reasons, at the conclusion of a workshop FCE leaders sometimes warn the participants not to take their newfound enthusiasm for community home with them lock, stock, and barrel. It is a teaching close to my heart. When Lily and I were first stumbling onto the concept of community almost two decades ago—but before we understood it in depth—we did some experimenting on our children. In a couple of instances, we pushed them (unsuccessfully) toward a depth of communication that was inappropriate for them and that was unfair, uncivil, of us. They have, I think, just about forgiven us.

Still, none of this means the principles of community have no applicability to families. Community building is the ideal vehicle for the teaching of civility, and FCE's workshop participants have generally found themselves, as a result, behaving more civilly toward their children, their spouses, their parents, their siblings—as well as toward their bosses, coworkers, employees, and many others. It only means that the nature of the family organization is such that not *all* principles apply.

Nor does it mean that children cannot be in community, or that the community building process doesn't work for them. Outside the family it does. Several workshop participants—dedicated teachers—have reportedly done community building in elementary school classrooms with notable success. FCE itself has done several CBWs with groups composed entirely of adolescents with great benefit. It has resisted the temptation, however, to develop a specific 'adolescent program' for two reasons. One is that there is something anticommunity about a youth group leader calling to ask that adolescents be isolated in this way so that community is *done* to them. The other reason is our experience in mixing adolescents with adults. A youth minister calling FCE will be told, 'Yes, we'll do a workshop for your youth group if that's the only way for you, but it works much better when the group is heterogeneous, when adults are willing to commit themselves to the same things that the kids do and participate alongside them.'

I have had the privilege to participate myself in half a dozen community building workshops where adults and adolescents have worked together, and they have invariably been healing experiences for every one of the adolescents involved. It is a wonderful thing for them to see that adults don't have it all together. This means, they realize, that at sixteen or seventeen they don't have to have it all together either.

There is another reason why adolescents take to community like ducks to water. In our ordinary materialistic culture, people have status according to very tangible measures: the amount of money they possess, the size of the house they own, the amount of their salary, or the position they hold and its attendant perks. Few adolescents have access to these things. Adolescence is not a high-status position, and rare is the adolescent in America who has much of material substance on which to base his or her self-esteem. But community is an entirely different kind of culture. In community no one gives a hoot about how much money you make or what your title might be. What people get admired and appreciated for in community are their soft skills: their sense of humor and timing, their ability to listen, their courage and honesty, their capacity for empathy—the kinds of 'things' that adolescents often possess in spades.

In summary, while they are profoundly, albeit only partially, applicable to families, the principles of community are best *formally* learned by children and adolescents, as well as by adults, within the other organizations to which they belong.

Although the majority of FCE's early work was in public workshops, in recent years, as its reputation spread, the primary focus has come to be work with business organizations. This more recent experience will comprise the theme of all that follows.

FCE did enough work with formal organizations in those early years to discover that a group of businesspeople, once they arrived at the stage of community, could make group decisions with phenomenal efficiency and collective wisdom. It quickly and quite naturally, therefore, developed a motto: 'Community building first, decision making second.'

It generally takes no more than two days to build a group into a functioning community—even in an organization where the members have been at one another's throats for years. But we also learned quickly that it is not enough to simply go into an organization and build community and then leave, because the whole thing will fall apart within hours.

Long before FCE, group facilitators recognized that if people did have an experience of community at a public workshop, they would often have a difficult time when they left. This phenomenon came to be known as 'the problem of reentry.' After learning how to relate with a group of fellow humans with affection and deep honesty while on a retreat, it can be painful to reenter the 'real world,' where people are customarily inauthentic with each other, where there is a prevailing lack of affection and trust cloaked behind a veneer of superficial politeness.

If the group is part of an ongoing organization, the problem of reentry is all the more severe. We have labeled it 'the problem of backlash.' Take a management group, for instance. The members have long been accustomed to relating with each other from a cautious distance, protecting their positions with subtle adversarialism. The CEO, tired of dealing with turf issues, brings in a facilitator for two days, with the hope of improving the group's functioning. It seems to work. The managers begin talking immediately about themselves and come to care for one another. The old turf issues seem ridiculous. Former enemies are hugging each other. An entirely new atmosphere of trust and cooperation pervades the group. They end their meeting Friday evening in a mood of joy and gentle hilarity. They feel they will never again be the same.

Then it is Monday morning and they are back at their desks. Yes, three days ago it was very different and felt like a good experience. But now they have years of tradition to buck and their departmental budgets to deal with. Yes, the new way seemed so much better, but they are accustomed to the old way. Without even being aware of it, they have been put in a position psychologists call 'cognitive dissonance.' There is a total dissonance between the old way and the new way. One of them has to go. Which? It is the new one. No matter how satisfying it was, it is still so much more tentative and foreign, uneasy and difficult, than the way they are used to. Hardly aware of what's happening, they are comfortably propelled back into their ruts as into a pair of old shoes.

So, even though it is obviously better, they discard the new way. How can they do this? They do it through a mechanism of emotional discounting. 'Yes, we thought it was good at the time,' they tell themselves and each other, 'but it was really all an illusion. That consultant the CEO brought from the West Coast managed to hoodwink us. In fact, she hoodwinked the CEO. She's not to be trusted with all her newfangled techniques and bag of tricks. Come to think of it, it's all a bunch of New Age crap. We thought the CEO was too smart to fall for some cheap gimmick. Well, now we know better. In fact, he had no business bringing in that charlatan to fool around with our minds. We won't put up with that kind of crazy thing again.'

The blacklash has set in, and the situation is irretrievable. No organization is more resistant to community building than one that once engaged in a similar kind of process without adequate completion. The problem is, unfortunately, common. I even know of the cabinet of an entire government that almost learned how to do it right through the intervention of a facilitator from a foreign country, but then retreated into even more rigid adversarialism because adequate follow-up was not built into the facilitation plan.

Consequently, FCE learned early on that it was often destructively insufficient in working with an organization to simply offer an experience of genuine community. (Its work building community over the course of two days has hence

343

come to be called a CBE—or 'community building experience'—and now is reserved for public workshops.) It set about developing various types of 'third days' in order to cement the initial learning, and established a policy of offering only CBWs (full community building workshops) to organizations for a minimum of three days.

It was at this point in its history, in June 1988, that FCE was contacted by the Valley Diagnostic and Surgical Clinic (VDC) of Harlingen, Texas. Harlingen is a large town located in the southern Rio Grande Valley. The term 'valley' is a misnomer. The landscape is dead flat and dry, its monotony relieved only by an occasional stunted cactus. Some residents say of the area, 'It isn't exactly the end of the world, but you can see it from here.' Yet by virtue of air-conditioning, lawn sprinklers, and modern buildings, the town itself is pleasant enough. But there are many outlying pockets of Mexican-Americans who live in considerable poverty with major medical needs and little capacity to pay for medical services. It is not an easy place to practice medicine conscientiously.

In the 1970's the VDC was a large and thriving group medical practice of approximately thirty physicians. With the onset of the eighties, however, it began a gradual decline. The economics of practice became more difficult. Conflicts emerged between surgeons and internists, between newcomers and old-timers. There was chronic turmoil over fee schedules and the decisions of the clinic's executive committee. Physicians gradually drifted away and it grew harder to find replacements. Finally morale plummeted. When it contracted FCE, the clinic was in the midst of losing six of its physicians over the course of six months, declining from twenty-three to seventeen in number. It knew the organization was in serious trouble, and thought community building might help. It asked FCE to provide them with a two-day workshop.

FCE responded by saying its experience with organizations was that two days were not enough, that three days was an absolute minimum: two to build community and a third day for the group to arrive at some consensual written commitments as to what they were going to do to maintain themselves in community. The contacting physician representative was aghast. 'My God,' he exclaimed, 'do you know how difficult it is to get seventeen physicians to take two full days off from their practice, and you're insisting we do it for three?' FCE understood the problem but was adamant. The clinic reluctantly agreed.

Another problem arose when FCE strongly urged that the clinic's top lay administrators be included in the workshop. This might not seem like much of a problem, but physicians have a long unwritten tradition of being a law unto themselves, of considering laypeople not only as their employees, but also as people before whom they should not be vulnerable. But they were desperate. Again it was with reluctance that they agreed.

The workshop began on the first day of Labor Day weekend, 1988, in a small conference room of a Harlingen hotel. Present throughout were sixteen of the seventeen physicians, the business manager and two other top lay administrators, and two FCE leaders. (FCE leaders virtually always work in teams.) The leaders instructed the group that their sole task over the next two days was to build themselves into a community, and that it was specifically *not* their task to deal with the clinic's issues. The issues would be dealt with on the third day, *after* the group had become a community.

For the next hour the group talked only about the clinic's organizational issues.

After a short break, the FCE leaders acknowledged that organizational issues could occasionally also become very personal ones. If a member was genuinely hurting over an issue, they instructed, he could talk about it only as it affected him personally. But there was to be no more talk about clinic issues on an abstract level.

For the next hour and a half the group continued to talk about VDC issues in a purely abstract fashion.

After lunch, the leaders told the group it was clearly focusing on clinic issues in order to avoid talking about the participants' individual personal issues. 'It's much safer,' they explained, 'to talk about issues "out there" than to talk about yourselves. But you've got to risk speaking personally about yourselves or there's no way you can ever become a community.'

Several physicians protested that they had no personal issues to talk about. 'Personally we're a very happy bunch of people,' they proclaimed. 'Every one of us is well adjusted. None of us has any personal problems. The only problems we have in our lives are those produced by the clinic.'

The FCE leaders said this was a bunch of bullshit. But it had no effect. The group persisted in talking only about its organizational issues in the abstract.

Finally, in the middle of that Saturday afternoon, the leaders voiced their despair. 'You're blowing it', they said. 'By refusing to talk personally, you're blowing any chance of getting to community. You're blowing the money you're paying us. You're blowing all the time you've taken off from work. And you're blowing the clinic right down the drain.'

The group continued to go in circles for the rest of the day, over and around the same impersonal issues. The FCE leaders began Sunday morning by addressing the group: 'You have consistently refused to follow our directions. We've pulled out all our stops and all our tricks. The only thing left for us to do is to hand the problem over to you. We're exhausted, trying unsuccessfully to police from you talking about issues. From now on you police yourselves—if at all.'

One of the physicians—a woman—offered to play the role of 'issue monitor,' and the group accepted. She was a genius at it. No one could even get through a complete abstract sentence before she would snap, 'Issue!' Within a half an hour, under her watchful, gifted eye, the group had painfully begun the shift out of chaos into emptiness. Slowly, one by one, these professionals began to talk of their disappointment in their children, the rejections they'd received from their parents, the hurts from their siblings, their divorces, their remarriages, their money struggles, their joys at their accomplishments, their love for their patients. They brought forth long-hidden resentments they'd harbored against one another for past put-downs, old committee decisions, unshared management. Some cried. All listened. 'I've learned more about you in the past ten minutes,' one said to another, 'than I have for the last fourteen years.' Then more tears alternating with waves of laughter. By mid-Sunday afternoon, the Valley Diagnostic and Surgical Clinic was deep into community.

Every group is different, unique, special. This group had a couple of particularly notable characteristics. As they spoke from the heart it emerged that they were a group of physicians who cared for their patients in unusually great depth. They were service oriented. And perhaps because they had been pared down by those who had left, despite their conflicts they possessed a high degree of loyalty both to one another and to the drab desert area they served. 'You requested our services,' the FCE leaders told them at the end of the day, 'because you were an unhealthy organization. Yet, paradoxically, as is often the case, you also requested our services because, in another dimension, you are a strangely healthy organization.'

There are many stories about the large egos of doctors. Ordinarily physicians do not work well together. But the next morning they amply demonstrated how a group that has become a community can function with extraordinary effectiveness. The first task the FCE leaders gave the group on the third day was to consensually arrive at a definition of consensus. It took them an hour and a half. A long time? This is what they came up with:

Consensus is a group decision (which some members may not feel is the best decision, but which they can all live with, support, and commit themselves not to undermine), arrived at without voting, through a process whereby the issues are fully aired, all members feel they have been adequately heard, in which everyone has equal power and responsibility, and different degrees of influence by virtue of individual stubbornness or charisma are avoided so that all are satisfied with the process. The process requires the members to be emotionally present and engaged, frank in a loving, mutually respectful manner, sensitive to each other; to be selfless, dispassionate, and capable of emptying themselves, and possessing a paradoxical awareness of the preciousness of both people and time (including knowing when the solution is satisfactory, and that it is time to stop and not reopen the discussion until such time as the group determines a need for revision).[3]

It was not all smooth sailing, however. The next task the FCE leaders gave the clinic was to brainstorm actions they might take to maintain themselves as a community. They came up with two dozen proposals—all of them modest and superficial. Just before lunch the FCE leaders commented it was remarkable that no one had proposed they might do another follow-up Community Building Workshop. The group suddenly descended into a full-blown group depression.

When they resumed work after lunch the group initially ascribed their low energy to the meal they'd just eaten; then to their fatigue after two and a half days of such intensity; then to their worry over the time they'd taken off from their practice. Only gradually were they able to face the real dynamic: the death of their collective fantasy that the workshop would be a full and complete quick fix. It began to dawn on them that to continue to function as a community

---

[3] Copyright by the Valley Diagnostic and Surgical Clinic of Harlingen, Texas, and The Foundation for Community Encouragement. This copyright exists only for credit. The definition may be duplicated with this credit and as widely as readers see fit.

It is not the only definition. I do believe it is the best. But for another and remarkably similar one (of which the VDC was unaware) the reader is referred to Edgar H. Schein, *Process Consultation*, 2nd ed. (Reading, Mass: Addison-Wesley, 1988), vol. I, pp. 73–74.

they were going to have to continue to devote considerable time and effort to the task. There would be a price to pay.

By the end of the day, as the reality sunk in, the group's depression lifted. There was hardly ecstasy, however. The workshop concluded on a cautious note. The clinic committed itself only to meet as a whole group one night every two weeks for an unspecified duration to continue to discuss the issue of community maintenance. 'I'm not sure I know how to run a business that's also some kind of church,' the business manager grumbled.

But the issues were clear, and they hung in together. They abolished much of their committee system so that thereafter all major decisions were made consensually by the group as a whole. Eventually they did come to recognize the need for a follow-up refresher workshop, which was held a year later. They also began to decisively use their definition of consensus in recruitment. When a headhunter brought them a new physician, they would immediately show her or him the definition. If the physician's eyes glazed over, they would say, 'We'll be in touch.' But if the physician's eyes lit up, they'd say, 'Let's go to lunch.' Within a year of its initial workshop, the medical staff of the VDC had grown from seventeen to twenty-five and morale was high. The Valley Diagnostic and Surgical Clinic can take credit not only for the extraordinary task of resurrecting itself—at least for the time being—but also for something else. The definition of consensus they arrived at in community in a mere hour and a half on the Labor Day morning is now starting to be used by other organizations throughout the English-speaking world.

Community building is the vehicle, par excellence, for both the teaching and the learning of civility.

Refer back to the second part of the definition of consenus: 'The process requires the members to be emotionally present and engaged, frank in a loving, mutually

349

respectful manner, sensitive to each other; to be selfless, dispassionate, and capable of emptying themselves, and possessing a paradoxical awareness of the preciousness of both people and time (including knowing when the solution is satisfactory, and that it is time to stop and not reopen the discussion until such time as the group determines a need for revision).' These are many of the virtues of civility. In other words, the process of consensual decision making requires a high level of civility from the participants.

This is the reason for FCE's motto: 'Community building first, decision making second.' It might sound as if consensual decision making is so demanding that only an unusually sophisticated group of people could possibly be capable of it. Yes and no. Yes because a sophisticated, civil group is required. But no because any group can become 'sophisticated' within a very short time—no more than two days— through the community building process. *Any* group. Previous individual psychological or spiritual sophistication or training is unnecessary. In fact, time and again, we have found it is easier to build community among supposedly unsophisticated people than among 'sophisticates.' Indeed, the community building process must and does cut through people's sophistication to their innocense. They must give up thinking they know all the answers; empty themselves of their degrees and diplomas and the smugness conferred upon them by their academic or other honors.

Most particularly the community building process teaches its participants civility by increasing their consciousness. For a full year the board of FCE struggled unsuccessfully to arrive at a vision statement, not for the organization but for its product of community. It would have been extremely helpful for us to have a catchy, visionary slogan like 'a chicken in every pot.' We failed, of course, since community is much too grand to ever be captured in a single adequate definition, much less a slogan. But at one point in the process our chairman asked each of us board members to come up with a single adjective and noun to describe community. My own individual offering was 'nine-dimensional consciousness.'

Length, width, and depth are the three ordinary dimensions, and the fourth is space/time. Everyone is conscious of these.

A fifth dimension is the absence of space/time, or emptiness—the critical stage of community building and the essence of the meditative state. Previously only the great mystics have been aware of this dimension. Yet it can be easily taught, and in a sense, community makes mystics of us all. But it is hard to talk about this momentary state of consciousness where the mind is utterly open and receptive and thereby totally alert.

The sixth dimension for me is that of the self. Discussing self-consciousness, it was noted how virtually everyone possesses its rudiments. But for most people their consciousness of themselves, of their own motives and passions, is rudimentary indeed. It was also noted that psychotherapy works in good part because it is a process that exercises and strengthens the observing ego, that is, our capacity to observe ourselves and thereby become progessively more self-aware. While the purpose of community building is not psychotherapy—it is to build community—it is also a process that profoundly encourages people to examine their motives, feelings, judgments, and reactions, and hence a process that expands the consciousness of self.

The seventh dimension in my schema is the other—that particular thing, creature, or person with whom you happen to be in relationship at any one moment in time. For Bruce, in a moment of emptiness, the other happened to be a lowly spider. For most of the time it is another human being. It has been repeatedly pointed out that the primary characteristic of narcissists is their unconsciousness of the other. It has also been pointed out that we are all narcissistic to a degree, that we all have a tendency to be remarkably unaware of the differentness, the separateness and uniqueness, of our fellow human beings. Community building is a process that dramatically teaches people to become more conscious of each other. Don't go into it unless you have some willingness to whittle away at your narcissism.

My eighth dimension is the group as a whole. At the same time in community that we are listening or responding to another person, we are doing so in the context of a group. When we speak to the other, whether we are aware of it or not, we are simultaneously speaking to the entire assembly. Yet our group consciousness is generally so lacking that I referred to this lack as 'the hole in the mind.' There are many learnings at FCE workshops, but perhaps the greatest is this often very new skill of keeping your eye on the group and your attention on its moods, its subtle fluctuations, and its dramatic shifts. So this chapter began by noting that the more we work in community, the more the hole in the mind begins to fill.

God, for me, is the ninth and final dimension. It has been recounted how when a group enters the stage of community, the members may sense the presence of God in the room. It is possible to have an abstract kind of faith in an abstract kind of God, but such faith is shallow. Deep faith can come only from personal experience of her actual presence. This experience is simultaneously gentle and earth-shattering, earth-shattering because God's position in our minds then moves from belief to knowledge, from theory to conscious fact. People do not have to be in community to experience the presence of God, and the secular-minded may spend years in community without ever having such an experience. But community is the way that groups and organizations can welcome God, and when sufficiently welcome she usually shows up 'for all those who have eyes to see.' I have fallen into the hands of the living God in many ways and places, but community has been the most frequent and consistent way and place he has leaped into my life and into my consciousness.

How exactly does the community building (and maintaining) process bring about such increasing consciousness? An entire book could be written to address this question thoroughly, and even then the adequacy of the answer would pale before that which you would receive through actually experiencing the process one or more times. But let me offer one little glimpse.

When I was still leading CBWs myself, I would give my final initial instruction to the group by recounting how at the age of sixteen I entered a Quaker school and there had my first experience of Quaker meetings and the silence of those meetings. 'And paradoxically,' I would continue, 'it was out of that silence that at the age of seventeen I first began to preach, that I first experienced something the Quakers called the "inner light" or what other Christians might call the Holy Spirit moving me to speak. Moving me to say things often wiser than I knew I had it in me to say. Community building has to do with communication. Among the innumerable sins of communication, one of the greatest is to speak when you are not moved—and we all know people who do this or else seem to somehow feel continually moved. The other greatest sin is to fail to speak when you are moved, which is a form of disobedience. We are now going to go into three minutes of silence, and when I let you know they are over then you will begin to speak as you are so moved.'

One way or another, in their own words, this has become a standard instruction for FCE leaders to give in introducing a workshop. Note all that it accomplishes. It instructs the participants to continually monitor themselves, to be conscious whether or not they are feeling moved. 'Do I feel like talking now,' they must ask themselves, 'just because the emptiness of the silence makes me nervous, or it is because I am genuinely moved? Is what I have to say a truly appropriate response to the person who has just spoken? Is it something that the group actually needs to hear?' Already the participants are beginning to learn to be more conscious of themselves, of the movement of God within themselves, of the emptiness of silence, of the needs of others and of the group as a whole.

It may seem like a tall order to operate with nine-dimensional consciousness, to be aware—virtually simultaneously—of all the aspects of the system. Yet everyone who wants to can do it. He and she can learn how to do it reasonably well quite quickly. No one ever learns to do it perfectly every second, every minute. But the more we work together in community, the better and better we become at it. And becoming every more conscious, we become ever more civil. And in short order we understand 'the glory of what it means to be human.'

A question needs to be raised at this point. It is an important—even burning—question.

Much has been said on the subject of consciousness, but it has all been examined from the standpoint of the individual. What about the group? Is there such a thing as collective group consciousness?

This question has tantalized almost all of us who have had the opportunity to repeatedly witness groups entering the stage of community. This shift in group process at such a time is so dramatic! Group decision making, previously clumsy, becomes profoundly efficient and wise. The individual members speak more concisely. The group is in a kind of harmony. It has developed an effective rhythm of its own that is so striking that even the members themselves are surprised by it, surprised by what has happened to them, as if it were not entirely their own creation.

At these times the individuals in the group are functioning in such perfect style it is hard to believe their consciousness has not changed. In fact, many of them feel that they are somehow thinking differently within themselves, yet they simultaneously have the feeling that they are participating in something much larger than themselves—as if they had become part of a group mind, of a kind of living organism much greater than the sum of its parts.

For these reasons, I myself do believe that there probably

is such a phenomenon as collective consciousness—that under the right conditions we human individuals can join together to form a larger system that is capable not only of something like thought but of a kind of thinking that is wiser than that of ordinary human mentation. But I can't prove it. I'm not even sure that it could be proved. Then again, no one has yet tried. The issue is of such significance I hope somebody we will be willing to bring sufficient coordinated financial and intellectual resources to bear on the problem so that it can be adequately scientifically researched.

We students of community are hardly the first to raise the issue of collective consciousness. People have been aware of lynch mobs and the reality of 'mob psychology.' Even 'groupthink' in the business world has been frequently criticized for producing conformist decisions less adequate than those that could be made by individuals functioning alone. Many, myself among them, have observed that groups are often likely to behave in a more primitive fashion than individuals, as if together their members had sacrificed their conscience, their mentality. Indeed, in community building workshops some hold themselves back precisely for this reason. They are fearful that if they relinquish a shred of their isolated detachment or desert their judgmental position, they will be sucked into the working of a group mind in a way that will cause them to lose their personal integrity.

In the end, however, most of them realize they need not be afraid. For eventually they come to recognize that the phenomenon of true community is the very opposite of a mob. Mob psychology is characterized by a lack of consciousness; community by an increase in consciousness. A mob is frightening; a community is a 'safe place.' Mobs are violent, uncivil. Genuine communities are mostly peaceful and profoundly civil. A community (as opposed to a cult) is always characterized by the room it makes for divergent opinion, and an individual member who feels even slightly bullied will often be the first to speak up. I repeat that mob psychology is characterized by authoritarianism and a lack of consciousness; a group in the phase of community is characterized by heightened consciousness and quite extraordinary inclusivity or egalitarianism.

In a different vein, the great psychiartrist Carl Jung posited a phemenon he called 'the collective unconscious.' This he described as a part of the individual mind that is not conscious but that is somehow shared with the same part of the minds of others. In his psychology this collective unconscious is a kind of semi-intellectual garden of delights that is owned by humanity in common, which every human being is free to visit in his dreams or roam in her deepest interior life. I said 'semi-intellectual' because the ideas, the delights, in this garden are in the form of energized, complex, mythic symbols rather than simple prosaic words. These collectively energized symbols Jung labeled 'archetypes.'

Although some early, supporting evidence is beginning to be accumulated, the notion of the collective unconscious is certainly not yet proven and remains very much a theory. Several of FCE's leaders, fascinated by the collective energy of community, have left their jobs to do research in academia on related subjects, such as 'group learning.' One of them, Kazimierz Gozdz, has hypothesized that community may be an archetype and that when a group enters the stage of community, its members somehow tap into this unconscious archetype and its collective power. Certainly, the energy of a group in community does have a mythic quality—literally as well as figuratively, since another characteristic of such groups is their capacity to creatively develop their own exquisitely appropriate and richly evocative myths.

Still, this is all highly theoretical, and the question of whether there is such a thing as collective consciousness simply cannot be answered for certain at this point. But the answer may have enormous implications. For instance, if an organization is particularly civil, is this merely because it happens to contain an unusual number of particularly civil employees in the right positions? Is its civility but the sum of the civility of its parts? Or might the organization actually have a *soul* of its own—a kind of collective mind and spirit that is greater than the average intelligence and vision of its individual members? Can a corporation have a conscience? Or can it only be conscientious to the degree that its leaders are willing to operate out of their individual consciences?

We don't know. But we do know that corporations have their own unique cultures, and these cultures do much to determine the civility or the incivility of organizations. We know that the organization's leaders have the greater power to create its own culture. But we also know that the culture in turn has a profound effect on the consciousness and behavior of all its members. A civil culture will do something to teach every employee civility. An uncivil culture will encourage all its participants to incivility. Moreover, cultures tend to perpetuate themselves. A CEO who has done much to create a particularly civil culture may leave behind her a legacy of civility long after she has retired or died.

Finally, whether there is or is not such a thing as collective consciousness, we do know—as the following chapters will amply demonstrate—that the introduction of community building and maintenance into organizations will vastly increase their civility. As has been pointed out, community is not only a highly civil form of organization but is also the ideal vehicle for teaching civility—teaching individuals *and* organizations. The technology or discipline of community is the single best means a top manager has at his disposal to develop and maintain on organizational culture of civility.

18

Rewalking the Tightrope

Ethics and Adversarialism in Business

Many chapters ago I quoted Richard Bolles's reference to us humans as 'the comparing creatures.' Sometimes I think we should also be called 'the forgetful creatures.'

It is, I believe, one of God's gifts to us that we naturally remember the good times in our lives and have a remarkable capacity to forget the bad—or at least lose touch with how bad the pain could be. But all gifts are potential curses, and the downside of our capacity to forget the unpleasant is our inefficient need to relearn and relearn and relearn yet again the more painful lessons of life.

One such lesson is that health is seldom painless and healing often hurts. We now revisit that lesson once more in terms of organizational health by focusing on the pain of tension. The reality is that the healthy business is not only one in tension but also one in which that tension is being fully experienced, where it is fully conscious.

We saw that tension or friction is inevitable in marriage and demonstrated that the most common marital problems arise out of the attempt to avoid this friction (or blame it on the partner) instead of dealing with it openly. In speaking of the tension between togetherness and separateness in marriage, the analogy was used of walking a tightrope. It is not easy to walk a tightrope. Skill and balance are required. It feels scary, even for the initiated. Every nerve is on the alert. Yet now we learn that healthy, civil businesses must also walk a tightrope. Daily. And that the greatest cause of organizational disease and incivility arises out of the attempts of top executives to escape this difficult reality. They forget that it is their job to face the tension head-on. If they forget long enough, they will doom their whole careers and probably their entire organizations to boot. Conversely, civil executives will recall and recall again that tension is the healthy norm in business, and they will remember to keep rewalking the tightrope.

From this point of view, the single greatest cause of business failure is the failure of a business to live in the tension. And the two most common varieties of this failure are adversarialism and 'pseudoconsensus,' which we will now examine in turn in the context of community.

Tension is conflict.

While nations still resort to war, groups to riot and pillage, and individuals to rape and murder, over the millennia civilization has developed procedures to resolve conflict without bloodshed. These procedures I call adversarial machinery. They are civil procedures. Indeed, it is the existence of adversarial machinery that makes civilization worthy of its name.

There are three broad categories of adversarial machinery: litigation, negotiation, and democracy. Each has its own set of traditions and prescribed rules and regulations. They are highly structured forms of communication. Seldom, however, are they entirely separate; two, and often all three, are employed in the process of the same battle. A trial, for instance, is the core of litigation. Yet at certain points in the litigation process the adversaries and their lawyers may *negotiate* a settlement. And if they don't, the trial may go to jury for a democratic *vote*. Similarly, the union membership will democratically vote on an agreement negotiated by its representatives. Or a senatorial committee may vote to confirm a nominee, but before doing so will conduct hearings that often come to resemble *trials*.

This adversarial machinery deserves enormous respect.

It has been refined over centuries as the most thorough, even elegant, formal means of discerning truth and arriving at effective, balanced judgments in matters of conflict of interest or ethics. It is also extremely expensive, unpleasant, and alienating.

What I call adversarialism may be defined as a profound tendency on the part of individuals, organizations, or societies to routinely resort to adversarial machinery when it is unnecessary and unproductive, even uncivil. But why? Why on earth would anyone—particularly an organization —want to unnecessarily employ procedures that are so unpleasant and alienating, time-consuming and expensive?

It is because tension is uncomfortable. Whether that tension is severely or only mildly painful, it is natural for us pain-avoiding creatures to want to get rid of it as quickly as possible. One way to do so is through a three-step process that can proceed with astonishing rapidity. When tension is experienced, the first step is to ascribe it to a conflict with another individual or organization. The second step is to blame the other for the conflict, ascribing to the other malicious or even insane motives. The third step is then to invoke the use of adversarial machinery to deal with the conflict. In approximately one case out of twenty this process is a proper and civil way to proceed. Ninety-five percent of the time it is unconscious, uncivil, and un-necessary. What makes it so frequently out of kilter?

First, because step one is often a misstep. The tension may have nothing to do with an external conflict. Let us suppose the tension is that experienced by an airline company under scrutiny by a federal aviation regulatory agency. The source of the tension may be guilt that the company has failed to follow regulations and has cheated in some way. Or fear that it will be found out. Or laziness that causes it to resent having to produce reasonable paperwork. Or greed that is frustrated by the regulations. Or trans-ference, causing the regulatory agency to automatically be regarded as a hated, autocratic father. In all these instances, the tension—or conflict, if you will—is entirely internal. To ascribe it to *genuine* conflict between the organization and the regulatory agency is to jump the gun. Which, in fact, is the point. To take the time to look seriously at—to examine—the tension requires that for at least a little while you live in the tension. But that is uncomfortable. The quicker you can ascribe the tension to a source, the shorter the period you need to live with it. Jumping the gun is a tension-relieving mechanism. A rush to judgment cuts short the pain. The problem is that the rushed judgment is usually wrong.

The second step is also likely to be a rush to judgment, for the same pain-avoiding motives. Let's say your airline company believes that thorough-overhaul engine maintenance should be conducted routinely after every 200 hours of flying time. The regulatory agency believes the figure should be every 150 hours. The conflict is clear. But does the agency take this position out of maliciousness? Or other spurious motives? How can you make a considered judgment without seriously attempting to understand the agency's position? Such understanding will inevitably require a reexamination of your own position. All this demands work and time spent in the midst of a period of ambiguity, of the tension of not knowing. It is emotionally so much less demanding to conclude without research that the agency is your enemy, persecuting you without regard to reality or reasonableness.

So you take step number three, and you call in your lawyers. Perhaps they are civil lawyers and will suggest you calmly rethink your position. But if they do, you, anxious to get on with it, are likely to direct them: 'Full speed ahead and damn the torpedoes. Go get 'em.' And if they are not so civil, they will be only too happy to jump into action on your behalf. The adversarial machinery has been set in gear.

All this discussion might seem academic were there not an obviously better way. So let us turn now to a story of how an ordinarily adversarial situation in business was dealt with very differently.

Among other things, this is a story about power on many levels, and we shall be returning to some of its morals throughout the remainder of the book. I like to begin it with Frank. At age eighteen, he was the youngest person, other than a child of a leader or board member, ever to come to one of FCE's public workshops. He liked the experience of that workshop so much that as soon as he returned to his home state, he began, in early 1989, to organize a public FCE workshop in the local area. He promoted it well, and fifty-five people attended in addition to Frank himself and the two FCE leaders.

Unbeknownst to Frank or FCE, one of those attendees was a high-ranking executive of a Fortune 500 corporation. That corporation was soon to be facing a two-month period of labor-management negotiations during which two labor-management teams, in two different cities, were to attempt to negotiate contracts with separate unions. One team was experienced and the other inexperienced. Approximately sixty thousand union employees were affected. It was anticipated that the negotiations would fail in each instance, and strikes seemed inevitable.

It would seem that the top executive liked what he saw because ten days later the coordinator of the experienced labor-management team contacted FCE's director of programs to request a community building workshop for the team. When she asked him how he'd heard of FCE's work, he answered, 'We were just told to do it by the vice-president for human resources. But he didn't seem to know much about it really. I don't know where or how it originated, except that it was somewhere very high up in the company.'

'How do you feel about being "just told" to do a workshop?' she inquired.

'Well, I'm a little uneasy, but that's just because I don't know anything about your workshops. They're not the kind of thing where people break down and cry, are they?'

'We don't have any whips, if that's what you mean,' she

answered. 'Most people think it's a very gentle process. Certainly we don't *make* people cry. But if they want to cry, which sometimes they do, we're also certainly not going to try to stop them unless they're being excessive about it.'

'Okay. I do have one other concern. It's not the kind of thing where people talk about God, is it?'

'I have to give you the same sort of answer,' she replied. 'We don't make people talk about anything. If they want to talk about God, they do. If there's any pattern in this regard, actually, it's that we tend to discourage *too much* "God talk." '

He seemed relieved.

A week later FCE was contacted by the second labor-management team. They'd heard that the first team was going to do a workshop, and they wanted to get in on the act and have one of their own, no questions asked.

The two workshops were held at the same time. Although facilitated by different FCE leaders in different cities and although one team was highly sophisticated and the other untrained, they were remarkably similar events. Within six hours members of each team were crying and talking about God, among other things. By the end of their workshops, both teams had spontaneously reached an identical set of determinations. Instead of 'coming to the table' they decided to get rid of the table. Management and labor, which had traditionally eaten separately, decided to eat together. Management vowed, if it could, to come in with its financial bottom line from the very beginning. And both vowed to try not to caucus throughout the two-month period.

These vows were successfully kept by each team.

Both teams specifically requested that their stories be kept confidential. The reason for this request was not that they didn't want the general public to know about them; it was that they wanted to keep their mode of functioning secret from their own labor force and their own management. They surmised, realistically, that neither would trust the outcome if it were learned that they were arrived at by consensus in community. How could either the bulk of union members or the company executives, themselves never exposed to genuine community, possibly believe that the teams could have arrived at what was best for them without drawing blood—indeed, while often having fun together?

In fact, a humorous moment of crisis came when one of the teams learned it was to be visited the next day by a high-ranking outside official to check on how things were going. What was to be done? The management and labor members agreed that their only recourse was to 'fake it.' Although they had been meeting for six weeks in an ordinary hotel parlor room, they succeeded in renting for that next day on the conference level a much larger venue entitled 'The Board Room,' which contained a huge, long table. They spent most of the night up dummying fake stacks of paper. By prearrangement, the next morning the management members arrived in ties and coats and behaved very coldly toward the labor members. The labor members similarly behaved coldly toward management. By the end of the morning, the visiting official pronounced himself most pleased by the progress of the proceedings.

I have not mentioned the name of the company because, four years later, the teams continue to desire that their manner of the operation must be kept confidential for the same reasons. These reasons will soon be examined more deeply. But the contract each team worked out proved acceptable to both labor and management. And, contrary to expectations, a strike was averted in both cases, saving everyone concerned vast amounts of money and agony.

Credit for this success story belongs to many. It belongs to FCE's leaders and the community building model they employed. The credit was given. At the end of their three-day workshop, the more sophisticated team proclaimed, 'We've been through every kind of team-building exercise up the kazoo, and what you guys are doing represents a whole new generation.'

Credit belongs even more to the labor and the management members of both teams. It was they, cooperatively, who took the experience of community and ran with it, who used it to break entirely new ground. They went out on a limb together, defying all the standard norms to such an extent that they had to operate in secrecy. It took great courage.

Credit must certainly go to that top executive who initially directed the first team to do the workshop. She or he did this because of his or her own anonymous workshop experience. It is an unusual top executive who takes a weekend to explore some newfangled process called community building where people might 'break down' and cry and talk about God.

Finally, it is an example of spiritual power. Remember the beginning of the story, of how it all evolved out of the efforts of an eighteen-year-old 'boy.' It is also an unusual eighteen-year-old who goes to such workshops. And had Frank not on his own initiative then returned home to organize a workshop for the public, none of this would have happened. In common with most adolescents, he possessed no political power. Yet by virtue of his discernment, initiative, and enthusiasm—his calling—he can take considerable credit for revolutionizing labor-management negotiations within a major corporation, at least for that year and perhaps eventually for longer and on a far wider scale.

Tension has been equated with conflict. It is extremely important for us to understand that conflict in human affairs is healthy and normal. Conflict is an inescapable part of life and is not inherently uncivil. Indeed, I must repeat that it is the essence of civility to openly deal with conflict in our organizational lives through respectful discussion and clarification. Conflict is uncivil only when it is either hidden or when, through the unnecessary use of the adversarial process, it is disrespectfully blown out of all proportion.

Ethical issues are at stake when the adversarial process is invoked. The process so often becomes the court of first resort instead of the court of last resort because, painful though it may be—often even ridiculous—it is less painful to take sides than to live in ethical tension for a substantial period of time. Yes, adversarialism puts the tension right out in the open, but it does so in a way that allows the participants to feel self-righteous. What I call 'living in the tension,' on the other hand, requires that we face our ethical dilemmas head-on without the balm of self-righteousness. It requires a certain amount of emotional and ethical maturity. This is the reason for the sentence in FCE's mission statement that its 'approach encourages tolerance of ambiguity, the experience of discovery and the tenson between holding on and letting go,' that is, between preserving one's integrity and relinquishing simplistic, rigid, self-righteous positions. It is the way of the tightrope.

What the labor management teams did, after their CBWs just described, was to choose to live in the tension rather than to blame it on the designated factions. There were clear factions on each team: the representatives of labor and the representatives of management. The tension between their differing needs was real; obviously it was in the interest of labor to 'get' as much as possible and of management to 'give' as little as possible. But in choosing to function as teams in more than name only, what these women and men did with the tension was to *play* with it. They bounced it back and forth. The reexamined their roles as 'givers' and 'getters.' They role-played each other's positions. Labor helped out management. Management helped out labor. They even 'emptied' themselves of positions. And eventually and consensually they arrived at what was fair.

How did they do this? Why were they able to 'internalize' the tension and live in it, rather than to 'externalize' it and clobber each other over the head with it? The answer is amazingly simple. Remember FCE's adage, 'Community building first, decision making second.' In the community building process people get real with each other. They are pushed not to hide behind the issues and their positions. They are encouraged to speak of what is closest to their hearts: their children, their marriages, their loneliness and frustration, their worries and insomnia and nightmares, their sexuality and strange feelings of connection to 'an unseen order of things.' And when they do so, something almost invariably happens: They come to care about each other.

This caring is real—and becomes ever more so the longer the group works together 'in community.' It is based on knowledge. It doesn't mean that everybody likes each other equally. It doesn't mean everyone trusts each other totally. To the contrary, it means one comes to know just where to trust the other and where not to trust him. Each person's gifts and weak points are revealed.

Part of the problem in the adversarial process is that the participants usually do not know each other well. Indeed, it is almost bizarre, when you come to think of it, that strangers should ever simply sit down and start negotiating. From a psychological standpoint they are not in the least ready to negotiate. Yet that is the standard way that things are done. Conversely, when people do know and care about one another, it becomes relatively difficult for them to be adversarial and relatively easy for them to behave co-operatively.

Anyone who has flown much commercially in the United States and scanned the airline magazines contained in the seat pocket in front of him has likely seen an advertisement for Karrass Seminars. Underneath the picture of Dr Chester L. Karrass, the ad states in huge type:

IN BUSINESS,
YOU DON'T GET
WHAT YOU DESERVE,
YOU GET
WHAT YOU NEGOTIATE.

Although ethical issues are always at stake in the adversarial process such as negotiations, the results are not necessarily fair or just.

In regard to the two labor-management teams described, purists would say that they didn't negotiate a contract at all; they *collaborated* a contract. What would ordinarily have been antagonistic was friendly; bumpy was smooth; agonizing was pleasant; ugly was beautiful. And just and fair. It was a magnificent example of healthy organizational behaviour, of civility.

Yet we live in such an adversarial society that neither team is willing, even four years after the fact, to make its extraordinary civility public. What a shame! But they are only being realistic. In U.S. society, where there are twice as many lawyers per capita as in any other nation, we are so accustomed to our adversarialism we seldom see it for what it is. In its excess, it is sick. Something is seriously wrong in a society when civility must be practiced in secret and organizational health must be hidden.

Not surprisingly, adversarialism has its opposite—an extreme just as unhealthy. I call it 'pseudoconsensus.' Here, instead of being blown all out of proportion, the ethical tension within an organization is 'stuffed.' Conflict is glossed over, submerged, denied. Real problems or issues, rather than being surfaced, are pushed into the organization's unconscious to become its organizational Shadow.

In this opposite type of failure to live in the tension—to walk the tightrope—the organization disallows any ethical debate whatsoever. It declares the tension to be nonexistent. Yet the tension is always there. Remember, life *is* tension. So the only way a business can declare it nonexistent is to make it unmentionable. Unfortunately, many top managers and corporate cultures do exactly this.

In May 1991, FCE, in conjunction with the University of Chicago Graduate School of Business, sponsored a conference, 'Business and Community,' attended by approximately one hundred and twenty businesspeople. Typical of community building events, where the outcomes are generally as unpredictable as they are positive, the conference was full of surprises. The participants did most of their work in four groups. It was the task of each group to build itself into a community during the first day and a half. Having become a community, each group was then assigned an issue and given a day to produce a product around that issue—a product it would present or market to the conference as a whole at the end.

One surprise was that while there were four distinct groups with different products, a single prevailing theme emerged from the conference. It was the theme of tension. Experienced in the world of business, the participants were realists and did not come up with any easy answers. What they came up with was the tension of living without such answers. For instance, the 'Yellow Group's' issue was that of pluralism in the workplace, that is, the issue of enabling men and women, blacks, whites, and Chicanos, Muslims, Jews, and Christians to work together effectively. It concluded that there was no way to eradicate the tension of pluralism; the key was to dignify it—even celebrate it—by giving it a forum, a time and space for it to not only be discussed but honored. In fact, the group suggested the primary reason to introduce community into business might be just this: to provide an adequate forum for all the tensions of business life to surface openly.

The 'Blue Group,' whose task was to develop a product on ethics in business, independently came up with a marketable exercise to demonstrate exactly this theme. The group elected one of its members, Mike, as its spokesperson. Mike herded the hundred and twenty of us participants out into the marble foyer of the administration building of the University of Chicago's business school. Standing on a table, he recounted the following ethical dilemma:

369

'There was a forty-year-old female middle manager in a large company. Her job performance was totally ineffective. Indeed, she was the laughingstock of the department. Her coworkers continually joked about her behind her back. Because the company had been in great turmoil due to a merger and a takeover, in the two years since her hire she had not received any supervision. At this point, a senior manager was brought in. He immediately discerned the situation and decided to embark on a twelve-month program of skilled, consistent supervision with the employee. Having had considerable success with similar cases, he was initially optimistic. However, she made zero progress, despite his considerable efforts, and after eight months, he was beginning to become pessimistic. At this point, he himself was ordered to another branch of the company in a distant city. He was therefore faced with the decision of whether to lay the woman off four months short of what he considered to be a fully adequate course of supervision, or to pass her on as a probably unsolvable problem to a new senior manager to start all over again.'

Mike gave a little hand signal, and six members of his Blue Group materialized out of the crowd and stretched three ropes tautly along the length of the foyer. Pointing to his left, Mike explained, 'The people holding the ropes on this side believe that the woman deserves a totally adequate course of supervision, and that, without question, she should be retained. The people holding the ropes to my right, on the other hand, feel that a perfectly reasonable effort has been made and she should obviously be fired. Now, I'd like you all to break into three groups and, as individuals, take a place on the rope according to where you would fall on the continuum between these opposite poles.'

I immediately went to the nearest rope and positioned myself on it two-thirds of the way toward the end held by the 'hard-liner.' When we had all clearly assumed our positions, Mike instructed us to talk with the person next to us as to why we had taken up that particular station. My neighbor on the rope was a woman of about the same age as the employee in question. We both agreed at once that we were tending toward a hard-line position because we were not the kind of executives who liked to pass problems on, but we could not be more certain because there was so much about the company that we did not know but that we felt needed to be factored into the equation.

'Now, I'd like each of you,' Mike directed, 'to go to that person on the rope that you most want to discuss the case with.' I made a beeline for the hard-liner. I wanted to tell him that I probably agreed with him, but I wanted to find out how he could be so certain. Did he know something that I didn't know? Something about the employee? Something about the company's employee assistance program or other programs it might have to aid people who were laid off in finding new jobs? A vocational testing program, perhaps?

The problem was that no sooner did I get to a spot three feet away from the hard-liner than he dropped his end of the rope. At the same instant the soft-liner at the other side of the foyer dropped his end. With the tension of the rope totally lost, the thirty of us became entangled in the rope, moving this way and that, not knowing where or how to proceed. The other two groups became similarly entangled in their ropes. The chaos turned hilarious.

When we had all finally disentangled ourselves, Mike informed us, 'The decision was made to lay the woman off. Seven months later, she committed suicide. The managers of the company were left with a great deal of guilt and self-blame.'

The point is not the very sad ending to the story, or even that the decision made was the wrong one. It may have been the right one. As have other executives, on two occasions I have had people I have fired come up to me years afterward and actually thank me. 'I just refused to believe I was in real difficulty,' they explained. 'It took your firing me for me to finally come to my senses.'

The point is the tension, and the fact that when it was lost, the conference, the organization, fell into utter chaos. Business is frequently faced with exquisite ethical dilemmas, and the purpose of this book is not to pretend otherwise. A business needs *both* its hard-liners and its soft-liners to maintain the tension. And it needs the forum of community to maintain that tension right in the forefront of the organization's collective consciousness.

Business fails ethically when either the soft-line or the hard-line positions are so in ascendancy that the debate between them becomes silenced. FCE itself almost once failed because all of us 'do-gooders' on the board had not yet learned how to take the hard-line positions that sometimes must be taken to ensure the survival of even the 'nicest' organizations.

The more common type of failure occurs, however, when top management is captured by a single hard-liner or small group so dedicated to one single position that ethical questioning is stifled as 'insubordination.' Time and again we see a situation in which a 'bottom line profitability this quarter' ethos rules a company so totally that more visionary approaches are silenced in the name of heresy. Sooner or later that kind of management either drives the company into the ground or is itself driven off to jail.

Community is the antidote or preventative for such incivility and ethical imbalance. Community is a 'safe place,' where all the players feel free to speak their mind and where their voices will be listened to with seriousness. It is an environment in which differences are not only allowed but encouraged. It is a group whose members have learned to fight gracefully so that ethical stones are not left unturned and the tension is not abandoned. Introduce genuine community into your business, and you will guarantee its ethical integrity.

Several times I have been asked, 'what would you do if an obviously uncivil or unethical organization, such as the Ku Klux Klan, request your community building services?'

'I'd explain to them what those services involve' is my

response; 'and then it is unlikely they'd continue to want them. But if they did, I'd certainly provide them.' When I'm met with a puzzled expression, I go on to point out, 'If the workshop succeeded—and I have not reason to believe it wouldn't—by the time it was over, it would no longer be the Ku Klux Klan.'

The question about the Ku Klux Klan arises because many who have never experienced community are skeptical about the ethicality of group decision making. The specters of conformity, 'groupthink,' and even mob psychology have already been raised. Aren't there consensual lynching mobs? This issue is the problem of pseudoconsensus.

As adversarialism is analogous to the stage of chaos in community building, so pseudoconsensus is analogous to the even more primitive stage of pseudocommunity. In pseudocommunity, the group members pretend that they have no issues, no differences. They avoid conflict and skirt tensions. Conformity is the order of the day. Consequently, when pseudocommunities make unanimous decisions, they usually do so by pseudoconsensus. It *looks* as if they had reached agreement. It *appears* that they have dealt with the issues when, in reality, the issues and tensions have been stuffed. A true community, on the other hand, is a group that truly does deal with its issues, that actually does face its organizational Shadow.

It is helpful at this point to recall the first part of Valley Diagnostic Clinic's definition of genuine consensus:

Consensus is a group decision (which some members may not feel is the best decision, but which they can all live with, support, and commit themselves to not undermine), arrived at without voting, through a process whereby the issues are fully aired, all members feel they have been adequately heard, in which everyone has equal power and responsibility, and different degrees of influence by virtue of individual stubbornness or charisma are avoided so that all are satisfied with the process.

Pseudoconsensus occurs when a group reaches an

apparently unanimous decision (and true consensus is not the same as unanimity) that has actually been subtly or not so subtly dictated by one or a few, where the issues have not been fully aired, and where other members do not feel they have been heard—indeed, where often they do not feel free to express their doubts or alternative ideas. It is a distressingly common situation, since so many organizations and their 'rubber-stamp' boards are pseudocommunities. I have talked on occasion to several autocratic presidents of large organizations who assured me that they led by 'consensus,' when in fact they didn't even begin to understand the meaning of the word.

So we're talking about real community and real consensus—and *real tension*. At the risk of mentioning the point *ad nauseum*, civility is never painless and life is tension and health can hurt. The reason to introduce community into a business has nothing to do with making it easier. It has a great deal to do, however, with making that business more ethical and civil, more painfully honest, more healthy and disturbingly alive.

Ethics is *one* of the major issues for private sector organizations—along with productivity, customer satisfaction, profits, and the like. For public sector organizations, ethics *is* the primary issue. Indeed, it might be said that ethics is the business of government.

I am not addressing here the ethics of individual public officials, upon which the media focus so much attention—issues of whether this official took a bribe or that one was sexually promiscuous. Rather, we are examining the ethical functioning of the organization as a whole. Does government behave ethically, and if not, why not?

Ethics are at the heart of all government decisions. To be specific, take the decision making involved in the determination of the federal government's budget. How much should be spent on federal regulatory agencies, much of whose work is based on the assumption that other organizations are not going to behave ethically unless they are so regulated? How much of that regulation should be directed toward protecting the environment, and how much toward favoring industrial expansion that might threaten the environment? What ethical right does the United States have to be the 'world's policeman,' and how large a 'defense' establishment should we support to protect our 'national interests'? What obligation does the federal government have to aid the states in further public education, and to what extent might this obligation take precedence over national defense? To what degree might the wealthy have a greater obligation to support these activities than the poor or middle class? What is a proper amount of debt for the government to incur for its sustenance? Such civic questions are all issues of values, and hence ethical issues and issues of civility.

Of all the organizations with which I have some acquaintance, the U.S. federal government is, in my estimation, the most unhealthy. I do not mean to imply that there are no governments more unhealthy or that there are not many equally unhealthy; only that I am not closely acquainted with them. I do mean to imply, however, that the ill health of our government is extraordinary indeed. This is not merely my perception. As I travel the country lecturing, one of the most common and painful questions I receive is, 'Dr Peck, to what degree is the sickness of our government caused by the apathy of the electorate, as opposed to the possibility that the people are so apathetic because the system is so hopelessly out of their control and so hopelessly out of control in general?'

I do not believe it was always this way. Yes, there have always been scandals in government, but it is only in the past thirty years that the scandalous in Washington has become the norm. It is not my purpose here to make any thorough analysis of the ills of our society. My intent is solely to relate the scandalous decline of civility in our government to a bizarre, recently normative combination of both adversarialism *and* pseudoconsensus in our national political life.

I would date the onset of our government's serious—very possibly fatal—illness as occurring in August 1964. The Department of Defense reported that North Vietnamese PT boats, without provocation, had attacked two U.S. destroyers in the Gulf of Tonkin. On the basis of this incident, President Lyndon Johnson sought and within three days obtained from Congress a virtually unanimous resolution authorizing him to openly wage war against North Vietnam. Within a year it had been established that the supposed 'Gulf of Tonkin Incident' had probably never happened. It was apparently an event completely trumped up by the administration. Yet Congress, which had granted Johnson authority to wage war on the basis of an utterly uncivil lie—a fabrication and a deliberate deception—never even lifted a finger to rescind that authority. Why not? Why did it compound uncivility with incivility?

There are many possible answers to that question, but they all bespeak a kind of insanity that had settled in upon Washington and has remained ever since. There is a rule in psychiatry that mental illness is 'overdetermined,' meaning it is the product of multiple causes operating simultaneously. As I have suggested, the two major cases of our government's illness—insanity, if you will—are adversarialism and pseudoconsensus operating in collusion.

Democracy, like litigation and negotiation, is by its nature an adversarial process. Candidates and parties campaign *against* each other. Indeed, whenever there is voting, there are going to be winners and losers. It is a process of what has come to be called 'win/lose decision making.' Better than autocracy or dictatorship, you might say. And so it is, though not necessarily better than nonadversarial group decision making using consensual or collaborative styles that have come to be designated as 'win/win decision making.' But American democracy has failed in recent years, I believe, not because it is adversarial, but because it has become excessively adversarial in some ways and insufficiently so in others. By this I mean we have developed an entrenched pattern of rapidly putting our most serious issues to an often meaningless vote without even first attempting consensual/collaborative decision making or seriously using the adversarial process to deeply consider the issues.

So it was, even though at the time the supposed facts of the Gulf of Tonkin Incident didn't add up, that Congress—operating in pseudocommunity—rushed to vote Johnson his desired war powers without seriously considering what it was doing. And so it was, when it emerged it had been duped, that again operating in pseudocommunity, it decided to gloss over its obvious failure and not reopen the discussion.

A year later, in 1966, the Johnson administration began a compaign to covertly force government employees to buy war bonds to pay for the escalation in Vietnam without having to raise taxes. The expansion of America's national debt had begun. In the ensuing twenty-six years, adjusted for inflation, that debt has increased by more than 250 percent. Reversing a tradition of maintaining a debt approximately equal to its annual budget, the federal government's debt now stands at three and a half times its budget.[1] Ostensibly in the interest of serving the public, our government has adroitly been hiding reality from the people by a fiscal sleight of hand that in ordinary business practice would be deemed criminal. Indeed, were it an ordinary business, it probably would have long since had to declare bankruptcy. Only because it has been the government has it been able to get away with such gross mismanagement.[2]

[1] In 1938, the Roosevelt administration openly decided to increase the national debt from its customary level equal to its annual income in order to pay for World War II. By the end of that war in 1945, our debt stood at twice our annual budget. Within a decade, however, despite the costs of the Marshall Plan and the Korean War, we managed to pay off the excess so that by 1955 the national debt once again was no more than the annual federal budget. It remained at that level until 1966, when we began our pattern of ever-increasing indebtedness without any publicly acknowledged or debated crisis to justify it.

[2] See James V. McTevia, *Bankrupt* (Ann Arbor, Mich.: Momentum Books, 1992).

Still, why? We see on our television screens the intensity with which Congress will adversarially consider the approval of a Supreme Court nominee or investigate a covert arms sale scandal. How then can it be guilty of such mismanagement? How can it so ill consider an entire war like Vietnam or annually vote to mortgage our children's future? How can it commit such gross incivilities? The answer, I believe, is that it focuses such care on relatively minor issues precisely in order to avoid caring deeply about the most important and truly *painful* issues. Its televised public hearings give the appearance that democracy is working when, in regard to the basic issues, it no longer is.

The key word is *painful*. It is characteristic of a pseudo-community to avoid painful issues. Seeking to be elected or reelected through an adversarial process, our representatives have become more interested in looking good than being good, in appearing civil than actually making civil decisions. They bounce back and forth between the adversarial chaos of campaigning and the pseudoconsensual collusion to make everything look smooth, to hide the real tension, to escape the real agony. Recall the mention of *folies*—shared, family, psychotic delusions—in Part Two. Could it be that in attempting to avoid the legitimate suffering demanded by fiscal responsibility, our government has descended into just such a form of collective insanity? I believe so.

There is no way that we can painlessly regain any semblance of national health. Some extremely painful fiscal decisions are going to need to be made by the government if the nation it governs is even to survive as such. And it seems clear from recent history that our democratic system, as it currently operates, is incapable of making such decisions.

Because of this apparent incapacity, some of my most thoughtful friends—extremely successful bankers and lawyers—have begun to foresee an eventual necessity for revolution. For my own part, as a peacemaker I shudder at the possibility. I'm not sure there are peaceful revolutions.

Consequently, my deepest hope is for reformation rather than revolution. I would very much like to see the democratic system be preserved, but I cannot imagine it being so without substantial reformation. Very specifically, I cannot imagine it unless we introduce some genuine community into the business of government, unless we are able to carve out within it an area—a forum—in which decision making can be exempt from adversarial politics and where the issues can really be grappled with in necessary depth without the pretense of pseudocommunity and the pressures of adversarialism. One such possible area, while otherwise preserving the beauty of the vote, might be that of congressional committees. These are potentially ideal places for the use of community building technology and genuine consensual functioning. Here is a vision of civility in government:

Let us consider a hypothetical senator from Michigan. He returns home after a Congress which, in the interests of a more responsible national budget and national future, has voted in favor of an Appropriations Committee recommendation to eliminate subsidies for automobile manufacturing in his state. A constituent tells him, 'The decision has hurt me and my family.' 'I'm terribly sorry,' he responds, 'but that was the vote of Congress.'

'Yes,' his constituent replies. 'But how did *you*, my representative, vote on the Appropriations Committee?'

The senator will be able to respond, 'Well, actually, I didn't vote; that's not the way it works, you see. We don't vote in committee anymore. We just collectively arrived, after deep consideration, at the very best consensual decision we could on behalf of the nation.'

Many react to any proposed reformation of our political process with knee-jerk cynicism: 'Sounds nice, but it's too idealistic; it'll never happen.' Maybe their cynicism is justified. I don't know. I do know it would be difficult for Congress to reject a legislative proposal coming out of community as a consensual recommendation. I also know there is no constitutional requirement for congressional committees to operate by vote or serve as adversarial partisan forums. There is only tradition. Yes, even those traditions that have become demonstrably ineffective and unhealthy may be extremely resistant to change. I must hope that lawmakers and citizenry alike will realize that bloody revolution or civil reformation are the only feasible options. Maintenance of the traditional status is no longer a viable alternative.

19

The Politics of Transformation

Introducing Community into Business

In the sixties and seventies, a body of skills and techniques emerged to gradually introduce greater participative management into business and improve communication at all levels of a company. This activity came to be known as Organizational Development, or OD. OD specialists quickly learned that if they were going to accomplish their goals, they had to start at the top. Even gentle interventions were doomed to failure unless the CEO and other senior management actively participated in them with clear enthusiasm for all to see.

Community building, which leads to much deeper changes in corporate culture, falls into a new category of activity at at the end of the eighties began to be called Organizational Transformation, or OT. When the sophisticated labor-management group said to its FCE leaders. 'We've been through every kind of team building exercise up the kazoo, but what you guys are doing is a whole new generation,' they were recognizing this distinction between OD and OT. Since building community in an organization is the more dramatic intervention, it is hardly surprising that the same principle applies: Any type of organizational transformation has to have the wholehearted support of the people at the top.

In its early days, FCE contracted with two junior ministers to conduct community building workshops within their churches. Both contracts fell through. What happened, essentially, was that when asked about the upcoming workshop, the senior minister replied, 'Well, that's Joe's thing. You know Joe. He's innovative but young. Is it some kind of New Age sort of thing? Well, I can't really tell you. I don't know anything about it, but it doesn't sound like my kind of thing.' Is it surprising that so few parishioners signed up that the workshop was canceled? Or that if a church is interested these days in a possible workshop, FCE will negotiate initially only with the senior minister?

Out of the hundred or more workshops FCE has conducted for organizations to date, just one has been a failure. It is instructive to examine it.

In 1989, the corporate director for marketing of a Fortune 500 company contacted FCE about a workshop for the top marketing executives of the corporation. The occasion was the reevaluation of the division's mission statement, and it was felt that community building would facilitate this critical group task. FCE selected its primary and secondary leaders with care. The primary leader then met in person for several hours with the corporate director, who seemed to be a most pleasant and dedicated individual. During the course of the meeting, however, the leader learned that, despite his title, this man was not at the top of the marketing hierarchy. He reported to a 'corporate manager' for marketing, who in turn reported to the vice-president for marketing. Both these men would be participants. Had they been fully informed as the nature and purpose of the workshop and were they in agreement with it? The leader was assured that they were. Would the corporate director mind if the leader spoke by phone with the vice-president just to make sure? It seemed no problem, and a phone appointment was set up. At the outset of that phone call, the vice-president apologized for being too busy to talk at any length, but he quickly stated he understood all about the workshop and was solidly behind it. The omens looked good.

The workshop began on schedule in an elegant hotel with all twenty-five of the top marketing executives and FCE's two leaders present. It was the usual dull pseudocommunity until the third hour, when the corporate director confessed he was unhappy in his position because the atmosphere of the department—indeed, of the whole corporate head-quarters—was fearful and oppressive.

The vice-president responded that he was saddened to hear that the corporate director was out of step, since everyone knew the corporation was 'one big happy family.' The group returned to its pseudocommunity.

During lunchtime, three executives came up to the leaders in private to say they agreed with the corporate director, that the atmosphere of the corporation was oppressive—so oppressive they were afraid to state this openly in the group.

When the workshop resumed after lunch, the corporate director said he felt 'not heard' by the vice-president, that he'd simply been written off as being 'out of step.' The vice-president said there was no other way to respond, since the corporation was, in fact, 'one big happy family.' Very uncomfortably, in the most gentle, muted terms, several of the more junior executives hinted at feelings that the vice-president might be slightly rigid and was not listening. It was clear he was visibly threatened. People retreated in inanities. The corporate manager, as from the beginning, said nothing. The group was bouncing back and forth between pseudocommunity and the most tenta-tive chaos.

During the midafternoon break, three more executives privately cornered the leaders to voice their agreement that the atmosphere was oppressive. The leaders called for an extra fifteen minutes of break time to discuss their strategy.

At the conclusion of the break, the secondary leader began. 'The issue of the workshop up until now seems not to be one of the individual conflict so much as one of corporate culture,' she said. 'The keystone of a culture is its myths. Myths can be true or they can be untrue. A major myth of this culture seems to be that the corporation is one big happy family. The tension seems to be around the question of whether this is a true or untrue corporate myth.'

The vice-president exploded at her. 'It is not the purpose of this workshop to criticize the culture of this corporation,' he shouted.

'What do you think the purpose is?' she asked.

'How should I know? I thought it was to facilitate us in rewriting a mission statement, but it clearly isn't going to do that. At this point, I have no idea, but I certainly wasn't informed it would be anything like this.'

'Nor was I,' the corporate manager chimed in. It was the first time he had spoken.

'I gave each of you a copy of Peck's book,' the director said. 'It described the process about as well as it can be.'

'Christ, you know I don't have the time to read books,' the vice-president retorted. 'You didn't tell me this thing would try to upset the whole applecart. You owed me that. And I wouldn't have permitted it if I'd known.'

The group returned to a kind of pseudocommunity, which was not merely boring; it was agonizing. Two members mildly suggested, 'I don't see how we can build ourselves into a community unless we're willing to look at our culture.' Their suggestions were met with uneasy silence.

Finally, the primary leader said, 'It is just a couple of minutes to five. Certainly we have done some work that has needed to be done, but I must admit it is very unclear whether we will get where we need to go. What I do know is that things go on overnight and have a way of becoming more clear on the second day. Unless there are any questions or one of you has something you feel needs to be said, we'll start work again at nine in the morning.' After a minute of silence he continued, 'Okay, dinner will be at six in Salon B. Otherwise, we'll see you in the morning.' There were some audible sighs of relief.

At dinner the vice-president came up to the leaders and said he wanted to meet with them in private as soon as they were finished. They agreed to go to his room. Once they were there, he faced the secondary leader. Was it because she was a woman or the one who'd raised the issue of corporate myth? 'I want you to stop this workshop,' he said in a demanding tone.

'Is that an order?' the primary leader asked.

'No.' He looked at them both. 'I want *you* to stop the workshop. It's your job to stop it.'

'I'm not sure we want to make that decision,' the primary leader said. 'Of course, if you ordered us to stop it, we'd have no choice but to do so, since you're the one who's paid for it.'

The vice-president looked profoundly discomfited. 'Actually the funds to pay for it have come out of some of the other people's subsidiary company budgets over which I have no direct control.'

There was a moment of silence. 'We *are* one big happy family,' he insisted. Then, almost as if in a trance, he told how he'd been abandoned by his parents as a young child and raised in a series of foster homes. 'This company's the only family I've ever had,' he concluded.

'That's fascinating,' the primary leader responded. 'And touching. Why don't you tell the group that in the morning? I think you'd be respected for it.'

'I'm not going to tell that to the group. Can't you idiots see that that bastard's trying to get my job?' he asked, referring to the corporate director. 'That he's set this whole thing up to be some kind of palace coup?'

'It's possible, I suppose,' the primary leader said. 'But unless you've got a very unique corporate structure, it seems to me more likely that he was simply hoping for a change in the culture, as he himself suggested. That doesn't necessarily mean he shouldn't have informed you better.'

The vice-president ignored him, suddenly pouncing on the secondary leader, prodding his index finger into her sternum just above her breasts. 'It's your job to make me look good,' he announced.

'I've been trained in how to build community,' she retorted. 'I've not had any training in how to selectively make someone look good.'

The vice-president appeared lost.

'I agree with what several participants suggested today,' the primary leader said, 'that there's no way for the group of you to build community without looking at your culture. I can see only three alternatives. One is for us to say that and continue with the workshop. A second is for you, as the highest-ranking person, to order us to stop it—in which case we will, but we will also make it clear, if you yourself don't, that it is under your orders and your authority alone. The only other alternative would be for me to announce you've requested us to stop it, but have agreed to put it to a vote, and to abide by the vote of the group.'

It didn't take the vice-president long to decide. 'I want the last alternative. Please,' he begged. 'Put it to a vote first thing in the morning. I want the workshop stopped, but I'll abide by the vote even if it costs me my job.'

They worked out the details.

When the group reassembled at nine the next morning, the primary leader announced, 'Your vice-president believes that this workshop was an inappropriate organizational decision and would like to see it stopped. He has agreed, however, to put it to a vote. If you vote to continue the workshop, then we will continue to attempt to build community, and in that attempt, we must continue to examine your corporate culture. He has agreed to abide by that condition if it is your vote. If it is your vote to stop the workshop, then we will simply decide whether you would like the two of us to depart so you can get on with your business or whether you would prefer for us to spend the rest of the day in a didactic mode telling you some things about community without actually doing it.'

The vice-president, the corporate manager, and twelve others—fourteen in all—voted to stop the workshop. The corporate director and ten others—eleven in all—voted to continue. The majority having voted to stop the workshop, the group unanimously requested that the leaders spend the remainder of the day lecturing them about the principles of the community. It went well. On the morning of the third day, with the FCE leaders present but not participating, the group quickly decided that their mission statement needed no revision. At lunchtime everyone, including the FCE leaders, went out to eat and drink and, in that manner, enjoy pleasant pseudofellowship for the rest of their allotted time.

FCE has heard no positive results from that 'workshop.' Its only feedback came from the corporate director who had initiated it. He reported that the vice-president continually referred to it as 'that debacle' and blamed him for it. Still stuck in the same corporate culture, and now fearful for his job as well, the corporate director in turn blamed FCE for the failure, although he could not be specific about what had been done wrong.

There were no real villains in this story. The vice-president was indeed a rigid man who, by virtue of personal psychopathology, had totally bought into a false corporate myth. He had failed to do his homework so as to have any understanding of what the workshop would be like. On the other hand, quiet research after the fact revealed that the myth of the company as 'one big happy family' had been initiated by the president and founder of the company—a silly yet very powerful myth, which pervaded not just the marketing division, but the entire huge corporation. Moreover, the vice-president had, I believe, been misinformed as to the real purpose of the workshop.

The corporate director had ample reason to be unhappy with the atmosphere of the company. It was oppressive — inevitably so, guided as it was by such an unrealistic myth. He was hardly alone in his unhappiness, as witnessed by the fact that almost half the executives voted openly against their superiors. Undoubtedly more would have voted to continue the workshop and scrutinize their culture had they felt free to do so. The corporate director's desire for change was most healthy. But he had never attempted individually, privately, to express this desire to the vice-president, nor had he been up-front about his motives for the workshop. Conscious or unconscious, it was an attempt at manipulation on his part.

Nor had he been up-front with FCE. Had he explained that he was unhappy with the culture and wanted to effect a change to which the vice-president was resistant, it is doubtful that FCE would have conducted the workshop at all. At the least it would have done more groundwork. But it was told only that the division was wholeheartedly behind the workshop to facilitate its mission statement work.

As with all of its workshops, FCE had sent a letter to the corporate director to be distributed to the participants beforehand informing them that the event was likely to be stressful. But was FCE also remiss? Should it have done more?

FCE makes a point of never guaranteeing the outcomes of its workshops. The community building process works so well in part because it is remarkably lacking in formulas and always full of surprises as the hidden becomes known. There is inevitably a degree of risk for the individuals involved and for the organization. This degree is relatively small, and the outcomes are usually dramatically positive.

The aborted workshop described above is one of the reasons FCE now offers a consulting service. If an organization desires, a skilled leader will come into it, spending many hours talking with the key players to assess the organizational culture and whether it is 'ready' for community building. In this way even the rare potential 'debacle' can probably be prevented. But this service is time-consuming. And even then, there cannot be an absolute guarantee that there will be no risk. If it is to be healthy, an organization, just like an individual, must be willing now and then to take a well-calculated risk in its life.

The primary moral of the preceding story is that it is impossible to introduce community into an organization unless there is wholehearted support at the top. The corollary of that moral is that if there is such support at the top, community can be effectively brought to an organization under almost any circumstances. It was not too surprising to us that there must be support from the top. What has been most surprising is that when there is support from the top, employees or others in an organizaton can essentially be *ordered* into the community building process with routine success. Recall that the first labor-management team, as described, requested its workshop purely because 'orders came down from on high.'

Let us now consider a different example of the same phenomenon. In 1987 the federal government set up a contest to award several ten-million-dollar grants to cities that competitively applied for them. The superintendent of schools of a middle-sized eastern city decided to enter the competition, but he quickly ran into difficulty. The grant application was sufficiently complex to require significant cooperation from all the other agencies and leaders of the city: drug abuse services, the city council, the hospitals, the department of welfare, the courts, the police, the ministerial association, and so on. But letters and phone calls went unanswered. The needed cooperation was not forthcoming. The superintendent decided that a community building workshop might be the tool to bring it about.

The workshop began in great confusion. The super-intendent had sent invitations, including FCE's standard informative letter, to the directors of these agencies. It emerged, however, that half the participants had never received this information because they had simply been ordered to attend the workshop by their supervisors. Typically, many of the agency directors had said to them, 'I'm supposed to go to this school grant workshop next week, and I'm all booked up with other things. But somebody from the agency has to attend. Here, you go,' and handed their subordinates the letter of invitation, neglecting to give them the letter explaining the nature of the event.

The leaders described to the group as best they could the purpose of the workshop, its format, and guidelines. 'It sounds like pretty weird stuff to me,' one of the participants, Marcia, responded. 'It doesn't seem to me the kind of thing anybody ought to be ordered to do. Frankly, I'm pissed about it, and I'm pissed at my director.'

The group ignored her and tried to switch to pleasantries. The primary leader interrupted them. 'I can really understand why Marcia is feeling pissed. If she's the only one who's annoyed, then that's one thing. But I wonder if many of you might not be feeling similarly angry.'

For the next hour, wave after wave of resentment came forth. But the tide turned when Marcia, a born leader, once again announced, 'First I was pissed. Now I'm getting bored. I don't know about the rest of you, but as far as I can see, I've got to spend the next two days here. I think I'd just as soon not spend all that time sitting around bitching about it. Maybe we might as well give this community building thing a try.'

There were calls of agreement, and within a few minutes the group got on to another kind of work. By the end of the first day they were in community.

I wish I could say this city was awarded the grant, but it wasn't. Months later, when the primary leader commiserated with the superintendent of the schools over this outcome, he said, 'I'm not feeling all that badly about it. It would have been nice, but at least we got the application done. That's almost a first in cooperation here, and there's no way it could have happened without the workshop. It's not the only reason we need cooperation, you know. I need it for many things, and we've got a whole network going now. My phone calls get returned these days. And when I occasionally can't get through to a department director, I simply talk to his designee from the group and then I hear back from the director in no time flat. Hell, as far as I'm concerned, the workshop was the best thing that ever happened to this town.'

In the following years this same scenario has been played out in at least two other workshops I know of intended to increase cooperation and coordination among city, county, and state agencies. Once they have with encouragement gotten their anger out onto the table, people ordered to these workshops have quickly and effectively participated in the community building process.[1]

The ways in which people may be 'ordered' into the process have hardly been exhausted. Let me tell a story about a different kind of ordering in a very different kind of workplace—a story once again with many morals, including the 'revolutionary' effects of community and the key role of politics in organizational transformation.

Dr Bob Roberts has been on an unusual career path as he has followed his calling. He was an ordinary dentist until he was intrigued by the human psyche and its capacity for healing. He soon became a noted specialist in the psycho-somatics of dentistry and, in particular, an authority on temporomandibular (TMJ) joint problems. Then he decided to obtain an additional degree in psychotherapy. This led him into an interest in group therapy, and that interest in turn brought him to his first public FCE workshop in 1987. He immediately asked if we thought it would be possible to build community in prisons. 'Theoretically, sure,' he was told, 'but, practically, we'll never know until someone actually tries. It would be nice if someone tried.'

As Bob finished his Ph.D., he attended several more workshops. He also began to talk to officials in the prison system of his home state of Louisiana. He learned that many

---

[1] The effectiveness of community building in breaking down interdepartmental barriers is also applicable to the private sector. Community building may be used by executives when they wish to introduce 'total quality management' into their companies. See Mary Walton, *The Deming Management Method* (New York: G. P. Putnam's Sons, 1986).

were deeply concerned by the low level of literacy of Louisiana prisoners, eighty percent of whom are black. Attempts to introduce literacy training programs into the prisons had been notably ineffective.

In early 1989 Bob made a $750,000 grant proposal to the Louisiana governor's office to do community building in one of the state's prisons and measure its effect on literacy training over the course of three years. Miraculously, it seemed to many, the proposal was approved.

Bob hired one of FCE's leaders to be his first deputy, and then he and his team consulted with FCE on how to begin. He was advised that the way to start was at the top, because the project was doomed if it didn't have understanding and support in high places. Bob took the advice and organized a workshop for the warden and other key staff, the commissioner of corrections, the assistant secretary of state, officials at the university through which the grant was being funneled, and other higher-ups likely to be involved. It worked. The officials got a good enough taste of community to like it and to understand the essence of the project. Bob had gotten the support he needed.

And need it he did. The team had done enough poking around at this point to learn that the climate within the ordinary cell-block was the antithesis of community. Far from even being an 'us against them' cohesive group of fifty-five prisoners locked in chronic struggle with the guards, what they found among the inmates was extraordinary fragmentation and mutual distrust. The usual prisoner would have one or two allies in the block and would do his best to stay clear of the others. The result was fifty-five men divided into thirty different, slightly over-lapping cliques.

The team proposed a community building workshop for the guards themselves to gain their understanding and support as well. The proposal was shot down on the basis of economics. It would require the guards to be paid overtime and funds simply weren't available. So the team did the next best thing: a community building workshop for a dormitory of trusties. These particularly 'trustworthy' prisoners did not constitute a typical inmate population, but it was thought that there would be lessons to be learned. So there were. It further helped that word of the success of this workshop started to filter down the grapevine to the cell-blocks.

Finally came the standard cell-block. As expected, the workshop began with immediate and intense racial confrontation. No pseudocommunity here. Bob and his team were all white. 'Why are you honkies coming in here to fuck with our minds?' the inmates demanded. 'What's in it for you?' But it took only a short time for them to pick up on the team's benign intent and lack of racism. After that, as workshops go, it was a piece of cake.

At the conclusion of the workshop, the team made it clear that the inmates had to make a decision whether they wanted to *voluntarily* maintain themselves in community or not. They chose to do so. The only significant obstacle to community maintenance proved to be no different from that in any other organization: time. Like almost everyone on the outside, the prisoners work, and the administration has no more reason to give them time off than does any other business. The system is quite dependent upon the output of and the income from prison industries. And then there are other mandated activities. But faced with a decision, the group chose to make the time.

After that they had an ongoing community for several months, the prisoners were introduced to a seven-week literacy training program. By 1991 three things had become clear. One is that it is possible to build community among ordinary prisoners in a standard cell-block. A second is that it is possible for such prisoners to successfully maintain their community for at least six months. Finally, these prisoners in community, when exposed to the literacy training program, had a low dropout rate, and at the end of the seven weeks demonstrated an average increase of more than one grade in their reading, writing, and vocabulary level. Two similar 'control' cell-blocks in the same prison, but not in community, when exposed to the same literacy training program had a high dropout rate, and at the end of the seven weeks measured absolutely no change in their reading level.

Everyone was naturally pleased by these findings. But more impressive than the statistics for Bob Robert's team were the unquantifiable stories: the men who have said to each other, 'I've been living in this block next to you for seven years now, man, and I never knew you before'; the almost mute and presumably dumb inmate who, in the midst of a community maintenance meeting, erupted into a ten-minute dance of exquisite beauty; the privilege of witnessing human beings, still behind bars, experience the joy of liberation that few supposedly free people every get to experience.

The results of this ground-breaking experiment, from a strictly scientific point of view, are hardly unimpeachable.[2] For instance, it could be countered that the cell-block in community received much more personal attention from the team before their exposure to the literacy training program than did the control cell-blocks (more because of funding constraints than scientific sloppiness) and that the control cell-blocks, therefore, do not represent an adequate scientific control. A basic tenet of the scientific method, moreover, is that any experimental findings remain in question unless they can be repeated—replicated—by different, independent researchers in a similar yet completely separate setting. How repeatable are these extraordinary results?

I don't know. I know—and I assume that by now the reader is also convinced—that community building in organizations works under the right circumstances. But what determines the right circumstances? This chapter sets forth the hypothesis that the primary determinant of

[2] Indeed, at this point they are anecdotal. Formal published results are not yet available although the project is now finished.

whether community building succeeds within an organization is the politics involved.

Above and beyond any questions of replicability, the Louisiana Prison Project proved itself to be a dramatic success. But why? One reason is not only the calling, but the personal political skills of Dr Bob Roberts. He is, on certain levels at least, a consummate politician, as anyone must be to initiate, negotiate, and maintain such an innovative program within a state government. There is, however, a different matter of politics involved.

Ordinarily it would be very threatening to the guards for a cell-block of fifty-five prisoners, previously fragmented in thirty-odd cliques, to become suddenly transformed into a cohesive, proud, and spirited group, potentially capable of fighting back. I have worked enough in prisons to know of the political power of the guards to squelch far less threatening projects. In this instance, however, not only were eighty percent of the inmates black, but so were fifty percent of the guards. The black guards tended to see the community as something distinctly positive that was being done for their people. Consequently, they were willing to assume the risk and they convinced their white colleagues to do likewise. Could the project have succeeded if most of the prisoners or the bulk of the guards were white? I don't know. Maybe. But I do know, as a political realist, that I am grateful in this constructive instance for racial loyalties and dynamics.

The *only* obstacle to introducing community into a business is politics. By politics I mean the configuration of personality and power within the organization. Specifically, if the top managers of a company are the kinds of people who want community, then they can have it. They may have to work hard for it. They may need to plan and strategize carefully. It may require a significant amount of time. But eventually any resistance down the hierarchy can be overcome.

Conversely, no matter how deeply those at the bottom or middle of the power structure desire it, community will be impossible to achieve if those at the top are resistant. Time and again I am asked by middle managers, 'What can I do to bring the community into my company?'

'Sell your superiors on it,' I answer.

'I can't. I've tried, but they won't buy it' is the almost invariable reply.'

'Forget about it then,' I must in all honesty—and with deep sadness—respond.

Some would claim that the only insurmountable obstacle to community is the nature of the organizational culture, but we are really saying the same thing. Remember that it is the personality of those at the top that primarily determines the culture. If those few people change, then the culture will change.

As previously noted, the purpose of a business may dictate a certain organizational structure, but within that structure there is room for great cultural variety or diversity of politics. Corporation A, which produces ball bearings, may be extremely open to the introduction of community. The sole difference is company politics—or culture, if you prefer.

Let us review the case of the aborted workshop for the marketing division leadership of that Fortune 500 company to illustrate the inseparable dynamics of culture and politics in these matters. It was the personality of the vice-president—molded by his childhood experience in foster homes—that determined his psychology of resistance to community building. Emotionally, he could not tolerate examining the corporate culture, given the fact that its basic myth—'We're one big happy family in this corporation'— was one upon which he was so psychologically dependent. Since genuine community is a group that deals with its own issues and since this cultural myth was such an issue for the group, his personality required him to oppose the community building process as soon as he realized what it would involve.

Had he not been the vice-president—had he instead been one of the lower-ranking members of the group—it is highly probable his opposition would have been ineffective. What would have happened to him then, forced to critically examine a cultural myth in which he had so much invested? A quite possible scenario is that he would have 'tuned out' the process and been one of that small minority that never gets in community. An equally likely scenario is that he would have eventually talked in the group about his childhood and experienced some significant healing as a result.

But he was not lower-ranking. Politically speaking, he was the group's most powerful member and, by virtue of that temporal power, was able to make his resistance to community the order of the day. The cultural status quo was preserved. This was hardly remarkable. The only thing remarkable in this instance was that it was such a close call. It was a measure of how far the myth was divorced from the reality that almost half his subordinates openly voted against him.

I have made it sound as if a middle manager is virtually impotent to introduce community or any other type of cultural change into an organization. This needs qualifying. The middle manager may be the top manager of a department or division. If this is the case, then she is in a position where she may well be able to initiate community within that portion of the organization under her charge. FCE has conducted a number of successful workshops at the request of department heads to initiate community within their departments. One, for instance, was for a university department where no attempt was made to change the culture of the university as a whole.

Still, such department heads usually must have a relatively high degree of autonomy within their purview. Moreover, it is also hopeful if the values of community are not too deviant from the cultural values of the larger organization. Had the vice-president of that huge company been receptive, I think it would have been possible for the marketing division to have learned how to routinely operate in community. But it would not have been without its dangers. Remember that the founder/owner of that corporation had created the myth that its employees were one big happy family. Given this fact, even if he had facilitated the development of community in the marketing division, the vice-president would have had to be quite cagey about it. The previously mentioned university department head, for instance, got into difficulty when she later attempted to involve faculty members from other departments in the community building process.

To repeat, the only obstacle to introducing community into a business is politics. It is, however, a most gigantic obstacle. Community building is transformational, and the plain fact of the matter is that most people in positions of power do not want their organizations or themselves transformed. They would like higher profits, yes. But transformation, no. No matter how healthy it might be, transformation is inherently painful. There isn't a CEO in the world who theoretically doesn't want his business to be healthier—painlessly. There are few who don't wish for a greater sense of community in their organizations—as long as they don't have to go through chaos, much less emptiness, to get it. What they really want is just to be able to 'do' pseudocommunity and pseudoconsensus a little bit better. They want cheap civility. Genuine community and genuine civility are transformational, however, precisely because they're the real thing, the genuine article.

The reality, therefore, is that while interest in community runs fairly high, the actual demand is low. Seldom is the political climate in an organization right. Rare indeed is the top management willing to risk such honesty or the unpredictable degree of radical change—of transformation—likely to result. And even when the political climate is just right, management must continue to remain *politic* in the most civil sense of the word—meaning wise as serpents and innocent as doves.

While politics is the only obstacle to introducing community into business that may be insurmountable, this does not mean that when the obstacle is overcome there won't be any problems. There are always problems in life. And there are certainly always problems in business life. The problems that may be involved in introducing community into a business involved that there is no point in discussing them in general. The point to remember is that none of them is insurmountable.

One problem, however, is so common—almost inevitable—that it does deserve specific mention. It is the effect of community in a business upon the marriages of its employees.

There is no such thing as a completely closed, isolated system. Just because the family and the workplace are very different settings does not mean that they are unrelated. Everything is related because everything is a part of a larger system. As has been stated, change part of a system, and the other parts must change. If there is a significant change in your family, your work is likely to be affected. And if there is a major change at work, your family will be affected. Many credit FCE for saving their marriages. A few blame it for their divorces. This isn't bad, it is simply in the nature of things.

The experience of community changes people, and the deeper, more prolonged the experience, the more significant the change will be. Community in the workplace, where we spend so much of our energy and time, is a deep and therefore profoundly transforming experience. The chief executive who creates community in her business will receive a good deal of gratitude, but she should also expect to have some angry spouses on her hands.

There are many different scenarios in this regard, but one is far and away the most common. The business world is usually not very intimate. Most people, therefore, are more accustomed to getting their needs for intimacy met within the bosom of their families—particularly within their marriages—than they are at work. If they have no intimacy in their workplace, then a small amount of intimacy in their homeplace may feel satisfactory. Once there is a lot of intimacy at work, however, returning home to little intimacy may be infuriating. The experience of community raises our standards for relationships. Many spouses adjust accordingly. Many do not.

Indeed, this may be an issue for CEO's themselves. Top executives interested in building sustained community within their organizations would be well-advised to discuss the issue in depth with their marriage partners before taking serious action. The partner of a CEO may otherwise be able to sabotage the entire endeavor.

In any case, it is the experience of businesses embarked upon this wonderful experience that community in the workplace tends to result in good marriages becoming better and bad marriages getting worse. As a result angry spouses may suggest it is the company's responsibility to somehow repair this damage or, at a minimum, provide a spouses' program to magically solve the problem. Such a program may, in fact, be a good idea. When it has not been attempted, however, it has emerged over time that some unhappy spouses exercised their own initiative to involve themselves, one way or another, in community and benefited accordingly. Others, with no less apparent resources, have not done so. It is something of a paradox that community leaves more, rather than less, up to the individual and his or her personal choice.

Finally, one aspect of introducing community into business is envisioned by many executives as a problem when, in fact, it is not. The top manager who considers bringing community to his company is likely to first attend a CBW himself. There he will see that titles are irrelevant. As a form of organization, community is 'lateral' rather than hierarchical. It is a 'group of all leaders.' Leaving a vast amount of space or time for 'emptiness,' the process may look extremely unstructured. No matter how creative it may be, it might seem to him utterly unsuitable to the day-to-day operation of a business. He will be concerned that community might destroy the hierarchy, the discipline and sense of order, within his company. But it is all a 'nonproblem.'

First, it is vitally important to understand that community is itself structure. The community building and maintaining process is one of *formal*, structure communication. The participants commit themselves to not walk away, to punctuality, to confidentiality. The space is carefully selected and the architecture of chairs diligently arranged in as small a circle as possible to facilitate acoustics and inclusivity. Newcomers are gently taught rules about when to speak, how to speak, and how to listen. Only one person can speak at a time. Leaders will monitor the tempo of talking and impose periods of silence when communication becomes too rapid to be thoughtful.

Compare this to the informal communication of a cocktail party. Guests come and leave as they please. Alcohol is used to diminish alertness. There usually aren't enough chairs. Eating and smoking are distractions. Subgroups of two to four instantly form and all talk at once. The noise level rises. It is hardly a structure to encourage meaningful communication. Indeed, one must wonder whether human beings don't unconsciously design such social gatherings so as to *avoid* communication.

There are many varieties of formal, structure group communication other than community. Court proceedings and public hearings. Lectures. Worship services. Business meetings with inflexible agendas. *Robert's Rules*. Some are designed for politeness. But none, other than community, are designed or structured to maximize genuine civility in communication.

Structure is the organizational incarnation of discipline. Liberty without discipline is license for destruction. We must have structure. As long as the spirit of an organization is healthy, clarity of titles, precision of job descriptions, and quantifiability of objectives are not stultifying; they are liberating. Community is a structured or disciplined form of communication and a way of being together. Consequently, the task of introducing community into an organization may be looked at as a task of integrating structures. It is not replacing an old structure with a new one. It is a task of reformation, not revolution. The original structure can — and usually should—stay very much in place as the structure of the community is piggybacked onto it.

When we look at it in this manner, it is no wonder that to be successful in an organization, community building must begin at the top. A new structure cannot be integrated with an old one without the consent—indeed, without the participation—of the director, the chief, of the original structure.

Until now, the word *community* has essentially been employed as a noun, albeit one with a definition different from that in the dictionary. Gradually, as we have become more experienced, however, we are increasingly using it as we would a verb. As a form of communication, a way of being together, we now see it more as something that a group does than something it invariably *is*. For instance, those of us who serve on the FCE board no longer think of it as a community. Instead we envision ourselves as a management body that chooses to function most of the time *in community*, that is, according to certain rules of communication that we use to structure our formal meetings. But when we are not formally meeting, we may function in a purely social way or communicate by memoranda and other modes.

A structure, for the most part, *is* a way of being together, a way of communication. Consider a hierarchal organization (which most organizations are). The manager of public relations, let us say, 'reports' to the vice-president for administration who, in turn, reports to the president. There are formal and informal rules that govern communication within this structure. As an example of the latter, the manager may address the vice-president by her first name, yet whenever the manager talks directly to the president, he calls him 'sir.' That rule is probably informal and unwritten. Yet it may be carried on through generations of managers, vice-presidents, and presidents.

As a way or mode of communication, community is virtually the opposite of the hierarchical mode. Usually (although this rule is not essential) everyone calls everyone else by their first name. No one has to get permission to speak from someone of a higher rank. In fact, rank is totally set aside and considered irrelevant. The voice of the highest-ranking member carries no more weight than that of the lowest. Each person is considered a leader with no more and no less inherent authority than any other leader.

Since the structures or modes of hierarchy and community are so diametrically different, how on earth can they ever be integrated? It would seem an impossible problem. The fact is that it's a snap. It's merely a matter of timing. The organization functions in a hierarchical mode some of the time and in a community mode some of the time. It switches back and forth. The problem is insurmountable only when the ranking member(s) of the organization insist on functioning only in the hierarchical mode. This is a political problem, not a structural one.

The question of timing is also not a problem. Issues of long-range or important planning, decision making, and organizational morale are generally best dealt with in a community mode. Less important and more immediate operational decisions are generally better made in the hierarchical mode. The flexible executive familiar with both modes quickly and easily—almost instinctively—learns which structure to use when.

This process of switching back and forth is the reason why it is actually easier to introduce community into a highly structured organization than into an unstructured one. If the hierarchy is not clear and people's roles not well defined, then there is likely to be a blurring between the hierarchical and community modes, which can create confusion. Indeed, a poorly structured organization that engages in community building will likely decide as a result that it quickly needs to do more work on its formal structure. If the hierarchy and its roles are well defined, however, then the switching is no more complex than that from standing up to sitting down or vice versa. People clearly know who, when, and where they are. But there will be difficulty if they try to assume a posture in between standing up and sitting down.

Given the right politics and a clear structure, the most significant problem introducing community into an organization is the flexibility of leadership style of the top-ranking executive(s). In the hierarchical mode, the president or CEO must be decisive, up-front, directive, and in control. In the community mode she must take a backseat, give up control to the group, become just one of the members, and be nondirective and facilitative. As was mentioned in the earlier discussion of participatory management, some executives have no trouble switching their leadership styles in this fashion. Others may have initial difficulty, but with a bit of practice or training or both, they can learn the skill relatively quickly. Occasionally top executives are so comfortable being dominant and so uncomfortable giving up the limelight or control that they are virtually unable to play a facilitative role.

Yet even this problem is surmountable if the top executive is willing. As long as he is agreeable to being told to shut up and ordered to take a backseat when in a community mode, then he can delegate the role of facilitator to another member of the group. And if no one else in the group is able to handle the job, then he can hire an outside facilitator, or else send one of the group off for facilitator training so he or she can become the group's skilled in-house facilitator.[3]

---

[3] The 'technology' of just how the president can take off his president's hat for meetings in the community mode, and then how he can put that hat back on when the mode is switched, is thoroughly described in *How to Make Meetings Work*, by Michael

This talk of functioning in two modes may make community in the workplace sound more complicated than life in the traditional workplace. It isn't. I suppose that an organization in community may be more complex than one that isn't, but only in the sense that an intelligent, mentally healthy human being is more complex than an unintelligent rigid person. Flexibility is one of the primary characteristics of mental health in organizations as well as individuals.[4] An organization capable of functioning solely in a hierarchical mode is unlikely to be particularly healthy, conscious, or civil. Community increases consciousness and vivacity. An organization flexible enough to vibrate between hierarchical and community modes of functioning will be a particularly vibrant one. Indeed, when it so evolves it becomes a higher organizational life-form.

Doyle and David Straus (New York: Berkley Publishing Group, 1976). 'Fellowship skills' for compulsive leaders are often gleaned from attending one or more FCE public workshops. (Contact the Foundation for Connecticut 06877, 203/431–9484.) Specific facilitator training is provided by Interaction Associates, located in San Francisco, California (415/777–0590), and Cambridge, Massachusetts (617/354–2000).
[4] See the discussion of 'flexible response systems' under the heading 'Balancing' in *The Road Less Traveled*, pp. 64–69.

20

No, Virginia, There Is No Quick Fix

Community Maintenance

Until now our focus has been on introducing community into business as the best way for teaching civility and assuring that the organization becomes a healthy and civil one. This chapter will address the issues of community maintenance. How does a business stay healthy and civil?

These issues are at the forefront of FCE's and my current interests. We *know* how to build community. We understand the ins and outs of it, and have the technology down pat—at least, as pat as a technology that leaves room for God is ever likely to be. There will always, thankfully, be a few surprises. But no big surprises anymore. The maintenance of community once it is built, however, is quite another matter. Here we are on a real frontier, wide open for research, new knowledge, and deeper understanding.

I have, for instance, presented some clear statistics about how people adjust to community building situations. Consistently, roughly five percent have grave difficulty whereas ninety-five percent don't. Consistently, ninety percent of people subjectively assess the process as personally rewarding. But what about people in *long-term* community? How do they do when they are part of an organization that practices the discipline of community month after month, year after year, even decade upon decade? We don't know.

The problem is that since community building is a relatively recent phenomenon, community maintenance is even more recent. We simply have not yet had the time to hardly begin to study it scientifically. So we have no statistics.

I do, however, have a few impressions. As best as I can discern it, the rare people to date who have experienced genuine community in their workplace over an extended period of time generally seem to do considerably better on average—to grow more psychospiritually—over the course of months and years than would be expected. It is my impression that a small minority do not do so well over the long haul and may, in fact, psychospiritually deteriorate.[1]

How is it that some people seem to deteriorate as a result of long-term participation within community? My impression is that these are people with hidden agendas that they are unwilling or unable to relinquish. Since community is an environment 'where the hidden becomes known,' if we have motives that we refuse to acknowledge, the intense light it casts will inevitably propel us to become more and more devious. Eventually a crisis point is reached. The devious individual is either expelled or quits just short of being found out. Disquieting though this reality is, it ultimately seems to be in the best interests of both the community and the individual involved. After such a rift, the person usually appears happier and more functional because he has more room in which to maneuver. On the whole, there is more freedom within community than without, but it is the freedom of 'soft' individualism, as opposed to the 'rugged' freedom to wheel and deal with less-than-total honesty.

So we have learned with sadness that community in the workplace does not mean an environment where no one ever needs to be fired. Community simply makes it more painful for those who do the firing. Once, when consulting to a huge corporation in regard to its culture, I was initially horrified to learn that its executives customarily referred to firing as 'excommunication,' because the word smacked of such total banishment. As I thought the matter out, however, it made considerable sense. It is my impression

[1] Jean Vanier, perhaps the world's expert on the subject of community maintenance, voices the same impression in his classic work, *Community and Growth* (London: Darton, Longman and Todd, 1979).

407

that when an individual is fired from a workplace of community, it is almost always not the fault of community but that of the individual, who has excluded himself from civil communication, who by his deviousness has made such communication impossible.

If it is correct that a few individuals will deteriorate in a business environment where there is no room to hide, then it is a fact of great significance. It means there can be no such thing as a 'perfect' workplace. I put the word *perfect* in quotes because in the next chapter we shall be reexamining our traditional notion of perfection. But perhaps this was what Jesus meant when he said, 'The poor will always be with us.'[2] Perhaps he was referring not so much to the economically poor. In any case, while I believe that genuine community in business provides the best possible working environment—the most healthy and civil, even ideal, environment—community can never be all things to all people.

Although it is a wide-open frontier, we do know some things about community maintenance with certainty.

A group in community will always perform better on a task than a group that is not in community. However, once a group is in community, it does not then always stay in community. In fact, if it lasts, it *never* stays in community for very long. The group will periodically, almost routinely, lapse back into chaos or, worse yet, pseudocommunity. This is par for the course. Many communities have unnecessarily self-destructed at this point simply because they didn't realize that community building for an ongoing group is, by necessity, an ongoing process. You don't just build community; you rebuild it and rebuild it and rebuild it for as long as you have reason to continue to be together. We call this ongoing process of rebuilding 'community maintenance.'

[2] Matthew 26:11; John 12:8.

Any long-term car owner or homeowner should immediately understand the concept. If a house must be continually worked on for its maintenance, why shouldn't the same reality hold true for a community?

Businesses like the Valley Diagnostic and Surgical Clinic (VDC) most commonly seek community building because they are in a crisis. Given the right political climate, the greatest problem is not introducing community into such an organization—building community—but maintaining it after it has been reached. Once a business has resolved its crisis through community, it naturally wants to sit back and relax, no longer doing the ongoing work of community, allowing this resolution to become a new rut. It doesn't want to have to relive choas or face further crises. So it was that on the third CBW day the VDC went into a three-hour group depression when the reality began to sink in that it was going to have to continue to work at maintaining itself in community if it was not going to regress—that there was going to be an ongoing price to pay. Perhaps the biggest problem FCE has in dealing with businesses is convincing them that community is not a quick, cheap fix or one-time magical solution.

The term 'magical solution' was coined by psychotherapists accustomed to seeing new patients seeking a quick fix for substantial psychospiritual distress related to their deep-seated personality problems. 'Isn't there some safe little pill that will take it all away?' such patients ask. Or some simple, facile formula for daily living? Therapists must then attempt to convince these sufferers that there is no such magical solution. Often the attempt fails and the patient soon departs to look elsewhere for an easy fix. Only the minority achieve real healing by staying and doing the real work of long-term, ongoing therapy.

So it is for businesses that come seeking FCE's services because of a current distress. It is a major task for FCE leaders to convince the organization that the work will need to be ongoing. Usually this requires that after they have led the organization into community, the leaders stay on in some kind of sporadic consultant role to assist it with its maintenance of community.

Businesses will then ask, 'How long? How long will we continue to need your consultant services?' The same question is asked by individuals of their psychotherapists: 'How do I know when to quit therapy?' The question is so common that therapists have a stock answer. 'When you have learned to be your own therapist; when therapy has become a way of life for you.' So it is for organizations. Organizational health is a continuing process. A business is ready to get rid of its community consultant when it knows so well how to build and rebuild and rebuild community that community maintenance has become a way of life for it.

To be healthy does not mean that an organization will be in the stage of genuine community every day of its existence. To the contrary, it will repeatedly lose it and fall out of community. Two things characterize the truly healthy organization functioning in an ongoing community mode. One is the rapidity with which it will recognize that it has lost it. The other is its sustained willingness to do the work to rapidly regain it.

And that is a lot of work. For a business involved in community maintenance, it is not like Organizational Development (OD), which would often conduct or advise personnel development programs (PDPs)—brief weekend or weeklong workshops that employees would attend to enhance their interpersonal skills. Rather we are speaking about something that an organization itself does—as a whole—week in and week out, month in and month out, year after year. We are speaking of work that is not only temporarily unsettling but chronically unsettling and always stretching. But it is work that an organization for which community has become a way of life would no longer even consider not doing.

An organization is most unlikely to do the hard work of community maintenance unless it has a task above and beyond community itself—a task so important that ongoing community is required for its accomplishment. For this reason I am doubtful how long organizations with relatively minor tasks—support groups or church congregations, for instance—can sustain themselves in real community. Usually the task must be major and complex.

Long before the term *community* came to be applied to the most effective of working groups, management consultants assisting task-oriented teams recognized that such groups, in order to function well, needed to work not only on their task but also on themselves as a team. To this group self-work they gave the name 'process.' And to describe the art of combining its work on a task and its work on itself, they coined the phrase 'integration of task and process.' It is my hope, as we struggle toward a much more civil future, that within a generation or two this seemingly abstract and esoteric phrase will be a standard part of the vocabulary of virtually all human beings by the time they emerge from adolescence.

I referred to the integration of task and process as an art. You bet. This business of building and maintaining community is, for the most part, enormously zestful and eventually fun, but that doesn't mean it is easy or doesn't continue to require the continued learning of new skills. There are several reasons that the integration of task and process requires such skill as to properly be considered an art form. The greatest reason is inertia. Inertia refers to two related phenomena. One is that it is hard—it takes energy—to get something moving in the first place. But the other is that once that something is moving in a certain direction, it is hard—it takes energy—either to stop it or to change its direction. And the faster this something is moving, the greater its momentum, the harder it is to counteract its inertia. It is like stopping or deflecting an oncoming freight train. Only in this case the something is a group.

411

There is a profound tendency for a group that is deep into working on a task to continue at it long after its work has become ineffective. Despite all manner of signs that the group needs to work on *itself*, it still plows ahead with its agenda. Conversely, once a group is engaged in community building or process work, it is often very difficult to get it to move on or back to its task. Perhaps the most salient distinguishing feature between a healthy, mature, ongoing community and an immature or unhealthy one is the efficiency with which it combats such inertia. Through training and experience, a mature group can become very quick at recognizing, 'Hey, guys, we've lost it. It's time we went back to community building,' or 'It feels as though we've ironed it out. Are we ready to get back to the agenda?'

All the training methods FCE use are gentle except one. That one seems almost brutal when it is used, occasionally, at workshops or conferences that are specifically addressing issues of community maintenance. It is an exercise in which the group is directed to build community for fifteen minutes—not a minute more or less—then immediately switch to working on a task for exactly fifteen minutes, and then instantly move back to process work. It can be wrenching when a group member is sobbing his guts out and the leader commands, 'It's time to return to your task. Right now.' Or when the group in the midst of effectively developing a policy statement is ordered, 'Stop. Go back to talking personally about yourselves. Immediately!' The art of integrating task and process is *not* brutal, but the point of this exercise is not to teach the entire art, only that part of it that is the capacity to switch gears against momentum. By the end of this experience, participants are amazed at how possible it is for the man who fifteen minutes before was sobbing to resume both his story and his tears. And how possible it is, after fifteen minutes of building community, for the group to pick right up again on constructing that particular sentence of its policy statement.

This exercise employs arbitrary timing. The *actual*

412

integration of task and process is an art form in large part because the timing involved is never arbitrary. Instead, it requires an adjustment of timing to the mood or energy of the group. If a member is sobbing and the rest of the group is listening to him intently, it is not the right time to interrupt the process. And if the group is working on a policy statement with high energy, it is definitely not the moment to interrupt its task work, even when the agenda calls for community building time. This sense of timing obviously requires great sensitivity to the group's mood or energy level. Such timing and sensitivity are learned skills of group facilitation. An immature group is often well-advised, therefore, to employ the skills of an outside trained facilitator or, if one of its members has these skills, to appoint that person to the role. In a mature community, practiced in the art of integrating task and process, the members are not only all leaders; they are also all facilitators, and it is usually unnecessary for a particular individual to assume the facilitator role more than any other member.

The final major component of the art of integrating task and process is a variation of the community skill of emptiness: the capacity of a group to empty itself of its agenda. Because I am a compulsive clock-watcher and an intensely goal-oriented person, this skill was particularly difficult for me to learn. For years I was in awe of our chairman's ability to start our board meetings with an agenda she had carefully prepared and, within a day at the most, throw it away and construct another one, only shortly to throw that away also. I learned the skill only after years at her feet, seeing that, by their end, our meetings had usually accomplished not only most of what was on her original agenda, but also a great deal more.

Since the art of integrating task and process is so much one of timing, of letting a group flow when it is working well on a task and interrupting the task when it isn't—and since such matters can never be predicted in advance—it is obvious that a truly effective group cannot be 'agenda-bound.' God—or inspiration, if you will—doesn't operate according to schedule. For meetings to be inspired, for God or the Spirit to be a participant, clearly the schedule or agenda, like community itself, must be built and rebuilt and rebuilt and rebuilt again. To have no agenda at all is to be unborn. To rigidly adhere to an agenda is to be in a state of rigor mortis.

When Jesus pointed out that man was not made to serve the Sabbath, but the Sabbath to serve man, he was essentially talking about agenda. He wasn't instructing us to do away with the Sabbath, only not to let it rule our lives. He was talking about an in-between place, a place of flexibility. As already pointed out, flexibility is one of the most salient characteristics not only of individual but also of corporate health. Just as I hope the phrase 'integration of task and process' will shortly become a part of everyone's vocabulary, so I also hope the neologism 'flex-agenda' will soon be in the dictionary.

Since it cannot operate according to schedule or any precise formula, the integration of task and process is not something that can ever be done with consistent perfection. As a learned skill it can only be done better and better. After eight years, the board of FCE is still learning this skill, but we have become relatively good at it. I keep referring to the integration of task and process as an art as well as a skill. Should you have the opportunity to observe a mature community doing it even relatively well, not only will you see civility or organizational behavior in its highest form but you will also witness a human phenomenon of great beauty.

21
Utopia Revisited

The Promise of Community in the Workplace

We knew very little about what we were doing when we started FCE. We knew there were some techniques to lead even remarkably large groups of people into community in a remarkably short period of time. We believed that carefully selected but otherwise ordinary women and men could be taught how to employ these techniques responsibly as our leaders. We knew that when strangers did become a community, the experience often transformed them beneficially not only as individuals but also, invariably and dramatically, as a group; they became able to work together with phenomenal effectiveness. We suspected that all this had something important to contribute in peacemaking. We felt that something was seriously wrong with our society, that it was deeply uncivil. We believed that community was a remedy for at least some of our social ills, and we wanted to establish an organization to help spread it.

Beyond that, we knew next to nothing. We did not know how community would work in frankly adversarial situations. We had no skill in introducing it into organizations. We didn't know whether it would work in other cultures or across cultures. We had little knowledge of the business world and not the least idea about how to manage a business ourselves.

But we learned. We learned that people of all races, religions, and cultures who came to our public workshops functioned equally well. We helped organize and facilitate two Jewish/Christian/Muslim workshops, discovering that community building dramatically diminished barriers between the invited authorities of these different faiths. Very recently three English-speaking FCE leaders travelled to Moscow to work with sixty-five 'conflictologists' gathered from around the already defunct Soviet Union to be trained in regional conflict resolution. The leaders not only succeeded in building community with this extraordinarily diverse cultural group, but did so entirely through the use of Russian translators.

We also learned about corporate cultures and that community had many roles to play in the business world. We learned how to manage our own organization as a rapidly growing business and then how to rapidly downsize and restructure it. Finally, we discovered that there was a great deal of work to be done in examining and reexamining our own organizational culture. We specified our norms and values. We added new ones as we learned. We deleted obsolete ones. We began not only to become expert in community building but also to gain experience in long-term community maintenance.

Slowly some exciting things dawned on us. We realized that the principles of community were the principles of civility. We realized these principles were sufficiently complex and interlocking as to constitute a culture in and of themselves. We realized that the citizens of all nations and people from all walks of life could quickly and fully participate in this culture. We discovered that it was a workaday culture. Finally, it began to dawn on us that we were deeply engaged in doing something even more visionary than that which we had set out to do: We were involved in forging the broad outlines of a planetary culture—and many of its details. And that this workable planetary culture, to which almost every human being can subscribe, is a culture of civility.

I would shudder at the grandiosity of this were it not for the fact that we have a significant body of evidence to substantiate it. A decade ago, in the chapter on group evil in

People of the Lie—which I designated as its most important chapter (since it is essentially the one that dealt with culture)—I quoted Daniel and Philip Berrigan as saying, 'The task before us is nothing less than to metaphorically exorcise our institutions.'[1] At the time, we had no idea how this tast might even be approached. Now we do. We have figured it out! We now have the technology; we know how to use it. The only problem left—and it is gigantic—is how to assist our institutions to desire their healing. An exorcism requires a willing patient. Enough small organizations have been willing for us to know not only that such exorcism is possible but that there are distinct rules for it and the outcome is institutional civility. Still, such instances have been very few and far between. The mass of our organizations or institutions, like individuals, thus far demonstrate little, if any, desire for healing. Is there some magic to make the sick want to be healed? Huge though it is, that is the only remaining question. There is no easy answer, but a few hints will follow shortly.

In retrospect, it is hardly remarkable that a planetary culture should be one of civility. How could there be a planetary culture of incivility, a culture of adversarialism and arrogant unconsciousness, to which all peoples could subscribe? Nor is it remarkable that the technology for institutional exorcism should be a technology of civility, given the fact that incivility is inherently unhealthy and civility a way of healing.

I began the introduction to *The Different Drum* six years ago by saying, 'In and through community lies the salvation of the world.' What a sweeping statement! Yet six years and hundreds of community experiences later, I am even more certain of that generalization. Community is the way—the means and the technology—to institute a planetary culture of civility.

But there are going to be lots of surprises along the way.

[1] *People of the Lie* (New York: Simon & Schuster, 1983), p. 251.

We are going to look at a few of them now as we come to terms with the reality that community is inherently full of surprises. It is time we returned to God.

My basic identity was (and still is) that of a scientist before that of a religious person. We scientists have a particular fondness for proof. Statistics is a major means we use to establish proof, and often we do so by measuring the statistical probability or improbability of events. If the occurrence of an event is highly improbable on the basis of chance alone, we find this significant. And when that statistically improbable event keeps occurring over and again, we feel we have proof that something is going on, proof of a meaningful connection.

Over the course of my life, as I have detailed elsewhere, I gradually discerned a pattern of statistically improbable events with beneficial outcomes occurring not only in my own day-to-day existence but also that of the people with whom I worked closely. Webster's dictionary defines *serendipity* as 'the gift of finding valuable or agreeable things not sought for.' As I pondered the surprising frequency with which this gift was bestowed, it seemed to me that it truly was a gift miraculously and metaphorically showered upon humanity from on high. A working scientist, I had stumbled upon a phenomenon most unfamiliar to science yet quite familiar to theologians: the grace of God. Amazing grace. Surprising grace, for which serendipity was my secular synonym.

The notion of a world in community with a planetary culture of civility is clearly a utopian vision. In recent years the notion of Utopia has generally become laughable. All attempts to create utopian societies have failed. But I think these attempts have been unrealistic. They have been based upon simplistic visions of a world where everyone is happy as well as financially secure, where there is little or no change because perfection has been achieved, of a society so well-designed by humans that there is no need for divine intervention. It is time we revisited the notion of Utopia in view of many things we have so recently learned through our experience with community.

On a Sunday morning in Salado, Texas, four years ago, I was to give one of the concluding addresses at a conference devoted to the subject of evil. I decided that I wanted to give the audience the good news that through community building we now had the technology, the know-how, to exorcise our institutions. So I knew I would be addressing something akin to 'Utopia construction.' Beyond that, however, I had deliberately not prepared my remarks any further because I wanted to hear first what the other speakers had to say.

Lily and I pulled into town late Thursday night. The conference was to begin on Friday evening. Friday afternoon I took a nap from which I awoke with one of those rare, revelatory dreams that occasionally slaps me awake—that Carl Jung used to refer to as a 'big dream.' It was my first and only *Star Trek* dream.

In it, I was a cultural anthropologist who had been hopping around the galaxy examining a number of different planetary societies. With considerable forethought I had saved the best for last: a distant society that, from my home planet and scholarly position, had seemed on paper to be ideally designed, a very probable Utopia. When I finally got there, however, I discovered that this society was no better or no worse than that of any of the other clearly inadequate and defective cultures I had visited. My disappointment was intense. I awoke from this dream screaming at my local guide in frustration, 'But I had assumed that on this planet the Laws of Serendipity would hold true as they do everywhere else.'

The dream—this gift—focused with exquisite clarity upon an issue that desperately needed to be addressed. The topic of 'social engineering' had already been touched upon twice in the conference before I spoke. I began my speech by recounting the dream. The moral of it, I explained, is that 'There is no question in my mind that we are called to build Utopia, but if we think we can do it solely by our design, we are sadly mistaken. We can do it only in cooperation with the grace of God. Any attempt at radical "social engineering" that does not incorporate God, that does not welcome grace and leave vast room for divine intervention, will utterly fail.' I was then able to go on to specify how the 'technology' of community building succeeds, in part, precisely because it takes God into mind, depends upon her, and deliberately produces space for the Holy Spirit to do her thing.

I am profoundly aware of how strange these words must sound to most executives. Even those who are deeply and personally religious, who have had considerable experience with letting God into their own individual lives, have in all probability never even thought of what it would be like to let God into their organizations. But there is no other way for me to talk about it. Uneasy over how to communicate with the hardheaded, intensely practical business world, FCE for several years struggled to develop some sort of marketing language that would not have to use such words as 'God' or 'love.' Eventually we gave up. We have to call a spade a spade.

And then we grow almost incoherent when asked, 'Well, what does it look like when God comes into an organization?' The answer is that nothing changes and everything changes. It is the sort of mystical response of Zen Buddhist language. 'Before I was enlightened,' one Zen master explained, 'the mountains looked like mountains and the rivers like rivers. At the moment of enlightenment I saw it all differently. And now that I am enlightened, the mountains look like mountains again and the rivers like rivers.' Or, when asked what it was like to be enlightened, another Zen master answered, 'I chop wood and carry water.'

If you build community and let God into your organization, on the outside it will look pretty much the same. You will probably continue to have exactly the same organizational structure. You will continue to chop wood and carry water. There will be the same sorts of budgets and inventories and action plans and dealines. But on the inside it will all be different. There will be a different spirit. There will be *more* spirit. It will be more alive.

So you need not be the least bit threatened by any radical change in titles, positions, lines of authority, or other structure for reasons that have already been elaborated. There is only one thing threatening about introducing community into your organization: a loss of control of *certain* outcomes. You won't lose control of 'bottom line' outcomes, such as profitability or fiscal accountability. Community is utterly realistic and would never lose sight of such things. But other 'things' will no longer be so predictable.

There is a common, perfectly human and understandable 'business mentality' that immediately focuses on outcomes. Natural though it may be, it causes considerable grief to FCE as it attempts to market its services to organizations. 'If I and my top management team do one of your community building workshops,' executives ask, 'what will be the outcomes?'

'We don't know,' FCE must reply.

'You don't know?' The questioner is aghast.

'No. Community is an adventure. We never can predict what will happen when a group becomes authentic and open to the Spirit. It's full of surprises. Thank God, because while the outcomes are usually quite different from what we imagined, they are often far better than we could have dreamed.'

By way of illustration, recall two examples from the preceding chapters. The labor-management team wanted some assurance they wouldn't cry or talk about God. FCE wouldn't give them that assurance, but they were satisfied on learning such behavior wasn't mandatory. Then shortly after the workshop began they were crying and speaking of God—the two outcomes they wanted to avoid. Neither they nor FCE could have predicted the ultimate outcome that they would so boldly and thoroughly revolutionize their way of working together. But what a salutary outcome it was!

The other was the example of failure. That workshop failed because the vice-president for marketing was so unwilling to be open to unpredictable outcomes. He was terrified of what might happen were the group to open talk about their corporate culture. Had he allowed it, I suspect the outcome would have been as salutary as it was for the labor-management teams. But he couldn't allow it. He couldn't give up that much control.

Community, within certain parameters, 'lets it happen.' This voluntary loss of control (or emptiness) feels scary at first, but the outcome is freedom and creativity. And God. Unexpected creativity. Unforeseen genius.

Remember the definition of serendipity as 'the gift of finding valuable or agreeable things *not sought for*.' It is, by definition, an unanticipated outcome. Recently a woman who had just undergone a religious conversion wrote to me saying that she wanted to 'learn grace-management skills.' I had to laugh, since on one level the basic grace-management skill is the skill of nonmanagement. You do not manage grace; you let it manage you. Actually, however, she was not entirely off base. There are grace-management skills. They are the skills of attention combined with surrender, of emptiness and, in an organizational setting, the skills of community.

But community does require this skill of nonmanagement, of voluntarily giving up some control within certain parameters. You cannot bring God onto your management team if you want to order everything yourself without asking any direction from him. Build community and welcome God into your organization, and you will be introducing a wild card. A good wild card. A creative wild card. The game will still look the same on the outside. But on the inside there will be that much more spice and excitement along with more 'valuable and agreeable things not sought for.'

When we began FCE, we assumed that the church would be a natural market for its services. Christians generally knew that the early church seemed to have had an extraordinary amount of community and that the notion of 'Christian community,' although largely lost, remained an ideal. Many clergy and laypeople bemoaned the lack of community within their churches. As an individual, Jesus had clearly transcended local culture, and the first major decision of his church was to peacefully go international. In recent years, the church in the United States has increasingly become involved in the peace movement. And what organization could possibly be more interested in welcoming the presence of God into its midst?

Conversely, we assumed that, with its competitive secular orientation and hierarchical structure, business would be the last place we would ever penetrate with our intimacy-demanding culture.

What has emerged over the past six years, however, has been an astonishing relative lack of interest on the part of the church in our community building services and an equally astonishing and burgeoning interest on the part of business.

The resistance on the part of the church has been so dramatic that a large and active volunteer 'FCE Task Force on Community and the Christian Church' sprang up to analyze the reasons for that resistance and, it is hoped, to develop effective strategies for overcoming it.[2] The outcome is still unknown, but as I have thought about it, the emerging trend actually makes a lot of sense. Community requires a good deal of time and work. The workplace is the center of most people's lives. Next comes the family. Church, if it comes in at all, is usually a poor third or fourth. Most churchgoers simply do not have the time to 'do' community at church. Nor do they want to do the often painful work of emotionally stretching at church that community requires. They want the worship service to be pleasantly uplifting, and if they do not like the pretentious-

---

[2] The task force includes a rabbi and is focusing on the Christian church only because a still larger focus would be unmanageable at the current time.

ness of the social hour, they are at least willing to put up with it in order to keep everything nice. Most want church to be pseudocommunity, and despite any protestations to the contrary, they have no real desire to see the boat, and their lives, rocked in the least. The minority who do invest their volunteer time more extensively in the church often do so out of their own leadership needs—that is, they use the church as a sphere of influence in which they can, at times, play very personal power games. The few who make attempts to actualize the church as a place of the Kingdom of God on earth may find themselves silenced by the congregation with an enormously powerful, subtle effectiveness.

Business is another matter. It is no one- or two-hour-a-week affair. Church is not where people's lives are on the line, but their workplace is. Here is where a single decision may cost them their employment, their livelihood. Here is where millions of dollars may be in play every day—sums of money a thousand times greater than their entire annual church budget. These decisions *count*. Here, therefore, of necessity, people may be willing to spend the time and effort to ensure that their decisions are the right ones. It is in business that they may be willing to pay the price of community.

I must emphasize this is a *relative* phenomenon. Here and there a most unusual church does work seriously toward community. Interest is not totally absent. FCE is doing some workshops with parts of congregations as well as for entire monastic groups. Its task force has found reason to believe that ten percent of the members of many congregations may be willing to meet community's high requirements of time, energy, and vulnerability. This 'tithe of persons' might well prove sufficient to achieve extraordinary results in God's service on behalf of the church as a whole.[3]

---

[3] Out of the Task Force evolved another nonprofit organization allied with but independent of FCE. Quest for Community is specifically designed to market community to the church. Clergy or lay ministers interested in bringing community to their congregations may wish to contact Quest for Community, P.O. Box 55810, Houston, Texas 77255–5810, (713) 932–8250, instead of FCE (which is nonsectarian and whose address appears at the end of the book).

At first, the dramatic, relative lack of interest on the part of the church and relative interest on the part of business distressed me. I had hoped the church would serve as a place where the Kingdom could be practiced and people would learn the skills of forging a planetary culture of civility. But then, as it occurred to me that God had possibly largely left the church and gone into business, I was struck by its appropriateness. What better place for God to do her work than in the workplace!

So I have a prophecy to make. If Utopia is to emerge, it will do so primarily from the world of business. This only makes sense. When defined as a condition of society as a whole, of an entire culture, Utopia cannot be instituted by an individual or small deviant group; it can only be instituted through our largest, best-organized, everyday institutions. Only such large organizations have the structure, the wherewithal, and the motive to provide and demand of their employees the continuing on-the-job training required.

But how is this to come about? Granted that community is the way to a planetary culture of civility, how will community be introduced into businesses? And why? Since community requires such a significant amount of time and often painful emotional work, what will motivate business to adopt it? The remainder of this chapter and book will be devoted to answering this question in detail. But there is one over-arching answer. It is why business is already evidencing so much more interest in community than the church. The bottom line in business is not saving souls. If healthy, it is not even immediate as opposed to long-term profitability. It is cost-effectiveness. Business will adopt community as a standard mode of operation for the sole reason that community is cost-effective.

How does one convince a business that an entirely different, emotionally challenging and time-consuming way of doing things is cost-effective? Usually even more than a truly visionary executive is required. Timing is crucial. A new and difficult way is not likely to be tried until it is clear that the old way is not working. The easiest point at which to introduce community into a business is a time of failure, a time of crisis.

So it was that the VDC sought community building services at a time of crisis. It had lost over twenty-five percent of its physicians in the preceding year. There was clearly a failure of retention. In the year following its instituting of community, its number of physicians increased more than forty percent. It had clearly done something that was highly cost-effective.

It is not accidental either, then, that the very first workshop FCE ever did in May 1985 was for a group of civic leaders of Peoria, Illinois, a 'one-company town' that was suffering from a twenty-two percent unemployment rate at the time because of the near failure of the Caterpillar Tractor Company under the stress of Japanese competition. We were very anxious. About the only thing we knew about the city was the cliché, 'If it will play in Peoria, it will play anywhere.' At the conclusion of the workshop, the leaders were presented with a drawing of a tractor overlaid in large letters with the words, 'Yes, it did play in Peoria.' FCE has since conducted workshops for groups of civic leaders of towns in Texas, Louisiana, and Montana also afflicted by poverty.

The 'opportunity of failure' may not be overtly financial. Bob Roberts was able to introduce community into the Louisiana prison system of the failure of its literacy training program (with the resultant high recidivism and an ultimate high cost to the state). The project demonstrated itself to be dramatically effective in enhancing literacy training, although its cost-effectiveness has not yet been calculated in terms of dollars and cents. FCE's services have been requested by a number of organizations because of a failure of morale. And as mentioned, we have done workshops for several groups of public agency managers who were

426

suffering from a failure of interagency cooperation. All such failures have their economic as well as social consequences.

A related window of opportunity arises when a business is not actually experiencing a failure but is anticipating one. It is unlikely that top executive would have directed the labor-management team to go through community building if he had anticipated that the negotiations would be successful. One such instance does not a science make, and it is impossible to state with certainty that the negotiations would have failed without the community building work that was done. FCE's fees for those two workshops totaled $18,000. Had the negotiations failed, it is likely the failure would have cost the company and its employees between $18 million and $180 million. *That's* cost-effectiveness. It was an example of preventive medicine at its most dramatic.

There is one critical time in business life when the preventive medicine of community building is obviously needed and would be extraordinarily cost-effective, but where it has not yet been employed. It is a time when failure can definitely be anticipated, a disaster waiting to happen. I am referring to corporate mergers. Mergers are relatively easy to accomplish on paper. The lawyers and accountants may charge huge fees, but when they are done the product looks letter-perfect. Yet from a functional point of view, most mergers are notoriously ineffective or inefficient. The problem is inherent in the very word, because it implies a squashing together of two different corporate cultures. Different cultures do not merge very well. As a rule, the result is both great turmoil and the destruction of the virtuous aspects of one or both cultures.

The key to solving the problem the moment the lawyers and accountants are finished is to begin to create a new culture at the very top: a 'supraculture' that, for the moment, leaves the two existing cultures (now 'subcultures') perfectly intact. The process of community building is the vehicle, par excellence, for the creation of a new culture. Moreover, such a top-management team operating in community would be the ideal body to make the wisest possible consensual decisions required to develop the complex plan necessary to deal coherently with a host of questions. Which aspects of the subcultures are assets and which are liabilities? To what extent can these assets be preserved while discarding the liabilities? What actions need to be taken to facilitate the transmission of cultural values from the top down or between the subcultures? What actions need to be taken to either integrate the subcultures or keep them separate? Should any new structures be developed? Should any old ones be abolished? Positions? Titles? Layoffs? Humane cost savings? What should be the timing and sequence of these actions? What are the possible measurements of their effectiveness, and what feedback loops can be established to allow, when appropriate, rapid strategic revisions?

When—and only when—there is such a carefully thought-out strategic plan can the merger actually be accomplished in a civil manner, as opposed to a mindless crushing together of two companies with uncivil and expensive results.

Related to mergers are acquisitions. It is a time of new beginning, a crisis not of failure or even anticipated failure but an opportunity for improvement. FCE has not yet been able to work on such a new beginning in the private sector. It has, however, successfully assisted in the initiation of several public sector programs—a somewhat analogous situation.

I have mentioned such opportunities as if they were somehow more important than individual leadership. To the contrary, the technology of community building and maintenance is currently so new there must be a visionary executive around to take advantage of them in this way. Our public sector work has invariably been made possible by unusually innovative, 'global' thinkers in government. There was a single physician at the Valley Diagnostic and Surgical Clinic who had the vision to lead his fellow

428

physicians to grudgingly set aside three days for their first experience of community building. The top executive who attended the public workshop young Frank organized was clearly visionary. No sooner did he experience his first public workshop than Bob Roberts was already inquiring, 'Do you think community building could work in prisons?'

Professor Michael Ray, an expert on 'the new paradigm in business,' contracted with FCE to do a Community Building Workshop in 1990 for a visionary class he was teaching at the Stanford University Graduate School of Business. In this course his students are required to form into relatively large work groups to develop innovative strategies and programs for real companies asking for this input. In the past he found that the groups did not work very well together and that strong disruptive conflicts developed. The class participating in the workshop—while diverse in terms of experience, skills, racial and ethnic background, and geographical origin (five continents and over twenty states were represented)—was able to work harmoniously over an extended period of time. The students utilized the diversity within each work group by honoring each individual in the context of group goals. Both morale and learning improved. The company sponsors were extremely pleased with the results. It would seem that not only the disadvantaged in a Louisiana prison can learn better when they are in community but also the relatively advantaged in a Californian graduate school. Indeed, one of the concepts of the new paradigm in business is that the workplace can be—and should be—a learning environment as well as a cost-effective, profit-making enterprise.

Several managers, familiar with FCE's work, have introduced community into their departments not because there was a failure or crisis or particular window of opportunity, but simply because they wanted to manage in the best way possible. A visionary leader can introduce community into her business at any time, given the right sort of political climate.

Still, there is often nothing like a crisis to create the right sort of climate.

In our pain-avoiding culture, most people think that the mentally healthy life is one characterized by an absence of crises. Nothing could be further from the truth. What characterizes mental health is how early we meet our crises.

The word *crisis* has become fashionable these days in terms of 'mid-life crisis.' It is a very real phenomenon. A huge variety of critical issues may be involved, but one way or another most of them relate to the issue of aging. I have yet to meet a man or woman who has entered old age without being afflicted by a mid-life crisis. What differs is timing.

The later in his life the mid-life crisis occurs, the less likely it is that one will be able to resolve it successfully. A man who is particularly fearful of the issues of aging will try to ignore them for as long as possible. I have known people who have avoided facing them not only during their thirties and forties but through their fifties as well. Ultimately, however, aging cannot be ignored, and it is not difficult to realize that the longer a man puts off facing the issues, the more they will then hit him like a ton of bricks. The blow may be permanently incapacitating. So, fearful of the issues to begin with, such people may never be able to resolve them. There are unfortunate millions who defer their mid-life crises to age sixty or more and then spend the remaining twenty years of their lives in chronic depression, even despair.

Conversely, the less fearful a person is of such issues, the earlier she will be able to meet them—even anticipate them—and the more easily she will be able to do the psychospiritual work necessary to resolve them. The healthiest people I know invariably begin this work in their forties—sometimes even late thirties—and have completed it by the end of their fifties. They have already finished what the unhealthy have not yet started.

Actually, it is possible for healthy people to have several mid-life crises of different flavors. The point is that what characterizes mental health is not an absence of crises in our lives but how quickly we can deal with each crisis so as to get on the next one. Indeed, the goal may be to see how many crises we can cram into a lifetime.

There is a devastating psychological disorder that afflicts perhaps one or two percent of the population that compels them to lead lives of compulsive histrionics. They can't function unless there is a crisis. But the far more devastating form of psychological disorder—which afflicts approximately ninety-five percent of individuals—is that they fail to live their lives with a sufficient sense of drama. They do not wake up and realize the critical nature of their lives until it is often too late.

As it is with individuals, so it is with organizations. A few managers love to operate in a mode of continual crisis, but it is a destructive style of management. Far more commonly, however, an organization will spend an enormous amount of effort trying to deny—ignore—the fact that it is in crisis. When it finally does wake up to the fact, it may be too late.

One way of looking at community building is to see it as a crisis-precipitating process. As we have seen, a group usually begins in pseudocommunity, pretending that everyone likes one another (even though they usually don't really know one another) and there is no problem. When this pretense no longer works, the group 'degenerates' into chaos. I put the word *degenerates* in quotes because while this feels like a deterioration, chaos is actually a step forward in the direction of reality and genuine civility. Consequently, it is the leaders' task early in the community building process to actually encourage chaos. The chaos then becomes a crisis that the group needs to work itself out of. The beginning of this work is the beginning of that stage we have called emptiness, where the members empty themselves of their old ways of relating and start experimenting with new and better ways. Change and growth have been precipitated.

I suspect another source of the resistance on the part of the church to community building is that congregations do not want to go through the pain of chaos. It may not be so much that they desire to be pseudo-communities as that they are instinctively terrified of disintegration, and lack the motivation to hang in together through a period of chaos where everything seems to be falling apart. While churches may get by on chronic pseudocommunity, however, business cannot. Changing external conditions in the marketplace or internal conditions in the workforce routinely force businesses into crisis, but they do not then look forward to the next crisis, and they tend then to forget about maintaining themselves in community.

One of the things we need to do as we push toward Utopia is to dignify organizational chaos. I do not mean structural chaos. I mean the psychospiritual chaos that erupts in an organization when there is sufficient confusion over its vision, mission, myths, norms, and patterns of communication as to produce overt conflict among its members.

The work to dignify chaos has already begun. At the level of organization of subatomic particles, Ilya Prigogine has won a Nobel prize for his study of 'dissipative structures,' his term for a period of organizational breakdown through which such particles pass as they move to a higher energy state.[4] And going up the system scale to our primary focus, there is Tom Peters's recent best-selling book about health and growth in business organizations, *Thriving on Chaos*.[5] Chaos may not be an ideal state, but as has been noted, it is one step ahead of pseudocommunity, and a group cannot mature from pseudocommunity into a genuine community without going through it. I believe the managers of the future will actually learn and deliberately employ techniques to precipitate certain amounts of chaos or crisis when they sense their organizations need revitalization.

---

[4] Ilya Prigogine, *Order Out of Chaos* (New York: Bantam, 1984).
[5] *Thriving on Chaos* (New York: Alfred A. Knopf, 1988).

As businesses consider paying the price of community maintenance—the price of organizational health, preventive medicine, or ongoing civility—it may help them to refer back to theology and the nature of God. An individual who has developed a conscious relationship with God will probably be engaged in developing that relationship—often with anguish and struggle—for the rest of his or her ever-changing life. Is it remarkable, then, that an organization that allows God into its midst will also need to continue to 'wrestle with the angel'?

The cutting edge in theology these days is called 'process theology.' Academicians tend to date the onset of this movement to the work of Alfred North Whitehead in the 1940's, although I suspect it goes way back before that.[6] However, I began my journey into the process theology not by reading Whitehead or learning about it from any other kind of book, but through a combination of experience, intuition, and perhaps even revelation.

The moment was fifteen years ago, as I was sitting in my office with a thirty-five-year-old patient. She was a very attractive person, perhaps as much as eight pounds over the standard weight for women of her age and height. The preceding evening at a joyful restaurant party, she was so relaxed she had ordered and eaten an ice cream sundae for dessert. Now she was lamenting, 'How could I have been so stupid? After only six days I broke my diet! Now I have to start all over again. I hate myself for being so undisciplined. An ice cream sundae, for Christ's sake! Butterscotch sauce. Thick, gooey. I mean, I couldn't have chosen anything that had more calories. One of these days I'll . . .'

As she went on and on in this vein I found myself drifting off slightly, thinking how utterly typical she was of a large category of women whom I found sexually appealing, yet who spent endless ergs of energy obsessing about their weight, even about the most minor deviations in it. What was

[6] Long before Whitehead the Mormons had a statement of pure process theology: 'As man is, God was; as God is, man will become.'

going on with them? In the midst of this wondering, I suddenly interrupted her, blurting out, 'What makes you think that God doesn't have to diet?'

She looked at me as if I'd gone crazy. 'Why'd you say that?' she asked.

I scratched my head, replying, 'I don't know.' But I had to think about why I'd said it, and as I did, I realized that I was onto something. I realized that my patient was laboring under a fantasy that if she read enough diet books or discovered just the right diet or received enough psycho-therapy, then she would achieve a state where she could either eat all she wanted without gaining an ounce or else whenever she did gain that ounce, be able instantly and effortlessly to lose it. A strange fantasy, come to think of it. 'Maybe God puts on five pounds,' I explained to her, 'and then has to take them off. Only he doesn't make a big deal out of it, which is perhaps why he's God.'

That's how I stumbled onto process theology.

The illusion my patient labored under was a static notion of perfection. It is a very common but very destructive notion that perfection is an unchanging state. It is so common because it is so purely logical. If something is perfect and it changes, it can only become imperfect. But if something is truly perfect, it cannot, by definition, become imperfect. Hence perfection must be unchanging. And so we think, 'God is as God was and always will be.'

But it's not the way I think anymore. It's also hardly what the Bible suggests. And increasingly it's not what theo-logians are beginning to think. Thank God! If there is anything that characterizes life, it is change. As already mentioned, what most distinguishes the animate moves when you poke at it. It doesn't just sit there. It's alive. It goes this way and that way. It grows, it decays, it gets reborn. It changes. All life is in process. And since I choose to have a living God, I believe that my God is also in process, learning and growing and perhaps even laughing and dancing.

Why is this new concept of process theology so critically

important? Because it means that it is good for organizations, like people, to be in a state of change. All organizations are in process, but the healthier they are, the more they will be in process. The more vibrant, the more lively they are, the more they will be changing. And the closer to perfection they are, the more rapidly they will be changing.

So, as we change our theology, we will come to expect our organizations to be in flux and in turmoil. We will know, not only in our heads but in our hearts, that if an organization lets God into itself, it will be welcoming even more flux and turmoil. We will know when we see a comfortable, complacent, particularly stable organization that it is undoubtedly in a state—or at least a phase—of decay. And if we see an organization that is suffering, struggling, searching this way and that for new solutions, one that is constantly revising and reviving itself, our tendency will not only be to give it the benefit of the doubt but to suspect that we may have stumbled upon a particularly godly institution.

For these same reasons, Utopia will not be stable or static. It will be evolving. It should not be thought of as a condition that we reach, because no sooner will we reach it than it will move on. It will not be a condition without suffering, without the stress and strain that inherently accompany change or development. Rather it will be a society moving with maximal vitality toward maximal vitality.

In summary, Utopia may not be impossible to achieve after all.

It *will* be impossible if we hold on to our traditional vision of perfection. In accord with this antiquated vision, Utopia in the past has generally been conceived as an isolated commune carved out within an otherwise imperfect world. Assets are held communally so that members are all economically equal. While the members work, the communal culture is antibusiness. There is no hierarchy, and consequently, no one is ever fired or 'excommunicated.'

The rules are so effective that the society is not only stable but unchanging. Although these rules may be considered to be divinely inspired, once in place there is no longer any role for God to play, any need for further divine intervention. There are no surprises and people need not struggle with each other toward a better future. In fact, there is no progress—since perfection has already been reached. Civility has been legislated; hence, it is not an ongoing process but an effortless, painless static state.

No wonder such utopian ventures have always failed. They were based on false, unrealistic assumptions. They were antithetical to everything we know about real civility and real community. Maybe they also failed because they were insufferably dull.

Based on what we know about civility and have learned thus far about community, let me consolidate what has been said by offering a radically different utopian vision.

My Utopia of the future will always be in the future. This is because Utopia is not a state arrived at but a state of becoming. Indeed, we might think of Utopia as having already started. Barely.

The distinguishing feature of the citizens of Utopia is not their location, nationality, religion, or occupation but their commitment to becoming ever more civil individuals and their membership in a planetary culture of civility. By virtue of this commitment and membership, regardless of their theology, they welcome the active presence of God into both their individual and their collective lives. They believe in progress. They see themselves as growing psychospiritually. They are willing to accept the pain of growth and are eager for any surprising assistance they can receive from a Higher Power. They know they cannot go it alone without God or their fellow humans. Although their primary allegiance is to the development of their own souls, they are all involved in teaching as well as learning civility and dedicated to inviting others into their planetary culture.

They will teach civility wherever they can, as parents in

families or educators in classrooms or parishioners in church. But as we move over toward Utopia, the primary role of teaching civility will be assumed by business. Business will assume this role out of self-interest as it learns the technology of community building and maintenance and just how cost-effective genuine civility is. Among their other missions, businesses will increasingly think of themselves as teaching and learning organizations. Eventually, the teaching of civility will become systematic—an integral part of the whole system of society—as the practice of community becomes endemic in business and the workplace. Every employee of any sizable business wil automatically receive ongoing, on-the-job training in community as businesses increasingly operate in a community mode.

This does not mean that all will then be sweetness and light. People will continue to differ in their levels of competence. There will continue to be economic cycles and the necessity of layoffs. There will still be mental illnesses and the occasional devious individual who must be fired. What it does mean, however, is that gradually real civility both in and outside the workplace will become ever more common and incivility ever less normative. The kinds of advertisements cited early in the book, appealing to our baser natures, will cease to sell.

But one last stumbling block needs consideration as business organizations begin to lead the way in forging a planetary culture of civility.

When the two labor-management teams, after building community, independently decided that instead of coming to the table they would get rid of the table, they were doing something not only revolutionary but utopian. They also independently requested FCE to keep it secret. Correctly, I believe, they surmised that their work in community would not be trusted by their constituencies, the labor union and management as a whole, who were accustomed to traditional adversarialism and utterly unfamiliar with community. But this raises a question. How does a utopian organization honestly introduce itself to the larger society? The answer is, 'carefully.'

I think this political problem of organizational civility can best be analyzed in relation to the essentially uncivil but prevailing ethic of rugged individualism. Just as this fallacious 'ethic' (so antithetical to the principles of community) governs the behavior of most individual human beings, even more does it currently govern the behavior of organizations. They must pretend that they have it all together, that they are utterly in control of the situation, that they are totally competent. General Electric does not announce its internal problems. The United States doesn't admit that it has been wrong.

In the course of the community building this ethic is shattered. Men and women drop their masks of composure. They confess their problems. They become, with great relief, publicly comfortable with themselves as imperfect, burdened, struggling people. In doing this they also reveal to themselves and to each other what I have come to call 'the routine heroism of human beings.' In the same way, organizations that build themselves into communities come to see themselves as imperfect, wounded, and struggling agencies, companies, or corporations. The problem is that they then become increasingly uncomfortable presenting to the world a facade of constant composure and ostensible perfection. They know it is a front, a lie. How long do they maintain the pretense? And what should their political strategy be in giving it up?

The difficulty is not internal. Individuals building themselves into a community have considerable assurance of confidentiality: the knowledge of their 'sins' will be maintained internally, will be kept within the group. Part of the problem of 'reentry,' however, is the issue of how they are going to behave when the workshop is over, when they leave it and reenter everyday society governed by the rules of rugged individualism. How do they now relate with the external world? They are usually a little more free, a little

438

more honest, with a few selected people, but generally they put their masks back on, albeit somewhat less rigidly.

The problem for organizations is of similar kind but far greater magnitude. It is not that difficult for an organization to build itself into a community—even at all levels—so that every employee knows the company is in some way fragile, some ways wounded and hurting, and very much struggling, and feels proud to belong to such a company. But how should such a human and humane business relate with the external world and present itself to a public that expects high-gloss images of smoothness and perfection?

It is an intensely real problem. Even FCE, a nonprofit organization whose very purpose is community, must wrestle with it. We know ourselves to be a wounded organization.[7] Yet our publications do not always reflect this reality. To what extent should our newsletter contain notes about how FCE's most recent Leaders' Roundtable was a meeting of unrelieved chaos? Or that the board member who recently resigned did so in anger? Or that the board and staff are in conflict? Or that we ended last year considerably in the red because of an absurdly optimistic misjudgment of how many new large donors we would attract? Do we tell potential major donors that we desperately need their help because our financial situation is so shaky? Yes, some might want to help out. But many more would surely think, 'I certainly wouldn't want to throw good money after bad, put it into a potentially sinking ship, or invest in an organization that doesn't have its act together!'

If FCE has this problem, think what it is like for a corporation whose shares sell on the New York Stock Exchange! How high-gloss do its publications need to be? How much attention must it pay to its image? (And how much of its profits must it divert from stockholders to maintain its image to these same stockholders?)

How are we, as a society, going to solve this problem of

[7] And a healing one: the two go together. Read Henri Nouwen's classic on the subject, *The Wounded Healer*.

corporate images and organizational hype? How do we get
to a world in which General Electric or General Motors or
the U.S. government can acknowledge internal problems
without being under the gun from investigatory reporters?
When the nations of the world can learn to apologize to one
another? If we are going to make any progress toward
Utopia, it is a problem that must be solved. For the present,
we are caught in a vicious cycle. In attempting to present
false fronts of perfection, organizations teach the public to
have unrealistic expectations of perfection, which further
compel the organizatons to create even glossier images to
feed those expectations. And so it goes, round and round.

The way the problem is going to be solved is by
organizational courage. The giant steps forward in the
community building process are taken by those individuals
of such courage that they are able to risk speaking at a level
of vulnerability and authenticity at which no one in the
group has spoken before. It only takes one individual at a
time. As soon as she speaks at that level, then others in the
group will follow, and shortly everyone will be talking that
way. Then after a while, another individual will start
speaking at a still deeper level of vulnerability and authenticity. Shortly he will be followed and everyone will be
talking at that level also. And so the process will go for
organizations. Someday an organization will be secure
enough in itself to have the courage to dramatically cast
away one of its images of invulnerability. As soon as other
businesses see how it has gotten away with it, they will start
to do likewise. And the whole culture will have begun to
shift.

Primarily the shift will occur not merely because the
world has seen that the vulnerable (internally as well as
externally) business has gotten away with it, but because it
has become extraordinarily successful in the process of
doing so. We return to the concept that community in the
workplace and organizational civility will succeed because it
is *cost-effective*. In his work on servant leadership, Greenleaf

posited that the world will be saved if it can develop just three truly well-managed, large institutions—one in the private sector, one in the public sector, and one in the nonprofit sector. Just one major profit-making corporation, one major government agency, and one charitable organization! He believed—and I know—that such excellence in management will be achieved through an organizational culture of civility routinely utilizing the mode of community. Such organizations will be so dramatically successful, that is, cost-effective, that their sister institutions—no matter how initially threatened—will flock to discover their secret and imitate them.

But we're far from there now. It's going to take us a long time before we can become such a civil society, before organizations as well as individuals are maximally vulnerable. Until then those organizations practicing community are going to have to wrestle continually with the political problem of how to function in a culture that is not yet comfortable with community or real civility. Until that time—and beyond that time—they will continue to need to struggle to figure out how to be, from moment to moment, organizations that are in the world but not of the world.

All who wish to explore FCE's services
or support its mission
are welcomed to write or call
The Foundation for Community Encouragement
P.O. Box 449
Ridgefield, Connecticut 06877
Phone: 203/431-9484
FAX: 203/431-9349

WHY ME WHY THIS WHY NOW

Robin Norwood

Robin Norwood's international bestseller *Women Who Love Too Much* changed forever the way we think about love.

Now, in *Why Me Why This Why Now*, writing for both men and women, she takes her readers on a deeper journey into the realm of Spirit, offering a revolutionary perspective on adversity that addresses our deepest and most disturbing questions:

- *Why is this happening to me?*
- *What is the point of pain?*
- *Why are relationships so difficult?*
- *What is my body trying to tell me?*
- *What does my life mean?*

Norwood tackles these questions head-on in this highly practical yet deeply spiritual book, illustrating them with concrete examples and clarifying such topics as:

- *Individual and family karma*
- *The destined nature of emotional attachments*
- *How we choose our parents and the circumstances of our birth*
- *Our past lives and present problems*
- *Addiction as a path to transformation*

By teaching us to recognise the soul's purpose behind our encounters with adversity, the author empowers us to cooperate with our own destiny, live a far more effective life and heal the deepest wounds of the heart.

LOVE, MEDICINE & MIRACLES

Bernie S. Siegel M.D.

The lessons learned about self-healing, written by a doctor who has watched 'terminal' patients take control of their illness and live.

'We do have biological "live" and "die" mechanisms within us . . . the state of mind changes the state of the body by working through the central nervous system, the endocrine system and the immune system. Exceptional patients manifest the will to live in its most potent form . . . ' writes Dr Bernie Siegel. Through the healing power of love, patients who have come under his care have learned to change, enrich and prolong their lives beyond medical expectation.

None of us know when illness will strike us or those we love, but we *can* do something about it. *Love, Medicine and Miracles* shows us how.

"A wonderful book that every patient and sceptic physician should read" –Elizabeth Kubler Ross

"His book is, and will be, a blessing to all humanity"
–Dr Carl Simonton

THE ROAD LESS TRAVELLED

M. Scott Peck

A new psychology of love, traditional values and spiritual growth.

Confronting and solving problems is a painful process which most of us attempt to avoid. And the very avoidance results in greater pain and an inability to grow both mentally and spiritually. Drawing heavily on his own professional experience, Dr. M. Scott Peck, a practising psychiatrist, suggests ways in which facing our difficulties – and suffering through the changes – can enable us to reach a higher level of self-understanding. He discusses the nature of loving relationships: how to recognize true compatibility; how to distinguish dependency from love: how to become one's own person and how to be a more sensitive parent.

This book is a phenomenon. Continuously on the US bestseller list for five years, it will change your life.

"Magnificent . . . This is not just a book, but a spontaneous act of generosity written by an author who leans towards the reader for the purpose of sharing something larger than himself"
– *Washington Post*

YOU'LL SEE IT WHEN YOU BELIEVE IT

Dr Wayne W. Dyer

The way to your personal transformation.

"Our thoughts are a magic part of us, and they carry us to places that have no boundaries, and no limitations"

In his most thought-provoking book yet, Dr Wayne Dyer stretches beyond self-help to self-realization. To do so, he embarks on a journey to activate our minds and shows us how to transform our lives by using our thoughts constructively: in other words, how to focus on a belief and *see* it.

Using anecdotes and examples, writing with wit and compassion, and drawing on his own amazing life story, Dr Dyer has, once again, written an inspiring book that explores the way to personal transformation through the visualization of thought — and teaches us that believing *is* seeing.

WOMEN WHO LOVE TOO MUCH

Robin Norwood

Is having "somebody to love" the most important thing in your life? Do you constantly believe that with "the right man" you would no longer feel depressed or lonely? Are you bored with "nice guys" who are open, honest and dependable?

If being in love means being *in pain*, this book is written for you. Therapist Robin Norwood describes loving *too much* as a pattern of thoughts and behaviour which certain women develop as a response to problems from childhood.

Many women find themselves repeatedly drawn into unhappy and destructive relationships with men. They then struggle to make these doomed relationships work. This bestselling book takes a hard look at how powerfully addictive these unhealthy relationships are — but also gives a very specific programme for recovery from the *disease* of loving too much.

"A life-changing book for women" — Erica Jong

BESTSELLING HEALTH AND SELF-HELP TITLES

☐	Aquarobics	Glenda Baum	£9.99
☐	Rosemary Conley's Whole Body Programme	Rosemary Conley	£9.99
☐	Rosemary Conley's Complete Hip and Thigh Diet	Rosemary Conley	£4.50
☐	No Change	Wendy Cooper	£3.99
☐	Understanding Osteoporosis	Wendy Cooper	£3.99
☐	Pulling Your Own Strings	Dr Wayne W. Dyer	£3.99
☐	You'll See It When You Believe It	Dr Wayne W. Dyer	£4.99
☐	The Vitamin and Mineral Encyclopedia	Dr Sheldon Saul Hendler	£8.99
☐	Feel the Fear and Do It Anyway	Susan Jeffers	£4.50
☐	Ageless Ageing	Leslie Kenton	£4.50
☐	The Joy of Beauty	Leslie Kenton	£8.99
☐	Raw Energy	Leslie Kenton	£3.99
☐	Sexual Cystitis	Angela Kilmartin	£3.99
☐	Understanding Cystitis	Angela Kilmartin	£4.99
☐	Who's Afraid	Alice Neville	£5.99
☐	Women Who Love Too Much	Robin Norwood	£4.99
☐	The Different Drum	M. Scott Peck	£4.99
☐	The Road Less Travelled	M. Scott Peck	£4.99
☐	Callanetics	Callan Pinckney	£7.99
☐	Love, Medicine and Miracles	Bernie Siegel	£4.50
☐	Peace, Love and Healing	Bernie Siegel	£3.99

ALL ARROW BOOKS ARE AVAILABLE THROUGH MAIL ORDER OR FROM YOUR LOCAL BOOKSHOP AND NEWSAGENT.

PLEASE SEND CHEQUE/EUROCHEQUE/POSTAL ORDER (STERLING ONLY) ACCESS, VISA OR MASTERCARD

EXPIRY DATE........................   SIGNATURE....................................

PLEASE ALLOW 75 PENCE PER BOOK FOR POST AND PACKING U.K. OVERSEAS CUSTOMERS PLEASE ALLOW £1.00 PER COPY FOR POST AND PACKING.

ALL ORDERS TO:
ARROW BOOKS, BOOK SERVICE BY POST, P.O. BOX 29, DOUGLAS, ISLE OF MAN, IM99 1BQ. TEL: 01624 675137 FAX: 01624 670 923

NAME..

ADDRESS ....

....

Please allow 28 days for delivery. Please tick box if you do not wish to receive any additional information ☐

Prices and availability subject to change without notice.